Key Issues

JOHN LOCKE AND CHRISTIANITY

Contemporary Responses to *The Reasonableness of Christianity*

Edited and Introduced by

VICTOR NUOVO

Middlebury College, Vermont

Series Editor

ANDREW PYLE

University of Bristol

THOEMMES PRESS

© Thoemmes Press 1997

Published in 1997 by
Thoemmes Press
11 Great George Street
Bristol BS1 5RR, England

US office: Distribution and Marketing
22883 Quicksilver Drive
Dulles, Virginia 20166, USA

ISBN
Paper : 1 85506 540 1
Cloth : 1 85506 539 8

John Locke and Christianity
Key Issues No. 16

British Library Cataloguing-in-Publication Data

A catalogue record of this title is available
from the British Library

The Publisher wishes to thank the Bodleian Library,
Oxford for the use of the manuscript review of *The
Reasonableness of Christianity* (shelfmark MS. Locke
c. 27, fols. 224 and following), the first item in this
collection.

Printed in Great Britain by Antony Rowe Ltd., Chippenham

CONTENTS

INTRODUCTION

The Reasonableness of Christianity as delivered in the Scriptures was the last constructive work written and published by John Locke during his lifetime. It is also one of the most important works of Christian theology produced during the Enlightenment. Perhaps its only rival is Schleiermacher's *On Religion*, published a century later, which ushered in a new age of religious sensibility, and which, significant differences notwithstanding, owed much to Locke.[1] Both works attempt, in different ways, to establish Christian revelation as a universally available truth. Both are basic to modern religion and to liberal Christianity.

The Reasonableness of Christianity was published anonymously in 1695.[2] Locke did not publicly acknowledge his authorship in his lifetime, but he arranged for its disclosure in a codicil to his will.[3]

---

[1] Friedrich Schleiermacher, *Uber die Religion*, 1799, translated with an introduction and notes by Richard Crouter (Cambridge University Press, 1988). Schleiermacher's dependence on Locke, which is indirect, is both sociological and psychological. See the translator's introduction, p. 52, and p. 152, n. 12.

[2] A second edition was published the following year, and it has become the standard for all subsequent editions. Locke also published two vindications of his book in 1696 and 1697. For a recent reprinting of the three works in one volume *The Reasonableness of Christianity* (Bristol: Thoemmes Press, 1997), with my introduction. Citations in this introduction will be to this text and will be signified by *TRC, 1V* and *2V*, followed by the page number. Citations in the documents of this collection will also be changed to refer to this text.

[3] E. S. de Beer (ed.), *The Correspondence of John Locke* (Oxford: Clarendon Press, 1989), vol. 8, p. 426.

ix

Publication of his book drew an almost immediate response. John Edwards, an Anglican clergyman of moderate Calvinist persuasion labelled it Socinian and accused its author of being 'altogether Socinianized'. Although he claimed not to know the author's identity, he suspected, almost ruefully, that it might be Locke, the famous philosopher and author of *An Essay concerning Human Understanding* and *Some Thoughts concerning Education*, works which he professed to admire.[4] The Socinian label stuck and the suspicion continues even today.[5] The key issue to be raised in this volume then is whether Locke intentionally wrote a Socinian book. But, although this is unquestionably an issue, it remains to be explained why it should be considered a *key* issue, why it is important.

First it must be made clear what it means to call a book or an author Socinian. John Edwards had a precise answer to this question. A Socinian is a deviant Christian, or a Christian whose faith is deficient and is more accurately represented by what he denies than by what he affirms. Socinians, according to Edwards, deny the divinity of Christ, original sin and the satisfaction rendered to God by the innocent death of Christ. There is no point to specifying and weighing the merits of what is left to the Christian faith once these doctrines have been deleted from it, for Socinianism is rather a method of unburdening the conscience of creedal oblig-

[4] John Edwards, *Some Thoughts concerning the Several Causes and Occasions of Atheism* (London: J. Robinson, 1695), pp. 93, 96.

[5] Maurice Cranston, *John Locke* (New York: Macmillan, 1957), p. 390 and J. R. Milton, 'Locke at Oxford', in G. A. J. Rogers, *Locke's Philosophy* (Oxford: Clarendon Press, 1994), p. 44, characterize Locke as a 'secret Unitarian', as does Mario Montuori, *John Locke on Toleration and the Unity of God* (Amsterdam: Gieben, 1983), p. 124. In *John Locke, Resistance, Religion and Responsibility* (Cambridge University Press, 1994), John Marshall claims to have shown Locke's development from orthodox Anglican to a secret Unitarian.

ations than a positive creed. Edwards believed that this
process continues beyond any positive Christian
assertion until it ends in atheism, although he equivo-
cates about whether Socinians wittingly pursue or
unwittingly are led to this goal. Nor is he clear about
what led the minds if not the hearts of Socinians towards
atheism. Recent historians have been more forthcoming
with explanations. Socinians practised a form of biblical
theology that relied on reason to interpret revelation.
The inevitable outcome of this practice was a reduction
of Christianity to a rational scheme.[6]

Suppose this account of Socinianism and its motive
were correct. It should not be hard to imagine why the
question, whether Locke intentionally wrote a Socinian
book, is important. Locke is one of the main modern
philosophers. *The Reasonableness of Christianity* is
arguably one of his main works and therefore a representative product of his philosophical programme.
Suppose also that Edwards's charges against Locke were
true. To those who believe that Christianity is true,
The Reasonableness of Christianity must be fundamentally in error, and not it only, but modern philosophy
also so far as it has been influenced by Locke. They
must expose this error and its philosophical hosts in
order to make way for a renewal of faith.[7] To those who
believe that Christianity is most likely false or at least no

[6] H. John McLachlan, *Socinianism in Seventeenth-Century England* (Oxford University Press, 1981), pp. 11f. H. R. Trevor-Roper, *Catholics, Anglicans and Puritans* (University of Chicago Press, 1987), pp. 95f.

[7] Locke's *Essay* was subjected to similar criticism. The Bishop of Worcester, Edward Stillingfleet (1635–99), was an early critic of the *Essay*, Peter Browne another. Stillingfleet, *A Discourse in Vindication of the Doctrine of the Trinity* (London, 1697), chap. 10 and the subsequent exchange between them of responses and counter-responses; [Peter Browne], *The Procedure, Extent, and Limits of Human Understanding* (London, 1728). For an account of twentieth-century theological criticism of Locke's philo-sophical programme, see Stephen N. Williams, *Revelation and Reconciliation* (Cambridge University Press, 1995).

longer properly credible, Locke's book may exemplify the wisdom of modernity. They would make it a milestone on the highway towards human enlightenment. They would see the irony in Edwards's attack against Locke, and judge him right about *The Reasonableness of Christianity*, although for the wrong reasons, and they would judge Locke to have been wrong about Christianity for the right reasons. Locke's attempt to make Christianity credible to an enlightened understanding in the end showed it to be incredible and probably false.

Suppose, on the other hand, that *The Reasonableness of Christianity* is not a Socinian book in this Edwardsian sense, then it must be asked just what sort of a book it is, and why it came to be viewed in this way. It would also seem fitting to re-examine the tendencies of modernity and to reconsider their likely outcomes, for if Locke was a major influence in giving them direction, then it may be that negative judgements about Locke, the Enlightenment and their consequences are not only premature but mistaken, and that far from subverting Christianity, along with morality and religion, Locke offered them a new lease on life whose benefits remain to be realized. This would be a reason to reconsider the prospects of liberal Christianity and the modern moral project.

The question of this book then is 'What is the meaning of *The Reasonableness of Christianity*?' Is it a Socinian book? Is it not? If not, what is it? If not, then is it likely also that Edwards was wrong not only about Locke but also about Socinianism? Up until now, the Edwardsian sense of Socinianism has been taken for granted. But it is far from certain that it should be. Socinians did indeed deny the divinity of Christ as this doctrine is defined in Nicene and Athanasian Creeds, and along with it the doctrines of the Trinity, Original Sin and Satisfaction. But they were sincere Christians whose intent was not to unburden the Christian conscience of the obligation of faith, but to fix it on its proper object as this came into view after a careful reading of Scripture. They affirmed without equivocation the unique office of Jesus of Nazareth, the Messiah and messenger of divine revelation, his miraculous birth and resurrection, his second coming, and the salvation that was begun and would be completed in these events. Although they set reason above tradition, they did not set it above revelation, and it is not obvious that there is any inconsistency in placing such a limitation on reason.

Notwithstanding the affinities that Locke shared with them, it seems very unlikely, given his methods, that he set out to promote their doctrine. It is more likely that, by setting aside traditions and applying the same historical method to determine the sense and authority of Scripture, he arrived at similar conclusions. But these agreements do not make Locke a Socinian. The historical method and the rejection of extra-biblical traditions are not unique to Socinianism. The former was a common benefit of Renaissance learning and the latter was common to all parties of the Protestant Reformation. Nor were Locke's conclusions about what constitutes fundamental Christianity peculiar to Socinianism. He didn't think so. We have a personal profession to this effect in a letter to Philippus van Limborch, where Locke claims to have found in Limborch's *Theologia Christiana* confirmation of his conclusion that faith in Christ involves no more than the historical belief that the man Jesus of Nazareth was the Messiah.[8] Limborch was not a Socinian but a

---

[8] Letter to Philip van Limborch, 10 May 1695, in de Beer (ed.), *op. cit.*, vol.

Trinitarian. Locke found that Limborch's account of faith in Christ was in perfect agreement with his own. That agreement was not about the Trinity, but the meaning of the Messianic office. He discovered Limborch's assertion that acceptance of Jesus as the Messiah does not entail acceptance of the doctrine of the two natures of Christ nor any other theological dogma that does not directly relate to the preaching of the Gospel.[9]

It was no accident that Locke should have sought confirmation in Limborch's theology. Philippus van Limborch (1633–1712) was Locke's host and protector and theological confidant during his years (1683–9) of exile in Holland. He was also the most eminent Dutch theologian during the late seventeenth and early eighteenth centuries and was leader of the Remonstrants, Dutch anti-Calvinists who were tried and condemned at the Synod of Dordrecht (1618–19) and who were subsequently expelled from the Dutch Reformed Church.[10] There is no doubt that Locke's views on toleration were influenced by Remonstrants, by Limborch and by his predecessor and father-in-law Simon Episcopius. Limborch acted as Locke's agent in the publication of his first letter on toleration, *Epistola de Tolerantia*. The Remonstrants were also tolerant of Socinians and did not doubt the sincerity and efficacy of their faith. It would be presumptuous to infer from this that Locke, having become a private Socinian, sought to hide the fact by associating his doctrine with

---

5, no. 1901. See also my introduction to *The Reasonableness of Christianity* (Bristol: Thoemmes Press, 1997).

[9] See this collection, Limborch's *Compleat System*, sect. 2.

[10] For a magisterial account of the Remonstrant Church, its leaders, the Calvinist reaction and the Synod of Dordrecht, see Jonathan Israel, *The Dutch Republic* (Oxford: Clarendon Press, 1996).

Limborch's. His agreement with Limborch was, after all, conveyed in a private letter, and the question he addressed there was not whether Unitarianism or Trinitarianism was true, but whether a commitment to either was necessary to the faith that makes one a Christian. It is clear that he was certain that it was not.

The title of *The Reasonableness of Christianity* asserts the proposition that Christianity as delivered in the Scriptures is reasonable. The subject of the book is biblical Christianity, or more precisely the Gospel of Jesus Christ, which is not merely recorded in Scripture but delivered as a sermon to an expectant world. Hence, it is not the whole of biblical doctrine that concerns Locke, but only that part of it represented in the preaching of Jesus and the Apostles. This preaching is taken as normative of fundamental or basic Christianity. Faith in Christ is the principal aim of this preaching. The content of this faith is the proposition that Jesus is the Messiah. Acceptance of this one proposition makes one a Christian.

This proposition requires interpretation if its meaning is to unfold for the believer. Locke's method is historical. The meaning of Jesus as Messiah derives from the biblical narrative, from the apostolic testimony concerning Jesus's birth, death, resurrection, his ministry, from prophecy and from the history of redemption narrated in Scripture. On account of his birth, Jesus is linked to Adam, for both are Sons of God, inasmuch as they had no human father. Episodes in the lives of both mark the beginning and end of Salvation. Everyone dies in Adam and is made alive in Jesus. But Jesus is not just the first fruits of resurrection, but the Messiah, the divine King, who will come again to judge the world and establish the manifest and everlasting reign of God. From this understanding of the Gospel as redemptive history, Locke derives the meaning and advantages of faith in Christ.

By predicating reasonableness to the Gospel of Jesus Christ, Locke did not mean that it is discoverable or verifiable by reason alone. The Gospel and all that it involved, at least Locke's account of it, consists of truths that are above reason, whose discovery depends upon divine revelation. Rather, 'reasonable' as Locke uses it in his title means primarily 'advantageous'. Locke's rationale seems to be something like this. Since the Gospel has been delivered to the world for the world's good, rational persons should be able to appreciate its benefits and therefore be inclined to accept it even though they cannot, apart from the assurance of revelation, be certain of its truth.[11] In the light of this interpretation of his title, one might describe Locke's work as apologetic, although evangelical might even be better.

According to Locke, the advantages of Christianity are of two sorts: particular, with respect to confessing Christians, and universal, with respect to the whole human race. The advantages made available to Christians, that is, to those who accept that Jesus is the Messiah, are the forgiveness of sins, the assurance of

---

[11] Locke's intention is to recommend acceptance of the Christian Gospel on account of its advantages and so he was aware that these advantages are reasons for acceptance. They make Christianity reasonable in a broader sense of being credible. But Locke makes clear elsewhere that the main reason why we take a revelation to be true is its author, God, who will not lie and cannot be deceived. In *An Essay concerning Human Understanding* (bk IV, chap. 16, sect. 4), however, he also observes that it remains for reason to decide whether something is a revelation. In *TRC*, authenticating revelation is largely a matter of weighing the reliability of testimony and in examining the biblical narrative for evidence of the wisdom of God in the unfolding of purported redemption. Locke's long discussion in *TRC* of the Messianic secret (pp. 35–100), is devoted to the question of authenticating revelation. The question of authentication is not treated in this volume because the controversies surrounding Locke's book were not about the authenticity of revelation but its meaning.

eternal life and bliss, and a new covenant with a new law, the Law of Faith, which is more lenient than the Law of Works or its natural counterpart, the Law of Nature, both of which require perfect obedience. Christianity is universally advantageous because it offers perfect confirmation of the principles of natural religion, which on account of human frailty, fallibility and depravity, had become obscure and uncertain. These principles are monotheism, an eternal and immutable Law of Nature, the promise of eternal life and happiness to all who perfectly keep this law, and the assurance of divine mercy to all who sincerely desire to obey the law of God yet who fall short of perfect obedience.[12] The two sets of advantages are intertwined, and once revealed, The Christian Gospel becomes a sort of public knowledge, whose advantages may be realized even by persons who do not acknowledge its truth.[13]

The last decade of the seventeenth century, during which *The Reasonableness of Christianity* appeared, was a period of chronic theological controversy and fluid partisan alignments. Under the circumstances, it is not surprising that Locke should have published his book anonymously. His concern in concealing his authorship was less about his safety than about his reputation, which at the time, on account of his *Essay concerning Human Understanding* and *Some Thoughts concerning Education*, was very high. The combat among theological writers, in England at least, was no longer mortal and in more than a few instances it was even civil, at least in tone. The weapon of choice was

---

[12] For more about Locke's argument see my introduction to TRC.

[13] See TRC, p. 145, where, in remarks possibly addressed to deists, Locke describes the illusion that knowledge once appropriated must have come from 'the strength and native light' on one's own mind and concludes that 'many are beholden to revelation, who do not acknowledge it'.

the non-lethal pamphlet, which became an easily available instrument for charges and countercharges.

Another reason for Locke's decision to publish anonymously was his desire to remain indifferent to the pamphlet wars that were waged about him. The indifference that he wanted to maintain was a philosophical indifference, one that would facilitate the pursuit of an impartial and unprejudiced inquiry. Although the claim of impartiality was commonly made by controversialists for their side and therefore should be suspect, in Locke's case, I think, it should be respected at the outset, at least until the reasons and arguments of *The Reasonableness of Christianity* have been identified and appraised.

This self-imposed philosophical indifference should not be taken to imply that Locke was unaware of the doctrinal skirmishes going on about him, or that he did not take them into account when writing *The Reasonableness of Christianity*. The Socinian challenge to the doctrine of the Trinity was met by several orthodox responses, which in turn gave rise to the Trinitarian conflict. Locke did not address this conflict in *The Reasonableness of Christianity*, and in the two *Vindications* that he wrote in defence of it, he attempted to avoid it. This attempt was unsuccessful. Two other ongoing conflicts did receive Locke's attention as much as to provide the themes of *The Reasonableness of Christianity*: justification by faith and other advantages of faith in Christ, or the efficacy and advantages of faith in Christ. One was the Antinomian Controversy, which was an episode in a continuing controversy among Calvinists concerning the meaning of justification by Faith. The second, which Locke regarded as an outcome of the first, involved deists and Calvinists. The Antinomian conflict was one between moderate and extreme Calvinists. It was about the efficacy of faith.

Extreme Calvinists denied that faith had any effect in the justification of the sinner. They argued that divine grace or the favour shown towards certain sinners and their election to salvation, as well as the reprobation of all the rest, was entirely a consequence of the eternal and altogether arbitrary decree of God. Hence, they concluded that the elect were justified even before they believed in Christ. Moderate Calvinists, while not disputing the priority of divine election, maintained that the justification of the sinner was nonetheless contingent upon faith in Christ. Deists reacted against Calvinism in both varieties. They considered the doctrine of predestination and unconditional election to be monstrous and demonic and destructive of a rational belief in God. They went on to deny any advantage, religious or moral, to faith in Christ. In Locke's view, the Calvinist crisis over the efficacy of faith in Christ led to the deist crisis which, if unresolved, could cause the decline of Christianity.[14] On the other hand, he supposed that deists, while justified in rejecting Calvinism, were wrong to suppose that Christianity had nothing more to offer.

Another conflict which was ongoing at the time deserves mention here. Although it is unmentioned in *The Reasonableness of Christianity*, Locke's outlook and method presuppose it. This was a conflict between Protestant and Catholic divines who made contrary claims about the nature of faith, whether it was an attitude of the believer founded on an honest understanding of Scripture, or whether faith required the mediation of the Roman Catholic Church.

All of these conflicts involved differing claims of what makes a person a Christian. All agree that faith in Christ is requisite, but just what the content of this faith

---

[14] See my Introduction to *TRC*.

is and how or by what authority it is to be decided, and what other obligations, if any, are attached to it, were matters of dispute.

The Antinomian and Trinitarian Controversies, as well as the deist and Socinian challenges are all Protestant conflicts, but the Reformation engendered not only a bundle of Protestant churches each with its confessional identity, it also produced the Roman Catholic Church reconstituted at the Council of Trent (1545–63) and the Tridentine faith, which even when it did not occupy Protestant divines, was a constant preoccupation to them. This faith interposed between the believer and Scripture an infallible Church as the only reliable interpreter of Scripture in this world, something that might seem advantageous to Christians perplexed by the multiplicity of Protestant confessions and the conflicts that they engendered.[15] William Chillingworth's *The Religion of Protestants a Safe Way to Salvation* is a defence of the Protestant principle of the sufficiency of Scripture against the challenge of the Tridentine faith.[16] During late decades of the seventeenth century this faith was ably defended in England by John Gother. His *A Papist Mis-represented and Represented: or, A Two-Fold Character of Popery* generated a flurry of pamphlets.[17] But Protestant pamphleteers were aware that it was not enough to

---

[15] See *The Profession of the Tridentine Faith* (1564), esp. art. 3. 'I also admit the holy Scriptures, according to that sense which our holy mother Church has held and does hold, to which it belongs to judge of the true sense and interpretation of the Scriptures', in Philip Schaff, *The Creeds of Christendom* (New York: Harper & Bros., 1919), vol. 2, p. 207.

[16] *The Works of William Chillingworth, M.A.*, 3 vols. (Oxford University Press, 1838). *The Religion of Protestants* is printed in the first two volumes.

[17] See [Edward Gee], *The Catalogue of all the Discourses published Against Popery, during the Reign of King James II* (London, 1689).

refute Gother by attacking the institutions, practices and special doctrines of Roman Catholicism. It was necessary also for them to overcome the scandal of doctrinal difference among Protestants. Two conflicting ways were proposed to achieve this. One was a way of toleration and broad comprehension. The other aimed to enforce comprehensive doctrinal uniformity. The latter way was advocated by William Sherlock in his *Apology.* He called for strict adherence to the 'Ancient Catholick Faith' and the excommunion of all who refuse explicitly to confess it. John Edwards advocated a similar policy. The former way, which might be called a latitudinarian as opposed to an orthodox policy, advocated tolerance of doctrinal differences so long as they did not bear on fundamentals. It should be noted that not just any different doctrine would do, but honest differences of belief that arose among Christians who maintained fidelity to Scripture. A theological justification for this strategy had been made by Simon Episcopius. He considered the diversity of opinion founded on Scripture to be providential. While the fundamental articles of faith are so clear that there is in fact no dispute among Christians about them, differences about other non-necessary beliefs that arise from an honest reading of Scripture merely illustrate the depth of divine wisdom and the limitations of human understanding. On this view, the aim of theology, beyond fundamentals, is not to produce a normative dogmatics but to promote a sort of collegial inquiry after truth.[18] Locke adopted a similar strategy, but he soon came to see that there is no easy agreement about what fundamental Christianity consists of, what doctrines are necessary and what although true are non-necessary to salvation.

[18] Jonathan Israel, *op. cit.*, p. 503.

Among the documents that might be classed as responses to *The Reasonableness of Christianity*, Locke contributed two, his first and second *Vindications*. The *Second Vindication of The Reasonableness of Christianity*, which is more than one and a half times the length of *The Reasonableness of Christianity*, is a polemical work, but it is also a treatise on fundamentals. Because the doctrine of fundamentals is central to his defence against Edwards's charge of Socinianism, and because it seems to contain original features that are not to be found elsewhere, it is important to have a clear understanding of just what Locke's doctrine is. The summary and interpretation that follows is based upon his remarks in *The Reasonableness of Christianity* (*TRC*, pp. 151–8) and the first and second *Vindications* (*1V*, pp. 167–72; *2V*, pp. 309–61).

A fundamental article of faith is a proposition that one must accept as true in order to be Christian. To be a Christian is to be a participant in a new covenant of grace, to live under the Law of Faith and to be able to enjoy its benefits, chief among which is justification by faith. The decision as to what propositions are fundamental is God's and it is communicated in the preaching of the Gospel. There is, according to Locke, as has been noted, one fundamental proposition, that Jesus is the Messiah. Locke insists that acceptance of this proposition does not require an extraordinary attitude of mind. What makes it a saving faith is that it has practical consequences. It is accompanied by repentance, as well as by an acceptance of divine mercy and a resolve, with divine assistance, to live in conformity to the divine law. It also involves certain presuppositions concerning the existence and attributes of God and the necessity of obedience to the divine law.

The belief that Jesus is the Christ is a historical belief.

It refers to certain events located in a particular place and time. These events comprise a moment of revelation. The proposition that Jesus is the Messiah, however, is unlike the assertion that he was crucified, or that he turned water into wine or restored sight to a blind man. The latter are assertions of fact made by persons claiming to have been eye and ear witnesses to the events reported in Scripture. The former is a proposition of revelation. It is a communication from God. Such communications disclose the meaning of these events as decisive moments in the history of redemption.

Locke believed that Scripture, and in particular the New Testament, contained many propositions of revelation, for the time of the beginning of Christianity was a time of special revelation. Jesus and later the Apostles were filled with the Spirit of God. They were infused with divine truth, and this truth, which could be discovered in no other way, became the content of their preaching and teaching, which has been recorded not only in the *Gospels* and *The Acts of the Apostles*, but in the letters of Peter and Paul and the rest. All Christians, that is, all who accept the fundamental proposition that Jesus is the Messiah, are obliged to study the Scriptures and are obliged also to accept as true every proposition of revelation that they read there and understand. But because Christians differ in natural wit and learning and experience and in leisure to pursue the study of divinity, and because judging or giving assent is an individual's business which can be accomplished only by understanding and not by compulsion, not all Christians have the same supplementary obligations of faith; and because Scripture is replete with hard sayings and profound mysteries and with particular teachings that were designed to meet all sorts of conditions and circumstances, any demand for uniformity of faith, beyond fundamentals would be unreasonable.

It follows that Locke's 'fundamentalism' is not a doctrinal minimalism, as Edwards made it out to be, for Christians individually are obliged to believe much more than this one article. Saving faith, then, varies among Christians, but it is unlikely, if the fundamental article is taken seriously, that it would consist of this proposition and nothing more. Thus, the distinction between necessary and non-necessary beliefs, which was basic to Episcopius's doctrine of fundamentals, does not apply very well to Locke. Nor is Locke's 'fundamentalism' a sort of foundationalism. The proposition that Jesus is the Messiah is not a basic belief. It is, as Locke conceived it, more like a threshold belief. This, I take it, is what Locke means when he says, repeatedly, that acceptance of this one proposition is what makes one a Christian. Hence, it is a different sort of belief from all the rest that Christians may be obliged to believe. His conviction that this difference was important, indeed absolutely so, may explain why he persisted single-mindedly defending his claim that all that it takes to make one a Christian is acceptance of Jesus as the Christ.

Daniel Waterland's *A Discourse of Fundamentals*, which appeared forty years after *The Reasonableness of Christianity*, was prepared by him, as archdeacon of Middlesex, for the clergy of the diocese. It contains what is supposed to be a definitive account of the doctrine of fundamentals, together with a critical survey of the concept of fundamentals in early modern theology. The learning and precision characteristic of all of Waterland's writings makes this an invaluable document, for it illuminates both the background against which Locke's work was written and the context in which it was received. In addition, Waterland offers a perceptive critique of Locke, and his own doctrine, becuase it is more ecclesial and more respective of tradition and yet distinctively Protestant, and may be considered by some as a desirable alternative to Locke's notion of normative Christianity.

Central to Waterland's doctrine is a distinction between a relative and an absolute or abstract consideration of fundamentals. Considered absolutely, fundamentals are the doctrines and practices, moral and religious, that all Christians must observe, all things being equal with respect to their intellectual capacities and situation in life. Scripture and reason are the primary sources for deciding what are fundamentals, but, since not all fundamentals are explicitly stated in Scripture yet may be inferred from what is given in it, tradition, so far as it can be derived from these two sources, is also an admissible source of fundamentals. Considered relatively, fundamentals or 'necessaries' are what an individual, with special limitations and in peculiar circumstances, might be expected to believe and practice. Fundamentals, considered absolutely comprise the essential constitution of the Church. They are the terms of the new covenant of grace.[19]

Locke's account is certainly covenantal. The Law of Faith, which is the basis of justification, replaces the older covenants and their respective duties represented in the Law of Nature and the Law of Works, and although this covenant, like its immediate predecessor, defines a community, the keeping of it is more a matter of individual responsibility and self-monitoring than an obligation imposed by a community on its members. Thus, for Locke, beyond the acceptance of the main proposition that Jesus is the Messiah, further accep-

---

[19] For more on Waterland's doctrine of fundamentals, see *The Importance of the Doctrine of the Trinity Asserted* (1735), *Works*, vol. 3.

tance of doctrine is a private matter, a matter of conscience.

It is not my intention to argue here the respective merits of Locke's and Waterland's doctrines of fundamentals. Yet it seems fair, since Locke is the subject of this book, to conclude with a word in his favour. Early in his *Discourse*, Waterland considers Bacon's distinction between perfect and imperfect points of doctrine as a possible way to clarify the difference between fundamental and non-fundamental doctrines, but he dismisses it as unprofitable.[20] Bacon's account of the distinction, as Waterland observes, lacks clarity, but I think that this deficiency can be overcome by comparing it with the distinction between perfect and imperfect duties. On this analogy, a fundamental or perfect doctrine is one that is cast with such clarity and directness that it evokes an unequivocal response of acceptance or rejection. An imperfect doctrine, on the other hand, is one whose meaning is such that it requires contemplation and reflection. In this respect, Locke's threshold belief that Jesus is the Messiah is a perfect doctrine, as indeed are the other doctrines of the Apostolic preaching, concerning Jesus's office, his death and resurrection, and so forth. One either accepts them or one does not. Accepting them, which makes one a Christian, involves an intellectual commitment to an inquiry about the Christian revelation, about what it means and what it requires. This inquiry, which is biblical and historical, ongoing, open-ended and non-dogmatic, is the substance of Christian theology. Its aim is truth that is beyond perfect definition.

---

[20] *The Advancement of Learning* (London: Dent, 1973), p. 212.

About the Collection

The first part of this introduction has been devoted to the context and meaning of *The Reasonableness of Christianity* and, in general terms, of the documents included in this volume. This second part gives bibliographical details of the sources and brief remarks concerning context and the relevance of the selection to the theme of John Locke and Christianity. Not all the documents are responses to *The Reasonableness of Christianity*. Some are here to provide background. All, I hope, will be found useful and germane.

1. *The Reasonableness of Christianity. Extract*, Bodleian MS Locke c. 27, fol. 224 (1703/1704).

This is a transcript of a handwritten review of the second edition of *The Reasonableness of Christianity* which now resides in the Bodleian Library as part of the Lovelace Collection of Locke's papers. The document offers a summary of the argument of Locke's book for the most part in Locke's own words. It is published here for the first time. The original is not in Locke's handwriting, although he wrote his endorsement on the back page, together with the date, 1703/4, and the title *The Reasonableness of Christianity. Extract*. It is in essence an extract of Locke's book, inasmuch as it consists mostly of sections taken from the second edition of *The Reasonableness of Christianity*. The extractor, whose identity, so far as I know, is unknown, has added connecting comments interspersed with favourable remarks about the book and its author.

2. *An Historical View of the State of the Protestant Dissenters in England, And of the Progress of Free Enquiry and Religious Liberty, From the Revolution to*

the Accession of Queen Anne, by Joshua Toulmin, D.D. (London, 1814).

Joshua Toulmin (1740–1815) was a dissenting minister who abandoned the strict Calvinism of his youth and became a leader of the Unitarian movement in England. His DD was awarded by Harvard on Priestley's recommendation. He was an accomplished biographer and historian. His publications include biographies of Faustus Socinus and John Biddle. The controversies that Toulmin narrates in *An Historical View* were still very much alive for him, as was the struggle for free inquiry and religious liberty. Yet he writes with a remarkable clarity if not detachment and shows an unsurpassed mastery of the sources.

3. *The Racovian Catechism, With Notes and Illustrations, translated from the Latin: to which is prefixed A Sketch of the History of Unitarianism in Poland and the Adjacent Countries*, by Thomas Rees, FSA (London, 1818).

The Racovian Catechism is a summary of the articles of faith of the Polish Brethren or the Minor Reformed Church. This small but intellectually active group of liberal Protestant mainly Unitarian congregations established a centre of learning and a printing press in the Polish City of Racow. Their leaders included a group of Italian refugees, among them Faustus Socinus (1539–1604). Hence the name 'Socinian'. *The Racovian Catechism* is a revision and expansion of a work begun by Socinus but left incomplete at his death. It was first published, in Latin, in 1609, with a dedication to James I of England who refused the honour. Another Latin edition was published in London

in 1651 and was condemned by Parliament.[21] The
Polish Brethren fell victim to the Counter-Reformation.
In 1638 they were forbidden to publish. In 1660 they
were forced into exile. They moved their centre to
Holland where they enjoyed the hospitality of the
Remonstrants. Locke did not have a copy of *The
Racovian Catechism* in his library. However, he did
own a copy of Socinus's prototype, which together with
other works by Faustus Socinus, he gave to Pierre
Coste.[22]

4. Philip van Limborch, *A Compleat System, or Body of
Divinity, both speculative and practical: founded on
Scripture and Reason* (London, 1702).

This is an English translation of Limborch's *Theologia
Christiana ad praxin pietatis ac promotionem pacis
Christianae unice directa* (*Christian Theology, drawn up
solely for the practice of piety and the promotion of
Christian peace*), 2nd ed. (Amsterdam, 1695). The
translation is not literal; some sections of the original are
transposed; and a different enumeration of sections is
followed. Locke was familiar with the first (1686) and
second Latin editions. It was the second to which he
turned to find confirmation of the conclusions set down
in *The Reasonableness of Christianity*.

5. This pamphlet, which is made up of extracts from
William Chillingworth's *The Religion of Protestants a
Safe Way of Salvation* (Oxford, 1638), appeared in *A*

---

[21] This account follows Rees. McLachlan's publication history of *The
Racovian Catechism* differs in detail. Chap. 1 of McLachlan, *op. cit.*,
presents a brief account of the origin and early development of
Socinianism.

[22] John Harrison and Peter Laslett, *The Library of John Locke* (Oxford: The
Oxford Bibliographical Society, 1965), p. 235, item 2704.

Collection of Tracts, proving The God and Father of our Lord Jesus Christ the only True God; and Jesus Christ the Son of God, him whom the Father sanctified and sent, raised from the Dead and exalted (publisher and date not known).

The compiler was most likely Stephen Nye (1648–1718), an Anglican clergyman and Unitarian sympathizer who was a prominent pamphleteer in the Trinitarian controversy of the late seventeenth century. This pamphlet was no doubt meant to establish a Socinian claim on Chillingworth and to portray Socinians as true Protestants. The most relevant of Nye's writings to Locke's biblical project is *An Accurate Examination of the Principal Texts usually alledged for the Divinity of our Saviour; and for the Satisfaction by him to the Justice of God, for the Sins of Men*. It was first published in London in 1692.[23] William Chillingworth (1602–44) was a member of the almost legendary Tew Circle and was its most formidable theologian.[24] *The Religion of Protestants a Safe Way to*

---

[23] Also informative about the main orthodox contenders in the Trinitarian conflict is Nye's *Considerations on the Explications of the doctrine of the Trinity occasioned by Four Sermons preached by his Grace, The Lord Arch-Bishop of Canterbury* [Tillotson]. *A Sermon preached by the Lord-Bishop of Worcester* [Stillingfleet]. *A Discourse by the Lord-Bishop of Salisbury* [Gilbert Burnet]. *A sheet by a very Learned Hand* [Edward Fowler], *containing twenty-eight Propositions. A Treatise by an Eminent Dissenting Minister* [John Howe], *being a calm Discourse concerning the Possibility of a Trinity. And by a Book in answer to the Animadversions on Dr. Sherlock's Vindication of the Trinity* (1694). Perhaps for reasons of economy, Nye preferred to have his pamphlets printed in double columns. This feature was noted with derision by John Edwards, who seemed to believe that the format itself is a sign of bad faith and worthy of a sneer.

[24] On the Tew Circle, see Edward Hyde, Earl of Clarendon, *The History of the Rebellion and Civil Wars in England* (Oxford: Clarendon Press, 1888), vol. 3, pp. 178–90; H. R. Trevor-Roper, 'The Great Tew Circle', in *Catholics, Anglicans & Puritans* (University of Chicago Press, 1989); Frederick C. Beiser, *The Sovereignty of Reason*, chap. 3; also on

Salvation is a response to a defence of Roman Catholicism by Edward Knott, aka Matthias Wilson, an English Jesuit.

6. *Roman-Catholick Principles, In Reference to God and the King* was printed as an Appendix to *A Papist Mis-represented and Represented: Or, A Two-Fold Character of Popery* (1685), by J. L. [John Gother, who went by the pseudonym Lovell].

Gother, born in Southampton into a Protestant family, converted to Roman Catholicism and was educated at the English College in Lisbon. He was ordained priest, and from 1682 until his death in 1704, he was active in the English mission.[25]

A Papist Mis-represented and Represented is an ingenious apology for Roman Catholicism. Gother's method is more therapeutic and conciliatory than disputational. His aim is not directly to refute charges of idolatry, superstition and sedition, but to dislodge the paranoia that conceived them in the first place. The imagination of Protestants harbours an image of a papist that is 'so deform'd and monstrous, that it justly deserves the hatred of as many as own *Christianity*'.

Tis a Papist, that is so abominable, so malicious, so unsufferable in any Civil Government, that for my part, I detest him from my heart; I conceiv'd an hatred against him and all his, from my Education, when as

---

Chillingworth, see John Tulloch, *Rational Theology and Christian Philosophy in England in the Seventeenth Century*, 2nd ed. (Edinburgh: William Blackwood and Sons, 1874), vol. 1, chap. 5.

[25] There is no article on John Gother in the *DNB*. For a brief biography and a bibliography of his writings, see Joseph Gillow, *Bibliographical Dictionary of the English Catholics* (London: Burnes & Oates, 1885), vol. 2, pp. 540ff.

yet a *Protestant*; and now, being a *Roman Catholick*, I am not in the least reconcil'd to him, nor his Principles; but hate him yet worse.

Insofar as English laws against Roman Catholic recusants are directed against Papists of this sort, he would wish them to be made more severe. In contrast to this abomination, which is an invention of the 'Father of Lies', Gother characterizes the true Papist, who 'lives and believes what is prescribed in the *Council of Trent*', and offers himself as evidence of the truth of this representation.[26]

7. *An Historical View of the State of the Protestant Dissenters in England, And of the Progress of Free Enquiry and Religious Liberty, From the Revolution to the Accession of Queen Anne*, by Joshua Toulmin, DD (London, 1814).

8. *An End to Discord: wherein is demonstrated, That no Doctrinal Controversy remains between the Presbyterian and Congregational Ministers, fit to justify longer Divisions. With a true Account of Socinianism As to the Satisfaction of Christ* (1699), from *Discourses on Several Important Subjects*, by the Late Reverend Daniel Williams, DD (London, 1750).

Williams (1644–1716) was a Presbyterian divine. He served as chief spokesman for the Moderate Calvinist Party during the Antinomian Controversy. *An End to Discord* was supposed to mark the end of the controversy, but it is not at all conciliatory. The juxtaposition of opposing propositions make it a convenient summary of questions at issue. Dr Williams's Library, a

---

[26] *A Papist Mis-represented, and Represented*, pp. 10f.

theological library located in London and devoted to works by dissenting divines, is named after the author.

9. *A Summary Account of the Deists Religion* from *The Oracles of Reason*, by Charles Blount, Esq; Mr. Gildon, and others (London, 1693). The *Summary* is prefaced by a letter addressed 'To the Most Ingenuous and Learned Dr. Sydenham'.

Charles Blount (1654–93) was an early deist writer.[27] It is likely that Locke had Blount's book and this summary in mind when he took up the deist challenge to Christianity. There seems to be an allusion to *The Oracles of Reason* in *The Reasonableness of Christianity*,[28] and Locke's case for the advantages of Christianity seems to have its counterpart in Blount's *Summary*. It is clear from Blount's letter to Sydenham that the *Summary* was in circulation at least since 1686. This was probably true of most of the contents of *The Oracles of Reason*. It seems unlikely that Locke would not have read some or many of them before he began work on *The Reasonableness of Christianity*, and that he was cognisant that they had been published together under the title *The Oracles of Reason*.[29]

Deism, as Blount presents it here, is a sort of ethical

---

[27] For a convenient account of Blount's life and writings see John Valdimir Price's introduction to the Routledge/Thoemmes Press reprint of *The Oracles of Reason* in *The History of British Deism*, 8 vols. (London, 1995).

[28] *TRC*, p. 144: '[Philosophers] depended on reason and her oracles, which contain nothing but truth: but yet some parts of that truth lie too deep for our natural powers easily to reach and make plain and visible to mankind; without one light from above to direct them.'

[29] Locke did not own a copy of the 1683 edition of *The Oracles of Reason*. The copy he possessed was included in Blount's *Miscellaneous Works* (London, 1695). He also possessed two other works by Blount that treated religious subjects: *Anima Mundi* (1679), and *Great is Diana of the Ephesians* (1695) (*The Library of John Locke*, items 353, 354, 355).

monotheism. He asserts the following: the sufficiency of monotheism: one God is enough; the perfection of God: 'God is whatsoever is Adorable, Amiable, and Imitable by Mankind'; the worship of God, which involves making our whole lives conform to whatever is by nature just; and the supreme confidence that God's mercy is sufficient to his justice. Hence there is need neither for a sacrifice nor a mediator to establish a proper relation to God. Whether Blount himself subscribed to this religion is an unresolved question. This summary seems far from the Hobbism and atheism with which he has been charged.[30]

Readers, however, should compare Blount's *Summary* with his letter 'To The Right Honourable, the Most Ingenious Strephon [John Wilmot, The Earl Rochester]' (dated 7 Feb. 1679/80). The subject of this letter is the immortality of the soul. Blount begins by quoting Pliny's Epicurean arguments against the immortality of the soul. He seems to accept these arguments as conclusive, for after remarking that some modern moralists argue, as though to refute Pliny's conclusion, that if the soul is not immortal then the whole world is deceived 'since all our Laws do now suppose it so', he presents a case that makes it at least plausible that the whole world is indeed deceived about the foundation of morality, and that politicians originated the deception.

> But to this [Modern moral argument] it has been reply'd, That if the whole be nothing but the parts, (as must be allow'd) then, since there is no Man who is not deceiv'd, as Plato saith, it is absolutely necessary to grant, either that the whole World is deceiv'd, or at least the greater part of it; for supposing that there be

---

[30] See David Berman, *A History of Atheism in Britain* (London: Croom Helm, 1988), pp. 93–5.

but three Laws, *viz.* that of *Moses*, that of Christ, and that of *Mahomet*; either all are false, and so the whole World is deceiv'd; or only two of them, and so the greater part is deceiv'd. But we must know, as Plato and Aristotle well observe, That a Politician is a Physician of Minds; and that his Aim is rather to make Men good, than knowing.[31]

Yet the deception has some basis, although not a sufficient one, in reason, for Blount goes on to say that neither the justice of God nor the happiness of mankind could be satisfied unless this doctrine of immortality and of eternal rewards and punishments were true. The conclusion is a sceptical one. However, it is not just reason, but revealed religion (Moses, Christ and Mahomet) that has failed to undeceive the whole world.

The question that concerns us is not what Blount believed but how Locke perceived deism. Suppose he perceived it as a moral religion burdened with scepticism about the foundation of morality and the immortality of the soul. This seems likely. But just so, deism provided him with an opportunity to promote the advantages of Christianity. The immortality of the soul cannot be proved because the soul, after Adam's sin, became mortal. Lacking this, it seems impossible to found morality, even though there seems to be some general knowledge of moral rules and a disposition, founded on utility and common sense, to be moral. Inasmuch as Christ restores immortality, and reveals that coming judgement of all mankind, and more perfectly discloses the eternal and immutable divine law, he provides the requisite reasons to found morality. Deism or natural

---

[31] *The Oracles of Reason*, p. 121. For a recent and illuminating discussion of this letter, and of Edwards and Locke as well, see J. A. I. Champion, *The Pillars of Priestcraft Shaken, The Church of England and its Enemies 1660–1730* (Cambridge University Press, 1992).

religion, then, is not denied by Christianity, rather is founded by it.[32]

10. *An Apology for Writing against Socinians, in Defence of the Doctrines of the Holy Trinity and Incarnation: In Answer to a Late Earnest and Compassionate Suit for Forbearance to the Learned Writers of some Controversies at present*, by William Sherlock, DD, Dean of St Pauls, Master of the Temple, and Chaplain in Ordinary to Their Majesties (London, 1693).

Sherlock's pamphlet was written in response to another by Edward Wetenhall (1636–1713), Bishop of Kilmore and Armagh: *An Earnest and Compassionate Suit for Forbearance, to the Learned Writers of some Controversies at present* by a Melancholy Stander-By (1691). Wetenhall was distressed by the Trinitarian controversy because it dishonoured the Reformation and put Protestants at a disadvantage in their controversy with Roman Catholics. Sherlock was a central figure in this controversy. He believed that he was bound to defend the doctrine of the Trinity, because it was a fundamental article of Christianity. Thus, he stands against Locke on this issue. Yet, in his defence of the doctrine of the Trinity, he relies on basic elements of Locke's philosophy, on his theory of ideas to establish the epistemological basis of his defence, and on his concept of personal identity to explicate the Trinitarian relations. This is not apparent in the *Apology*, for Sherlock had other purposes there, but it is apparent in his *Vindication of the Ever Blessed Doctrine of the Trinity*.[33]

---

[32] See my introduction to TRC for a more detailed development of this argument.

[33] London: W. Rogers, 1690. I have used the 3rd edition of 1694. Locke's

11. Samuel Bold, *A Short Discourse of the True Knowledge of Christ Jesus. To which are Added, Some Passages in the Reasonableness of Christianity, &c.* (London, 1695).

Samuel Bold (1649–1737), an Anglican divine, was rector of Steeple on the Isle of Purbeck. Most of his published writings were written in defence of Locke, who gratefully acknowledged Bold's unsolicited support in an open letter included in the preface to the *Second Vindication* (2V, pp. 185–9).[34] *A Short Discourse* is not one of Bold's defences, but an independent work. However, its argument coincides with Locke's on one important point: both assert that the belief that Jesus is the Messiah is sufficient to make one a Christian. It is unlikely that Bold was deliberately following Locke here, for he remarks that he had not read *The Reasonableness of Christianity* carefully until after reading Edwards's *Socinianism Unmask'd*. Until then, he admits to having read it only cursorily. Another reason to conclude that *A Short Discourse* was written without Locke's influence is the remarkable difference between Bold's concept of the covenant of grace and Locke's. Whereas Locke emphasizes the continuing legal obligations under the new covenant, modified, to be sure, by the assurance of pardon and the promise of spiritual assistance, Bold draws attention to its newness. Christians are endowed with a new nature, with a new 'vital principle' or agency that takes possession of all their faculties. In this respect, Bold has greater affinities

---

Essay was published in 1689.

[34] Samuel Bold, *A Collection of Tracts, publish'd in Vindication of Mr. Locke Reasonableness of Christianity, &c. And of his Essay concerning Humane Understanding* (London: A & J. Churchill, 1706). This collection includes all of Bold's defences of Locke.

with the Calvinist Edwards than with Locke, a fact that does not go unnoticed in his defences.

12. John Edwards, *Some Thoughts Concerning the Several Causes and Occasions of Atheism, Especially in the Present Age. With some Brief Reflections on Socinianism: and on a Late Book entituled, The Reasonableness of Christianity...* (London: J. Robinson, 1695).

The discussion of Locke's book appears as a last-minute addition, although there is a progression from end to beginning, that is, from Locke, et al., to Socinianism, to atheism, that coincides with Edwards's line of argument. According to this construction, Locke and some others, in particular, Jeremy Taylor, Herbert Croft, and Arthur Bury, are not Socinians but their books are gladly received by them, on account of the 'Plausible Conceit' that has come to maturity in their works: that there is 'one Article of Faith necessary to Salvation'.[35] Locke didn't mind at all being associated with Taylor and Croft, both of whom had been Bishops of the Church of England. In an epilogue to the first *Vindication*, he added Simon Patrick to their number as one who also practised this 'plausible conceit' (*V1*, pp. 179f).[36]

---

[35] Jeremy Taylor, *A Discourse of the Liberty of Prophesying* (London: R. Royston, 1647); [Herbert Croft, Bishop of Hereford], *The Naked Truth. Or, The True State of the Primitive Church*, by an Humble Moderator (1675); [Arthur Bury], *The Naked Gospel, Part I, of Faith*, by a True Son of the Church of England (1690). Bury, Rector of Exeter College Oxford, lost his post on account of this publication, and his book was publicly burnt. This action was condemned by Locke's friend, Jean Le Clerc in an anonymous pamphlet: *An Historical Vindication of the Naked Gospel* (1690).

[36] Simon Patrick, *The Witnesses to Christianity; or, The Certainty of Our Faith and Hope*, in two parts (1st ed., 1676; 2nd ed., 1703, retitled: *Jesus and the Resurrection justified by Witnesses in Heaven and in Earth*, in *Works*, ed. A. Taylor (Oxford, 1858), vol. 3).

13. From *The Exceptions of Mr. Edwards, in his Causes of Atheism, Against the Reasonableness of Christianity, as deliver'd in the Scriptures, Examin'd; And found Unreasonable, Unscripture, and Injurious. Also It's clearly proved by many Testimonies of Holy Scripture, That the God and Father of our Lord Jesus Christ, is the only God and Father of Christians* (London, 1695).

This defence of Locke's book is also a defence of Socinianism. It is printed in the characteristic Socinian format of double columns. I have been unable to discover the identity of the author.

14. John Edwards, *Socinianism Unmask'd. A Discourse shewing the Unreasonableness of a Late Writer's Opinion Concerning the Necessity of only One Article of Christian Faith...,With a Brief Reply to another (professed) Socinian Writer* (London, 1696).

Unlike its predecessor, this book is devoted almost entirely to *The Reasonableness of Christianity*. Edwards wants to unmask the author's Socinian intentions and to show their dangerous consequence namely, the devolution of Christian faith from orthodoxy to the mere 'faith of a Turk', and from there to a state of mind that is beneath even what devils are capable of. Of interest also is Edwards's own account of fundamental Christianity and a brief defence of the doctrine of the Trinity. In an appendix he responds to *The Exceptions of Mr. Edwards*.

15. Samuel Bold, *Some Passages in the Reasonableness of Christianity &c. and its Vindication. With some Animadversions on Mr. Edwards's Reflections on the Reasonableness of Christianity, and on his Book, Entituled, Socinianism Unmask'd* (London, 1697).

16. *A Discourse of Fundamentals, being the substance of Two Charges delivered to the Middlesex Clergy, at the Easter Visitations of 1734 and 1735,* in *The Works of The Reverend Daniel Waterland, DD,* 3rd ed., 6 vols., ed. William A. Van Mildert, DD (Oxford University Press, 1856).

The *Discourse* is complete with the exception of the notes, most of which have been deleted here.

Daniel Waterland (1686–1740) was Master of Magdalen College, Cambridge and Archdeacon of Middlesex. A scholar of immense learning and formidable intellect, Waterland devoted these talents to a defence of orthodoxy, especially of the doctrine of the Trinity. The occasion of his defence was the revival of Arianism. His principal opponent was Samuel Clarke (1675–1729).[37] His dispute with Clarke went beyond dogma to issues of natural theology. He argued that Clarke's a priori theistic proof made the existence of God dependent upon an antecedent necessity, and that his moral theory, based upon the essential fitness of things, separated morality from religion. In both cases he feared that Clarke's natural theology might lead to atheism. Waterland's collaborator in these last two disputes was Edmund Law (1702–87), who was at the time a fellow at Christ's College, and later became Master of Peterhouse, Cambridge and Bishop of Carlisle. Law was also editor of Locke's works and a promoter of his philosophy. Waterland adopted Law's Lockean positions in epistemology and moral philosophy. Thus he, like William Sherlock, may also

---

[37] See Maurice Wiles, *Archetypal Heresy, Arianism through the Centuries* (Oxford: Clarendon Press, 1996). Chapter 4 of this excellent book is a lengthy account of British Arianism during the seventeenth and eighteenth centuries; also J. P. Ferguson, *An Eighteenth Century Heretic, Dr. Samuel Clarke* (Kineton: The Roundwood Press, 1976).

be regarded as a Lockean theologian of Trinitarian persuasion.[38]

Victor Nuovo
Middlebury College,
Vermont, 1997

---

[38] For some products of the collaboration between Waterland and Law, see my introduction to *The Collected Works of Edmund Law* (Bristol: Thoemmes Press, 1997).

ACKNOWLEDGMENTS

I am grateful to my friends Torrance Kirby, Peter Scott, Maurice Wiles and Avihu Zakai for helpful advice in preparing this book and its introduction; to Jane Williamson, editor of Thoemmes Press, and Andrew Pyle, editor of the Key Issues series, for their advice and constant support; to the directors of the Center of Theological Inquiry, old and new: Daniel Hardy, William Lazareth and Wallace Alston, for counsel and support; to the Keeper of the Western Manuscripts of the Bodleian Library for permission to publish the *The Reasonablenes of Christianity. Extract*; and especially to William Harris, Librarian for Special Collections at Speer Library, Princeton Theological Seminary, whose generosity enabled me to complete this work.

EDITORIAL NOTE

All citations of *The Reasonableness of Christianity* in this collection have been amended to correspond to the 1794 edition reprinted by Thoemmes Press, 1997.

In addition, where the featured pieces refer to other items in the collection the citations have been amended to correspond to the new typesetting.

THE REASONABLENESS OF CHRISTIANITY. EXTRACT

The Reasonableness of Christianity as delivered in the Scriptures. The Second Edition: to which is added *a Vindication of the same from Mr. Edwards Exceptions.* London* 1696 8º pagg. 307 & 40. *printed for Awnsham & John Churchill at the Black Swan in Pater-Noster Row.

The Author of this Book being little satisfied with most of the Systems of Divinity betook himself to the sole reading of the Scripture, for the understanding of the Christian Religion. He read the Sacred Writings with great care & attention, & after an impartial search after truth, he found that the Christian Religion, *as it is delivered in the Scriptures*, is more plain & intelligible than it is commonly believed. This subject being Therefore of great moment, the Reader will without doubt expect from me an Exact Account of this Treatise.

The doctrine of Redemption, sayth the Author, & consequently of the Gospel is founded on the supposition of *Adam's* Fall. That which *Adam* fell from was the State of perfect Obedience, which is called *Justice* in the New Testament, though the word which in the Original signifies *Justice*, be translated *Righteousness*. And by this Fall he lost paradise, wherein was Tranquillity and the Tree of Life, i.e. he lost Bliss & Immortality. He might have been happy & immortal in paradise, but as soon as he eat the

1

forbidden Fruit, his Life began to shorten, & waste, & to have an end. 'Tis in this sense that we are to take these words *Gen.* 11 *In the day that thou eatest thereof, thou shalt surely die.*

As *Adam* was turned out of paradise, so all his posterity was born out of it. All like their Father *Adam* are in a state of Mortality, & deprived of the Tranquillity and Bliss of paradise. *Rom.* v. 12. *By one Man sin entered into the world, & death by Sin* i.e. a state of Death and Mortality. Whereupon the Author observes, to prevent a common objection, that the state of Immortality in paradise is not due to the posterity of *Adam* more than to any other Creature, & that therefore keeping Men from what they have no right to, cannot be called a *Punishment.* This temporary mortal life is the Gift of God, & he does not injure Men, when he takes it from them. So that Death is not a punishment inflicted upon Men by reason of the sin of *Adam:* which will the more clearly appear, if we consider that though *all die in Adam,* yet none are truly punished but for their own deeds, as it is manifest from the doctrine of Christ & his Apostles. *Matt.* VII. 23 & XXV. 42. *Rom.* II. 6. 2 *Cor.* V. 10.

Men had remained under death forever, & had been utterly lost, if Christ had not been restored to life by the Resurrection; 1 *Cor.* XV. 22. *As in Adam all die, so in Christ shall all be made alive:* & in the foregoing verse *by Man Death came, by Man also came the Resurrection of the dead.* If Men had lived in an *Exact Conformity* to the Law of God, they had been out of the reach of death. But Loss of immortality is the portion of sinners of all those who have *any way* broke the divine Law, & failed of a *compleat* obedience by the guilt of *any one* Transgression. From whence it follows, that all Men being Sinners, they were all to die & cease to be. But God has found a way to justify Some, i.e. as many as obey another Law, which God has given, which in the New Testament is called *the Law of Faith, Rom.* III. 27. & is opposed to *the Law of Works.*

The *Law of Works* is that Law, which requires *perfect* obedience, without any remission or abatement; so that by that Law a Man cannot be Just, or justified without an *Exact* performance of every tittle. The Language of this Law is Do this & live, Transgress & die, as it appears from several places of the Scripture. This *Law of Works*, was to be found in the Law delivered by *Moses*, & it comprehends not only the Law delivered by *Moses*, but also the Law of Nature, knowable by reason to all Mankind, which all men have transgresst.

The difference between the *Law of Works* & the *Law of Faith* is only this, that the *Law of Works* makes no allowance for failing on any occasion. Those that obey are Righteous, those that in any part disobey are Unrighteous, & must not expect Life the Reward of Righteousness. But by the *Law of Faith*, Faith is allowed to supply the defect of full obedience, & so the Believers are admitted to Life & Immortality as if they were Righteous. God does justify or make Just those who by their Works are not so: which he does by counting their Faith for Righteousness i.e. for a compleat performance of the Law. *Rom.* IV. 3. *Abraham believed God, & it was counted to him for Righteousness.* See also the following verses. This faith for which God justified Abraham was the believing God, when he engaged his promise in the Covenant he made with him. Now this, says St. *Paul, Rom.* IV. 23, 24 *was not writ for his* [Abraham's] *sake alone; but for us also;* teaching us that as Abraham was justified for his Faith, so also ours shall be accounted to us for Righteousness, if we believe God, as Abraham believed him. In short the Law of Faith is for every one, to believe what God requires him to believe, as a condition of the covenant he makes with him; & not to doubt of the performance of his promises.

The Author having laid down the Foundation, says that what we are required to believe to obtain Eternal Life is plainly set down in the Gospel. As *John* tells us, *John* III, 36. *He that believeth on the Son, hath eternal Life*; & *he that believeth not the Son, shall not see Life*. & it appears says the Author, by the next chapter v. 25 &c. that *believing on the Son*, is the *believing that Jesus is the Messiah*, giving credit to the miracles he did, and the profession he made of himself. For those who were said to BELIEVE ON HIM for the saying of the Woman of *Samaria* v. 39 tell the Woman that they now believed not any longer because of her saying; but that having heard him themselves they knew, i.e. BELIEVED past doubt THAT HE WAS THE MESSIAH.

The Author observes that this was the great proposition that was then controverted concerning Jesus of *Nazareth*, whether he was the *Messiah* or no; & the assent to that, was that which distinguished Believers from Unbelievers. He wrought Miracles to convince Men of this truth, & the great point insisted on & promulgated in the Gospel was, that he was the *Messiah*. This was the great Truth he took pains to convince his Disciples & Apostles of, appearing to them after the Resurrection, And the preaching of the Apostles everywhere in the *Acts*, tended to this one point to prove that Jesus was the *Messiah*. The Author quotes a great many passages to prove all these things, & shews at the same time that the title of *Son of God* which is given to Christ, imports no more than his being the *Messiah* & the King of Israel.

Afterwards he oberves that there is a threefold declaration of the *Messiah*: 1. by Miracles. The Jews expected a *Messiah*, who was to be an extraordinary Man sent from God, who with an extraordinary Divine power & Miracles should evidence his Mission & work their deliverance. Accordingly we find that the people justified their *believing in Him*, i.e. their believing him to be the *Messiah* because of the Miracles he did, *John*. VII. 31. & Christ himself refers the Jews to his miracles to convince them that he was the *Messiah, John*. X. 24, 25. & elsewhere.

2. By phrases & circumlocutions, that did signify or intimate the coming of the *Messiah*; though not in direct words pointing out the person. The most usual of these were, *the Kingdom of God & of Heaven*; because it was that which was oftenest spoken of the *Messiah* in the Old Testament: & a Kingdom was that which the Jews most looked after, & wished for. So that *the Kingdom of God & the Kingdom of Heaven* were common phrases among the Jews, to signify the times of the *Messiah*. See *Luke* XIV. 15. & XVII. 20.

3. By plain & direct words, declaring that Jesus was the *Messiah*: as we see the Apostles did, when they went about preaching the Gospel after our Saviours Resurrection.

Now the reasons why Jesus for the most part made no other discovery of himself, at least in *Judea*, & at the beginning of his ministry, but in the two former ways; & why he forbad his Apostles to declare openly that he was the Messiah, were these. 1. Christ was to fill out the time foretold of his ministry, & after a life illustrious in Miracles & good Works, & every way conformable to the prophecies of him, was to be lead as a Sheep to the Slaughter, & with all quiet and submission be brought to the Cross, though there were no guilt nor fault found in him. But if as soon as he appeared in publick, he had professed himself to have been the *Messiah*, the King that owned that kingdom he published to be at hand; the *Sanhedrim* would then have laid hold on it, to have got him into their power, & thereby have taken away his life; at least they would have disturbed his Ministry & hindered the work he was about. And therefore he was very cautious to avoid the occasions of provoking them, & falling into their hands. Besides, if Christ had publicly preached that he was the King whom the Jews expected, the Roman Governour of *Judea* could not have forborne to have taken notice of it, & would have stopt him in the Course of his Ministry. 2. Another reason that hindered him as much as the former from professing himself in express words that he was the *Messiah*, was that the whole Nation of the Jews expecting at this time their *Messiah*, & deliverance by him from the subjection they were in to a Foreign Yoke, the body of the people would certainly upon his declaring himself to be the *Messiah* their King, have rose up in rebellion, & set him at the head of them. I need not tell the Reader that the Author proves & illustrates all this (as he does all along in this Treatise) by several passages of the New Testament, which cannot be set down in an Extract.

This being premised, the Author takes a View of the promulgation of the Gospel by Christ himself. Therefore he runs through the Four Gospels & carefully examines, according to the order of times, every Text that relates to the matter at hand. He finds the Christ preached *the Kingdom of God*, and *the Kingdom of Heaven*, that is, the Kingdom of the *Messiah*, though he very seldom said in express words that he was the *Messiah*, for the reasons above mentioned; but instanced upon his Miracles, & by several other estimations, gave them to understand, that he was the *Messiah*, & the King whom they expected. In short it appears by a careful reading of the Four Gospels, that such was the manifestation of Christ as everyone at present could not understand; but yet it carried such an evidence with those who were well disposed now, or would reflect on it, when the whole Course of his Ministry was over, as was sufficient clearly to convince them that he was the *Messiah*. This part of the Author's Book does very much deserve to be carefully read. He explains each passage with great clearness, & what he says affords a great light towards the understanding of the New Testament. The Reader cannot expect that I should give him an account of the explication of those many passages: for then I must transcribe a great part of the Author's Book, & consequently exceed the bounds of an Extract. I refer him therefore to the Book it self.

The Author having thus explained what Men are required to believe by the preaching of the Gospel, viz. that Jesus is the *Messiah*, adds that this *Faith*, & *Repentence*, i.e. believing Jesus to be the *Messiah*, & a good Life, are the indispensible conditions of the New Covenant to be performed by all those, who would obtain eternal Life. God, out of his mercy to Mankind, & for the erecting of the Kingdom of his Son, proposed to the Children of Men, that as many of them as would believe *Jesus* his Son to be the *Messiah*, the promised Deliverer; & would receive him for their King & Ruler, should have all their past sins, disobedience & rebellion forgiven them: And if for the future they lived in a sincere obedience to his Son, to the utmost of their power; the sins of human frailty for the time to come, as well as all those of their past lives, should for his Son's Sake, because they gave themselves up to him to be his Subjects, be forgiven them.

The Author proceeds therefore to shew, that besides believing Christ to be the *Messiah*, it was farther required

that those who would have the priviledge, advantages &
deliverance of his Kingdom, should enter themselves into
it; & by Baptism being made Denisons, & solemnly incor-
porated into that Kingdom, live as became Subjects
obedient to the Laws of it. & therefore St. Paul tells the
Galatians, That that which availeth is *Faith*; but *Faith
working by Love*. & St. *James* shews at large, Chap. 11.
that *Faith* without *Works*, i.e. the works of sincere
obedience to the Law & will of Christ, is not sufficient for
our justification.

Our Author observes, before he comes to treat of the
Several Laws, which Christ delivers to those who
acknowledge him for their King, that amongst the Jews
Anointing was used for three sorts of persons, at their
Inauguration; whereby they were set apart to three great
offices, viz. of priests, prophets, & Kings. Though these
three Offices be in Holy Writ attributed to our Saviour, yet
I do not remember, (says he), that he anywhere assumes
to himself, the Title of a priest, or mentions any thing
relating to his priesthood: Nor does he Speak of his being
a prophet, but very Sparingly, & once or twice, as it were,
by the by. But the Gospel or the good news of the
Kingdom of the *Messiah*, is what he preaches every where,
& makes it his great business to publish to the World.

In order to know what Christ requires of those, who
believe him to be the *Messiah*, the Author examines all the
passages of the Four Gospels, which contain some Moral
precepts, too long to be here inserted, & shews that a
sincere Obedience to the several Laws & Commands of
Christ is a condition of the New Covenant as well as
Faith. The Apostles taught the same thing, as it appears
by several places of the *Acts* quoted by the Author. The
same is also evident from all the Texts, where Christ
mentions the Last Judgement, & describes his way of

proceeding in that great Day.

All that was required of the Jews before the coming of the *Messiah*, was to believe what God had revealed to them concerning him, & to rely with a full assurance on God for the performance of his promise, & to believe that in due time he would send them that *Messiah* according to his word. If it be objected, What will become of the rest of all Mankind, who never heard a word of a *Messiah* to be sent, or that was sent, & consequently could not believe on Him? The Author answers, That God will require of every Man, *according to what a Man hath, & not according to what he hath not*; that God had by the light of reason, revealed to all Mankind, who would make use of that Light, that he was Good & Merciful, & therefore would forgive them, if they acknowledged their faults, begg'd his pardon, & resolved in earnest for the future to conform their actions to his Law, which they owned to be just and right. This way of Reconciliation, this hope of Atonement the Light of Nature revealed to them: & the Revelation of the Gospel having said nothing to the contrary, leaves them to stand & Fall to their own Father & Master, whose Goodness & Mercy is over all his Works. Some urge this place of the Acts, chap. IV. v. 12. *Neither is there Salvation in any other: for there is none other Name under Heaven given among men, in which we must be saved.* But the Author answers that the meaning of it, is; that *Jesus* is the only true *Messiah*; neither is there any other person but he given to be a Mediator between God & Man, in whose name we may ask & hope for Salvation.

Some are apt to ask, what need was there of a Saviour? What advantage have we by *Jesus Christ*? To this our Author's General Answer is, that it is enough to justify, the fitness of any thing to be done by resolving it into the

Wisdom of God, who has done it; though our short view & narrow understanding may utterly incapacitate us to see that Wisdom, & to judge rightly of it. We know little of this visible, & nothing at all of the State of that Intellectual World, wherein are infinite numbers & degrees of Spirits out of the reach of our ken or guess: & therefore know not what transactions there were between God & our Saviour, in reference to his Kingdom. We know not what need there was to set up a Head & a Chieftain, in opposition *to the prince of this world, the prince of the power of the Air*, &c. Whereof there are more than obscure intimations in the Scripture. &c.

But this is only a general Answer: what follows from page 134 to page 155 concerning the Excellency & Usefulness of the Christian Revelation, seems to me to be so admirable, that If I had not this Book by me, I would buy it upon the account of this most excellent part of it. I shall find it a difficult thing to give the Substance of what the Author says on this Subject; because every line is of great weight, & the Whole can scarce bear an Abridgment without great disadvantage.

1. Though all the Works of Nature sufficiently manifest the Being of a God, yet the greatest part of Mankind Knew him not. Some were careless & unthinking; others were blinded by their Lust & Passions: but most out [of] a fearful apprehension of some Superiour unknown Beings, gave up themselves into the hands of their priests, who filled their heads with false notions of the Deity, & their Worship with foolish Rites: & what Dread and Craft once began, Devotion soon made sacred, & Religion immutable. In this state of Darkness & Ignorance the World was filled with Vice & Superstition. The priests, to secure their Empire, excluded *Reason* from having any thing to do in Religion. 'Tis true that thinking Men found

the One, Supream, Invisible God; but they kept this truth lockt up in their own breasts as a Secret, & durst not publish it among the people, much less among the priests. Hence it is that *Reason* could never prevail on the Multitude, & perswade the Societies of Men that there was but one God, who alone was to be worshipped. The *Israelites* were the only Nation that believed & Worshipped One only God, for which they were beholden to *Revelation*. The *Athenians* exceeded all other Nations in parts, knowledge & Learning; & yet we find but one *Socrates* amongst them, that opposed their polytheism, & wrong opinions of the Deity; & we know how he was rewarded for it. The philosophers were forced to comply with the Crowd, & profess the Religion established by Law. St. *Paul* tells us how great was the Superstition of the Athenians, & their ignorance concerning the true God, in that remarkable place of the *Acts* XVII. 22–29.

Such was the State of the World, when Christ appeared in it. The Revelation he brought with him, made the true God known to Men. *Polytheism* & *Idolatry* were not able to withstand that Light. In effect we see that since our Saviours coming, the belief of *one God* has prevailed & spread itself over the face of the Earth. If the *Mahometans* believe but one God, we must ascribe to it the Religion taught by Christ, part of which they adopted into theirs. Though the *Israelites* had a clear Revelation of the Unity of God, yet they were not able to propagate that truth in the World; because their Law excluded them from communicating with the rest of Mankind. Besides it was a Nation shut up in a little corner of the World, Scarce known to any people but their Neighbours, by whom they were contemned & unregarded. But Christ did not confine his Doctrine to the Land of *Canaan*; he sent his Apostles amongst the Nations accompanied with Miracles so certain & undeniable that the Enemies of Christianity never dared to deny them, no, not *Julian* himself, who wanted neither skill nor power to enquire into the truth.

2. Next to the Knowledge of One God, Maker of all things, Mankind wanted a clear *Knowledge of their Duty*. This part of knowledge was cultivated by some of the Heathen philosophers, but it got little footing among the people. All men indeed were to frequent the Temples, & offer sacrifices; but the priests made it not their business to teach them *Virtue*. If the people took care to observe the Ceremonies, Feasts & Solemnities, & all the tricks of Religion; they were told by the Holy Tribe that the Gods were pleased. Few went to the schools of the philosophers to be instructed in their Duties. The priests sold the better penny worths, & therefore, had all the custom. Lustrations & processions were much easier than a clean Conscience, & a steady course of Life. An Expiatory Sacrifice was much more convenient than a strict & Holy Life. *Natural Religion* in its full extent was no where taken care of by the force of Natural Reason. It should seem by the little that has hitherto been done in it, that 'tis too hard a thing for unassisted Reason, to establish Morality in all its parts upon its true foundations, with a clear & convincing Light. & 'tis at least a surer & shorter way for the greater part of Mankind, that one manifestly sent from God should as a King & Law-maker tell them their duties & require their obedience; than leave it to the long and sometimes intricate Deductions of Reason to be made out to them. Most Men have neither leisure to weigh, nor skill to judge of such Strains of Reasonings. The attempts of the Heathen Philosophers have been very unsuccessful in this respect. Their systems came very short of a true & compleat *Morality*. In short 'tis plain matter of fact, that Humane Reason unassisted failed

Men in *Morality*. It never from unquestionable principles, by clear deductions made out an entire Body of the *Law of Nature* & if all the Moral Rules of the Philosophers were collected & compared with those contained in the New Testament, they would be found to come short of the Morality delivered by Christ & his Apostles.

The Author goes on, & says, Let it be granted (though not true) that all the *Moral Precepts* of the Gospel were known by somebody or other, amongst Mankind, before the coming of Christ. *Suppose they may be pikt up here & there; some from* Solon *&* Bias *in* Greece; *others from* Tully *in* Italy: *& to compleat the work, let* Confucius *as far as* China *be consulted, &* Ancharsis *the* Scythian *contribute his share. What will all this do to give the World a* Compleat Morality, *that may be to Mankind the unquestionable Rule of Life & manner?* The Sayings & Opinions of these philosophers gave them no authority, & Mankind might receive or reject them as they pleased. The moral precepts of the philosophers & Wise Men, though never so excellent in themselves, could never make a Morality, whereof the World could be convinced, & with certainty depend on. Whoever will have his Rules pass for Authentique Directions, must shew that either he builds his Doctrine upon self evident principles of Reason, & deduces all the part of it from thence, by clear & evident Demonstration: Or must shew his Comission from heaven, that he comes with Authority from God, to deliver his will & commands to the World. 'Tis true that there is a *Law of Nature*. But, who ever made out all the parts of it; put them together, & shewed the World their Obligation? Was there any such Code, that Mankind might have recourse to, as their unerring Rule, before our Saviour's time? If there was not, 'tis plain there was need of one. Such a *Law of Morality* Jesus Christ has given us in the New Testament, by the latter of these ways, *viz*. by Revelation. He was sent by God, his Miracles shew it; & as his precepts are grounded upon the Divine Authority, so they are found altogether agreeable with Reason.

Some will perhaps say, that it was Men's *negligence*, if they did not carry Morality to an Higher pitch, & make out every part of it with that clearness of Demonstration, which it is capable of. But, be the Cause what it will. It cannot be denied that Christ found Mankind under a great corruption of manners & principles, & that they stood very much in need of his Coming. Where Truths are once known to us, which way soever we come by them, we are apt to flatter our selves, & think that we have discovered them, though we are often beholden to others for that Discovery. There are a great many things, many Notions, which we have been bred upon from our Cradles, & are, as it were, become natural to us under the Gospel, which we take for plain, & obvious Truths, & easily demonstrable; without considering how long we might have been in doubt or ignorance of them, had Revelation been silent. *And many are beholden to Revelation, who do not acknowledge it.* To conclude, the Author says that one coming from heaven in the power of God, in full & clear evidence & demonstration of Miracles, giving plain & direct Rules of Morality & obedience, is likelier to Enlighten the bulk of Mankind, & bring them to do their Duties, than by reasoning with them from general Notions & Principles of Humane Reason. & were all the Duties of Humane Life clearly demonstrated, yet he concludes, when well considered, that Method of teaching Men their Duties, would be proper only for a few, who have much leisure, improved understandings, & are used to abstract Reasonings. But the best way would be to leave the Instruction of the people to the precepts & principles of the Gospel. To one who is once persuaded of the Miracles of Christ, (which are matters of Fact he can without difficulty conceive,) that he was sent by God to be a King, & a Saviour of those, who do believe in him; all his Commands become principles; there needs no other proof for the truth of what he says, but that he said it.

3. The outward forms of worshipping the Deity wanted a Reformation. Amongst the Heathens the principal part, if not the whole of Religion did consist in having stately Temples, rich ornaments, peculiar habits, & in a numerous train of pompous Ceremonies. The Gospel of Christ brought also a remedy to this by teaching Men that God must be worshipped *in the Spirit & in Truth*, & that he seeks such Worshippers. God requires now to be worshipped by a pure Heart every where; praises & prayers humbly offered up to him, are the sacrifices he demands. In a word, the inward disposition of the Mind is that which God will regard to, & accept of his Creatures.

4. Before the coming of Christ, the doctrine of a Future Life was not clearly known in the World. The philosophers spoke seldom, or doubtfully of it. The people heard indeed the names of *Styx* & *Acheron*: they were told of the *Elysian Fields*, &c. But these notions they had generally from their priests, who mixed them with Fables; & so they could make no great impression in order to a good Life. But this great Truth, that there is another Life after this, rewards & punishments, has been clearly revealed by the Gospel of Christ, & by his Resurrection & Ascension in to Heaven, & consequently Men have now a more powerful motive to love & practice Virtue, notwithstanding all the dangers & discouragements which

good & virtuous Men are apt to meet with in this World.
  5. Lastly, there is another advantage which accrues to
Men by the Gospel, & it is the promise of Assistance.
Christ has promised us, that if we do what we can, he will
give us his Spirit to help us to overcome all temptations,
& perfect the Holiness & Virtue we desire to attain to.

The Author having thus shewn the Excellency & great
Usefulness of the Gospel, has thought fit to Answer an
Objection, which some will be ready to make. The
Objection is this. If to believe Jesus of *Nazareth* to be the
Messiah, together with those concomitant Articles of his
Resurrection, Rule & coming again to judge the world, be
all the Faith required as necessary to Justification, to what
purpose were the Epistles written; if the belief of those
many Doctrines contained in them be not also necessary
to salvation? And if what is there delivered, a Christian
may believe or disbelieve, & yet nevertheless be a member
of Christ's Church, & one of the Faithful?

Our Author answers, that the Epistles were writ to
those, who were in the Faith & true Christians already, &
so could not be designed to teach them the Fundamental
Articles, & points necessary to Salvation. They were writ
upon particular occasions; & without those occasions
had not been writ; & so cannot be thought necessary to
salvation: though they resolving doubts & reforming
mistakes, are of great advantage to our knowledge &
practice. The Author does not deny, but that the great
Doctrines of the Christian Faith are scattered up & down
in most of the Epistles. But he says that 'tis not in the
Epistles we are to learn what are the Fundamental Articles
of Faith, where they are promiscuously & without
distinction mixed with other Truths in Discourses that
were (though for edification indeed, yet) only Occasional.
Those great & necessary points he says shall be found &

discerned best in the preaching of our Saviour & the Apostles, to those who were yet strangers & ignorant of the Faith, to bring them in, & convert them to it. This is what the Author has done, as we have seen before. He observes that the Epistles to particular Churches do in many places explain the Fundamentals of the Christian Religion, & that wisely, by proper Accommodation to the apprehension of those they were writ to, the better to make them imbibe of Christian Doctrine, & the more easily to comprehend the Method, Reasons & Grounds of the great Work of Salvation. Thus, says he, we see in the Epistle to the *Romans*, Adoption (a custom well known among those at Rome) is much made use of to explain to them the Grace & Favour of God in giving them Eternal Life, to help them to conceive how they became the children of God, & to assure them of a share in the Kingdom of Heaven, as Heirs to an Inheritance. Whereas the setting out & confirming the Christian Faith to the *Hebrews*, in the Epistle to them, is by Allusions & Arguments from the Ceremonies, Sacrifices, & Oeconomy of the Jews, & reference to the records of the Old Testament. The Holy Writers, says our Author, Inspired from above writ nothing but truth: but he does not think that every sentence of theirs must be looked on as a Fundamental Article necessary to salvation. We have seen before what are the Fundamental Articles of Faith, according to our Author. He grants that an Explicit Belief of them is absolutely required of all those to whom the Gospel is preached. As for the other parts of Divine Revelation, they are Truths none of which, that is once known, ought to be disbelieved. But there are a great many Truths revealed in the Gospel, which one may be ignorant of, nay disbelieve without danger to his Salvation.

The Writers & Wranglers in Religion, says our Author, *fill it with niceties, & dress it up with notions; which they make necessary and fundamental parts of it; As if there were no way in to the Church but through the* Academy *or* Lyceum. *The bulk of Mankind have not leisure for Learning & Logick, & Superfine Distinctions of the Schools. Where the hand is used to the plough & the spade, the Head is seldom elevated to sublime notions; or exercised in Mysterious Reasonings. 'Tis well if Men of that rank (to say nothing of the other sex) can comprehend plain propositions, & a short reasoning about things familiar to their Minds, & nearly allied to their daily experience. Go beyond this, & you amaze the greatest part of Mankind: & may as well talk* Arabick *to a poor Day Labourer, as the Notions & Language that the Books & Disputes of Religion are filled with, & as soon you will be understood. The Dissenting Congregations are supposed by their Teachers to be more accurately instructed in matters of Faith, & better to understand the Christian Religion, than the Vulgar Conformists, who are charged with great ignorance; How truly, I will not here determine. But I ask them to tell me seriously, whether half their people have leisure to study? Nay, whether one in ten of those, who come to their Meetings in the Country, if they had time to study them, do or can understand the controversies at this time so warmly managed amongst them, about Justification, the subject of this present Treatise? I have talked with some of their Teachers, who confess themselves not to understand the difference in debate between them. And yet the points they stand on, are reckoned of so great weight, so material, so fundamental in Religion, that they divide communions & separate upon them.*

The Gospel was chiefly designed for the poor, ignorant,

& illiterate Men, who heard & believed the promises of a Deliverer, & believed *Jesus* to be Him; who could conceive dead & made alive again, & believe, that he should at the end of the world come again, & pass sentence on all Men, according to their deeds. In short, the Gospel was preached to the poor: Christ makes it a mark as well as the business of his Mission, *Mat.* XI. 5. & if the poor had the Gospel preached to them, says our Author, it was without doubt, such a Gospel, as the poor could understand, Plain & Intelligible.

The Author's Vindication is short, & though it deserves to be read, it does not appear to me necessary to give an Extract of it.

Extract [17]03/4 [Locke's Endorsement]

AN HISTORICAL VIEW
OF THE STATE OF THE
PROTESTANT DISSENTERS
IN ENGLAND
Joshua Toulmin

In the year 1695, appeared from the press a production, of
the first excellence as a specimen of didactic theology, and of
the first importance as to its object, the christian religion
itself, a subject of evident superiority to any question
concerning discipline and ceremonies, or even the explanation of any particular doctrinal principle; and it was soon
discovered to have proceeded from the first pen of the age,
though it was anonymous, and the author carried the point
of secrecy so far as to conceal his concern in it from his most
intimate friends. This work was entitled, "The Reasonableness of Christianity, as delivered in the Scriptures." It
excited much attention, as appears from a letter which its
author, Mr. Locke, wrote to Mr. Molyneaux at Dublin,
desiring to know what people thought of it there: "for here,"
says he, "at its first coming out it was received with no
indifferency, some speaking of it with great commendation,
and most censuring it as a very bad book." His friend, in
reply, "informed him that a very learned and ingenious
prelate said he liked it very well; and that if Mr. Locke writ
it, it was the best book he ever laboured at. But," says he, "if
I should be known to think so, I should have my lawn sleeves
torn from my shoulders." Abroad it was greatly esteemed by
two of the best divines who were then living, Le Clerc and
Limborch. Le Clerc pronounced it one of the most excellent
works on the subject that had for a long time appeared.[1]
Limborch preferred it to all the systems of divinity he had

---

[1] "Un des plus excellens ouvrages qui ait été fait depuis longtems sur celle
matiere et dans cette vue."

ever read. Soon after its publication it was translated into French and Dutch. But we are informed it was extremely offensive to the corrupt and selfish part of the clergy, both high and low. Its doctrine, it seems, militated too strongly against the foundation of their favourite idols, power and interest, inasmuch as it teaches *salvation by Christ alone.*[2]

The principal design of this treatise is to shew, by a review of the Gospel and the Acts, that Jesus Christ and his Apostles required nothing of those to whom they preached, as the condition of their being baptized and acknowledged as converts, but faith in Jesus of Nazareth, as the Messiah; for the belief of this article necessarily includes a readiness to be instructed in the history, doctrine, and commands of this heavenly king; to receive the truths he taught, and to obey the precepts he delivered, when known and understood.

This principle the author illustrated and proved by a great number of passages; but in the discussion of his main argument he was lead to treat on several other points, which had not been handled by any writer before him. The first was, the reason why Jesus did not, from the beginning of his ministry, explicitly and openly declare himself to be the Messiah, but only by degrees opened his character, till when near his death, he avowed it without reserve. This caution was practised on account of the impatient expectation of a temporal Messiah, who would deliver them from a foreign yoke, having been entertained by the Jews, to prevent a seditious rising; and to guard against his religion being considered as a political faction, instead of an heavenly doctrine.

Another point which, in connection with this, the author illustrates, is the reason which determined Christ to select for his disciples and attendants men of low rank, unlearned and unpractised in the wisdom and ways of the world. Men of higher birth, of aspiring genius and enterprize, would have been less submissive to the restraints of caution and reserve; would hardly have been hindered from whispering, at least to their friends and relations, that their master was the Messiah; and would have been too ready to form schemes to announce him to the world, and to enlist numbers under his standard.

[2] See the preface to a late edition of this treatise in 1810, p. 12.

It is also a subject of enquiry discussed in this work, whether we are to seek in the epistles of the apostles other and new articles of faith, which are not taught in the gospels? The author answers in the negative, and supports his decision by many arguments which deserve to be well weighed. There are many who think with him that the holy spirit which the apostles received, did not instruct them in any new doctrines, but only enabled them better to understand and comprehend those which they had heard from the lips of their divine master.[3]

Several other topics are incidentally touched upon in this work, that claim the reader's attention; such as, the nature of justifying faith, the laws and requirements of the gospel, the final doom of those who lived before our Saviour's time, and of all the rest of mankind who never heard of him; and lastly, the advantages we have received by Jesus Christ. Under this last head the author takes a fine and comprehensive view of the excellence and superiority of a system of morals by revelation; in which he displays "a vast knowledge of human nature, an extensive acquaintance with antiquity, and a prodigious sagacity and penetration of mind."[4]

Neither the candour of the author, nor the clearness and strength with which he treated his subjects of enquiry could procure "The Reasonableness of Christianity" a fair hearing. It alarmed the advocates for the jargon of the schools and the established systems of theology. "He," it is justly observed, "who has to combat with prejudices supported by bigotry and power, will find the talk difficult. Some zealous hireling," or blind adherent to systems, "will attack him with the venom of the serpent, misrepresent him, and answer what he has not written. Such treatment did Mr. Locke receive from Dr. Edwards, a divine of the Church of England, though the son of a furious presbyterian, the author of 'The Gangrena,' a curious picture of religious opinions and sects of his day." Dr. Edwards stated various objections against Mr. Locke's principles, in a desultory manner, encumbered with repetitions, in a language that was not merely low but scurrilous in the extreme; and not satisfied with the

---

3 Bibliotheque Choisie, par Le Clerc, tom. ii. p. 288–292.
4 Benson's Reasonableness of the Christian Religion, vol. ii. p. 322 3d edition.

declarations and words of scriptures, as ambiguous and common to the orthodox and heretics, he blended with them the decisions of the father of schoolmen. Mr. Locke replied in two vindications of his work, in a masterly manner, and in language becoming the gentleman and the christian; and contrary to his antagonist's manner of writing, preserved through the whole answer a pure respect and attachment both to the words and sentiments of the New Testament, scrupulously adhering to them in every instance.[5]

"The Reasonableness of Christianity" found also an advocate in a worthy and pious clergyman, Mr. Samuel Bold, rector of Steeple in Dorsetshire; who, unconnected with its author, and unknown to him, and embracing the popular sentiments of the times concerning the deity of Christ, the doctrine of the Trinity, and other points, and who had before this suffered by a legal prosecution for preaching a sermon against persecution, stepped forward, with a firmness and laudable liberality of mind in the cause of free enquiry and moderation, in vindication of Mr. Locke's performance, and in answer to Dr. Edwards, and did not hesitate to pronounce it "one of the best books that had been published for at least sixteen hundred years." Mr. Bold, on whose defence the learned Le Clerc passed an encomium, as being well and ably written, ingeniously observes, "Were the 'Reasonableness of Christianity, &c.' generally read with deliberation, and rightly understood, and (what I apprehend to be) its main design well followed, it would be of eminent use, amongst other good purposes, of these two: first, to effect a happy alteration in particular persons; for if more time and pains were employed in bringing people to a sound conviction and full persuasion that *Jesus* is the *Christ* and *only saviour* of sinners, and of their own personal need of him; and less of each in squabbling about terms *men have devised to express their own conceits*, relating to points which Christ and his apostles have delivered in easy and unaffected words, there would not be such great numbers every where who pretend to be christians, merely because it is the fashion and mode of the country to make that profession;

5 Bibliotheque Choisie, p. 304.

but we might, upon good grounds, expect that multitudes would be *christians* upon a *rational* and *wise* choice."[6]

Mr. Locke's work, while Dr. Edwards's Reflections on it have long since been forgotten, maintains its credit by its perspicuous reasoning and intrinsic merit to this day; and a neat and new edition of it was published, in 1810, by a Society for promoting Christian Knowledge and the practice of virtue. It has also a place in Dr. Watson's, bishop of Llandaff, valuable "Collection of Theological Tracts."

[6] See the preface to the edition of 1810; and Memoirs of Mr. Bold, in the Monthly Magazine for September 1806, p. 150.

THE RACOVIAN CATECHISM, WITH NOTES AND ILLUSTRATIONS, TRANSLATED FROM THE LATIN: TO WHICH IS PREFIXED A SKETCH OF THE HISTORY OF UNITARIANISM IN POLAND AND THE ADJACENT COUNTRIES
Thomas Rees

Preface
[By Andrew Wissowatius and Joachim Stegman the Younger.]

To The Pious Reader, Health and favour from God, the Father, and Our Lord Jesus Christ.

We here publish a Catechism, or Institute of the Christian Religion, drawn from the Holy Scriptures, as it is professed by our Church. It must not be thought, because in many things it departs from the standard of all other Christians, that, in sending it forth to the public, differing in their perceptions upon all matters, we intend, as it were by a herald, to proclaim hostility, or sound the trumpet for the combat, and, as the poet sings,

> *Ære ciere viros, Martemque accendere cantu:*
> The warrior trumpet in the field to sound,
> With breathing brass to kindle fierce alarms.   DRYDEN

It was not without reason that Hilary, bishop of Poictiers, heavily complained of old, that after the Council of Nice nothing was written but CREEDS, and these indeed annually and monthly; "by which," he observes, "one after another, we are bitten until we are almost devoured." The same writer elsewhere styles the bishops of Gaul, *beati* and *felices*, blessed and happy, because they had neither composed, nor received, nor acknowledged any other Confession besides that first and most simple one, which has been delivered to the Universal Church from the very days of the apostles. It is not without just cause that many pious and learned men complain at present also, that the Confessions and Catechisms which are now put forth, and published by different Christian Churches, are hardly any thing else than apples of Eris, trumpets of discord, ensigns of immortal enmities and factions among men. The reason of this is, that those Confessions and Catechisms are proposed in such a manner that the conscience is bound by them, that a yoke is imposed upon Christians to swear to the words and opinions of men; and that they are established as a Rule of Faith, from which, every one who deviates in the least is immediately assailed by the thunderbolt of an anathema, is treated as a heretic, as a most vile and mischievous person, is excluded from heaven, consigned to hell, and doomed to be tormented with infernal fires.

Far be from us this disposition, or rather this madness. Whilst we compose a Catechism, we prescribe nothing to any man: whilst we declare our own opinions, we oppress no one. Let every person enjoy the freedom of his own judgment in religion; only let it be permitted to us also to exhibit our view of divine things, without injuring and calumniating others. For this is the golden Liberty of Prophesying which the sacred books of the New Testament so earnestly recommend to us, and wherein we are instructed by the example of the primitive apostolic church. "Quench not the spirit," says the apostle (1 Thess. v. 19, 20); "Despise not prophesying; prove all things, hold fast that which is good."

THE RACOVIAN CATECHISM

Section I. Of the Holy Scriptures.

I wish to be informed by you what the Christian Religion is?

The Christian Religion is the way of attaining eternal life, which God has pointed out by Jesus Christ: or, in other words, It is the method of serving God, which he has himself delivered by Jesus Christ.

Where may it be learnt?

In the Holy Scriptures; especially those of the New Testament.

Chapter II. Of the Sufficiency of the Holy Scriptures.

You have proved to my satisfaction that the Scriptures of the Old and the New Testament are authentic and credible; – I wish to know, further, whether they are of themselves sufficient, – so that in things necessary to salvation they alone are to be depended upon?

They are in this respect amply sufficient; because Faith that "worketh by love," which alone, the apostle Paul asserts (Gal. v. 6.), "availeth anything in Christ Jesus," is in them sufficiently inculcated and explained.

How do you prove that Faith is sufficiently inculcated and explained in the Holy Scriptures?

From hence:– because Faith, which is directed to God and Christ, is nothing else than the belief "that God is, and that he is the rewarder of them that seek him." (Heb. xi. 6.) And this Faith is most fully inculcated in the Scriptures.

How do you prove the same in respect to Love?

This appears from hence, that the duties of Love, whether towards God, or Christ, or our neighbour, are so fully explained, either in general or in particular precepts, as to place it beyond doubt, that he who practically observes them is endued with perfect love: and the same may also be asserted of the other duties of piety.

Have you any other reasons to prove this perfection of the Holy Scriptures?

There are, indeed, several other reasons; but I shall content myself on the present occasion with noticing only two. The first is, that every thing which, in addition to the Law delivered by Moses, it is necessary to believe under the Gospel, in order to salvation, has been declared by the authors of the Evangelical History. For Christ, as he himself testifies, taught all these things: and whatever he taught as necessary to be known, it was the express object of these writers faithfully to record. And Luke asserts in respect to himself (Acts i. 1, 2, compared with his Gospel, chap. i. 3, 4.) that he had declared "all that Jesus began both to do and teach, until the day in which he was taken up." So also John xx. 31; "But these are written, that ye might believe that Jesus is the Christ the Son of God; and that believing ye might have life through his name."

What is the second of these reasons?

It is this:– that it is wholly incredible, that in so large a body of sacred literature, which God caused to be written and preserved with the express view of furnishing men with the knowledge of saving truths, those few particulars with which it is necessary for every person, even the most ignorant, to be acquainted, in order to his salvation, should not all have been included: and that, while a great number of things are written, the knowledge of which is not essential to salvation, – any one of those particulars should have have been omitted, without which all the rest are of no avail.

Of what use then is right reason, if it be of any, in those matters which relate to salvation?

It is, indeed, of great service, since without it we could neither perceive with certainty the authority of the sacred writings, understand their contents, discriminate one thing from another, nor apply them to any practical purpose. When therefore I stated that the Holy Scriptures were sufficient for our salvation so far from excluding right reason, I certainly assumed its presence.

If then such be the state of the case, what need is there of Traditions, which, by the Church of Rome, are pronounced to be necessary to salvation, and which it denominates the unwritten word of God?

You rightly perceive, that they are not necessary to salvation.

What then is to be thought concerning them?

That some of them are not to be reckoned under the name of traditions, in the sense in which the Papists employ the term; – but that many of them were not only invented, without just reason, but are also productive of great injury to the Christian Faith.

What are the traditions of the former class?

They are those whose origin may be deduced from historical writings, or other authentic testimonies and sources of information, independent of the authority of the Church, and of the spirit, by which it is itself continually directed. For there is a certain medium between sacred scripture and what they call tradition.

What are the injury and danger resulting from the traditions of the latter class?

That they furnish occasion to draw men from divine truth to falsehood, and to fables of human device.

But the Papists appear to maintain these traditions on the authority of the Scriptures?

Some of the testimonies which they adduce from the Scriptures, in support of their traditions, do indeed demonstrate, that several things were said and done by Christ and his apostles which are not included in the sacred volume: but they by no means prove that those things are essential to salvation; much less, that they are the identical matters which the Church of Rome obtrudes upon our belief. Some of those testimonies, as evidently appears from several passages of Scripture, do not refer to traditions which were never committed to writing; but to such as were not written with an exclusive view to particular persons and seasons; but which, nevertheless, might have been written by the same individuals or by others, in respect of other times, and of other, or even of the same, persons. Moreover, though some traditions were to be admitted, those ought on no account to be received which are repugnant to the written word of God, or to sound reason;– of which kind are not a few maintained by the Roman Church.

Chapter III. Of the Perspicuity of the Holy Scriptures.

You have now shown that the Holy Scriptures are both authentic and sufficient; – what is your opinion as to their perspicuity?

Although some difficulties do certainly occur in them; nevertheless, those things which are necessary to salvation, as well as many others, are so plainly declared in different passages, that every one may understand them; especially if he be earnestly seeking after truth and piety, and implore divine assistance.

How will you prove this?

By the following considerations:– first, that since it was the design of God, when it pleased him to give the Holy Scriptures to mankind, that they should from them acquaint themselves with his will; it is not to be believed that the writings he would furnish them with for this purpose, should be of so defective a kind, that his will could not be perceived and understood from them by all. Secondly, that the apostles, even at the very first promulgation of the Christian Religion, addressed their epistles, which comprise the chief mysteries of Christianity, to men of plain understandings.

Whence then arise such differences in ascertaining the sense of the Scriptures?

These differences, so far as they relate to the parts of Sacred Writ which are necessary to salvation, are not very numerous; though the contrary is commonly supposed. And where differences do really exist, although some of them may arise from the obscurity of particular texts, yet the greatest number must be charged to men's own fault. For either they read the Scriptures with negligence, or bring not with them a sincere heart, disengaged from all corrupt desires; or have their minds warped by prejudice; or seek not divine assistance with becoming earnestness; or else, finally, are perplexed by their ignorance of the languages in which the Scriptures are written. This last circumstance, however, can hardly exist in reference to those particulars which are essential to salvation: for, if some of these be conveyed in more obscure, the rest are delivered in the plainest, declarations of Scripture.

By what means may the more obscure passages of Scripture be understood?

By carefully ascertaining, in the first instance, the scope, and other circumstances, of those passages, in the way which ought to be pursued in the interpretation of the language of all other written compositions. Secondly, by an attentive comparison of them with similar phrases and sentences of less ambiguous meaning. Thirdly, by submitting our interpretation of the more obscure passages to the test of the doctrines which are most clearly inculcated in the Scriptures, as to certain first principles; and admitting nothing that disagrees with these. And lastly, by rejecting every interpretation which is repugnant to right reason, or involves a contradiction.

Are the same rules of interpretation to be applied to the predictions of the Prophets?

Not altogether: for the meaning of the more obscure prophecies cannot be ascertained without the immediate aid of the divine spirit, unless men divinely inspired have furnished us with their proper explanation, or communicated to us the information by which we may be enabled to understand them; – or unless their true interpretation have been shown in their accomplishment. This is what the apostle meant to assert, when he observed (2 Peter i. 20,) that "no prophecy of the Scripture is of any private interpretation."

If the proper mode of interpreting the Scriptures be such as you have stated, of what service are religious teachers?

To propose and inculcate those things which are necessary to salvation, notwithstanding they may be already plainly declared in the Scriptures; – since all men are not able, or, if able, are not of their own accord disposed, to peruse them; and since it will be easier to acquire a clear apprehension of these things after the detached passages relating to them, which are dispersed throughout the sacred volume, have been collected by such teachers into one view. Further, to excite men to maintain, and reduce to practice, the knowledge they have once acquired: and lastly, to assist them to understand those matters which are more difficult.

Section IV. Of the Knowledge of Christ.
Chapter I. Of the Person of Christ.

As you have stated that there are some things relating to the Will of God, which were first revealed by Jesus Christ, and also asserted, at the commencement, that the way of salvation consisted in the knowledge of him, – I now wish you to specify what those particulars are, concerning Jesus Christ, which I ought to know?

Certainly: You must be informed, then, that there are some things relating to the PERSON, or nature, of Jesus Christ, and some, to his OFFICE, with which you ought to be acquainted.

What are the things relating to his Person, which I ought to know?

This one particular alone, – that by nature he was truly a man; a mortal man while he lived on earth, but now immortal. That he was a real man the Scriptures testify in several places: Thus 1 Timothy ii. 5, "There is one God, and one mediator between God and men, the MAN Christ Jesus." 1 Corinthians xv. 21, 22, "Since by MAN came death, by MAN came also the resurrection of the dead. For as in ADAM all die, even so in CHRIST shall all be made alive."

Was, then, the Lord Jesus a mere or common man?

By no means: because, first, though by nature he was a man, he was nevertheless, at the same time, and even from his earliest origin, the only begotten Son of God. For being conceived of the Holy Spirit, and born of a virgin, without the intervention of any human being, he had properly no father besides God: though considered in another light, simply according to the flesh, without respect to the Holy Spirit, of which he was conceived, and with which he was anointed, he had David for his father, and was therefore his son. Concerning his supernatural conception, the angel thus speaks to Mary, Luke i. 35, "The Holy Ghost shall come upon thee, and the Power of the Highest shall overshadow thee; therefore also that holy thing which shall be born of thee shall be called the Son of God." Secondly, because, as Christ testifies of himself, he was sanctified and sent into the world by the Father; that is, being in a most remarkable manner separated from all other men, and, besides being distinguished by the perfect holiness of his life, endued with divine wisdom and power, was sent by the Father, with supreme authority, on an embassy to mankind. Thirdly, because, as the apostle Paul testifies, both in the Acts of the Apostles, and in his Epistle to the Romans, he was raised from the dead by God, and thus as it were begotten a second time; – particularly as by this event he became like God immortal. Fourthly, because by his dominion and supreme authority over all things, he is made to resemble, or, indeed, to equal God: on which account, "a king anointed by God," and "Son of God," are used in several passages of Scripture as phrases of the same import. And the sacred author of the Epistle to the Hebrews (chap. i. ver. 5) shows from the words of the Psalmist (Psalm ii. 7), "Thou art my Son, this day have I begotten thee," that Christ was glorified by God, in order that he might be made a Priest, that is, the chief director of our religion and salvation, – in which office are comprised his supreme authority and dominion. He was, however, not merely the only begotten Son of God, but also A GOD, on account of the divine power and authority which he displayed even while he was yet mortal: much more may he be so denominated now that he has received all power in heaven and earth, and that all things, God himself alone excepted, have been put under his feet. – But of this you shall hear in its proper place.

But do you not acknowledge in Christ a divine, as well as a human nature or substance?

If by the terms divine nature or substance I am to understand the very essence of God, I do not acknowledge such a divine nature in Christ; for this were repugnant both to right reason and to the Holy Scriptures. But if, on the other hand, you intend by a divine nature the Holy Spirit which dwelt in Christ, united, by an indissoluble bond, to his human nature, and displayed in him the wonderful effects of its extraordinary presence; or if you understand the words in the sense in which Peter employs them (2 Peter i. 4), when he asserts that "we are partakers of a divine nature," that is, endued by the favour of God with divinity, or divine properties, – I certainly do so far acknowledge such a nature in Christ as to believe that next after God it belonged to no one in a higher degree.

Show me how the first mentioned opinion is repugnant to right reason?

First, on this account, That two substances endued with opposite and discordant properties, such as are God and man, cannot be ascribed to one and the same individual, much less be predicated the one of the other. For you cannot call one and the same thing first fire, and then water, and afterwards say that the fire is water, and the water fire. And such is the way in which it is usually affirmed; – first, that Christ is God, and afterwards that he is a man; and then that God is man, and that man is God.

But what ought to be replied, when it is alleged that Christ is constituted of a divine and human nature, in the same way as man is composed of a soul and body?

The cases are essentially different: – for it is stated that the two natures are so united in Christ, that he is both God and man: whereas the union between the soul and body is of such a kind that the man is neither the soul nor the body. Again, neither the soul nor the body, separately, constitutes a person: but as the divine nature, by itself, constitutes a person, so also must the human nature, by itself, constitute a person; since it is a primary or single intelligent substance.

Show me, in the next place, how it appears to be repugnant to the Scriptures, that Christ possesses the divine nature which is claimed for him?

First, because the Scriptures propose to us but one only God; whom I have already proved to be the Father of Christ. And this reason is rendered the more evident from Christ's being in several passages of Scripture not only distinguished from God absolutely so called, but often also expressly from the one or only god. Thus 1 Cor. viii. 6, "There is but one God, the Father, of whom are all things, and we in him; and one Lord, Jesus Christ, by whom are all things, and we by him." And John xvii. 3, "This is life eternal, that they might know thee, the only true God, and Jesus Christ whom thou hast sent." Secondly, because the same Scriptures assert, as I have already shown, that Jesus Christ is a man; which itself deprives him of the divine nature that would render him the supreme God. Thirdly, because the Scriptures explicitly declare that whatever of a divine nature Christ possessed, he had received as a gift from the Father; and refer it to the Holy Spirit, with which he had by the Father been anointed and filled. Thus Phil. ii. 9,

"God hath highly exalted him, and GIVEN him a name which is above every name." 1 Cor. xv. 27, "When he saith all things ARE PUT UNDER HIM, it is manifest that HE is excepted which DID PUT ALL THINGS UNDER HIM." Luke iv. 14 and 18, "Jesus returned in the power of the Spirit into Galilee." "The spirit of the Lord is upon me, because he hath anointed me to preach the gospel to the poor." Matt. xxviii. 18, "All power is GIVEN unto me in heaven and in earth." Acts x. 38, "God anointed Jesus of Nazareth with the Holy Ghost and with power." Isaiah xi. 2, "And the spirit of the Lord shall rest upon him, the spirit of wisdom and understanding, the spirit of counsel and might, the spirit of knowledge and of the fear of the Lord." John v. 19 and 36, "The Son can do nothing of himself, but what he seeth the Father do: for what things soever he doeth, these also doeth the son likewise." "The works which the Father hath given me to finish, the same works that I do bear witness of me, that the Father hath sent me." John vii. 16, "My doctrine is not mine, but his that sent me." John viii. 26, "He that sent me is true; and I speak to the world those things which I have heard of him." John x. 25, "The works that I do in my Father's name, they bear witness of me." And, moreover, because the same Scriptures plainly show that Jesus Christ was accustomed to ascribe all his divine words and works, not to himself, nor to any divine nature which he possessed distinct from the Holy Spirit, but to his Father; which renders it evident that the divine nature which some would claim for Christ must have been wholly inactive and useless. Fourthly, because Christ repeatedly prayed to the Father: whence it is evident that he had not in himself a nature of that kind which would have made him the supreme God. For why should he have recourse to another person, and supplicate of him, what he might have obtained from himself? Fifthly, because Christ explicitly declares, that he is not himself the ultimate object of our Faith; for he thus speaks, John xii. 44, "He that believeth on me, believeth not on me, but on Him that sent me." On this account Peter (1st Epist. i. 21) states that it is "by Christ we do believe in God." Sixthly, because Christ frequently asserts that he came not of himself, but was sent by the Father (John viii. 42). That he spoke not of himself, but that the Father which sent him gave him a commandment, what he should say, and what he should speak (John xii. 49). That he came not to do his own will, but the will of him that sent him (John vi. 38). Neither of which could have happened in respect to the supreme God. Seventhly, because Christ while he was yet living on earth affirmed of himself, that he was ignorant of the day of judgement; and stated that the knowledge of it was confined to the Father alone. "But of that day and that hour knoweth no man, no, not the angels which are in heaven, NEITHER THE SON, but the Father" (Mark xiii. 32. See also Matt. xxiv. 36). But the supreme God could not have been wholly ignorant of any thing. Eighthly, to omit other reasons, because Christ distinctly affirms (John xiv. 28), that his Father was greater than he – by which he intimates that he is not equal to his Father. He also, on several occasions, calls the Father his God. Matt. xxvii. 46; Mark xv. 34, "My God, my God, why hast thou forsaken me?" John xx. 17, "I ascend unto my Father and your Father, to my God and your God." Revel. iii. 12, "Him that overcometh will I make a pillar in the temple of my God, and he shall go no more out; and I will write upon him the name of my God, and the name of the city of my God, which is New Jerusalem, which cometh down out of heaven from my God." The Father is called the God of Christ by other sacred writers, particularly by Paul: thus Ephes. i. 17, "The God of our Lord Jesus Christ, the Father of Glory," &c. And the same apostle observes (1 Cor. xi. 3), that God is the head of Christ; (1 Cor. iii. 23), that as we are Christ's, so in like manner, "Christ is God's." And (1 Cor. xv. 28), that at a certain period "the Son himself would be subject unto him, that had put all things under him:" – things which could not have been predicated of Christ, had he possessed a divine nature.

But to these arguments, and others of a similar kind, it is replied, that such things are spoken of Christ in reference to his human, and not his divine nature?

But this is done without reason: partly because those who so assert, take for granted the very point in dispute; namely, that Christ is possessed of a divine nature; – and partly because there is no room for such a distinction when any thing is absolutely, and without any limitation, denied, or might be denied, concerning Christ. For otherwise I might at one time be allowed to say, that Christ was not a man, that he did not die, that he was not raised; and at another, on the contrary, that he was not the only begotten Son of God, that he was not, as themselves pretend, the supreme God, and that he was not possessed of this divine nature: – because the former circumstances would be incompatible with the divine, the latter with human, nature. The reason of this is, that those things which may be, and usually are, affirmed absolutely of any whole, without any limitation being expressly stated, cannot be denied absolutely of the same whole, although in respect to some part those things may not appertain to it. Thus when we affirm absolutely that a man is tall, that he is corruptible, that he eats and drinks, and the like; we cannot at the same time deny these things absolutely concerning him, because they do not appertain to one, and that the nobler part of him, – his soul. Much less then ought any thing to be denied absolutely concerning Christ, which may be affirmed absolutely of him, although it may not comport with his human nature, which is infinitely inferior to the divine; the more particularly in those places where Christ is thought to be described and designated from his divine nature; such as when he is called "the Son," that is "of God." It appears then, from these considerations, that that cannot be affirmed absolutely of any whole which may be denied absolutely of it; and also, that things cannot be attributed absolutely to Christ on account of one nature, if they may in terms equally unqualified be denied of him on account of another: – for though we read of many things attributed absolutely to Christ on account of his human nature, which might and ought to be in terms equally unqualified denied of him in relation to his divine nature; as, because it may and usually is denied concerning man that he is endued with a spiritual or incorruptible nature; the same thing cannot, on this account, be affirmed absolutely of him, notwithstanding such may be the case in respect to one of his parts.

But in what sense is it asserted that the Word was in the beginning of the Gospel?

In the following, that any one might learn that Jesus, even at the very beginning of the Gospel, was invested with his office, though he had not as yet entered on its duties, being at that time communing with God: – Wherefore the Baptist was on no account to be preferred before him, because, when he was preaching the Gospel, Jesus was not present and publicly seen. The evangelist therefore distinguishes him by the appropriate title of the WORD, that is, of God, in order to show that even in this very respect the office of Christ was long anterior, more ancient, and more excellent than that of John the Baptist. And with what propriety he ascribes this title to Jesus, and asserts that he is, by virtue of his office, the first in the concerns of the Gospel, he evinces by the creation effected by him of all things under the Gospel: And who this Baptist was, and wherefore he cannot be compared with Jesus, or preferred before him, he explains in verses the third to the ninth of this chapter; and confirms his observations further on by the personal testimony of the Baptist himself.

What answer do you make to the second testimony, which alleges that he was in heaven?

That there is no mention here of the eternity spoken of. For the Scriptures expressly assert in this place, that the SON OF MAN, that is, A MAN, was in heaven; who, it is beyond all dispute certain, had not existed from eternity.

What reply do you make to the third testimony, wherein Christ asserts that he was before Abraham?

That in this place it is not only not stated that Christ had existed from eternity (since it is one thing to have been before Abraham, and another to have been from eternity) – but also that it is not declared even that he had existed before the Virgin Mary. For that these words might be otherwise rendered (namely, "Verily, verily I say unto you, before he becomes ABRAHAM I am HE") is evident from those passages in this evangelist, where the same or similar forms of speech are found in the Greek. Thus chap. xiii. 19, "Now I tell you before it come, that when it is come to pass ye may believe that I am he." And xiv. 29, "And now I have told you before it come to pass, that when it is come to pass ye might believe."

What would be the sense of this reading?

It would be very excellent. For Christ admonishes the Jews, who sought to entrap him in his discourse, to believe that he was the light of the world, while yet an opportunity was afforded them, and before the divine favour, which he offered to them, was taken from them, and transferred to the Gentiles. For that the words I AM (εγω ειμι) are to be construed as if he had explicitly stated, "I am the light of the world," appears from the commencement of his address, verse 12, – and also from hence, that Christ twice designates himself by the same words, I AM or I AM HE (εγω ειμι), in verses 24 and 28. That the words "before Abraham was I am" mean what I have already intimated, may be shown from the signification of the name Abraham, which is on all hands agreed to denote THE FATHER OF MANY NATIONS, Genesis xvii. 5. But since he was not actually made the Father of many nations until after the grace of God having been manifested to the world by Christ, many nations had become, through faith, the sons of one Father, who was in token thereof called Abraham, – it is apparent that Christ might with propriety admonish the Jews to believe that he was the light of the world before Abraham should become the Father of many nations, and thus the divine grace be transferred from them to other nations.

Chapter VIII. Of the Death of Christ.

Of what kind was the death of Christ?

It was such a death as was preceded by various afflictions, and was in itself most dreadful and ignominious; so that the Scriptures testify (Heb. ii. 17) that he was on account of it "made in all things like unto his brethren."

But why was it necessary that Christ should suffer so many afflictions, and undergo so cruel a death?

First, because Christ, by the divine will and purpose, suffered for our sins, and underwent a bloody death as an expiatory sacrifice. Secondly, because they who are to be saved by him, are for the most part obnoxious to the same afflictions and death.

What was the ground of the divine will and purpose that Christ should suffer for our sins?

First, that a most certain right to, and consequently a sure hope of, the remission of their sins, and of eternal life, might by this means be created for all sinners. "For if God spared not his own Son, but delivered him up for us all, how shall he not with him also freely give us all things?" (Rom. viii. 32.) "And if while we were yet sinners Christ died for us, much more then, being now justified by his blood, we shall be saved from wrath through him. For if when we were enemies, we were reconciled to God by the death of his son, much more being reconciled shall we be saved by his life" (Rom. v. 8, 9, 10). Secondly, that all sinners might be incited and drawn to Christ, seeking salvation in and by him alone who died for them. Thirdly, that God might in this manner testify his boundless love to the human race, and might wholly reconcile them to himself. All which things are comprised in that divine declaration of Christ (John iii. 16), "God so loved the world that he gave his only-begotten son, that whosoever believeth in him should not perish, but have everlasting life."

But what reason was there that Christ should suffer the same afflictions, and the same kind of death, as those to which believers are exposed?

There are two reasons for this, as there are two methods whereby Christ saves us: for, first, he inspires us with a certain hope of salvation, and also incites us both to enter upon the way of salvation and to persevere in it. In the next place, he is with us in every struggle of temptation, suffering, or danger, affords us assistance, and at length delivers us from eternal death. It was exceedingly conducive to both these methods of saving us that Christ our captain should not enter upon his eternal life and glory, otherwise than through sufferings, and through a death of this kind. For as to the former, since we perceive in his case that the termination of that way which seemed to lead to destruction is so happy, – following our leader with the utmost firmness, we enter this way and persevere in it, with the certain hope that the same end remains for us also: and as to the latter, since having himself experienced how heavy, and of themselves intolerable to human nature, such trials are, and being not ignorant of sufferings, he might learn to succour the distressed. The former cause of the sufferings and death of Christ is intimated in the words of Peter (1 Epist. ii. 21), "Christ also suffered for us, leaving us an example that we should follow his steps." And also in Hebr. ii. 10, where the sacred author asserts that "it became God, in bringing many sons unto glory;" that is, as is to be understood from what follows, by afflictions and death, "to make the captain of their salvation perfect," or to conduct him to eternal glory, "through sufferings:" that thus, the happy termination of their afflictions, and of a death so dreadful, being perceived, those persons might shake off the fear of death, who through this fear had been all their lifetime subject to bondage. The latter cause is proved by what we read in the same chapter (Heb. ii. 17, 18), that "in all things it behoved Christ to be made like unto his brethren, that he might be a merciful and faithful high-priest in things pertaining to God, to make reconciliation for the sins of the people. For in that he himself hath suffered, being tempted, he is able to succour them that are tempted." And also further on in the same epistle (chap. iv. 15), "For we have not an high-priest which cannot be touched with the feeling of our infirmities; but was in all points tempted like as we are, yet without sin." And (chap. v. 8),

"Though he were a son, yet learned he obedience by the things which he suffered:" that is, how hard and difficult soever it was, he was obedient to God in every adversity, in suffering, and a dreadful and ignominious death.

Could not God have caused that believers should not be exposed to afflictions and a violent death?

He could indeed, had he thought proper to change the nature of things. But God has not done this, except sometimes, and that very rarely, in some remarkable cases and for a time; not always nor commonly, as would in this instance be absolutely necessary, if he purposed that believers in Christ should be exempted from afflictions and a violent death: and God has done this the less, where he would as far as possible exercise and prove their faith and their devotion to him.

But why was it absolutely necessary to change the nature of things, if believers in Christ were to be exempted from afflictions and a violent death?

Because believers in Christ are endued with singular piety and innocence of life, and also with patience. Of these, the former naturally cause them to be exposed to the hatred of all wicked men, of whom both the number and the power are the greatest; so that they are vexed by them, and also, if occasion or opportunity offer, put to death: and the latter is even a greater incitement to the wicked, and furnishes them with the power of carrying all these things into execution.

But how has the blood or the death of Christ confirmed to us the will of God?

In two ways. First, because he did not suffer himself to be deterred from inculcating his doctrine even by the most painful death; but particularly, because he ratified the New Covenant by his blood, and confirmed the New Testament by his death (Heb. xiii. 20). Hence the blood of Christ is called "the blood of the New Testament, which speaketh better things than that of Abel" (Matth. xxvi. 28; Heb. xii. 24). And Christ is himself called "the true and faithful witness" (Rev. i. 5, iii. 14). Secondly, because through his death he was led to his resurrection, from which principally arises the confirmation of the divine will, and the most certain persuasion of our resurrection and the obtaining of eternal life.

Explain more at large – in what manner we are assured by the resurrection of Christ, and consequently by his death, of our own resurrection and eternal life?

First, we are assured by the death and resurrection of Christ, of our own resurrection, because we behold placed before our view, in the example of Christ, what is promised in his doctrine – that they who serve God shall be delivered from every kind of death, however violent. Secondly, since Christ was thus raised in order that he might obtain supreme authority over all things, every cause of doubt concerning our salvation has been taken away.

But in what manner?

In two ways. First, because we perceive a certain beginning of the fulfilment of God's promises, particularly as God has made an especial promise that Christ himself should deliver us from death, and confer upon us eternal life. Secondly, because we see that the power of fulfilling the divine promises made to us is placed in the hands of him who is not ashamed to call us brethren, and who so greatly loved us, – though until then wicked, and enemies to him, – that, with a view to our everlasting salvation, he submitted to a death as cruel as it was infamous; who endured in himself all those afflictions to which we must be exposed if we would obey him; and can therefore commiserate us, and be touched with a feeling of our infirmities, as I have before shown. Having then our salvation in his hands, how should he not bestow it upon us, especially as the conferring of it is connected with the highest glory both of himself and of his Father?

I observe then from hence, that in the business of our salvation more depends upon the resurrection than upon the death of Christ?

Certainly, in as much as the death of Christ would have been useless and inefficacious, unless it had been followed by his resurrection (which indeed, in respect to the divine decrees, could not but have happened), which also, in a wonderful manner, gave force to his death, and rendered it effectual in the business of our salvation. Hence Paul writes (1 Cor. xv. 17), "If Christ be not raised, your faith is vain, you are yet in your sins." That is to say, as the same apostle intimates Romans iv. 25, connecting together the effects of his death and of his resurrection, Christ "was delivered for our offences, and was raised for our justification." And again (Rom. viii. 33, 34), "Who shall lay any thing to the charge of God's elect? It is God that justifieth, who is he that condemneth? It is Christ that died, yea rather that is risen again, who is even at the right hand of God, who also maketh intercession for us."

But why do the Scriptures so often ascribe all these things to the death of Christ?

Because the death of Christ the Son of God, made effective, as I have stated, by his resurrection (which principally declared him to be the Son of God), had of itself, as I have shown, great and extraordinary power in effecting our salvation. And, in the next place, because it was the way to the resurrection and exaltation of Christ; for, from the nature of the thing, his death was necessary to the former, and, through the divine will and purpose, was essential to the latter. Lastly, because of all the things done by God and Christ with a view to our salvation, the death of Christ was the most difficult work, and the most evident proof of the love of God and of Christ towards us.

But did not Christ die also, in order, properly speaking, to purchase our salvation, and literally to pay the debt of our sins?

Although Christians at this time commonly so believe, yet this notion is false, erroneous, and exceedingly pernicious; since they conceive that Christ suffered an equivalent punishment for our sins, and by the price of his obedience exactly compensated our disobedience. There is no doubt, however, but that Christ so satisfied God by his obedience, as that he completely fulfilled the whole of his will, and by his obedience obtained, through the grace of God, for all of us who believe in him, the remission of our sins, and eternal salvation.

How do you make it appear that the common notion is false and erroneous?

Not only because the Scriptures are silent concerning it, but also because it is repugnant to the Scriptures and to right reason.

Prove this, in order.

That nothing concerning it is to be found in the Scriptures appears from hence; that they who maintain this opinion never adduce explicit texts of Scripture in proof of it, but string together certain inferences by which they endeavour to maintain their assertions. But, besides that a matter of this kind, whereon they themselves conceive the whole business of salvation to turn, ought certainly to be demonstrated not by inferences alone but by clear testimonies of Scripture, it might easily be shown that these inferences have no force whatever:

otherwise, inferences which necessarily spring from the Scriptures, I readily admit.

How is this opinion repugnant to the Scriptures?

Because the Scriptures every where testify that God forgives men their sins freely, and especially under the New Covenant (2 Cor. v. 19; Rom. iii. 24, 25; Matth. xviii. 23, &c.) But to a free forgiveness nothing is more opposite than such a satisfaction as they contend for, and the payment of an equivalent price. For where a creditor is satisfied, either by the debtor himself, or by another person on the debtor's behalf, it cannot with truth be said of him that he freely forgives the debt.

How is this repugnant to reason?

This is evident from hence; that it would follow that Christ, if he has satisfied God for our sins, has submitted to eternal death; since it appears that the penalty which men had incurred by their offences was eternal death; not to say that one death, though it were eternal in duration, – much less one so short, – could not of itself be equal to innumerable eternal deaths. For if you say that the death of Christ, because he was a God infinite in nature, was equal to the infinite deaths of the infinite race of men, – besides that I have already refuted this opinion concerning the nature of Christ, – it would follow that God's infinite nature itself suffered death. But as death cannot any way belong to the infinity of the divine nature, so neither, literally speaking (as must necessarily be done here where we are treating of a real compensation and payment), can the infinity of the divine nature any way belong to death. In the next place, it would follow that there was no necessity that Christ should endure such sufferings, and so dreadful a death; and that God – be it spoken without offence, – was unjust, who, when he might well have been contented with one drop (as they say) of the blood of Christ, would have him so severely tormented. Lastly, it would follow that we were more obliged to Christ than to God, and owed him more, indeed owed him every thing; since he, by this satisfaction, showed us much kindness; whereas God, by exacting his debt, showed us no kindness at all.

State in what manner this opinion is pernicious?

Because it opens a door to licentiousness, or, at least, invites men to indolence in the practice of piety, in what way soever they urge the piety of their patron. For if full payment have been made to God by Christ for all our sins, even those which are future, we are absolutely freed from all liability to punishment, and therefore no further condition can by right be exacted from us to deliver us from the penalties of sin. What necessity then would there be for living religiously? But the Scripture testifies (Tit. ii. 14; Gal. i. 4; 1 Pet. i. 18; Heb. ix. 14; 2 Cor. v. 15; Eph. v. 26) that Christ died for this end, among others, that he might "redeem us from all iniquity, and purify us unto himself a peculiar people zealous of good works;" "that he might deliver us from the present evil world;" "might redeem us from our vain conversation, received by tradition from our fathers," in order that being "dead to sin" we might "live unto righteousness," that our consciences might be "purged from dead works to serve the living God."

But how do they maintain their opinion?

They endeavour to do this first by a certain reason, and then by the authority of Scripture.

What is this reason?

They say that there are in God, by nature, justice and mercy: that as it is the property of mercy to forgive sins, so is it, they state, the property of justice to punish every sin whatever. But since God willed that both his mercy and justice should be satisfied together, he devised this plan, that Christ should suffer death in our stead, and thus satisfy God's justice in the human nature, by which he had been offended; and that his mercy should at the same time be displayed in forgiving sin.

What reply do you make to this reason?

This reason bears the appearance of plausibility, but in reality has in it nothing of truth or solidity; and indeed involves a self-contradiction. For although we confess, and hence exceedingly rejoice, that our God is wonderfully merciful and just, nevertheless we deny that there are in him the mercy and justice which our adversaries imagine, since the one would wholly annihilate the other. For, according to them, the one requires that God should punish no sin; the other, that he should leave no sin unpunished. If then it were naturally a property of God to punish no sin, he could not act against his nature in order that he might punish sin: in like manner also, if it were naturally a property of God to leave no sin unpunished, he could not, any more, contrary to his nature, refrain from punishing every sin. For God can never do any thing repugnant to those properties which pertain to him by nature. For instance, since wisdom belongs naturally to God, he can never do any thing contrary to it, but whatever he does he does wisely. But as it is evident that God forgives and punishes sins whenever he deems fit, it appears that the mercy which commands to spare, and the justice which commands to destroy, do so exist in him as that both are tempered by his will, and by the wisdom, the benignity, and holiness of his nature. Besides, the Scriptures are not wont to designate the justice, which is opposed to mercy, and is discernible in punishments inflicted in wrath, by his term, but style it the SEVERITY, the ANGER, the WRATH of God: – indeed, it is attributed to the justice of God in the Scriptures that he forgives sins: 1 John iv. 9; Rom. iii. 25, 26; and frequently in the Psalms.

What then is your opinion concerning this matter?

It is this; – that since I have shown that the mercy and justice which our adversaries conceive to pertain to God by nature, certainly do not belong to him, there was no need of that plan whereby he might satisfy such mercy and justice, and by which they might, as it were by a certain tempering, be reconciled to each other: which tempering nevertheless is such that it satisfies neither, and indeed destroys both; – For what is that justice, and what too that mercy, which punishes the innocent, and absolves the guilty? I do not, indeed, deny that there is a natural justice in God, which is called rectitude, and is opposed to wickedness: this shines in all his works, and hence they all appear just and right and perfect; and that, no less when he forgives than when he punishes our transgressions.

What are the passages of Scripture whereby they endeavour to support their opinion?

Those which testify that Christ died for us, or for our sins; that he took away our sins; that he hath redeemed us; that he has given himself, or given his soul, a ransom for many: also that he is our mediator; that he has reconciled us to God; that he is the propitiation for our sins: and lastly, they infer it from the death of Christ being compared with the sacrifices of the law, as with figures whereby it was shadowed.

What do you reply to these passages?

As to those testimonies wherein it is affirmed that Christ dies for us – that no satisfaction can be inferred from the phraseology itself, much more that it could not be such satisfaction as they contend for, is manifest from hence, that the Scriptures declare (1 John iii. 16), that "we also ought to lay down our lives for the brethren:" and Paul wrote concerning himself (Col. i. 24), "I now rejoice in my sufferings for you, and fill up that which is behind of the afflictions of Christ in my flesh for his body's sake which is the Church." But it is certain both that the believers did not give satisfaction for the brethren, and that Paul did not give satisfaction for the Church.

A COMPLEAT SYSTEM, OR BODY OF DIVINITY
Philippus van Limborch

Sect. III. Of the Effects which Adam's first Transgression had upon his Posterity; and first of the Imputation thereof.

Adam, as being the common Parent of all Mankind, expos'd all his posterity to the same Miseries to which himself was liable. For 'tis not to be suppos'd that *Adam*'s Sin had no effect but upon himself alone, which is said to be the Error of *Pelagius*: But all the Miseries into which he fell by his Sin, are entail'd upon his Posterity. For they are all excluded from the Terrestrial Paradise, as well as *Adam* and *Eve*: The Women bring forth Children with Pain, and are subject to their Husbands, even the most morose; and Men eat their Bread with the sweat of their Brows; and all are subject to the same Fate, *viz.* Death. However this Death is not to be look'd upon as properly a Punishment inflicted on *Adam*'s Posterity; for 'tis impossible that the Innocent should be punish'd for another's Offence; but it is only a natural Necessity of dying, deriv'd from *Adam* on whom it was inflicted as a Punishment.

Death in itself Eternal.
And this Death, as in *Adam*, is in its own Nature Eternal, from which none can be exempted by any Vertue of their own, but only by our Lord Jesus Christ; for by Grace they are to be saved.

As to Eternal Torments, so manifestly denounc'd against the Impenitent in the Gospel, we have already evinc'd that they are not comprehended under the Threatening made to *Adam*. As therefore *Adam* by his first Transgression was not liable to their Guilt; so likewise he cannot be said to transmit his Guilt to his Posterity. However we do not by any means infer that all the Wicked, who sin without the knowledg of the Gospel, shall remain under Everlasting Death without any Resurrection to a future Punishment; but all that we contend for is, that this Punishment was not the Effect of *Adam*'s Transgression.

Query answer'd.

But here it may be ask'd, whether there be not any Original Sin, with which all Men are tainted at their Birth? In answer to this we say, that the Phrase *Original Sin* is no where to be met with in Scripture; and it is likewise very improper, since it cannot properly be said that Sin which is voluntary, is innate to us. But if by *Original Sin* they mean the Misfortune which happen'd to Mankind upon *Adam*'s Transgression, we very readily grant it, tho it cannot in any proper sense be said to be Sin. We likewise own that Infants are born in a less degree of Purity than *Adam* was created, and have a certain Inclination to Sin, which they deriv'd not from *Adam*, but from their next immediate Parents.

Sect. II. Of the Person of Jesus Christ.

From what has been said of the Dignity of the Forerunner of our Saviour, may be infer'd in some measure the Dignity of our Redeemer. But for the clearer apprehending thereof, we shall in this Section treat more distinctly of his Person.

Christ signifies Anointed.

Our Saviour is stiled *Jesus Christ*; *Jesus* denotes Saviour, and *Christ* Anointed. For God was pleas'd that the Redeemer should perform his Offices of Prophet, Priest, and King, as was most usual among the *Jews*. Now both Kings and Prophets were by the express Command of God anointed with Oil. Accordingly our *Jesus*, for the due Performance of those Offices, was to be Anointed; or the Christ; from whence We of his Religion are call'd *Christians*. However he was not anointed with material Oil, but with the Holy Ghost.

Is God and Man in one Person.

But in treating of the Person of our Saviour, 'tis necessary to take notice of the Dignity thereof. He is therefore the True and Eternal God by a secret and ineffable Generation from the Father, and upon this account is stiled *the only begotten Son of God*. He is likewise in the same Person, by the Hypostatical Union, perfect Man, or the Son of Man. But having already (*B. 2 Ch. 5. Sect.* I.) discours'd of the Divine Nature of Jesus Christ, we shall at present confine our selves to those things that more immediately relate to his Human Nature.

Is truly Man.

That he was true Man, and really partook of the same Human Nature with other Men, is very evident from Scripture, wherein he is call'd, not only *the Man Christ Jesus*[1], but also *the Seed of the Woman*[2], *the Seed of* Abraham[3], *made of the Seed of* David *according to the Flesh*[4], and *made of a Woman*[5]. Hence it is that he stiles himself very often *the Son of Man*, thereby denoting that he was truly Man. Add to this, that his Mother bore him in her womb; and when her full time, according to the manner of other Women, was come, she brought him forth into the World. Nor is it a less Argument of his Humanity, that he was subject to the same Infirmities of Body, and the same Passions of Mind as we are; so that he was in all things made like unto us, Sin only excepted.

The Opinion of the 'Eutychians' concerning the Humanity of Christ refuted.

Tho this be so evident a Truth, yet we thought it requisite to establish it by the foregoing Texts of Scripture, in order to refute the Opinion of some Christians, call'd *Eutychians*, who maintain that the Human Nature of Christ was not produc'd of the Flesh and Blood of the Virgin *Mary*; but that the Divine Essence of the Son of God, or the Eternal Word, was transubstantiated into Flesh, and that it was derived from some celestial or uncreated Matter, and transmitted into the Virgin's Womb; and by this means the Son of God remain'd what he was, and was made what he was not.

Now the Weakness of this Opinion appears not only from the Texts of Scripture before alledg'd, but also from its own Absurdity. For (1.) it is a manifest Contradiction for any thing to remain what it is, and to be changed into what it is not. (2.) 'Tis as absurd to say that a Material Essence was made of one purely Immaterial, Mortal of Immortal, Flesh and Bones of mere Spirit. (3.) For as much as Man is compos'd of a Body and a Soul, it was requisite that the Divine Essence of the Son should be changed partly into an Immortal Soul, partly into Mortal Flesh: Or if they would have it chang'd only into Flesh, because 'tis said, *the Word was made Flesh*, it follows that it was turn'd into Flesh devoid of Soul and Spirit, which alone was the Son of God; and that a Soul was infus'd into it, which

[1] 1 Tim. 2. 5.
[2] Gen. 3. 15.
[3] Gal. 3. 16.
[4] Rom. 1. 3. Tim. 2. 8. Acts 2. 30.
[5] Gal. 4. 4.

should quicken and govern it. (4.) And lastly, 'tis necessary that they own one of these two things, either that the Essence of the Son was not the same with the Father, which they do not assert; or if it be the same, then when the Essence of the Son was chang'd into Flesh, the Essence of the Father was chang'd into Flesh likewise; and when the Son died, the whole Divine Essence died too: and by this means, upon the Death of Christ, the World was without a God for three days together. All these, with several others of the like nature, are monstrous Absurdities: Not that we charge it upon them as their genuine Opinion, but as the Consequences thereof; and therefore would desire them to beware of an Opinion, which has such fatal and absurd Consequences flowing from it.

Some Objections answer'd.
However in defence of their Opinion they usually produce some Places of Scripture, which we shall briefly examine.

In the first place they say, that the Lord Jesus was not born after the manner of other Men, but conceived of the Holy Ghost. *Answ.* There can no Inference be drawn from hence in favour of their Opinion; for Christ is only said to be conceived of the Holy Ghost, because the Holy Ghost by a peculiar Power made the Flesh and Blood of *Mary* so fruitful, as out of it, as the Material Cause, the Body of Christ should be form'd.

Secondly they produce *John* 1. 14; where we read, *The Word was made Flesh*; which they say signifies nothing else but that the Word was chang'd into Flesh; for that is the meaning of being made. *Answ.* The true and genuine Sense of this Place is, that the Word was Flesh, that is, a true fleshly Substance, subject to all those Infirmities to which our Flesh is liable: That is to say, Jesus Christ was mortal, of a mean and despicable Condition; which more especially appear'd in the Days of his Passion and Death, which are therefore call'd *the Days of his Flesh*.[6]

Thirdly they alledg the Words of the Apostle, 1 Cor. 15. 47. *The first Man is of the Earth earthy, the second Man is the Lord from Heaven. Answ.* The Apostle does not here speak of Christ as born of the Virgin *Mary*, nor of the Body which he deriv'd from her; but of Christ as rais'd from the Dead to Eternal Life, and of his glorified Body which he has now in Heaven. This is very plain from the whole Series of this

[6] Heb. 5. 7.

Chapter, not to mention the Absurdities which follow from their Interpretation of the Words.

Upon the whole matter therefore we conclude, that the Flesh of the Lord Jesus, like that of other Men, was produc'd of the Flesh and Blood of his Mother *Mary*; only with this Difference, that he was not born, as other Men are, by the Conjunction of a Man and a Woman, but by the Power of the Holy Ghost miraculously overshadowing the Virgin *Mary*; upon which account it is, even with respect to his Human Nature, that he was call'd by the Angel *the Son of God*.[7] And we are firmly to believe that Jesus Christ was true MAN, not only because he is in Scripture expressly so call'd; but also, because he died for us, and by his Death procured a Reconciliation for us with the Father, and saved us from our Sins: which we could never believe of him, had he not been MAN. Add to this, that God exhibited him to us as an Example of Obedience, and of attaining Everlasting Salvation by the Resurrection from the Dead, if we endeavour by persevering in Holiness to tread in his Steps: But if he had not been MAN, he could have given us no Example of this Gracious and Divine Will. So that they who antiently in the Christian Church denied our Lord Jesus to be truly Flesh, and to partake of our Human Nature, such as the *Marcionites*, *Cerdonians*, *Manichees*, and others, and who asserted that our Lord did not really die, but only in appearance seem'd in the Apprehension of the *Jews* to suffer, have miserably perverted the Oeconomy of our Salvation, and subverted the very Foundation of it.

Sect. III. The Opinion of Socinus concerning the Satisfaction of Jesus Christ examin'd and refuted.

From what was said in the foregoing Section it appears what was the Act of Christ's Priestly Office, *viz.* the obtaining the Remission of Sins, and our Redemption. But wherein this consists, Divines are not very well agreed.

The Opinion of Socinus refuted.
Socinus and his Followers give us this account of it, "That Christ entring into Heaven by his own Blood, has received from the Father a Power over all things, by virtue of which he should convert Men from Sin to Righteousness; and thus he expiates their Sins, and reconciles them to God."

[7] Luke 1. 35.

1. By Reason.

But this is too loose an account of the Priestly Office of Christ; for what they attribute to him, he may do as he is a Prophet and a King. Where then is the Sacerdotal Act? What Oblation do they assign to Christ, whereby to denominate him a Priest? For every High Priest is ordain'd to offer Gifts and Sacrifices; wherefore (as the Apostle argues[8]) it is of necessity that this Man (*viz.* the Man Christ Jesus) have somewhat also to offer, that thereby he might be truly a Priest. We ought not then to confound the Offices of Christ one with the other, but to consider them as distinct: As he is a King and a Prophet, he is the Vicegerent of God, and declares his Will and Pleasure to Men: But as he is a Priest, his Business is with God alone, in order to render him propitious and merciful to sinful Man.

2. By Scripture.

For a fuller Refutation of the *Socinian* Doctrine, we will consider what Force and Energy the Scripture does all along attribute to the Death of Christ; whereby it will appear, that it was a real and proper Sacrifice, by which God's Anger was appeas'd, and he was pleas'd to pardon the Sins which were the occasion of his Anger. (1.) This is evident from all those Texts wherein Christ is stiled *an Offering* and *Sacrifice for Men*, or *for the Sins of Men*.[9] (2.) From those Places where he is call'd ἱλαστήριον and ἱλασμος, *the Propitiation for our Sins*[10], and said ἱλασχεσδαι, *to make Reconciliation for the Sins of the People*[11]: All which Expressions plainly denote that our Saviour had reconciled the Father to us, and that the whole Force and Efficacy of this Propitiation was deriv'd from his Death. (3.) From all those Places wherein Christ is said *to die for our Sins*[12]. (4.) And lastly, in those from which we are said to have ἀπολύτρωσιν, *Redemption by him*[13], and those other Places where Christ is stiled λύτρον and ἀντίλυτρον, *a Ransom for many*[14]. By which Phrases it is evident, that the Blood of Christ

---

8   Heb. 8. 3.

9   Is. 53. 10. Eph. 5. 3. Heb. 9. 14, 26. & 10. 10.

10 Rom. 3. 25. 1 John 2. 2. & 4. 10.

11 Heb. 2. 17.

12 Is. 53. 4, 5, 6. 1 Cor. 15. 3. Gal. 1. 4. 1 Pet. 3. 18.

13 Eph. 1. 7. Coloss. 1. 14.

14 Mat. 20. 28. 1 Tim. 2. 6.

was the Price of our Redemption, which he paid down for us, that we might be deliver'd from the Guilt of Sin.

Before we dismiss this Argument, it will not be amiss to answer some Objections that are alledg'd in favour of the *Socinians* Opinion.

Answer to two Objections.

In the first Place then they urge, "That God when he deliver'd up his Son to Death was not angry with us, but out of Love sent us his Son: For the Scripture, when it speaks of this Mission of the Son into the World, never makes mention of the Wrath, but always of the Love of God." *Answ.* (1.) That God was angry with Men for their Sins is too notorious, and needs no Proof; see to this purpose among other Places, *Psal. 5.5. Isa. 59. 2.* and *Coloss. 3. 6.* Nay at that very time, wherein he sent his Son into the World, the Apostle informs us that *the Wrath of God was kindled against Sin*[15]. (2.) But farther, the Wrath of God is not always taken in the same sense. Sometimes it denotes his Affection or Inclination to punish, rais'd by the Greatness and Heinousness of the Offence; yet not so join'd with an immutable purpose of punishing, but that it is often suspended by the Interposition of his Love, whereby he waits for the Repentance of a Sinner, and pardons the Penitent. Sometimes it signifies the firm and immutable purpose of God to punish the Sinner[16]. Now in this latter sense God cannot be said to have been angry with us, when out of Love he sent his Son to us, because such Anger allows of no mixture of Love: Wrath is only ascribed in the former sense, which has some Alloy of Love and Mercy mix'd with it; that is, God shewed himself reconcilable to, and a Lover of Mankind; and therefore he deliver'd up his Son to die for us, that he might at the same time manifest his Love to Justice, and express his Willingness to be reconcil'd fully with Men, upon the Atonement made by the bloody and cruel Death of his Son. And because in this Mixture of Justice and Mercy, or of Wrath and Love, the one exceeded the other, and God out of Love to Men gave his Son to be a propitiatory Sacrifice for their Sins; hence it is that the Scripture on this Subject, never makes mention of the Anger, but always of the Love of God.

[15] Rom. 1. 18. Eph. 2. 3.
[16] John 3. 36.

Again they object, "That the Scripture declares, that Jesus Christ died for the Confirmation and Sanction of the New Covenant, and of the Divine Promises contain'd therein, the chief of which is Remission of Sins, and Eternal Life; that by this means he might bestow upon us some sort of Right of obtaining those Promises; and then that he might prevail upon all men to lay hold on and perform the Conditions annex'd to this Covenant." *Answ.* This is true; but the Death of Christ consider'd thus belongs to his Prophetical Office, which does both these things, as he by his Death has given an Attestation to the Truth which he preach'd. His Death then in this case is that of a Martyr, and not of a Priest; nor can the Remission of Sins be ascribed thereto, unless in a remote and improper sense, *viz.* as it confirms a Doctrine by the Observation of which we attain Remission of Sins. Now Remission of Sins might in this case be likewise ascribed to all that innumerable Company of Martyrs, who laid down their Lives for the Truth of the Gospel which we suppose the *Socinians* themselves will never allow of. The Death of Christ therefore must be look'd upon in another sense, *viz.* that of an Offering and a propitiatory Sacrifice for our Sins; and in this sense it belongs to his Priestly Office, of which we now treat.

Sect. IV. The Opinion of the Contra-Remonstrants concerning the Satisfaction of Jesus Christ, examin'd and refuted.

The *Contra-Remonstrants* or *Calvinists* are of a quite contrary Opinion to the *Socinians*, for they maintain that Christ has satisfied the Divine Justice for our Sins. But they are not all of a mind in the manner of explaining this Opinion. Some distinguish this Act of Christ into two Parts, *viz. Merit*, which regards the perfect Righteousness of Christ, which (as they say) he perform'd in our stead, and by which he merited for us the Imputation thereof, and Eternal Life; and *Satisfaction*, whereby he endur'd in our stead all the Punishments due to our Sins, and by the suffering of them fully satisfied the Divine Justice. But others will not allow of any distinct Action in the Case, but include the Merit in the Satisfaction of Jesus Christ, saying that his Satisfaction merited Salvation and Eternal Life. As to the Words *Merit* and *Satisfaction*, they are no where to be met with in Scripture, when mention is made of the Obedience and

Death of Christ, as *Maresius* himself acknowledges[17]; but are deduc'd from the word *Price*, ascribed to the Death of Christ, whereby Heaven is purchas'd for us[18]. Since therefore these Words are not extant in Holy Scripture, but are of Human Invention, no Man is bound to the Explication of them any farther than as it can be founded on those Scripture-Expressions, to the illustrating of which they are applied.

Refuted, 1. Concerning the Merit of Christ.

As to the Word *Merit*, it is usually plac'd in the perfect Obedience of Christ, whereby he is said to have fulfilled the Law for us, and by his Righteousness perform'd in our stead, has merited that it should be imputed to us by God the Father. But now, if Christ has by this means merited Righteousness, and so perform'd it for us, that we might in him be conformable in all things to the Law of God, nothing can be requir'd of us in order to be Partakers of that Righteousness, no not so much as that we should apprehend this Merit by Faith. We have already in Christ all that Righteousness, and Christ has already perform'd all things for us, which are necessary to our Salvation. But on the contrary, it appears from several Places of Scripture[19], that Faith and Holiness of Life are requir'd as necessary Conditions of attaining Eternal Life.

Several Objections answer'd.

But to this it may be objected, If Christ has not fulfill'd the Law in our stead, how is it necessary that he should be Holy and without Spot? *Answ.* Several Reasons may be assign'd for it, but those which more immediately relate to his Priestly Office, are these; That he might be a Sacrifice without Blemish, and a Holy High Priest. For he who was to offer up himself to God as a propitiatory Sacrifice for the Sins of Men, ought in all respects to be free from Sin; otherwise (as the Apostle argues[20]) *he would have needed a Sacrifice for the Expiation of his own Sins.* Hence it is that he is frequently said *to be without Sin*[21], and is call'd *the Lamb without Blemish and without Spot*[22].

---

[17] Loc. 10. de Officio Mediatoris, §. 29.

[18] Ibid. §. 44.

[19] Mat. 5. 20. 1 Cor. 6. 9, 10, 11. Heb. 12. 14. 1 John 3. 7. Rom. 8. 13. Revel. 22. 14.

[20] Heb. 7. 26, 27.

[21] 2 Cor. 5. 21. Heb. 4. 15. 1 Pet. 2. 22, 23.

[22] 1 Pet. 1. 19.

Rom. 5. 10. explain'd.

Again, they urge Rom. 5. 10. *For if when we were Enemies we were reconcil'd to God by the Death of his Son; much more being reconcil'd, we shall be sav'd by his Life. Answ.* We are not here to understand by the Life of Christ opposed to his Death, the Obedience which he shew'd to the Father, or his active Righteousness, as they phrase it; but the Life which he liv'd in Heaven after his Resurrection from the Dead, that he might fully and faithfully discharge the Office of our Priest before the Father, and expiate our Sins. The meaning therefore of the Words is this: If God did that which was greater, *viz.* gave his Son to die, that he might by his Death reconcile us to himself, whilst we were his Enemies; much more will he give Eternal Life to us who are reconcil'd unto him by his Son, who is rais'd from the Dead to Immortal Life, and appears before him in our behalf.

Rom. 5. 18, 19 explain'd.

They add, that in the same Chapter, *Ver.* 18, 19, 'tis said, *As by the Offence of one, Judgment came upon all Men to Condemnation, even so by the Righteousness of one, the Free Gift came upon all Men unto Justification of Life,* &c. *Answ.* In this Passage it is not said, that our Saviour lived righteously in our stead, or that his Righteousness is imputed to us, whilst we are yet in our Sins: but only that the Righteousness of Christ is the Cause of our Justification; or that God would impute Righteousness to us, who believe and are spiritually born again of him.

1. Cor. 1. 30. explain'd.

Lastly they object, 1. Cor. 1. 30. *Christ is made unto us Wisdom, and Righteousness, and Sanctification, and Redemption. Answ.* It is not likewise said in this Place, that Jesus Christ liv'd righteously in our stead, or that his Righteousness is ours, and imputed to us: for then for the same reason the Wisdom of Christ should be imputed to us, since he is said to be made Wisdom as well as Righteousness to us. The meaning therefore is, that Christ was appointed by God the Father to be the Author of Wisdom, Righteousness, &c. for by him alone can we attain to true and saving Wisdom, Righteousness, &c.

2. Concerning the Satisfaction of Christ.

The Satisfaction of Christ is said to be that whereby he has suffered all the Punishments due to our Sins, and by this

Suffering has fully satisfied the Divine Justice. But this Opinion has no Foundation in Scripture, and that for the following Reasons. (1.) The Death of Christ is called a Sacrifice for Sin: Now Sacrifices are no Discharge, nor plenary Satisfaction for Sins. (2.) Christ did not suffer Eternal Death, neither in Intenseness nor Extent, as we have already observ'd (*B.* 3. *C.* 3. §. 3) and yet this was the Punishment due to our Sins. (3.) If Christ did fully and entirely suffer all the Punishments due to our Sins, God then could grant nothing gratuitously to us: for if Christ has made a full Payment for us, even to the utmost Farthing, nothing is left for the Father to bestow upon us *gratis*, since his Justice is already fully satisfied. But the Scripture[23] teaches us that God out of his own Grace and Mercy grants us Remission of Sins in Christ. (4.) If Christ has made such a Satisfaction for us, then neither could God justly require of us Faith and Obedience (which 'tis plain he does[24]) as the means of obtaining Remission of Sins; nor could we be justly deprived of the Benefit of Christ's Death, or be punished for our Sins, tho we do not perform this Condition; for God would be unjust in exacting a double Punishment for one and the same Sin, first of Christ, and then of us. Now this is very absurd, and not only contrary to Scripture[25], but destructive of a Holy Life.

Objection answer'd. In what sense Christ is call'd the Surety of the New Covenant.

To what we have said, several Objections lie, which require an answer. In the first place they say, that Jesus is called *our Surety*, Heb. 7. 22. and that it is the Office of a Surety, where the Debtor is insolvent, to pay the whole Debt to the Creditor. *Answ.* (1.) Christ in the foremention'd Place is not properly call'd our Surety, but *the Surety of the New Testament*, or Covenant. (2.) Tho it were certain that Christ is our Surety in the Sanction of the New Covenant, yet he is not to be consider'd as a Security betwixt Debtor and Creditor, but as a Guarantee of the Covenant or Contract between God and Man, who undertakes to see that the Conditions of the Covenant be perform'd on both sides. So that the true Meaning of Christ's being a Surety seems to be this, not that he engages

23   Eph. 1. 7. & 4. 32. Coloss. 1. 14.

24   John 3. 16. Acts 3. 19. 1 John 1. 7. Mat. 6. 14, 15.

25   Heb. 10. 28, 29. 2 Pet. 2. 1, 2.

for Sinners, and takes all their Debts, and all the Punishments due to their Sins upon himself, but as he is a Surety or Mediator of the New Covenant, he by his Presence in Heaven intercedes for Men with God, and promises that sinful Men shall be converted to God, and that he by his Word and Spirit will effect it, that so the Wrath of God may not fall upon Sinners, nor they be cut off in a moment, and excluded from Salvation.

Again 'tis objected, that our Saviour is often stiled λύτρον and ἀντίλυτρον, or *the price of Redemption*; which can never be said, unless he had fully satisfied the Divine Justice, and suffer'd all those things which we deserv'd. *Answ.* They are egregiously mistaken in this, that they would have the Price of Redemption equivalent in all things to the Misery from which one is redeem'd; whereas it is usually set according to the voluntary Estimate of the Conqueror, and not according to the Worth of the Captive; one and the same Person being sometimes redeem'd for a greater, sometimes with a lesser Sum, and a meaner Person paying a greater, whilst one more noble pays a lesser Ransom, according as he who detains them is pleas'd to set a Price upon their Heads. Just thus the Price which Christ paid, was such as God the Father was pleas'd to accept of; not that it did in all things equal the Offence and Misery from whence we are thereby redeem'd.

They add, that *Gal.* 3. 13. we read, *Christ hath redeemed us from the Curse of the Law, being made a Curse for us*. Now, say they, to be made a Curse for any one, is the same thing as if he should take upon himself, and suffer in his stead all that Curse which the other was to endure. Wherefore since the Curse which hung over our Heads for our Sins, was Eternal Death, if Christ was made a Curse for us, it follows that he suffer'd Eternal Death for us, else he could not have redeem'd us from the Curse. *Answ.* We have just now observ'd, that in Redemption it is not necessary that the Price should in all things be equivalent to the Evil and Misery from whence we are redeem'd, but that it depends upon the Estimate of him, to whom the Price is to be paid; who may be satisfied with any Price that he is pleas'd to require. Now that our Saviour did not suffer Eternal Death, is too evident to need any Proof: nay, the Apostle himself sufficiently declares that he did not mean, that Christ took upon himself the Eternal Curse, but only the accursed Death of the Cross; for he immediately adds, *Cursed is every one who hangeth on a Tree*.

Sect. V. The true Opinion of the Satisfaction of Jesus Christ establish'd and maintain'd.

It now remains that we should set down our own Opinion, which is a Medium between the two other Extremes, and it is this: "That our Saviour Jesus Christ was a Sacrifice for our Sins, truly and properly so call'd; since he suffered most grievous Torments, and the accursed Death of the Cross, and after his Resurrection enter'd by his own Blood into the Celestial Tabernacle, and there presented himself before the Father: By which Sacrifice he appeas'd the Wrath of God, reconciled us to him, and averted from us the Punishment we deserv'd." This is evident from all those Places of Scripture formerly mention'd, wherein Christ is said to be *an Oblation, a Sacrifice*, to *die for us*, to *have redeem'd us*, to *have reconciled us to God*, to *have given himself a Ransom for many*, &c.

A Query answer'd.
But here it may be ask'd, What was the Evil which Christ suffer'd, was it the Punishment due to our Sins? *Answ.* We have already shewn that our Saviour did not suffer the same Punishment which we deserv'd for our Sins, for he did not suffer Eternal Death. But he endur'd great Misery and a bloody Death in our place, which was instead of that Punishment which might justly have been inflicted upon us. So that tho we had deserv'd Eternal Death, yet God was pleas'd by this voluntary Sacrifice, which his innocent Son offer'd for us, to be reconcil'd and to receive us into his Favour. We had deserv'd a greater and severer Punishment for our Sins; but God accepted of this Atonement made by the Death of Jesus Christ, and thereby displayed the Greatness of his Grace and Mercy, even whilst he requir'd Satisfaction to be made to his affronted and injured Justice.

Objections answer'd. Christ did not merit Faith and Regeneration for us.
To this it may be objected, If Christ made Satisfaction for us only in this manner, then he did not merit Faith and Regeneration for us. *Answ.* This is true; he merited, *i.e.* obtain'd of God for us a Suspension of his Wrath, an Allowance of farther time of Repentance, and a gracious Call to Faith and Regeneration; nay, and bestow'd upon us all the Assistances of Grace whereby we might be able to hearken to

the Divine Call: but he did not merit for us Faith and Regeneration it self. Had this been so, God could not have requir'd it of us under the Denunciation of Death; he would then by virtue of Christ's Merit have been oblig'd to have wrought it in us by his Almighty Power; and so it would not have been our Duty, but the Act of God alone.

Absurdity in God's requiring the Death of his Son as a Sacrifice.
It may be urged farther, that it seems absurd and repugnant to the Nature of God, that he should require a Human Sacrifice, nay even that of his own only begotten Son; and that this savours of Cruelty. *Answ.* By no means; for the Absurdity, if any arises from hence, is either because God will'd the Death of his Son; or because he will'd him to suffer Death as an Expiatory Sacrifice for our Sins. But there is no Absurdity in either of these. Not in the former; because God the Father having an uncontroulable Power over all Men as to Life and Death, has also a Right of delivering up his Son to Death. Nor is there any Absurdity in the latter; since if God might deliver his Son to die as a Prophet, that he might by his Blood as of a federal Victim establish the New Covenant (which the Objectors themselves own) why was it less allowable to the Father to require, that his Son should die as a Propitiatory Sacrifice for Sins, and thereby intercede for Sinners as a sanctified Priest? For certainly if he could have put his Son to Death, he had also a Right of directing his Death to such an End, as was most suitable to his Glory and the Salvation of Mankind.

Further evinc'd.
But here again it may be retorted; Since God forbad any Human Sacrifices to be offer'd to him, it seems absurd that he should will Christ to die as a Sacrifice for Men. *Answ.* (1.) God in prescribing a Law to Men of not offering Human Sacrifices, did not prescribe a Law to himself of never requiring a Human Sacrifice, as is plain from the Instance of *Isaac*[26]. (2.) God did not command Men to offer Jesus Christ to him as a Sacrifice for their Sins; that Thought be far from us: But he only left him to the Power of wicked Men, and Christ freely deliver'd himself into their Hands, that they might out of Envy kill him: And this

---

[26]   Gen. 22.

ignominious Death of his Son, tho design'd to another End by the *Jews*, was the Father pleas'd to allow of as an Expiatory Sacrifice for Sins.

A Query answer'd.
Very likely it may be demanded; How could, and really did, the Sacrifice of one Man suffice for the expiating the innumerable Sins of so many Myriads of Men in the World? *Answ.* It was sufficient upon these two accounts. (1.) Upon the account of the Divine Will, which requir'd nothing more for the Redemption of Mankind, but was satisfied with this single Sacrifice. And certainly if God (who, as we observ'd before, has an absolute Power of declaring what Ransom will satisfy him) was pleas'd to accept of the Sacrifices under the Law as expiatory of the Sins of the People[27]; why should not, by the same Divine Will, the Blood of Jesus Christ be sufficient to atone for all the Sins of the whole World? (2) Upon the account of the Dignity of the Person of Jesus Christ, who is the Son of God, nay who is over all, God blessed for ever[28]. True it is, he suffered only in his Human Nature; yet since it was united to the Divine, the very Eternal Son of God may rightly be said to have suffered whatsoever the Man Christ Jesus endur'd in the Flesh for Sinners. Besides, if Christ be consider'd only as a MAN, the Excellency of his Person upon several accounts was so great, that he surpass'd in a high measure all the rest of Mankind. Now who can question, but that this Dignity of the Person of Christ did mightily enhance the Merit of his Passion?

Chap. VI. Of Vertues relating to the Will, and first of FAITH in Jesus Christ.

A Distribution of all the Christian Vertues.
Next to the two Intellectual Vertues follow those of the Will or Manners, comprehending Holiness of Life in general, and all the Parts of it in particular. These respect either all Men in general, or only some particular Persons, according to the Diversity of their Ranks and Stations in the civil Society of which they are Members. Again, those Vertues which affect all Men, are either about things necessary, wherein properly and truly Holiness consists; or about things indifferent. Of the Vertues relating to things necessary, some are general, others

---

[27] Lev. 16.

[28] Rom. 9. 5.

more special. The general ones are such as comprehend summarily the whole Duty of a Christian, and are these two, Faith in Jesus Christ, and Repentance. Having thus distributed the several Vertues of a Christian into their several Classes, we shall now proceed to give a more particular view of them, and in this Chapter shall consider the first general Vertue, *viz. Faith in Jesus Christ,* with all that is proper for a Christian to know of it; which we shall do in several distinct Sections.

Sect. I. Of the Antecedent Act of Faith, viz. Knowledg.

Faith in Christ defin'd, with its several Acts.

Without taking notice of the various Acceptations of the word FAITH in Scripture, and the Perfection or Imperfection of it, according to more or less Degrees of Revelation communicated to Men; we shall confine our selves only to give an account of that sort of Faith which is most proper to be known and understood by a Christian. *Faith then in Jesus Christ is not only a Knowledg and Assent, whereby we believe that Jesus is the Christ, the only Saviour of all who live according to the Gospel-Rule; but likewise the Confidence and Assurance we put in him as our Prophet, Priest and King, whereby we are fully persuaded, if we obey his Doctrine, that we shall by him attain Remission of Sins and Eternal Life: producing of it self a serious and effectual Purpose of performing that Obedience he requires of us.* From this Definition it appears, that Faith is not a single Habit or Act, but consists of several Parts, and comprehends under it several Acts. (1.) An antecedent Act, *viz.* Knowledg. (2.) Its formal Act, *viz.* Assent, to which is annexed Assurance. (3.) Its consequent Act, Obedience, which is not only a constituent part of Faith, but the immediate Effect thereof, and that which renders it a lively Faith.

Its antecedent Act, Knowledg.

The antecedent Act of Faith is Knowledg, on which Faith it self is founded, and which being taken away, is effectually destroyed; *for how,* says the Apostle[29], *shall they believe in him, of whom they have not heard?* &c. Hence 'tis that by a *Synecdoche* of the Part for the Whole, Faith it self is sometimes described by the word Knowledg[30]. Now the Object of this Knowledg is all those things that are necessary to be known in

[29] Rom. 10. 14.

[30] Tit. 1. 2. Joh. 17.3.

order to Salvation, such as God, his Attributes and Works, Jesus Christ, with his Person and Offices, and the Divine Precepts, Promises and Threatenings. But we do not here reckon as things necessary, all such as are controverted in the Schools, but only such, without which, Faith in God, and in Jesus Christ as our Saviour, the Observation of the Divine Precepts, and Belief of the Promises cannot be of any force; a Summary of which we have exhibited to us in that which is called *the Apostles Creed*. However, we do not pretend to discourage any Christian from making a further Progress in the Knowledg of Divine things; but what we mean is, that they who know and believe the things necessary to Salvation, and live according to that Knowledg and Belief, are really of the number of the Faithful, tho they are ignorant of, or do not rightly understand some other things that are not precisely necessary.

An Implicit Faith what.
This Knowledg is requisite in opposition to that implicit and blind Faith of the *Romanists*, whereby a Man is said to be obliged to believe as the Church believes, tho he knows nothing of it: For an implicit Faith is as it were under a Cloud, by which a thing is believed in general, contrary to an explicit Faith, whereby a Man believes any thing distinctly and particularly. But for a full Confutation of the *Romanists* implicit Faith, we say, that this implicit Faith may admit of a twofold Sense. (1.) As it relates to the Holy Scripture, and all the things contained therein: Thus when we explicitly believe in general, that the Scripture is Divine, and consequently all and every thing contain'd in it must be credited; we likewise implicitly believe all the Histories and Doctrines delivered therein: it being enough to shew that they are in Scripture, in order to create Belief. However this is not a saving Faith, unless all the particular things necessary to Salvation are believed distinctly and explicitly. (2.) As it relates to the Church of *Rome*, and as it is joined with the Ignorance of the Doctrines of Religion, and of things necessary to be believed in order to Salvation. So that *Implicit Faith* in the *Popish* Sense, is that whereby the Laity, who either know not, or as yet do not understand the Articles of Faith, do believe implicitly in this General, *That all things are true which the Church of* Rome *believes and holds as true.* But in such a sense *Implicit Faith* is by no means tolerable;

(1.) Because this is not a *Divine* but *Human* Faith, built upon a rotten Foundation, *viz.* the Authority of Men subject to Error, and consequently so fallacious that no Man who valued his Salvation would rely upon it. (2.) We are commanded in Scripture to get Knowledg for our selves[31], *to try all things, and hold fast that which is good*[32], that so we may *beware of false Prophets that come in Sheeps Clothing*[33], &c. and *not believe every Spirit, but try the Spirits whether they are of God*[34]. This is our indispensible Duty, and no Excuse will serve the Turn if we are negligent therein.

Two Objections answer'd.

To this they make two Objections: First, they say that the Priests of their Church stake down their own Souls for the Truth of their Doctrine. *Answ.* (1.) There is no relying safely on such a Security; for it is possible that this Surety may be so far indebted to the Divine Justice by his own Sins, as not to be able to discharge himself from Guilt and Condemnation, and how then can he be responsible for the Errors of others? (2) God denies to accept of any such Security, but will make a Retribution *to every Man according to his own Works*[35]. (3.) Nor is it a certain evidence that any Doctrine is true, because the Teacher of it pledges his own Soul for it; but only, that he himself does not in the least question the Truth of his Doctrine. Nor has the Church of *Rome* any Preeminence herein over the rest of the Churches, since every Christian Teacher is bound to lay down his Life for the Profession of his Doctrine.

Again the *Romanists* object, That the Understanding ought to be brought into Captivity[36], which cannot be where Knowledg is required. *Answ.* The contrary of this is true, *viz.* That because the Understanding is to be brought into Captivity, therefore a Knowledg is required of those things, which the Understanding ought to be subjected to; else this Captivity would not be a rational, but a blind and brutal one. Thus the Understanding of Man is brought into Captivity,

---

31   1 Cor. 14. 20. Eph. 5. 15.

32   1 Thess. 5. 21.

33   Mat. 7. 15.

34   1 John 4. 1.

35   Gal. 9. 5. 2 Cor. 5. 10.

36   2 Cor. 10. 5.

when relying on Divine Revelation it searches for true Wisdom in that alone, laying aside its own Wisdom which he finds is no true Guide to the supreme Good. And 'tis after this manner that the Apostle brought every Understanding into Captivity to the Obedience of Christ; drawing Men to the Christian Faith by the Efficacy of his Doctrine and the Power of Miracles, that denying their own Wisdom with which they were puffed up, they might yield themselves the Disciples of Christ, and learn out of his Gospel true Wisdom for the Salvation of their own Souls.

Sect. II. Of Assent, the Formal Act of Faith, and its Adjunct Assurance.

The *Formal Act* of *Faith* is *Assent*, which ought to have a close Connection with *Knowledg*; since without it *Knowledg* is unavailable to Salvation, it being to be seen not only in many wicked Men[37], but also in the Devils themselves[38]. But every kind of *Assent* is not sufficient; that which is truly an Act of Faith must be solid and firm, founded on the rational Judgment of the Will, produced in us by a serious and accurate Meditation of those things, which render us fully persuaded of the certainty of what we are to believe. Any other *Assent* raised upon slight Grounds cannot be effectual or lasting, 'tis rather Opinion than *Faith*, more a blind than a rational Obedience, and rather a brutal *Impetus* of the Mind than sound Judgment.

Its Object in general, Truth.
The Object of *Faith* in general ought, (1.) to be the TRUTH; for no Man can be obliged to believe a LYE, and God himself who is faithful and holy, nay TRUTH it self, cannot injoin any Man to give his Assent to a LYE. (2.) Those things are only to be believed, which God in his Word declares to be true; for *Faith* is an *Assent* relying on the Testimony of God, but he neither does nor can declare what is false to be true. (3.) The Divine Law does not command us to err, because every Error is repugnant to the Divine Rectitude; but to believe a Falshood is to err. (4.) Lastly it would follow, if the Object of *Faith* can be a Falshood, Divine Faith may sometimes be an Error, *viz.* an *Assent* to what is false; which is egregiously absurd.

[37] Luk. 12. 47. Tit. 1. 16.
[38] Luk. 4. 33, 34. Acts 16. 17.

God cannot oblige a Man to believe a Lye.

This we thought fit to observe, in opposition to some Divines, who for the maintenance of this their Doctrine [*That the Reprobate are bound to believe that Christ died for them, tho he did not*] are not ashamed openly to assert, that God can, nay sometimes does oblige a Man to believe that which is false; nay they are not afraid, for the defence of this horrid and blasphemous Notion, to invent some Pretences for it: *Adam* (say they) was obliged in his State of Innocence to believe that he shou'd obtain Eternal Life, which was false. *Answ. Adam* was not bound to believe this absolutely, but only conditionally, if he persevered in that State; else he could not have believed the Divine Threatning, that on the Day wherein he should eat of the forbidden Fruit, he should surely die. Again they urge, that *Abraham* was bound to believe, that God was willing he should sacrifice his Son; but this was likewise false. *Answ.* (1.) This Command is expressly called a *Temptation*, and consequently is of a quite different nature from the rest of the Divine Precepts; unless they will be so hardy as to say, that God when he commands the Reprobate to believe in Christ, does it only to tempt them. (2.) Properly speaking, *Abraham* was not commanded to believe that God was willing that he should really kill his Son, but only that he should sacrifice him. This latter he did believe, and accordingly prepared himself to obey the Command; but it was not his business to enquire whether God intended that he should really kill his Son, or whether he commanded it only to try him.

Its Object in particular, that Jesus is the Christ.

The *Object* of a *Christian Faith* in particular is every *Truth* necessary to be believed in order to eternal Salvation: But whereas this is comprehended under one single Truth, that *Jesus is the Christ*, therefore that alone in Scripture is commonly said to be the *Object* of a *Christian's Faith*, as if nothing besides was required of us to believe. This is expressed under various Terms in Scripture[39], all amounting to this, "That *Jesus* of *Nazareth* who preach'd the Gospel in *Judea*, excelled in Miracles, was crucified, rose the third day from the Dead, and ascended into Heaven, was the Christ, or the

[39]   Mat. 16. 16. Joh. 20. 3. Acts 8. 37. 1 Joh. 5. 1. Rom. 10. 9. Acts 16. 31. Joh. 3. 16–36.

Saviour promised before the Prophets, and to be owned as such."

Two things considerable herein.
But it is worth our while to enquire more distinctly what is necessarily required for our believing that *Jesus is the Christ.* Now this Proposition, *Jesus is the Christ*, which is the *Object* of a saving Faith, comprehends two things, the *Subject*, *Jesus*, and the *Predicate*, *Christ*; the one denoting the Person, the other the Office of our Saviour.

1. The Predicate, Christ, what it means.
The *Predicate* of the Proposition is *Christ*, or the *Son of God*; which according to the usual Style of the Writers of the New Testament, signifies the *Messiah* promised to the *Jews*, by whom Salvation was to be obtained: Who not only directed us in the way that leads to Eternal Life, but also by his accursed Death delivered us from the Curse, being made a Propitiatory Sacrifice for us, strengthens us by his Spirit against all the Insults and Temptations of the Devil, and at last by his Almighty Power will raise us from the Dead, and bring us to Eternal Life and glory. This Dignity is sometimes expressed by the word *Christ*, sometimes by the *Son of God*, which are equivalent in the Scripture-Phrase. The Words of *David* seem to have given rise to this Title, *Thou art my Son, this day have I begotten thee*[40]; and again, *I will be to him a Father, and he shall be to me a Son*[41]: Which Expressions were applied by the Apostles to the *Messiah*[42] in a more sublime and mystical Sense, and so understood by the *Jews*. This is evident from the Acknowledgment of *Nathaniel*[43], *Peter*[44], the other Disciples[45], and the Eunuch of *Candace*[46]: But the greatest Testimony of all is that which *Jesus* himself gives us of this Truth when he was examin'd by the High Priest[47], and which he confirms in

[40]   Ps. 2. 7.

[41]   2 Sam. 7. 14.

[42]   Acts 13. 33. Heb. 1. 5.

[43]   Joh. 1. 50.

[44]   Mat. 16. 16. Luk. 9. 20.

[45]   Mat. 14. 33.

[46]   Acts 8. 37.

[47]   Mat. 26. 33.

another place[48]. To believe then that *Jesus is the Christ*, or *the Son of God*, signifies nothing else than that *Jesus* is that extraordinary Saviour promised so long before, to whom the Office of saving Men was committed by the Father, in which Office he was inaugurated by being anointed with the Holy Ghost.

2. The Subject, Jesus.

As to the *Subject* of this Proposition, the full and perfect Knowledg thereof does not seem to be absolutely necessary for the Truth and Evidence of it. True it is, the Person to whom the Office of a Saviour is committed by God, ought to be apprehended, who is denoted by the Name of JESUS; which Name signifies a certain Man Anointed by God the Father, and installed in that Office. But whether this Person consists of two Natures, one *Eternal* and *Divine*, the other *Human*, both united in one Person, has no reference to the Truth of this Proposition, but ought to be enquired after in other Places of Scripture.

The Eternal Filiation not a necessary Object of Christian Faith. We do indeed believe that this Person is *the Son of God*, upon the account of his Divine Nature, and the *Eternal Filiation*; but whether this *Filiation* be the Object of a Christian's Faith, cannot be concluded from this Proposition, but must be proved from other places of Scripture. Since therefore no Text, as we know of, maintains that the Union of the Divine with the Human Nature is the necessary Object of Faith, and the Office of Christ is to be believed concerning *Jesus*; yet tho we own and acknowledg this truth, we dare not say 'tis necessary to be believed in order to Salvation: And that for these two Reasons; (1.) Because this Doctrine is so full of Obscurities and Niceties, that the most learned and wise have taken pains to no purpose, after all confessing their Ignorance in this matter. Now 'tis not at all likely that God should annex our Salvation to a Doctrine so obscure and intricate, that hardly one in a thousand, perhaps no Man, can distinctly apprehend. (2.) Because without the special Knowledg of the two Natures in Christ, and the manner of their being United, we may believe that *Jesus is the Christ*; that is, we may have a right Apprehension of the Office, tho we have not a full and clear knowledg of the Person of Jesus, as he is *God-Man*.

---

48   John 10. 34, 35, 36.

Nor the Eternal Word made Flesh.
But there are some Christians, *viz.* the more rigid ANA-
BAPTISTS of foreign Parts, who require that in order to make
it an essentially saving Faith, we shou'd believe that the Eternal
Word of the Father was made Flesh, *i.e.* that the very Divine
Essence of the Word was changed and transubstantiated into
Flesh. But these Men are egregiously mistaken: for (1.) the
Scripture does not inform us of any such manner of our Lord's
Incarnation; and tho we should grant what is not to be granted,
that some things are somewhere contain'd in Scripture in
favour of this Opinion, yet it would not from thence follow,
that in it consists the Essence of a saving Faith. (2.) This Faith
is not necessary for the acknowledging our Jesus to be the
Christ, or for believing in and obeying him; nay it has no
respect to Piety, or Obedience to the Divine Commands, since a
saving Faith produces this of itself, being that which
overcometh the world[49]. (3.) It may be prejudicial to Piety,
since it tends to the destruction of the Article concerning the
Resurrection of the Dead; for since his Resurrection is the
Foundation of ours, and according to them the Flesh of Christ
is of another nature than ours, what hope can we have of being
raised again, from the Consideration of the Resurrection of
Jesus Christ? And being deprived of such a Hope, our Piety
must needs sink to the ground.

But the Offices of Christ, as Prophet, Priest and King.
Since therefore the *Object* of a Christian's Faith does properly
regard the Offices of Christ, Faith in a Profession of them is
also necessary; for by them Christ is, and without the
Knowledg of them the Worship due to God and Christ cannot
be performed. Now these Offices are, as we elsewhere
observed, the *Prophetical, Priestly* and *Kingly*, to which our
Faith must be applied. (1.) As to the *Prophetical* Office, by
Faith we believe *Jesus* was a true Teacher sent forth from God;
by whom alone, or by whose Gospel alone, the full Knowledg
of the Divine Will is to be fought for, and whose Doctrine is to
be received, with a full persuasion of Mind, That if we obey his
Precepts, we shall attain the Salvation promised to us by him.
(2.) As to his *Sacerdotal* Office, we are to believe, that by his
own Blood shed for us here for the Remission of Sins, he is
enter'd into the Heavenly Sanctuary, there to offer up himself

[49]   1 Joh. 5. 4.

continually, and intercede for us. Which Oblation and Intercession is of so great Avail, as to obtain a plenary Expiation of all our Sins, and on whose single Sacrifice we are to rely, in exemption of all other Mediators. (3.) As to his *Kingly* Office, we must believe, that he is risen from the Dead, taken up into Heaven, where he has Power over all things both in Heaven and Earth; governs us by his Word and Spirit, protects and defends us against all Temptations and Adversities, and at last, if we persevere in Faith and Obedience, will advance us to Eternal Felicity.

True Faith consistent with a small Error.
Beside these, many other things are usually enquired into about the Offices of *Jesus Christ*; however they are not all necessary to Salvation, but only such as without which the Worship due to God and Jesus Christ cannot consist. Now if any one with sincerity admits of those things, he is endued with a saving and true Faith, tho he should err in some matters of less moment.

What is contained in this Assent.
Having thus at large explained the Nature of a saving Faith, it appears that there are two things contained in it in general. (1.) Some Truths which God affirms to us, and to which he requires our assent. (2.) Some Duties which he enjoins us under a promised Reward, and a threatened Punishment. From hence arise two Acts of Faith; First, an Assent applied to God, who affirms such things as we suppose to be credible. And secondly, such an Assent as is given to God, who commands that those things we know to be credible, we should look upon to be most certain. From hence 'tis easy to solve that Question which is usually started, whether Faith be the Act of the Understanding or Will? To which we answer, That 'tis not a mere Act either of the Understanding or the Will, but a mixt one, partly of the one and partly of the other.

Assurance.
To an *Assent*, as its necessary Adjunct, flowing from it, is annex'd *Assurance*; which is not only a strong Hope, but *Confidence*, whereby we are ascertain'd that we shall attain to Eternal Salvation according to the Divine Promise. That this *Assurance* is an Act of Faith, appears from hence, that 'tis nothing else but a firm Assent of one, who without disputes relies on the Divine Promises.

Its Object not a special Mercy of God.
As to the *Object* of this *Assurance*, a great Question is started:
The *Contra-Remonstrants* maintain that 'tis the *special Mercy*
of God, whereby he irrevocably had elected some certain
Persons to Salvation, without any regard had to their Faith,
and has sent Christ as their Saviour, who has made satisfaction
for their Sins; and therefore they make the Righteousness of
Christ performed for the Elect the *Object* of *Faith*. Now this
Opinion is very absurd; since (1.) there is no such *special
Mercy* in God, the Promise annexed to the Divine Covenant
being universal, and under the Condition of Faith and
Obedience[50]. (2.) Nor could such a special Mercy be promised
to Man, because according to their Opinion, it was before the
Promise peculiar to the Elect, as being destined to them from
all Eternity, by virtue of the Divine Decree. (3.) It is not a
Mercy which happens to the Elect for the sake of Christ, of
which nature however are all the Blessings, which are the
Object of a Christian's Assurance or Faith; but Christ was
given to the Elect for the Sake of that Mercy. (4.) Such a Faith
is destructive of Piety, because it takes away the necessity
thereof, in order to our attaining the Divine Promises: For if
God without any regard had to Faith or Piety has predestinated
Eternal Life to the Elect, what necessity is there of believing
and obeying, that they might attain a Happiness, irrevocably
destined to them, without any consideration of Faith or
Obedience?

But his Universal and Conditional Mercy.
The *Object* therefore of *Assurance* is the *Universal Mercy of
God*, offered to all Men, provided they believe in Christ, and
live according to the Rule he has prescribed them: So that this
Assurance is the Act of Man, whereby he stedfastly believes
that God will pardon his Sins, and bestow upon him Eternal
Life, if he believes in and obeys his son *Jesus Christ*. This
Assurance is the immediate Product of Assent; for the Believer
giving his Assent to the Doctrine of *Jesus Christ*, whereby
Eternal Life is promised to all Men on the Conditions of Faith
and Obedience, does hence, by a Reflection made to himself,
trust, That Eternal Life will likewise be bestowed upon him by
Christ, provided he believes and obeys.

---

[50] Joh. 3. 16. 1 Joh. 1. 7.

Sect. III. Of the Consequential Act of Faith, Obedience.

Its Consequential Act, Obedience.

The *Consequential Act*, or rather the immediate Effect of *Faith*, is *Obedience*, which proceeds from the former; for he who believes with Assurance, that God will bestow Eternal Life on the Believing and Obedient Soul, will also obey God, that he may attain that Life. And because the Virtue and Efficacy of Faith shews forth it self in such an Obedience, hence it is called the Life of Faith, without which Faith is ineffectual to Salvation[51], nay is accounted as no Faith[52].

The Nature of Faith.

To make this the more plain, we must consider the Nature of Faith a little more thorowly. The Apostle *Heb.* 11. 1. tells us, that *Faith is the* ὑπόστασις, *the Substance of things hop'd for, the* ἔλεγχος, *the Evidence or Conviction of things not seen*; because by its Certainty and Solidity it bestows a sort of Being on things future which do not as yet exist, and places and presents them as it were before the Eyes of the Believer. For Faith takes it for granted that future good things will at one time or other be present; and by this Representation it renders them as efficacious, as if they were really present. Now those future Blessings are Eternal Life, the Beatifick Vision, and all the other Enjoyments of the other World, in opposition to Eternal Death, Misery and Torment.

How it works Obedience.

If then *Faith* renders future things as efficacious as if they were present, it follows that one who has such a stedfast Faith must obey Christ: *i.e.* He who believes with a firm Faith, that he shall attain those Blessings, if he obeys Christ according to the Rule prescribed him in the Gospel; and if he is disobedient, must suffer Eternal Death and Misery, and represents this future Happiness or Misery to himself as present and before his eyes, will certainly pay a ready Obedience to his great Master's Commands. Now the reason is plainly this: Because there is no Comparison to be made between the Enjoyments of this World, whereby we are tempted to sin, and the Happiness of a future State; nor between the Pain we may suffer in restraining our Appetites,

---

51   Jam. 2. 14.

52   1 Joh. 2. 4.

and the Eternal Torment of Hell-fire. For all the things of this Life are of an inconstant, transitory nature, and perish even in the Enjoyment: But Eternal Life is a solid, lasting, and perfect Happiness. What can be compared to it in this World? Can the good things of it? Alas! no: They are of a fading perishing nature, and have too great an Alloy of Unhappiness and Misery, which render them unsatisfactory Enjoyments. Can the Evils of it? No; they are not to be compared to the Glory which shall hereafter be reveal'd, nor do they bear any proportion to Eternal Misery. True it is, we are most affected with those Objects that are present, and strike immediately upon our Senses; and this is the great Cause why so many who walk by Sight not by Faith, are carnal and mind worldly things. But the Man who by the Eye of Faith brings those future Enjoyments closer to himself, and beholds them as if present, must needs be more strongly affected with this View, than with all the Allurements offer'd him by the false appearance and glittering of the perishable Enjoyments of this World: and consequently such an one will be inclined to pay a ready Obedience, when he has such powerful Motives to excite him thereto.

A Query answer'd.
But here it may be asked, whether a sound Judgment can be made of any Man's *Faith* by his *Obedience*, so that whoever does not live conformably to the Gospel, ought to be esteem'd as having no Faith? *Answ.* Faith may be consider'd either as a *Habit* or as an *Act.* In the former sense *Faith* is consider'd in the general, and may be perfect, tho it does not produce Works of Obedience. For notwithstanding the *Habit* of *Faith*, it may so happen that a Man allur'd by the Sweetness of present Enjoyments, may be pinion'd down to them, and so disregard the Happiness of Heaven, as not to exert his Virtue in resisting the Prevalency of his Lusts; which might have been done, if Faith had had its perfect Work. But *Faith* consider'd in the latter sense, as actually apprehending future good things, if it be solid and strong, cannot be barren of good Works: and consequently a neglect of what is good, and a customary doing of Evil, is a certain and infallible Sign of Man's having no true and sound Faith in him.

Sect. IV. Of the Causes and Effects of Faith.

God the efficient Cause of Faith.

The Primary and *Efficient Cause* of Faith is God, from whom, as from *the Father of Lights, every good and perfect Gift cometh*[53]. But the Divine Gifts are various; some are bestowed by God absolutely on Men, without any Operation requir'd on Man's part; such as Creation, Preservation, Redemption, *&c.* Others are given by him, but then the Labour of Man is requisite for his obtaining them; thus God gives Corn, but the Industry of the Husbandman must be us'd in sowing the Grain in the Earth: Others again are commanded by God, for the performance of which he bestows upon us sufficient Helps; but the free Obedience of Man is requir'd, whereby he obeys, by the Divine Assistance, the Commands of God, and so obtains the Gift offer'd to him: and of this nature are *Faith* and *Repentance.*

It is not an infus'd Habit.

Faith is not then such a Divine Gift as is wrought in us without our Co-operation, nor a Habit infus'd into us by God; but an Act of our Obedience proceeding from the Will, which is excited and assisted by the Divine Grace. This will more evidently appear if we consider the following Particulars: (1.) *Faith* is commanded us by God, with the addition of a promis'd Reward, and a threatned Punishment[54]: But Habits infus'd by God cannot be prescrib'd to Man, because they cannot be reckon'd as his Acts. (2.) *Faith* proceeds from hearing the Word of God; but a Habit infus'd by him proceeds not from Hearing, but from the Divine Omnipotent Power. (3.) If *Faith* were a Habit infus'd into us by God, then we should be Believers before we actually believe; which is absurd. (4.) Faith is according to the Scripture-Acceptation taken wholly as an Act of Obedience, as being commanded; but an infus'd Habit is not so, being produc'd by an external Principle. (5.) With respect to an infus'd Habit the Will is purely passive, which is repugnant to the Nature of the Will and a free Obedience. (6.) Faith would at this rate be the entire Work of God alone, and Man would contribute nothing at all to the first Production of it, and so in some sense God might be said to

---

[53] Jam. 1. 17.

[54] Joh. 3. 36. Rom. 10. 9. Eph. 4. 22, *&c.*

believe in us. (7.) And lastly, The Reason why some do not believe, would not be a Man's own fault, but it lies upon God in not infusing into him the Habit of Faith.

But an Act at the very first.

We therefore say that *Faith* is at the very first an Act even of the Will, not indeed acting by its own natural Faculty alone, but excited and render'd capable of Believing by the Divine Grace preventing and assisting it: that by many repeated Acts a perfect Habit of Faith is wrought in us.

Objections answer'd.

Contrary to this Opinion 'tis objected, "(1.) That if Faith be an Act, then that whereby a regenerate differs from an unregenerate Man, must be attributed to our Actions; which are not permanent, but transient and inconstant. (2.) It will follow that the Regenerate when they sleep and do not actually believe, do displease God, and are not in a State of Grace, since without Faith it is impossible to please God. (3.) Nor can Men persist in Grace, so much as for one night, whilst they are out of Action." *Answ.* All these Objections may be solv'd by one single Reply, which is this: That all our Actions contribute something towards a Habit, and that every first Act is a Beginning of it; especially if that first Act be not single, but compounded of many other Acts concurring in the Production thereof. For such Acts are the Beginning of a Habit, and tend so far to Perfection that in a short time by some subsequent Acts the Habit becomes compleat. Of this nature is *Faith*, for the producing of which not one single, but several concurrent Acts are requisite, *viz.* a *Knowledg* of the Divine Will, a *Judgment* pass'd after a nice Inquisition into the Reasons and Grounds of our Faith, and an Inclination of the Will in *assenting* to those Reasons. Such an Act cannot be perform'd without the manifest Beginning of a Habit; and so the very first Act of Faith, if it does not leave a perfect, yet at least leaves a Habit begun behind it, which is continually carried on to perfection by subsequent Acts. Hence it is plain that the Difference between a Believer and an Infidel consists not in Actions only, but in the Habit; so that Believers, tho they do not actually believe in their Sleep, yet are endued with the Habit of Faith, and remain in the Favour, as well as under the Protection of God.

Its Instrument the Word of God.
The *Instrument* or Means God makes use of whereby to
product *Faith* in us, is his *Word*, whether spoken by him, or
committed to writing, and read or explain'd by Men; which is
always attended with the spiritual Influence of the Holy Ghost.
Now this *Word* not only requires *Faith*, but likewise contains
in it many Reasons and Tokens, by which a Man may be
certain of the Divinity thereof. These Arguments are not only
the Sanctity of the Doctrine, and Excellency of the Promises,
but likewise Miracles of all kinds, for the Confirmation of that
Doctrine, and several other things which tend to establish the
Divine Authority of the Scriptures.

What Arguments requisite for the producing of it.
Now whoever rightly considers the Nature of *Faith*, that it is a
voluntary Act of Obedience, will be far from expecting on
God's part such Arguments for the producing of Faith, as are
mathematically demonstrable and self-evident; but only such as
are convincing to sincere and teachable Minds, and against
which nothing can be urg'd. For *Faith* ought to be fix'd on a
solid Foundation, else it would be no wonder if all Men were
Infidels; nor can our Salvation depend on a sandy Bottom.
True it is, there are several things in Christianity which seem at
first blush to be absurd to a carnal Reasoner; as that *Jesus* of
Nazareth crucified by the *Jews* is the *Christ*, in whom we ought
to believe; that the Cross and Afflictions are the direct Road to
Eternal Happiness, *&c*. But by the Resurrection of our Saviour
from the Dead, and his Ascension into Heaven, all this is so
abundantly evinc'd, that there is no room left for doubting of
it. However the Nature of *Faith* does not require such evident
Arguments as should remove all manner of pretence for
prevaricating: for then it would not be an Act of free
Obedience, nor consequently deserve Praise or a Reward. By
this then it is plain, that God by the means of his Word does
not so work *Faith* in us, but that a teachable Disposition is
requir'd on Man's part, that the Operation of the Word may be
effectual. This is all along recommended by our Saviour in St.
John's Gospel[55], and it requires that the Mind should be free
from *Passion*, *Prejudice* and *Malice*, the three main Obstacles
of a Christian Faith. *Passion* disturbs, and draws a Veil over
the Mind, that it cannot discern the Truth: *Prejudice* has such a

[55]   *Ch*. 3. 20, 21. *& Ch*. 7. 17. *& Ch*. 8. 47. *& Ch*. 10. 26, 27.

Prepossession in our Minds, and so strong a Biass on our Judgments, that so long as we are sway'd by it, we cannot but think, and judg just as it directs and inclines us: But *Malice* is the greatest Hindrance of all. For the Doctrine of *Jesus Christ*, to which we are by Faith to assent, is diametrically opposite to the Lusts of the Flesh, prescribing the Denial and Mortification of them, and requiring that our Righteousness should exceed that of the *Scribes* and *Pharisees*; with the Promises of Eternal Life, and future Enjoyments annexed unto it. These Precepts are ungrateful, these Promises unknown to Flesh and Blood, which cannot tell how to hope for any such things; its Desire is only bent upon present Enjoyments, which it sees, and feels, and tastes, and is sensible of: no wonder then if the *Carnal Mind*, besotted with sensual Pleasures, has no relish for the Christian Religion, no Knowledg of Spiritual things, and no Inclination to believe in a future State, or in *Jesus* the Author and Finisher of our Faith.

In what sense Justification is attributed to Faith.

Hitherto we have consider'd the *Causes* of *Faith*, a word or two now of its *Effects*. We have already demonstrated that good Works are the genuine Effects of *Faith*: But besides them, *Justification* is likewise attributed to it in Scripture, especially in the Epistles to the *Romans* and *Galatians*; tho this be not the Effect of Faith after the same manner that good Works are. For Faith does not produce in us *Justification*, as the *Efficient Cause* of it, that being the internal and judicial Act of God; nor is it the *Meritorious Cause* of *Justification*, since Faith excludes all Merit. How Faith produces *Justification*, is therefore a controverted Point. Some there are who teach us that Faith in the Business of *Justification* is taken by way of *Metonymy* for its Object, *viz.* the Righteousness of Christ; so that by being justified by Faith, we are to understand being justified by Christ's Righteousness, as it is comprehended and apply'd to the Believer by Faith. But they would not have this Faith to be an Act of our Obedience, but only a means of apprehending the Righteousness of Christ, oppos'd to Faith as it is an Act. This Opinion labours under a great many Difficulties, and does not seem to be consistent with it self. (1.) Because 'tis unusual for Faith to be taken in Scripture by way of *Metonymy* for its Object; nor can any one Instance be produc'd of such a Signification, tho some are urg'd by Men of that side, which are misunderstood, and as wrongly applied by them. (2.) 'Tis unconceivable, how Faith can be the Means of apprehending Christ's Righteousness, and not be our Act. (3.) Nor is the Righteousness of Christ properly imputed to us, but for the sake of it is God pleas'd to justify us. Faith therefore in those Epistles can admit of no other sense, than that it is a Condition prescrib'd us by God in order to attain *Justification*, not by any Virtue or Merit of its own, but by the gracious Promise of God, by which he is willing to impute Faith to us as Righteousness for the sake of Christ. Nay, Faith is so far from not being an Act of Obedience in the Business of Justification, that it implies the Works it produces, and the whole Evangelical Obedience. But these short hints may suffice for the present, designing hereafter when we come to treat particularly of *Justification*, to handle this Point more at large.

Sect. V. Of the several Branches into which Faith is divided.

The vulgar Distinction of Faith how far allowable.
Faith is commonly distinguished into an *Historical*, a *Temporary*, a *Justifying*, and a *Faith of Miracles*. This Distinction might be admitted, if the several Parts of it are said to differ not in kind but degree. For an *Historical*, and a *Temporary Faith*, as they term it, differs only in degree from that which is *Justifying*. As to the *Temporary Faith*, 'tis not a Scriptural Expression, that taking notice only of the Faith of some temporizing Men, who fell away when Persecution arose for the Gospel's sake[56]. But that even this Faith differ'd only in degree from a *Justifying* one, and was a true Faith, appears from hence: (1.) Because they are threatned with a sorer Condemnation if they fall from the Faith[57]; now what occasion would there have been for a more grievous Punishment, for forsaking a Faith that was not true, saving, and which would necessarily cease? (2.) Nor is Perseverance essential to, but the Consequence of Faith; else no Man can be said to be a Believer before his Death.

Faith of Miracles what.
As to the *Faith of Miracles*, this I confess is a distinct kind of Faith, and such as does not affect all Men at all Times: for 'tis

[56] Mat. 13. 21.

[57] Heb. 6. 4, 5, 6.

a peculiar Gift of working Miracles, which is not communicated to all. However this is not without an *Historical Faith*,
but is a more eminent degree of it. Now this Faith is twofold;
the former *Active*, whereby a Man stedfastly relies upon God,
that some Miracle will be wrought at his Desire and Intreaty, of
which our Saviour and St. *Paul* makes mention[58]: the latter
Passive, by which he believes that a Miracle will be wrought in
him by the means of another Person, whom he fully believes to
be sent by God. This was the Condition which our Saviour
frequently requir'd of those on whom, and for whose sake he
wrought his Miracles; as appears by those Expressions
recorded in the Gospel, where he says, *Dost thou believe that I
am able to do this? According to thy Faith be it unto thee*, &c.

1. Faith either Lively or Dead.

But not to insist on this *Faith of Miracles*, which was a Gift of
God peculiar to those Times wherein they were wrought, we
distinguish *Faith*, according to the Acceptation of it in
Scripture, into a *Lively* and a *Dead Faith*. A *Lively Faith* is that
which produces good Works, and thereby attains Justification;
whilst a *Dead Faith* is destitute of Works, and consequently is
ineffectual for the obtaining of Justification. Now these differ
only in degree, and the Effects of both; all Faith consider'd in it
self being dead, till Works quicken it, tho before them it is a
true and sound Faith. For (1.) the Apostle tells us[59], *Thou
believest that there is one God, thou dost well*; tho that Faith
was without Works. (2.) The same Apostle does in part
attribute Justification to such a Faith; *Ye then see* (says he) *how
that by Works a Man is justified, and not by Faith only*[60].
(3.) *Abraham*'s Faith was genuine, tho it preceded his Works;
and yet it could not justify him without Works[61].

An Objection answer'd.

We shall now reply to an Objection that may be made to what
we have advanced. A *Dead Faith* (say they) is no true Faith; as
a Dead Man is not truly a Man. *Answ.* (1.) Faith is not stiled
Dead upon the account of its Nature, but Effects. (2.) A *Dead*

---

[58] Mat. 21. 21. 1 Cor. 13. 2.

[59] Jam. 2. 19.

[60] *Ibid. v.* 24.

[61] *Ibid. v.* 21.

Faith is not compared to a dead Man, but to a Body without a Soul; which is a real Body, tho it exerts no vital Action: and so is Faith without Works a true Faith, tho it be fruitless and unavailable to Eternal Life. (3.) A Body, if animated with a Spirit, would be a living Body; so Faith by the addition of good Works becomes lively, and is conducive to Salvation.

2. Either Weak or Strong.

Faith is likewise divided, according to the degrees of it, into a *Strong* and a *Weak* Faith: which takes place in all the four Acts of it, *viz. Knowledg, Assent, Assurance,* and *Obedience.* (1.) With respect to *Knowledg,* that is a *Weak* Faith, which knows only the Rudiments and first Principles of Christianity; or which has not as yet attained a thorow Apprehension of some one Doctrine of great moment in Religion. On the contrary, they have a *Strong* Faith, who have made a considerable Proficiency in the Knowledg of the Gospel; who to their Knowledg of things necessary have added that of things useful, and being fully persuaded of the Certainty of them, can give an account of the Hope that is in them, and convince the Gainsayers. (2.) With respect to *Assent,* that is a *Weak* Faith, which is either backward, or rash and injudicious, in assenting to those things which God has reveal'd to us in the Gospel, whether Promises or Threatnings, or any thing else which is remote from our Senses. On the contrary, that is a *Strong* Faith, which assents not only readily, but also with Judgment to all the Mysteries of the Christian Religion, tho above our Comprehension; which could not have been discover'd by Natural Reason, but are knowable by Divine Revelation only. (3.) With respect to *Assurance,* his is a *Weak* Faith, who is with some difficulty brought to rely upon God and Christ in Adversity, and whose Mind being fearful does not fully acquiesce in God and his Providence; such a *Weak* Faith as this were the Disciples[62], *Peter*[63], and the Father of him that was possess'd[64], endued with. Whilst on the other hand their Faith is *Strong,* who depend stedfastly upon God, expecting a Completion of the Divine Promises, overlook all Obstacles and Difficulties, and cast not away their Confidence, tho they can

---

[62]   Mat. 8. 24, *&c.*

[63]   *Ch.* 14. 28, &c.

[64]   Mar. 9. 22, *&c.*

see no natural Means for the obtaining of the thing hoped for. (4.) With respect to *Obedience*, that is a *Weak* Faith, which does not produce the requisite Fruits of good Works, but is deficient in many things: On the contrary, that is a *Strong* Faith which makes us pay a willing and extraordinary Obedience to God, even in things that are not only uneasy to Flesh and Blood, but also seem to thwart our Expectation of the Promises of God.

A Caution.
However this is to be observed: As those Acts of Faith are subordinate to one another, the former being the Foundation of the rest that follow; so the Weakness or Imperfection of the antecedent Act renders the subsequent Act weak also; but not *vice versâ*. That is, he who is *weak* in *Knowledge*, will be so likewise in *Assent*, *Assurance*, and *Obedience*; but it does not follow that he who is *weak* in the last, is so in the first of these Acts. But this is to be understood only of that point of Doctrine, in the Knowledg of which a Man is weak. For in other Cases, one who is ignorant of many things, may and often does assent to the Fundamentals of Religion, which he understands, and thereby is excited to a sincere Obedience. Hence it is that we see so many ignorant Souls excel in Piety, because they firmly believe the Divine Precepts and Promises, without nicely enquiring or apprehending the particular Doctrines of the Christian Religion.

3. Either of Beginners, Proficients, or Men perfect in Religion.
Lastly, *Faith* with respect to Obedience may be said to be *Initial*, *Progressive*, or *Consummative* and *Perfect*. (1.) *Initial Faith* is that of *Beginners*, who do indeed assent to the Gospel, and heartily resolve to bid adieu to their Lusts, and endeavour after Holiness; but yet by the inveterate Habit of Sin so deeply rooted in them, they are put to some trouble and reluctancy in conquering the Motions of it, the Flesh ever now and then rising up and fighting against the Spirit. And hence it sometimes happens that they relapse into Sin, but immediately recover themselves by Repentance, and renew their former Practice of Piety. (2.) We call a *Progressive Faith* that of those, who have made some Progress in Religion, who by the Benefit of Faith being for some time accustomed to a stricter Course of Life, abstain from Sin with more ease and less reluctancy of the Flesh: However they still perceive some small strugglings of the

Flesh against the Spirit, for the subduing of which they are chearfully to set themselves. (3.) A *Consummative* or *Perfect Faith* they are endued with, who being corroborated by a long Perseverance in Piety, and by the Assistance of Faith, not only meet with less Difficulties in the Practice of Religion, but also feel a certain sort of Pleasure and Delight in Vertue and in abstaining from Sin; nay, perceive as much reluctancy against Sin, as the Beginners met with in their first Practice of Piety. These are called *Perfect*, not because they have attain'd a compleat Perfection, and are free from all the Defilements of Sin (since 'tis possible they may sometimes fall through Mistake, Infirmity, Inadvertency, or a sudden Passion, especially upon a strong Temptation offer'd) but because they have quite abandon'd all vicious Habits, and are no longer under the Power and Dominion of any one Sin.

All these in a State of Salvation.

These are all of them Believers and in a State of Salvation, since they are all fully inclin'd to do whatever they do, or can know to be commanded by God: which Resolution they all put into practice alike, tho in different degrees according to the proportion of their Strength. So that shou'd one newly converted to the Faith, die before he has made any further Progress in it, he would be no less a Partaker of Eternal Happiness, than he who has attained to the second or third degree of Faith. However, should his Life be spared, he must press on to the other degrees of Perfection, else he is not to be accounted a Believer that heartily discharges his Duty, and truly endeavours to grow in Grace, and in the Knowledg, and Fear, and Love of God.

Sect. VI. Of the Opposites to Faith.

Opposites to Faith in general.

The *Opposites* to *Faith* are such as affect *Faith in general*, or such as are contrary to that particular Act of it call'd *Assurance*. Again, the *Opposites* to *Faith in general* are some in the *Defect*, others in the *Excess*. Those in the *Defect* are either imperfectly, or else perfectly opposite thereto.

1. In Defect, either Doubtfulness;

The *imperfect Opposite* to *Faith* is *Doubting*, which is a suspending of the Assent to, or a Hesitation about Divine things. Now this is not a mere Defect of the Understanding, which arises from an equal weight of the Arguments brought on both sides, and is faultless so long as the Ballance is kept in an even Poise, and no greater weight be added to sway it on either side: But it is chiefly a fault of the Will, when a Man will not give his Assent to a thing, unless convinc'd by demonstrative Arguments; tho there are other evidences enough to render the matter credible to a sincere and teachable Mind. *Faith* does not pretend to *Demonstration*, that belonging to *Science* only, but to Credibility: So that if a Man after all the Arguments us'd proper to persuade him that such or such a thing is credible, will not believe it, but withholds his Assent, he is guilty of that Doubtfulness or rather *Scepticism*, which is opposite to Faith, and will, if continued in, lead him directly to Infidelity. Let a Man then forbear indulging himself in such a captious Humour, for fear of the fatal Consequences thereof.

Or Incredulity, which is Infidelity, or Apostacy.

The *perfect Opposite* to *Faith* is *Incredulity, when a Man will not assent to a Divine Truth, tho he has an opportunity of assenting thereto:* I say, *tho he has an opportunity of assenting thereto,* in exception of those to whom Christ was never reveal'd, and consequently had no opportunity of believing in him. I say, *That he will not assent to the Truth,* to intimate that *Incredulity* is chiefly an Act of the Will, in not assenting to a Truth when rendred credible to him by proper Arguments. Now this *Incredulity* is twofold: (1.) That which precedes, or rather excludes Faith, when they to whom the Gospel is preached, and who have an opportunity offered them of believing, yet reject it. (2.) That which follows Faith, when they who have for some time assented to the Gospel, will not afterwards assent to it. This is worse than the former, and their State is expressly said to be more miserable than the Infidels[65], and is usually call'd *Defection* or *Apostacy*. This *Defection*, if it consists in denying only some part of the Christian Religion, or some one Doctrine necessary to be believed in order to Salvation, tho it does not destroy and subvert all Religion, yet it is destructive of Salvation, and is commonly call'd HERESY, of which more hereafter: But if it consists in the Denial of the whole, or the principal part of the Christian Truth, upon which the whole Force of our Religion depends, then 'tis emphatically stiled Ἀποστασία, APOSTACY.

[65] 2 Pet. 2. 20, 21.

To this may be refer'd a Relapse into a wicked course of Life.
But whereas we have already shewn that the subsequent and
inseparable Act of *Faith* is *Obedience*; it follows, that the
abandoning a Pious and Christian course of Life, and relapsing
into the Defilements of our former Conversation, is a falling
from the Faith. A Believer then, and one that is regenerate, may
depart from the Faith several ways. (1.) By being seduced into a
false Opinion, and hearkning to the Doctrine of false Teachers
and Deceivers. (2.) By the Allurements of this World and the
Deceitfulness of Sin, which has likewise its Degrees, as first a
Coldness or want of Charity, or an Omission of Works of
Piety; and then a Commission of the contrary Acts, either what
is not a Sin in it self, but on the Confines of, and an Inducement
thereto; or of Sins actually such, beginning with smaller ones,
and going on to the more gross. (3.) By some great and sudden
Temptation, often repeated, which by its Violence bends and
forces the Mind to that which is proposed to it, and by frequent
Assaults conquers the Will, and makes it commit the Act.
(4.) By Persecution for the Gospel's sake, especially if it be
more grievous and painful than ordinary: The fear of this may
shock the Man, put him upon renouncing his Faith, and upon
embracing his old course of Life again.

But as the Habit of Faith is not acquired, so neither is it lost
in a moment, but by degrees 'tis weakned, till at last it expires.
For (1.) the Habit of Faith is not immediately extinguished, but
only broken by vicious Practices. (2.) An Assent to a Truth may
for some time be lost, tho the Man degenerates into a contrary
Habit of sinning. (3.) When this Assent is gone, some
Knowledg may still remain in the Understanding, by which as a
Spur a Man may sometimes be excited to re-assume new
Strength, and to implore the Divine Assistance. (4.) If he does
not this, and Impiety is got to its greatest height, then all
Remedies become ineffectual, and the Man is at last deserted
by God; who in just Judgment gives him over to strong
Delusions, that he should believe a Lye, and be deliver'd up to
the Power of Satan, to be led captive by him at his Will.

Damnation the Effect of Incredulity.
The *Effect* of *Incredulity* is Eternal Damnation, and an
Exclusion, from all hopes of Eternal Life; as is plain from
sundry Passages of the New Testament[66]. But the Effect of

---

[66]   Joh. 3. 36. Mar. 16. 16. Joh. 3. 18, 19. & 8. 24.

Apostacy is still a sorer Punishment[67]; the case of such as fall into it being represented as desperate, *it being impossible to renew such again by Repentance*[68]: and they are compar'd to a Man out of whom a wicked Spirit was cast, and into whom he entred again with a train of seven worse Spirits than himself[69].

2. In Excess, too great Credulity.
The *Opposite* to *Faith* in the *Excess* is *too great a Credulity*, whereby a Man without passing a previous Judgment, and examining the Reasons offer'd, is forward to assent to any Doctrine, and by this means embraces human Inventions and Errors instead of the Divine Truth. This usually proceeds from want of Experience and Wisdom; for Men who are ignorant of things, are easily imposed upon by the bare appearance of Credulity: which is the case of the meaner sort, who depend and rely wholly upon the Sayings and Opinions of their Teachers. Hence it is that they are sometimes *Inconstant*, carried about by every wind of Doctrine, by the cunning craftiness of Men, who lie in wait to deceive; and sometimes *Obstinate*, in adhering strictly to an Opinion, the Truth of which they think they have sufficiently learned, tho they were blindly led into and wedded to it by the Authority of him that taught them.

Opposites to Assurance in particular: 1. In the Defect.
The *Opposites* to *Faith*, as taken for *Assurance*, are likewise Faults, either in the *Defect* or the *Excess* thereof. To Assurance as opposed in the *Defect*, either (1.) A small Assurance, when a Man does not put that Confidence in God, and in Jesus Christ, which he ought to do, considering the Circumstances he is in, and the Arguments used to excite him to a stronger Assurance. Or (2.) *Diffidence*, which is a total renouncing of Assurance; when a Man puts not his Trust in God, tho he has sufficient grounds for so doing. This Distrust is an Affront offered to the Power, Goodness, Wisdom and Veracity of God, since it puts no Confidence on the express Promises of God, as if he were not able, or willing, or faithful, or wise enough to perform what he had promised.

[67] 2 Pet. 2. 20, 21. Heb. 10. 26, 27, 28, 29.

[68] Heb. 6. 4, 5, 6.

[69] Mat. 12. 44, 45, 46.

A small or weak Assurance, from whence it proceeds.
But it is possible, (1.) That in the Business of Salvation, a weak
or small Assurance may sometimes proceed from a pious
Cause, *viz.* from a Mind desirous of Salvation, but finding in it
self still some Defects remaining, or at least not very well
satisfied of its own Constancy. Hence arise those Scruples
which some Men make, whether they have a true Faith in God,
whether they obey him as they ought, whether they are in a
State of Salvation, or not, *&c.* Now all these Jealousies might
be removed, would they but examine the Frame and Temper of
their own Minds, and duly consider the Nature of the new
Covenant made between God and us; wherein he is no hard
Master, requires no more than he has given, and is ready to
give larger Measures of his Grace to those who sincerely make
use of what they have, and desire it of him in Prayer. (2.) It is
possible that this Uncertainty or weak Assurance may in some
Men proceed from a mere Error of the Understanding, in that
they have not a right Apprehension of the Nature of Faith, and
know not how to distinguish it from its Effects. For since
Remission of Sins, and Peace of Conscience is promised to
Believers, those Men conclude themselves destitute of Faith,
and dare not apply the Hopes of Salvation to themselves,
because sometimes they are troubled in Mind, or at least are
not sensible of that Joy, which is (as they think) peculiar to the
Faithful. Now this Error or Uncertainty might be removed by
duly distinguishing between Faith, and its Consequences or
Effects. For First, "Faith is a strong Assent of the Mind,
whereby we believe that *Jesus* of *Nazareth* is *the Christ*, sent
into the World by the Father, as the true and only Saviour:
That in him alone God has reconciled the World to himself, by
not imputing their Sins to them: And that this *Jesus* has
received from the Father a Power of remitting Sins how great
soever, and of bestowing the Spirit of Adoption upon all those
who believe in him and sincerely obey his Commands; which
Power he is ready, nay has solemnly promised to make use of,
for the Salvation of his faithful Members." Secondly, as for
Remission of Sins, it is the Consequence of Faith, being
obtain'd by it. But then the being sensible of this Remission,
with the Joy of the Holy Ghost that attends it, ought to be
distinguished from Remission it self: For such a Sense, if not in
time, yet in order of Nature, follows not only Faith, but also
Remission, since it is a special Application of the Promise made

in general to Believers. But thirdly, tho commonly the Faithful, to whom God has granted the Remission of Sins, are sensible thereof, by making a closer Application of the Divine Promises to themselves, and are inwardly moved with a spiritual Joy at the certainty of being in such a State, wherein if they persevere they shall undoubtedly attain everlasting Salvation: Yet it may sometimes happen, that for a while they cannot perceive in their Breasts that inward Consolation and Satisfaction; whether it may arise from any false arguing of the Mind, or from the wise Disposal of God, in order to try their Faith and Constancy, and render it the more exemplary to others; or that by this means he might make known to them the greatness of this Spiritual Enjoyment; which is never better apprehended than by having the Sense of it withheld for a time, that they might be more fervent in their Prayers for it, and filled with a greater Joy, when that Blessing is granted to them. That God has a right of thus dealing with us, no Man can question, since he hereby withholds nothing that is expressly necessary to Salvation. For this spiritual Joy is not prescribed to a Believer, as an indispensible Duty, but only Faith and Obedience: This Joy being a gratuitous Gift of God, whereby he rewards the Piety of Believers, and excites them to a further degree of loving it, by the Sense and Apprehension of a future Reward.

2. In Excess.

The *Opposite* to *Assurance*, which is criminal in the *Excess*, is *Over-Confidence* or *Presumption*; when a Man conceives an Assurance of obtaining Eternal Salvation, and supposes himself to be in the Favour of God, tho by reason of his Sins he ought to be afraid of an angry God, and to dread his Punishments; at least cannot apprehend such an Assurance, as he rashly arrogates to himself. Of this nature are those Men, who having led a profane and wicked Life without any Repentance, do yet in Sickness, or at the point of Death, with the highest Assurance apply to themselves all the Promises made to the Faithful alone. We do not indeed deny but that even those Men, if they sincerely turn to God (and how hard a matter that is, every one cannot but be sensible) have some Refuge still left in the extraordinary Grace of God, whereby they may be encouraged and kept from falling into Despair. However we now here read of any Promises of Eternal Life made to such Men, by which they may with the same πληγοφογία, or *full*

Assurance of Mind, apply Salvation to themselves, as the Faithful and truly Regenrate can. These Promises are only made to the truly penitent, who testify the sincerity of their Repentance, not only by Sorrow for, or Detestation of Sin, or by a Barren Resolution of Amendment of Life, but by a real and thorow Change of their whole Lives[70]. The Assurance therefore which those Men conceive, tho it may keep them from Despair, yet at most is inferiour to that of true Believers, which is founded on the clear Promises of God. Hence it is that applying the Divine Promises to themselves, they conceive a rash Assurance, whereby being deceived and render'd secure, they do not express such a humiliation of Mind and detestation of Sin as they ought; and consequently are not absolved of the Guilt, but whilst they promise Peace to themselves, they too often meet with unavoidable Destruction. To these Men the Words of the Apostle[71] are very applicable; *For when they shall say, Peace and Safety, then sudden Destruction cometh upon them as Travail upon a Woman with Child, and they shall not escape.* And thus God has declared by the Prophet, that *there is no Peace to the wicked*[72]; that is, to those who continue in an impenitent course, and when they come to die flatter themselves with a vain Assurance of Peace, when no Peace belongs unto them.

---

[70]   Mat. 3. 8. & 7. 21. Rom. 12. 2. Eph. 4. 22, 23, 24.

[71]   1 Thess. 5. 3.

[72]   Is. 48. 22.

MR. CHILLINGWORTH'S JUDGMENT OF THE RELIGION OF PROTESTANTS, &c.

[Edited by Stephen Nye?]

The Preface

I Presume, there's no Protestant acquainted in any measure with Books that defend his Religion against the Papists, who has not a high Esteem of Mr. *Chillingworth*'s Book, entitled, *The Religion of Protestants a safe Way to Salvation*: a Man singled out from among all the learned Men of those times, as best qualified for that undertaking against a most learned Jesuit. His Book in order to Printing, was not only approved by those of greatest Learning and Authority in the Church, but was commended to the Press by the suffrages of the then Vice-Chancellor, and both the *King*'s and *Margaret* Professor of Divinity in the University of *Oxon*: and since its Publication has had the highest Commendations of most, if not all learned Protestants, as the most learned and judicious Work of any that had been published before upon that subject. It was first printed in the year 1637, and dedicated to King *Charles* the First; and then reprinted 1663, and for more common Use made shorter, by leaving out personal Matters; was printed again Anno 1685, as a most rational Defence against Popery, then breaking in upon us like a Land-Flood.

Out of this excellent Book, I have collected these excellent Passages which give a brief Account of the Religion of Protestants, what it is; what Errors are dangerous, what not; that differing Protestants agree in all things necessary to Salvation: that it's Unchristian to use Force in Matters merely Religious: what is the Fountain of all the Schisms of the Church, and the Calamities that have infested Christendom about Opinions in Religion: and that universal Liberty well moderated is the way to reduce Christians to Truth and Unity.

OF THE RELIGION OF PROTESTANTS.

Chap. 6. Num. 56. Know then, Sir, that when I say the Religion of Protestants is in Prudence to be preferred before yours: As on the one side I do not understand by your Religion the Doctrine of *Bellarmine* or *Baronius*, or any other private Man amongst you; nor the Doctrine of the *Sorbon*, or of the Jesuits, or of the Dominicans, or of any other particular Company amongst you, but that wherein you all agree, or profess to agree, *The Doctrine of the Council of* Trent. So accordingly on the other side, by *the Religion of Protestants*, I do not understand the Doctrine of *Luther* or *Calvin*, or *Melancthon*, nor the Confession of *Augusta* or *Geneva*, nor the Catechism of *Heidelberg*, nor the Articles of the Church of *England*, no, nor the Harmony of Protestant Confessions; but that wherein they all agree, and which they all subscribe with a greater Harmony, as a perfect Rule of their Faith and Actions; that is, the BIBLE, the BIBLE, I say the BIBLE only is the Religion of Protestants! Whatsoever else they believe besides it, and the plain irrefragable, indubitable Consequences of it, well may they hold it as a Matter of Opinion, but not as a Matter of Faith and Religion; neither can they with Coherence to their own Grounds believe it themselves, nor require the Belief of it of others, without most high and most schismatical Presumption. I, for my part, after a long (and as I verily believe and hope) impartial Search of *the true way to Eternal Happiness*, do profess plainly, that I cannot find any Rest for the Sole of my Foot, but upon this Rock only. I see plainly and with mine own Eyes, that there are Popes against Popes, Councils against Councils, some Fathers against others, the same Fathers against themselves, a Consent of Fathers of one Age, against a Consent of Fathers of another Age; the Church of one Age against the Church of another Age; traditive Interpretations of Scripture are pretended, but there are few or none to be found: No Tradition but only of Scripture can derive it self from the Fountain, but may be plainly proved, either to have been brought in, in such an Age after Christ, or that in such an Age it was not in. In a word, there is no sufficient Certainty but to the Scripture only, for any considering Man to build upon. This therefore, and this only, I have Reason to believe; this I will profess, according to this I will live, and for this, if there be Occasion, I will not only willingly, but even gladly lose my

Life, though I should be sorry that Christians should take it from me. Propose me any thing out of this Book, and require whether I believe it or no; and seem it never so incomprehensible to humane Reason, I will subscribe it with Hand and Heart, as knowing no Demonstration can be stronger than this, *God hath said so, therefore it is true.* In other things I will take no Man's Liberty of Judgment from him, neither shall any Man take mine from me; I will think no Man the worse Man or the worse Christian; I will love no Man the less for differing in Opinion from me; and what measure I meet to others, I expect from them again: I am fully assured that God does not, and therefore that Men ought not to require any more of any Man than this, to believe the Scripture to be God's Word, to endeavour to find the true Sense of it, and to live according to it.

N. 57. This is the Religion which I have chosen, after a long Deliberation, and I am verily perswaded that I have chosen wisely, much more wisely than if I had guided my self according to your Churches Authority; for the Scripture being all true, I am secured by believing nothing else, that I shall believe no Falshood as Matter of Faith: And if I mistake the Sense of Scripture, and so fall into Error, yet I am secure from any Danger thereby, if but your Grounds be true; because endeavouring to find the true Sense of Scripture, I cannot but hold my Error without Pertinacy, and be ready to forsake it, when a more true and a more probable Sense shall appear unto me. And then all necessary Truth being, as I have proved, plainly set down in Scripture, I am certain by believing Scripture to believe all necessary Truth; and he that does so, if his Life be answerable to his Faith, how is it possible he should fail of Salvation?

SCRIPTURE THE ONLY RULE WHEREBY TO JUDG OF CONTROVERSIES.

Chap. 2. N. 11. – To speak properly (as Men shou'd speak when they write of Controversies in Religion) the Scripture is not a Judg of Controversies, but a *Rule only*, and *the only Rule for Christians to judg them by*: Every Man is to judg for himself with the Judgment of Discretion, and to chuse either his Religion first, and then his Church, as we say; or as you, his Church first, and then his Religion. But by the Consent of both sides, every Man is to judg and chuse; and the Rule whereby he is to direct his Choice, if he be a natural Man, is Reason; if he be already a Christian, Scripture, which we say is the Rule to judg all Controversies by, yet not all simply, but all the Controversies of Christians, of those that are already agreed upon this first Principle, that *the Scripture is the Word of God.* But that there is any Man, or any Company of Men, appointed to be Judg for all Men, that we deny; and that I believe you will never prove.

EVERY MAN TO JUDG FOR HIMSELF IN MATTERS OF RELIGION.

Chap. 2. N. 16. In civil and criminal Causes the Parties have for the most part so much Interest, and very often so little Honesty, that they will not submit to a Law though never so plain, if it be against them; or will not see it to be against them, though it be never so plainly: Whereas if Men were honest, and the Law were plain and extended to all Cases, there would be little need of Judges. Now in Matters of Religion, when the Question is, Whether every Man be a fit Judg and Chuser for himself? we suppose Men honest, and such as understand the Difference between a Moment and Eternity; and such Men, we conceive, will think it highly concerns them to be of the true Religion, but nothing at all that this or that Religion should be the true: And then we suppose that all the necessary Points of Religion are plain and easy, and consequently every Man in this Case to be a competent Judg for himself; because it concerns himself to judg right as much as Eternal Happiness is worth; and if through his own Default he judg amiss, he alone shall suffer for it.

Ch. 3. N. 81. – If they [Men] would be themselves, and be content that others should be, in the choice of their Religion, the Servants of God and not of Men; if they would allow, that the Way to Heaven is no narrower now than Christ left it, his Yoak no heavier than he made it; that the Belief of no more Difficulties is required now to Salvation, than was in the Primitive Church; that no Error is in it self destructive, and exclusive from Salvation now, which was not then; if instead of being Zealous Papists, earnest Calvinists, rigid Lutherans, they would become themselves, and be content that others should be plain and honest Christians; if all Men would believe the Scripture, and freeing themselves from Prejudice and Passion, would sincerely endeavour to find the true Sense of it, and live according to it, and require no more of others but to do so, not denying their Communion to any that do so; would so order their publick Service of God, that all which do so may without Scruple or Hypocrisy, or Protestation against any Part of it, join with them in it; who does not see that (seeing as we suppose here, and shall prove hereafter) all necessary Truths are plainly and evidently set down in Scripture; there would of necessity be among all Men, in all things necessary, Unity of Opinion? And notwithstanding any other Differences that are or could be, Unity of Communion, and Charity, and mutual Toleration; by which means all Schism and Heresy would be banished the World, and those wretched Contentions which now rend and tear in pieces not the Coat, but the Members and Bowels of Christ, which mutual Pride and Tyranny, and cursing, killing and damning, would fain make immortal, should speedily receive a most blessed Catastrophe. But of this hereafter, when we shall come to the Question of Schism, wherein I perswade my self that I shall plainly shew, that the most vehement Accusers are the greatest Offenders, and that they are indeed at this time the greatest Schismaticks, who make the Way to Heaven narrower, the Yoke of Christ heavier, the Differences of Faith greater, the Conditions of Ecclesiastical Government harder and stricter, than they were made at the Beginning by Christ and his Apostles; they who talk of Unity, and aim at Tyranny, and will have Peace with none but with their Slaves and Vassals.

Pref. N. 30. – For what one Conclusion is there in the whole Fabrick of my Discourse, that is not naturally deducible out of this one Principle, *That all things necessary to Salvation are evidently contained in the Scriptures?* Or what one Conclusion almost of Importance is there in your Book, which is not by this one clearly confutable? Grant this, and it will presently follow, in opposition to your first Conclusion, and the Argument of your first Chapter, That amongst Men of different Opinions, touching the obscure and controverted Questions of Religion, such as may with Probability be disputed on both sides (and such are the Disputes of Protestants) good Men and Lovers of Truth of all sides may be saved, because all necessary things being supposed evident concerning them, with Men so qualified, there will be no Difference; there being no more certain Sign that a Point is not evident, than that honest and understanding and indifferent Men, and such as give themselves Liberty of Judgment, after a mature Consideration of the Matter, differ about it.

OF DISAGREEING PROTESTANTS.

Ans. to Pref. N. 26. 1. The most disagreeing Protestants that are, yet thus far agree, that these Books of Scripture which were never doubted of in the Church, are the undoubted Word of God, and a perfect Rule of Faith. 2. That the Sense of them which God intended, whatsoever it is, is certainly true; so that they believe implicitly even those very Truths against which they err; and why an implicit Faith in Christ and his Word should not suffice as well as an implicit Faith in your Church, I have desired to be resolved by many of your side, but never could. 3. That they are to use their best Endeavours to believe the Scripture in the true Sense, and to live according to it. This, if they perform (as I hope many on all sides do) truly and sincerely, it is impossible but that they should believe aright in all things necessary to Salvation, that is, in all those things that pertain to the Covenant between God and Man in Christ; for so much is not only plainly, but frequently contained in Scripture; and believing aright the Covenant, if they for their Parts perform the Condition required of them, which is sincere Obedience, why should they not expect that God will perform his Promise, and give them Salvation? For, as for other things which lie without the Covenant, and are therefore less necessary, if by reason of the seeming Conflict which is oftentimes between Scripture, Reason, and Authority on the one side, and Scripture, Reason, and Authority on the other; if by reason of the Variety of Tempers, Abilities, and Educations, and unavoidable Prejudices, whereby Mens Understandings are variously formed and fashioned, they do embrace several Opinions, whereof some must be erroneous: to say that God will damn them for such Errors, who are Lovers of him, and Lovers of Truth, is to rob Man of his Comfort, and God of his Goodness; it is to make Man desperate, and God a Tyrant.

Ib. N. 27. That it is sufficient for any Man's Salvation, that he believe the Scripture, that he endeavour to believe it in the true Sense of it as far as concerns his Duty; and that he conform his Life unto it, either by Obedience or Repentance: He that does so, (and all Protestants, according to the *Dictamen* of their Religion, should do so) may be secured that he cannot err Fundamentally; so that notwithstanding their Differences, and your Presumption, *the same Heaven may receive them all.*

Ib. N. 29. Who can find fault with him [Dr. *Potter*] for saying; If through want of Means of Instruction, Incapacity, invincible or probable Ignorance, a Man die in Error, he may be saved: But if he be negligent in seeking Truth, unwilling to find it, either doth see it and will not, or might see it and will not, that his Case is dangerous, and without Repentance desperate?

Ch. 1. N. 11. Methinks, with much more Reason, and much more Charity, you must suppose that many of these Controversies which are now disputed among Christians, (all of which profess themselves Lovers of Christ, and truly desirous to know his Will and do it) are either *not decidable* by that Means which God hath provided, and so not necessary to be decided; or if they be, yet *not so plainly and evidently*, as to oblige Men to hold one way: Or lastly, if decidable, and evidently decided, yet you may hope that the erring Part, by reason of some Veil before their Eyes, *some excusable Ignorance, or unavoidable Prejudice*, does not see the Question to be decided against him, and so opposes not that which he doth know to be the Word of God, but only that which you know to be so, and which he might know, were he void of Prejudice: which is a Fault, I confess, but a Fault which is incident even to good and honest Men very often; and not of such a Gigantick Disposition as you make it, to fly directly upon God Almighty, and to give him the Lie to his Face.

OF THE NECESSITY OF A VISIBLE JUDG IN CONTROVERSIES OF RELIGION, AS WELL AS IN CIVIL MATTERS.

Ch. 2. N. 17. – In Civil Controversies we are obliged only to external Passive Obedience, and not to an internal and active. We are bound to obey the Sentence of the Judg, or not to resist it, but not always to believe it just. But in Matters of Religion, such a Judg is required whom we should be obliged to believe to have judged right: so that in Civil Controversies every honest and understanding Man is fit to be a Judg, but in religion none but he that is infallible.

5. In Civil Causes there is Means and Power, when the Judg has decreed to compel Men to obey his Sentence: otherwise I believe Laws alone would be to as much Purpose for the ending of Differences, as Laws and Judges both. But all the Power in the World is neither fit to convince, nor able to compel a Man's Conscience to consent to any thing: Worldly Terror may prevail so far, as to make Men profess a Religion which they

believe not, (such Men, I mean, who know not that there is a Heaven provided for Martyrs, and a Hell for those that dissemble such Truths as are necessary to be professed) but to force either any Man to believe what he believes not, or any honest Man to dissemble what he does believe, (if God commands him to profess it) or to profess what he does not believe, all the Powers in the World are too weak, with all the Powers of Hell to assist them.

7. In Civil Matters it is impossible *Titius* should hold the Land in question, and *Sempronius* too; and therefore either the Plaintiff must injure the Defendant by Disquieting his Possession, or the Defendant wrong the Plaintiff, by keeping his Right from him. But in Controversies of Religion the Case is otherwise; I may hold my Opinion, and do you no Wrong, and you yours, and do me none. Nay, we may both of us hold our Opinion, and yet do our selves no harm, provided the Difference be not touching any thing necessary to Salvation, and that we love Truth so well, as to be diligent to inform our Conscience, and constant in following it.

CONCERNING ERRORS DAMNABLE, OR NOT DAMNABLE.

Ch. 3. N. 52. I answer, that these Differences between Protestants concerning Errors damnable, and not damnable, Truths fundamental, and not fundamental, may be easily reconciled; for either the Error they speak of may be *purely and simply involuntary*, or it may be, in respect of *the Cause of it, voluntary*: If the Cause of it be some voluntary and avoidable Fault, the Error is it self sinful, and consequently in its own Nature damnable; as if by Negligence in seeking the Truth, by Unwillingness to find it, by Pride, by Obstinacy, by desiring that Religion should be true which sutes best with my Ends, by Fear of Mens ill Opinion, or any other worldly Fear, or any worldly Hope, I betray my self to any Error contrary to any Divine revealed Truth, that Error may be justly stiled a Sin, and consequently of it self to such an one damnable. But if I be guilty of none of these Faults, but be desirous to know the Truth, and diligent in seeking it, and advise not at all with Flesh and Blood about the Choice of my Opinions, but only with God, and that Reason that he hath given me: If I be thus qualified, and yet through humane Infirmity fall into Error, that Error cannot be damnable. Again, the Party erring, may be conceived either to die with Contrition, for all his Sins known and unknown, or without it: If he die without it, this Error in it self, if damnable, will be likewise so unto him; if he die with Contrition, (as his Error can be no Impediment but he may) his Error, though in it self damnable to him, according to your Doctrine, will not prove so.

OF USING FORCE IN MATTERS OF RELIGION.

Ch. 5. N. 96. But they *endeavoured to force the Society, whereof they were Parts, to be healed and reformed as they were; and if it refused, they did, when they had Power, drive them away, even their Superiors, both spiritual and temporal, as is notorious.* The Proofs hereof are wanting, and therefore I might defer my Answer until they were produced, yet take this before hand: If they did so, then herein, in my Opinion, they did amiss; for I have learnt, from the antient Fathers of the Church, that *nothing is more against Religion, than to force Religion*; and of St. *Paul, The Weapons of the Christian Warfare are not carnal*: And great Reason; for humane Violence may make Men counterfeit, but cannot make them believe, and is therefore fit for nothing, but to breed Form without, and Atheism within. Besides, if this Means of bringing Men to imbrace any Religion were generally used, (as if it may be justly used in any Place, by those that have Power, and think they have Truth, certainly they cannot with Reason deny, but that it may be used in every Place by those that have Power as well as they, and think they have Truth as well as they) what could follow but the Maintenance perhaps of Truth, but perhaps only of the Profession of it in one Place, and the Oppression of it in an hundred? What will follow from it, but the Preservation perhaps of Unity, but peradventure only of Uniformity in particular States and Churches; but the immortalizing the greater and more lamentable Divisions of Christendom and the World? And therefore what can follow from it, but perhaps in the Judgment of carnal Policy, the temporal Benefit and Tranquillity of temporal States and Kingdoms, but the infinite Prejudice, if not the Dissolution of the Kingdom of Christ? And therefore it well becomes them who have their Portion in this Life, who serve no higher State than that of *England*, or *Spain*, or *France*, nor this neither, any further than they may serve themselves by it; who think of no other Happiness but the Preservation of their own Fortunes and Tranquillity in this World; who think of no other Means to preserve States but humane Power and Machiavilian Policy, and believe no other Creed but this, *Regi aut Civitati Imperium habenti nihil injustum quod utile*! Such Men as these it may become to maintain by worldly Power and Violence, their State-Instrument, Religion: For if all be vain and false (as in their Judgment it is) the present whatsoever, is better than any, because it is already settled: An Alteration of it may draw with it Change of States, and the Change of State the Subversion of their Fortune; but they that are indeed Servants and Lovers of Christ, of Truth, of the Church, and of Mankind, ought, with all Courage, to oppose themselves against it as a common Enemy of all these.

They that know there is a King of Kings, and Lord of Lords, by whose Will and Pleasure Kings and Kingdoms stand and fall; they know that to no King or State any thing can be profitable which is unjust and that nothing can be more evidently unjust, than to force weak Men by the Profession of a Religion which they believe not, to lose their own eternal Happiness, out of a vain and needless Fear, lest they may possibly disturb their temporal Quietness, there being no Danger to any State from any Man's Opinion, unless it be such an Opinion by which Disobedience to Authority or Impiety is taught or licensed; which sort I confess may justly be punish'd as well as other Faults; or unless this sanguinary Doctrine be joined with it, That it is lawful for him by humane Violence to enforce others to it.

Chap. 4. N. 16. This presumptuous imposing of the Senses of Men upon the Words of God, the special Senses of Men upon the General Words of God, and laying them upon Mens Consciences together under the equal Penalty of Death and Damnation: This vain Conceit, that we can speak of the things of God better than the Words of God; this deifying our own Interpretations, and tyrannous enforcing them upon others; this restraining of the Word of God, from that Latitude and Generality, and the Understandings of Men from that Liberty wherein Christ and the Apostles left them,[1] is, and hath been

---

1   *This Persuasion is no Singularity of mine, but the Doctrine which I have learned from Divines of great Learning and Judgment. Let the Reader be pleased to peruse the seventh Book of* Acont. de Strat. Satanæ, & Zanch. *his last Oration delivered by him after the composing of the Discord between him and* Amervachius, *and he shall confess as much.*

the only Fountain of all the Schisms of the Church, and that which makes them immortal: The common Incendiary of *Christendom*, and that which (as I said before) tears in pieces not the Coat, but the Bowels and Members of Christ; *Ridente Turca, nec dolente Judæo*: take away these Walls of Separation, and all will quickly be one. Take away this *Persecuting*, *Burning*, *Cursing*, *Damning of Men* for not subscribing to the *Words of Men*, as the Words of God; require of Christians only to believe Christ, and to call no Man Master but him only; let those leave claiming Infallibility, that have no Title to it; and let them that in their Words disclaim it, disclaim it likewise in their Actions. In a word, take away Tyranny, which is the Devil's Instrument to support Errors and Superstitions, and Impieties, in the several Parts of the World, which could not otherwise long withstand the Power of Truth.

I say, take away Tyranny, and restore Christians to their just and full Liberty of captivating their Understanding to Scripture only: and as Rivers, when they have a free Passage, run all to the Ocean; so it may well be hoped by God's Blessing, that universal Liberty thus moderated, may quickly reduce *Christendom* to Truth and Unity. These Thoughts of Peace (I am perswaded) may come from the God of Peace, and to his Blessing I recommend them.

FINIS

ROMAN-CATHOLICK PRINCIPLES, IN REFERENCE TO GOD AND THE KING

J. L. [John Gother]

Paragraph I. Of the Catholic Faith, and Church in General.

Redemption in Christ, *

I. The Fruition of God, and Remission of Sin is not attainable by Man, otherwise then ([1]) *in and by the Merits of Jesus Christ,* who (*gratis*) Purchas'd it for Us.

applicable by Faith.

II. These Merits of Christ are not apply'd to Us, otherwise than by a *Right* ([2]) *Faith* in Christ.

Which is but One,

III. This *Faith is but* ([3]) *One*, Entire and Conformable to its Object, being *Divine Revelations*; to all which ([4]) *Faith* gives an undoubted assent.

Supernatural,

IV. These *Revelations* contain many *Mysteries* ([5]) *transcending the Natural Reach of Human Wit or Industry*; Wherefore,

By the Divine Providence to be learnt,

V. It became the *Divine Wisdom* and *Goodness*, to provide Man of some ([6]) *Way or Means* whereby he might Arrive to the *Knowledge* of these *Mysteries*; Means ([7]) *Visible* and *Apparent* to all; Means ([8]) *proportionable* to the Capacities of all; Means ([9]) *Sure* and Certain to all.

[1] Eph. 2. 8. 1 Cor. 15. 22.
[2] Mark 16. 16. Heb. 11. 6.
[3] Eph. 4. 4.
[4] Ja. 2. 10.
[5] 1 Cor. 1. 20. Mat. 16. 17.
[6] Isa. 35. 8.
[7] Jo. 9. 41.
[8] Mat. 11. 25.
[9] Joh. 15. 22.
* Italicized headings were marginal comments in the original text and were meant to be read in sequence – ed.

Not from private Interpretation of Scripture.
VI. This Way or Means is not the *Reading of Scripture*, Interpreted according to the *Private* ([10]) *Reason* or ([11]) *Spirit* of every Disjunctive Person, or Nation in particular; But,

and guided by the Holy Ghost for that end.
VII. It is an *Attention* and ([12]) *Submission* to the *Doctrine* of the *Catholick or Universal Church*, established by Christ for the Instruction of all. ([13]) *Spread* for that end throughout all *Nations*, and *visibly continu'd* in the Succession of Pastors, and People throughout all *Ages*: From which Church ([14]) *Guided in Truth, and secur'd from Errour* in Matters of *Faith*, by the ([15]) *promis'd Assistance of the Holy Ghost*, every one may, and ought to ([16]) *Learn* both the Right Sense of the *Scripture*, and all other Christian *Mysteries* and *Duties*, respectively necessary to Salvation.

This Church is the same with the Roman Catholick.
VIII. This Church, thus Spread, thus Guided, thus visibly Continu'd, ([17]) in *One Uniform Faith*, and *Subordination of Government*, is that self-same which is term'd the *Roman-Catholick Church*, the *Qualifications* above-mentioned, *viz.* Unity, Indeficiency, Visibility, Succession, and Universality, being applicable to no other *Church*, or *Assembly*, whatsoever.

From the Testimony of which, we receive the Scripture to be Gods Word.
IX. From the *Testimony* and *Authority* of this *Church*, it is, that we Receive, and Believe the *Scriptures* to be God's Word: And as She can ([18]) *assuredly* tell Us, This or That Book is *God's Word*, so can she with the like *Assurance* tell us also the True *Sense* and *Meaning* of it in Controverted Points of *Faith*;

10   2 Pet. 3. 16. Pro. 14. 12. Matth. 22. 29.
11   1 Jo. 4. 1. & 6. Pro. 12. 15.
12   Matth. 18. 17. Lu. 10. 16.
13   Ps. 2. 8. Isa. 2. 2. &c. cap. 49 6. Mat. 5. 14.
14   Is. 59. 21. Joh. 16. 13. Eze. 37. 26. Eph. 5. 25. 1 Tim. 3. 15. Mat. 16. 18.
15   Matth. 28. 23. Jo. 14. 16.
16   Deu. 17. 8. Mat. 23. 2.
17   Can. 6. 8. Jo. 10. 16. Rom. 15. 5. Jo. 17. 22. Phil. 2. 2.
18   Mat. 16. 18. 1 Tim. 3. 15. Mat. 18. 17.

the same *Spirit* that Writ the *Scripture*, ([19]) *Enlightning Her* to understand, both *It*, and all matters necessary to *Salvation* From these grounds it follows,

Divine Revelations only Matters of Faith.
X. All, and only *Divine Revelations* deliver'd by God unto the *Church*, and propos'd by her to be believ'd *as such*, are, and ought to be esteem'd *Articles of Faith*; and the contrary *Opinions*, Heresie. And,

What Heresie, and what Schism.
XI. As an *Obstinate Separation* from the *Unity* of the Church, in known declar'd *Matters of Faith*, is *Formal* ([20]) *Heresie*: So a wilful *Separation* from the *Visible Unity* of the same *Church*, in matters of *Subordination* and *Government*, is *Formal* ([21]) *Schism*.

How Matters of Faith are proposed by the Church.
XII. The Church proposes unto us matters of *Faith*: First, and chiefly, by the ([22]) *Holy Scripture*, in Points plain and intelligible in it. Secondly, By ([23]) *Definitions of General Councils*, in points not sufficiently Explain'd in *Scripture*. Thirdly, By ([24]) *Apostolical Traditions*, deriv'd from *Christ* and his *Apostles*, to all Succeeding Ages. Fourthly, By her ([25]) *Practice, Worship* and *Ceremonies*, confirming her *Doctrine*.

Sect. II. Of Spiritual and Temporal Authority.

What is the Authority of General Councils.
I. *General Councils* (which are the Church of God Representative) [Gal. 1. 7, 8.] have no Commission from Christ to Frame *New Matters* of Faith, (these being sole *Divine Revelations*,) but only to ([26]) *Explain* and *Ascertain* unto Us, what anciently was, and is Receiv'd and Retain'd, as of *Faith* in the Church, upon arising *Debates* and *Controversies* about them. The

---

[19] Isai. 59. 21. Jo. 14. 26.

[20] 1 Cor. 11. 19. Mat. 18. 17.

[21] Tit. 3. 10. 1 Cor. 1. 10. cap. 12. 25.

[22] Jo. 5. 39.

[23] Acts 15 *per tot.*

[24] 2 Thes. 2. 15. cap 3. 6. 2 Tim. 2. 2.

[25] Ja. 2. 18.

[26] Deu. 17. 8. Mat. 18. 17. Act. 15. *per tot.* Luc. 10. 16. Heb. 13. 7. 17.

Definitions of which *General Councils* in *Matters of Faith* only, and propos'd *as such*, oblige, under pain of *Heresie*, all the *Faithful*, to a *Submission of Judgment*. But,

An Explanation of the same Authority.
II. It is no Article of Faith to believe, That *General Councils* cannot *Err*, either in matters of *Fact* or *Discipline*, alterable by circumstances of Time and Place, or in matters of *Speculation* or *civil Policy*, depending on meer humane Judgment or Testimony. Neither of these being Divine *Revelations* ([27]) *deposited* in the *Catholick Church*, in regard to which alone, she hath the ([28]) *promised Assistance of the Holy Ghost*. Hence it is deduc'd,

A Deduction from thence concerning Allegiance.
III. If a *General Council* (much less a *Papal Consistory*) should undertake to *depose a King*, and *absolve his Subjects* from their *Allegiance*, no *Catholick* (*as Catholick*) is bound to *submit* to such a *Decree*. Hence also it follows,

A second Deduction, concerning the same.
IV. The Subjects of the King of *England* lawfully may, without the least breach of any *Catholick Principle*, Renounce, (even upon Oath,) the Teaching or Practising the *Doctrine of deposing Kings* Excommunicated for Heresie, by any Authority whatsoever, [*Declar. fac. Sorb.*] as repugnant to the *fundamental Laws* of the Nation, *Injurious to Sovereign Power*, Destructive to the *Peace and Government*, and by consequence, in His Majesties Subjects, *Impious and Damnable*: Yet not properly *Heretical*, taking the Word *Heretical* in that connatural, genuine *sense*, as it is usually understood in the *Catholick Church*; on account of which, and other Expressions, (no-wise appertaining to Loyalty,) it is, that *Catholicks* of *tender Consciences* refuse the *Oath* commonly call'd *the Oath of Allegiance*.

The Bishop of Rome Supreme Head of the Church,
V. *Catholicks* believe, That the Bishop of *Rome* is the Successor of S. *Peter*, ([29]) Vicar of *Jesus Christ* upon Earth, and the *Head of the whole Catholick Church*; which *Church* is

27 1 Tim. 6. 20.
28 Jo. 14. 16.
29 Matth. 16. 17. Lu. 22. 31. Jo. 21. 17.

therefore fitly stil'd *Roman-Catholick*, being an *universal Body* ([30]) united under *one visible Head*. Nevertheless,

but not Infallible.

VI. It is *no matter of Faith* to believe, That the *Pope* is in himself *Infallible*, separated from a General Council, even in *Expounding the Faith*: By consequence *Papal Definitions* or *Decrees*, though *ex Cathedra*, as they term them, (taken exclusively from a *General Council*, or *Universal Acceptance of the Church*,) oblige none under *Pain of Heresie*, to an interior Assent.

Nor hath any Temporal Authority over Princes.

VII. Nor do *Catholicks* (*as Catholicks*) believe that the *Pope* hath any direct, or indirect *Authority* over the *Temporal Power* and Jurisdiction of *Princes*. Hence, if the *Pope* should pretend to *Absolve* or *Dispense* with His Majesties Subjects from their *Allegiance*, upon account of *Heresie* or *Schism*, such *Dispensation* would be *vain and null*: and all *Catholick* Subjects (notwithstanding such *Dispensation* or *Absolution*,) would be still bound in Conscience to defend their King and Country, at the hazard of their Lives and Fortunes, even *against the Pope* himself, in case he should invade the Nation [1 Pet. 2. *v.* 12 &c.].

The Church not responsible for the Errors of particular Divines.

VIII. And as for the *Problematical Disputes*, or Errors of particular *Divines*, in this or any other matter whatsoever, the *Catholick* Church is no wise *responsible* for them: Nor, are *Catholicks* (*as Catholicks*,) justly *punishable* on their account. But,

King-killing Doctrine, damnable Heresie.

IX. As for the *King-killing Doctrine*, or Murder of Princes, Excommunicated for Heresie; It is an *Article of Faith* in the *Catholick* Church, and expressly declar'd in the General Council of *Constance*, that such Doctrine is *Damnable* and *Heretical*, being contrary to the known *Laws* of God and Nature (*Conc. Const. Sess. 15.*).

Personal misdemeanours not to be imputed to the Church.

X. *Personal Misdemeanours*, of what Nature soever, ought not to be *Imputed* to the *Catholick* Church, when not Justifiable by

[30] Eph. 4. 11, &c.

the *Tenents* of her Faith and Doctrine: For which Reason, though the Stories of the *Paris Massacre*, the *Irish Cruelties*, or *Powder-Plot*, had been exactly true, (which yet for the most part are notoriously mis-related) nevertheless *Catholicks* (*as Catholicks*) ought not to suffer for such *Offences*, any more than the Eleven *Apostles* ought to have suffer'd for *Judas's Treachery*.

No Power on Earth can authorise Men to Lie, Forswear, Murther, &c.

XI. It is an *Article of the Catholick Faith* to believe, that no *Power* on Earth can *License* Men to *Lie*, to *forswear*, and *Perjure* themselves, to *Massacre* their Neighbours, or Destroy their Native Country, on pretence of *promoting the Catholick Cause or Religion*: Furthermore, all *Pardons and Dispensations* granted, or pretended to be granted, in order to any such *Ends* or Designs, have no other Validity or Effect, than to add *sacriledge* and *blasphemy* to the above mention'd Crimes.

Equivocation not allowed in the Church.

XII. The Doctrine of *Equivocation* or Mental Reservation, however wrongfully impos'd upon the *Catholick Religion*, is notwithstanding, neither taught, nor approv'd by the Church, as any part of her Belief. On the contrary, *simplicity and Godly sincerity* are constantly recommended by her as truly *Christian Virtues*, necessary to the conservation of *Justice, Faith, and Common-security* [2 Cor. 1. 12.].

Sect. III. Of some Particular controverted Points of Faith.

Of Sacramental Absolution.

I. Every *Catholick is oblig'd to believe*, that when a Sinner (31) Repents him of his Sins from the *bottom* of his *Heart*, and (32) *Acknowledges* his Transgressions to God and his (33) *Ministers, the Dispensers of the Mysteries of Christ*, resolving to turn from his evil ways, (34) and *bring forth Fruits worthy of Penance*; there is (then, and no otherwise) an *Authority* left by Christ to *Absolve* such a *Penitent Sinner* from his Sins; which

31 Ez. 18. 21. 2 Cor. 7. 10.
32 Ps. 32. 5. Pro. 28. 13.
33 Act. 19. 18. 1 Cor. 4. 1. Jam. 5. 16.
34 Lu. 3. 8.

Authority Christ gave his ([35]) *Apostles*, and their *Successors*, the *Bishops* and *Priests* of the *Catholick Church*, in those words, when he said, Receive ye the *Holy Ghost*, whose Sins you shall *forgive*, they are *forgiven* unto them, &c.

Of Satisfaction by penitential Works.
II. Though no Creature whatsoever can make ([36]) condign *satisfaction*, either for the *Guilt* of Sin, or the *pain Eternal* due to it; ([37]) This *satisfaction* being proper to Christ our Saviour only; Yet *penitent Sinners* Redeemed by Christ, may, as *Members* of Christ, in some measure ([38]) *satisfie* by Prayer, Fasting, Alms-Deeds, and other *Works* of *Piety*, for the *Temporal Pain*, which by order of Divine Justice sometimes remains due, after the *Guilt* of Sin, and *Pains Eternal* and (*gratis*) *remitted*. These *Penitential Works*, are, notwithstanding, *satisfactory* no otherwise than as *joyned* and apply'd to that *satisfaction* which *Jesus made upon the* Cross, *in virtue of which alone, all our good Works find a grateful* ([39]) *acceptance in God's sight.*

Indulgences are not Remission of Sins, but only of Canonical Penances.
III. The Guilt of Sin, or Pain Eternal due to it, is never remitted by *Indulgences*; but only such ([40]) *Temporal punishments* as remain due after the Guilt is remitted; These *Indulgences* being nothing else than a ([41]) *Mitigation* or *Relaxation* upon just causes, of *Canonical Penances*, enjoyn'd by the Pastors of the Church on Penitent Sinners, according to their several Degrees of Demerit.

Abuses herein not to be charged on the Church.
And if any abuses or mistakes be sometimes committed, in point either of granting or gaining *Indulgences*, through the Remisness or Ignorance of particular Persons, contrary to the

35   Joh. 20. 21, &c. Matth. 18. 18.
36   Tit. 3. 5.
37   2 Cor. 5. 3.
38   Acts 26. 20. Jonas 3. 5. &c. Psal. 102. 9. &c. Ps. 109. 23. Dan. 9. 3. Joel. 2. 12. Luk. 11. 41. Act. 10. 41.
39   1 Pe. 2. 5.
40   1 Cor. 5. 5. &c.
41   2 Cor. 2. 6.

ancient Custom and Disciple of the Church; such abuses or mistakes cannot rationally be charged on the Church, not rendred matter of derision, in prejudice to her Faith and doctrine.

There is a Purgatory or State where Souls departing this Life with some blemish, are purify'd.

IV. *Catholicks* hold there is a *Purgatory*, that is to say, a place or State, where Souls departing this Life, with Remission of their Sins, as to the Eternal Guilt or Pain, or yet ([42]) *Obnoxious* to some temporal *Punishment* still remaining due, or not perfectly freed from the Blemish of some ([43]) *Defects* or *Deordinations*, (as idle Words, &c. not liable to *Damnation*) are ([44]) *purg'd* before their admitance into Heaven, where nothing that is ([45]) *defil'd* can *enter*. Furthermore,

Prayers for the Dead available to them. Superfluous Questions about Purgatory.

V. *Catholicks* also hold, That such Souls so detained in *Purgatory*, being the *Living Members* of Christ Jesus, are *Reliev'd* by the ([46]) *Prayers* and *suffrages* of their *Fellow-members* here on Earth: But where this place is? Of what Nature or Quality the Pains are? How long each Soul is detained there? After what manner the *suffrages* made in their behalf, are apply'd? Whether by way of *satisfaction* or *Intercession, &c.* are Questions superfluous, and impertinent as to *Faith*.

Of the Merit of good Works through the merits of Christ.

VI. No Man, though *just*, ([47]) can Merit either an Increase of Sanctity or Happiness in this Life, or Eternal Glory in the next, independent on the Merits and Passion of Christ Jesus, ([48]) the *Good Works* of a just Man, proceeding from *Grace* and *Charity*, are *acceptable* to God, so far forth as to be, through his goodness and Sacred *Promise*, truly *meritorious* of Eternal Life.

[42] Num. 14. 20, &c. 2 Sam. 12. 13, &c.

[43] Pro. 24. 16. Ma. 12. 36. and cap. 5. 22, 26.

[44] Mat. 5. 26. 1 Cor. 3. 15.

[45] Rev. 21. 27.

[46] 1 Cor. 15. 29. Col. 1. 24. 2 Mac. 12. 42. &c. 1 Jo. 5. 16.

[47] Jo. 15. 5. 16.

[48] Mat. 16. 27. cap. 5. 12. cap. 10. 42. 2 Cor. 5. 10. 2 Tim. 4. 8.

Christ really present in the Sacrament of the Eucharist.
VII. It is an Article of the *Catholick Faith*, That in the most
Holy Sacrament of the *Eucharist*, there is truly and really
contain'd the ([49]) *Body of* Christ, *which was deliver'd for us,
and his Blood, which was shed for the Remission of Sins*; the
substance of *Bread and Wine* being by the powerful Words of
Christ *chang'd* into the *substance* of his Blessed Body and
Blood, the *Species* or Accidents of *Bread* and *Wine* still
remaining. Thus.

But after a Supernatural Manner.
VIII. Christ is not present in this Sacrament, according to his
Natural way of Existence, that is, with extention of parts, in
order to place, &c. but after a *supernatural* manner, one and
the same in many places, and whole in every part of the
Symbols. This therefore is a real, *substantial*, yet *Sacramental*
presence of Christ's Body and Blood, not expos'd to the
External Senses, or obnoxious to Corporal Contingences.

*Whole Christ in either Species. Hence Communicants under
one kind no wise depriv'd either of the Body or Blood of Christ.*
IX. Neither is the Body of Christ in this Holy Sacrament,
separated from his Blood, or his Blood from his Body, or either
of both disjoyn'd from his Soul and Divinity, but all and whole
([50]) *living* Jesus is *entirely* contain'd under *either* Species; so that
whosoever receives under *one kind*, is truly partaker of the
whole Sacrament, and no wise depriv'd *either* of the Body or
Blood of Christ. True it is,

Of the Sacrifice of the Mass.
X. Our Saviour Jesus Christ, left unto us his Body and Blood,
under two *distinct Species* or Kinds; in doing of which, he
instituted not only a *Sacrament*, but also a *Sacrifice*; ([51]) a
Commemorative Sacrifice distinctly ([52]) *shewing* his Death or
Bloody Passion, *until he come*. For as the *Sacrifice of the Cross*
was performed by a distinct *Effusion of Blood,* so is the same
Sacrifice commemorated in that of the ([53]) *Altar*, by a
distinction of the Symbols. Jesus therefore is here *given*, not

[49] Mat. 26. 26. Mar. 14. 22. Lu. 22. 19. 1 Cor. 11. 23, &c. cap. 10. 16.

[50] Jo. 6. 48. 50, 51, 57, 58. Acts 2. 42.

[51] Luk. 22. 19, &c.

[52] 1 Cor. 11. 26.

[53] Heb. 13. 10.

only *to us*, but (⁵⁴) *for us*; and the Church thereby enriched with a true, proper, and propitiatory (⁵⁵) sacrifice, usually term'd *Mass*.

Worship of Images wrongfully Imposed on Catholicks.
XI. *Catholicks* renounce all *Divine Worship*, and Adoration of *Images* or *Pictures*. (⁵⁶) *God alone we worship and adore*; Nevertheless we make use of Pictures, and place them in (⁵⁷) Churches and Oratories, to reduce our wandring thoughts, and enliven our Memories towards *Heavenly things.*

Yet there is some Veneration due both to Pictures,
And further, we allow a certain *Honour* and *Veneration* to the Picture of Christ, of the Virgin *Mary*, &c. beyond what is due to every *prophane* Figure; not that we believe any *Divinity* or Virtue in the Pictures themselves, for which they ought to be Honour'd, but because the Honour given to Pictures is referr'd to the *Prototype*, or things represented. In like manner,

And other sacred things.
XII. There is a kind of Honour and Veneration respectively due to the *Bible*, to the *Cross*, to the Name of *Jesus*, to *Churches*, to the *Sacraments*, &c. as (⁵⁸) things peculiarly appertaining to God; also to the (⁵⁹) *glorify'd* Saints in Heaven, as Domestick Friends of God; yea, (⁶⁰) to *Kings*, *Magistrates*, and *Superiours* on Earth, as the *Vicegerents* of God, to whom Honour is due, Honour may be given, without any Derogation to the Majesty of God, or that *Divine Worship* appropriate to him. Furthermore,

Prayers to Saints lawful,
XIII. *Catholicks* believe, That the Blessed Saints in Heaven replenish'd with Charity (⁶¹) *pray* for us their *fellow-members*

---

54   Lu. 22. 19.
55   Mal. 1. 11.
56   Luk. 4. 8.
57   Ex. 25. 18. 1 Kin. 6. 35. Luke 3. 22. Num. 21. 8. Acts 5. 15.
58   Jos. 7. 6. Exod. 3. 5. Psal. 99. 5. Phil. 2. 10. Luk. 3. 16. Acts 19. 12.
59   Jo. 12. 26.
60   1 Pet. 2. 17. Rom. 13. 7.
61   Rev. 5. 8.

here on Earth; that they ([62]) *Rejoyce at our conversion*; that seeing God, they ([63]) *see and know in him* all things suitable to their *happy state*; but God is inclinable to hear their *Requests* made in our behalf, ([64]) and for their sakes grants us many favours; That therefore it is good and profitable to *Desire* their *Intercession*; And that this manner of *Invocation* is no more injurious to Christ our *Mediator*, or *superabundant* in it self, than it is for one Christian to beg the *Prayers* and *assistance* of ([65]) *another* in this World.

Yet so as not to neglect our Duties.
Notwithstanding all which, *Catholicks* are not taught so to rely on the *prayers of Others*, as to neglect their own ([66]) *Duty* to *God*; in *Imploring* his *Divine mercy* and *Goodness*, ([67]) in *mortifying* the *Deeds of the flesh*; in ([68]) *Despising the World*; in *loving and* ([69]) *serving God and their Neighbour*; in *following the footsteps of Christ our Lord*, who is the ([70]) *Way*, the *Truth*, and the *Life*: to whom be Honour and Glory for ever and ever, *Amen.*

FINIS

---

[62] Lu. 15. 7.

[63] 1 Cor. 13. 12.

[64] Ex. 32. 13. 2 Chron. 6. 42.

[65] Romans 15. 30.

[66] Jam. 2. 17. 30, &c.

[67] Rom. 13. 14.

[68] Ro. 12. 2.

[69] Gal. 5. 6.

[70] Joh. 14. 6.

AN HISTORICAL VIEW OF THE STATE OF THE PROTESTANT DISSENTERS IN ENGLAND

Joshua Toulmin

THE TRINITARIAN CONTROVERSY

Soon after the Revolution, the public mind was agitated by various publications on the questions that owe their origin to the doctrine of the Trinity; a doctrine ever involved in intricacies by abstruse, metaphysical, and indefinite terms. In 1690, the learned mathematician, Dr. John Wallis, Savilian professor of geometry in Oxford, who professed to have paid a studious attention to the subject for more than forty years, offered to the public a pamphlet, entitled, "The Doctrine of the ever-blessed Trinity explained." His explanation amounted to this, that the blessed Trinity was three *somewhats*, commonly called "*persons*; but the true notion and name of that distinction," he said, "are unknown to us. The word *persons*, when applied to GOD, is but metaphorical; not signifying just the same as when applied to men." This tract engaged the author for that and the following year in a controversy with the Unitarians; nor were the Trinitarians more satisfied than they were, with an explanation which explained nothing. In 1691, there issued from the press a new edition of several tracts written by Mr. John Biddle, first published in 1648, and reprinted in 1653. Another publication of the same year was "A Brief History of the Unitarians, called also *Socinians*; in four letters to a friend." Dr. Sherlock, who had the character of being a polite, clear, and strong writer, and who, by his writings against popery in the former reign, had obtained great reputation, took up his pen, this year, on the Trinitarian question, in "A Vindication of the doctrine of the holy and ever-blessed Trinity;" in which he expressly asserted, that the three persons in the Trinity are three distinct infinite minds or spirits, and three individual substances; two of these issuing from the Father; and that these three are one by a mutual consciousness. This tract was intended as an answer to the "Brief History of the Unitarians." A defence of that history against Dr. Sherlock's answer soon appeared. Another reply to his tract was published under the title of "Some Thoughts upon Dr. Sherlock's Vindication of the doctrine of the Holy Trinity, in a letter. 4to." Observations on it were annexed to a tract in 4to. entitled "The Acts of Great Athanasius; with notes, by way of illustration on his Creed." In this tract the doctor was charged with reviving paganism by such an explication of the Trinity, as undeniably introduced tritheism, or the doctrine of three gods; an error condemned by the ancients in the person of Philoponus; in the middle ages, in the person and writings of Abbot Joachim; but more severely, since the Reformation, in the person of Valentinus Gentilis, who for this very doctrine was condemned at Geneva, and beheaded at Berne. It was generally acknowledged that Dr. Sherlock had exceeded all proper bounds; and his friends used their influence to engage him to be silent in future. He had given the Unitarians such an advantage, that politicians feared the issue of a war, the beginnings of which had been so inauspicious. For some time a stop was put to the publication of any sermons or tracts written against that sect. The language held between the champions of what is called the orthodox faith was, that being masters of all the pulpits, they could sufficiently dispose the people to receive and adhere to that belief without the aid of printed answers and replies; and that they need not trouble themselves about the Socinians.[1]

Several years before, the very learned Dr. Cudworth, in his elaborate performance, entitled, "The Intellectual System," had expressed the same apprehensions concerning the three divine persons, as Doctor Sherlock advanced: they both apprehended the three persons to be as distinct and different, and as really three several intelligent beings and substances, as three angels, or as Peter, James, and John are. Dr. Cudworth professed to follow, in accounting for the doctrine of the Trinity, the platonic philosophers; with whom he said the orthodox fathers perfectly agreed. He contended, that the unity of sameness of substance of the three divine persons consisted not in *number*, but in *kind* or *nature*: he represented the Son and Spirit,

[1]   Considerations on the Explications of the Doctrine of the Trinity, written by a person of quality; in 4to. 1693. p. 12.

however, as in every way inferior to the Father. He did not allow them to be omnipotent in any other respect than *externally*; i.e. because the Father concurreth omnipotently to all their external actions, whether of creation or providence. He desired to distinguish his explication from all others of the moderns by this mark; that it allowed not the three persons to be, in any respect but duration, *coequal*. For he said, "three distinct intelligent natures or essences, each pre-eternal, self-existent, and equally omnipotent *ad intra*, are of necessity three Gods: but if only the first person be indeed internally omnipotent, and the other two subordinate in authority and power to him, you leave them but one God, only in three divine persons."[2] Though Dr. Cudworth and Dr. Sherlock appear to have been of the same opinion concerning the three divine persons, each conceiving of them as three several intelligences; it seems that the former learned writer did not entertain the same idea concerning their unity, which the latter afterwards advanced: for he called the union of will and affection only a moral union, not a physical or real unity; as three *human* persons would be three distinct men, notwithstanding the moral union in affection and will, so also three divine persons would be three distinct Gods, notwithstanding such an union in will and affection.[3]

Not long after the Revolution, the civil power interfered in theological debates, and converted what ought to have been considered only as fair discussion in order to ascertain and discover truth, into an offence against the community, and regarded it as the ground of a criminal charge. In 1693 was published a Treatise, entitled, "A brief but clear Confutation of the Doctrine of the Trinity." It was industriously dispersed, and copies of it under cover were directed to several peers, and to some members of the House of Commons. The attention of the legislature being called to it, their prejudices were awakened, and their fears of the spread of the sentiments it defended were alarmed. The House of Lords voted it to be an infamous and scandalous libel; it was ordered to be burnt in

---

[2] Considerations on the explications of the Doctrine of the Trinity, 1693; p. 13, 14. The correspondence of Dr. Cudworth's sentiments with Plato, or their origin in the platonic philosophy, has been examined in the Theological Repository, vol. iv. p. 77, 97. Priestley's early opinions, vol. i. p. 349.

[3] Considerations, &c. p. 14.

Old Palace-yard by the hands of the common hangman; an enquiry after the author, printer, and publisher was instituted; and the attorney-general was directed to prosecute them.[4]

But notwithstanding the prosecutions to which, as in this instance, the publication of tracts in favour of Unitarian sentiments was exposed, and the discountenance given to sermons and tracts directed against such opinions, after a temporary pause the Trinitarian controversy was revived. In 1693, Dr. South, rector of Islip in Oxfordshire, a man of great talents and learning, but of a violent and domineering temper, attacked Dr. Sherlock's book on the Trinity in "Animadversions on it, together with a more necessary vindication of that sacred and prime article of the Christian faith from Dr. Sherlock's new notions and false explications of it: humbly offered to his admirers, and to himself the chief of them." "This pamphlet was written," says Bishop Burnet, "not without wit and learning, but without any measure of Christian charity; and without any regard either to the dignity of the subject or the decencies of his profession."[5] Dr. South explained the doctrine in the common method, that the Deity was one essence and three subsistencies. In 1694, ·Dr. Sherlock published a defence of himself against the "Animadversions;" and charged his opponent with Sabellianism. Dr. South replied in a treatise, entitled, "Tritheism charged upon Dr. Sherlock's new notion of the Trinity, and the charge made good in answer to the defence." Others went into the dispute with some learning, but with more warmth; and great men espoused the side of each. Dr. Sherlock was accused of polytheism, or holding the doctrine of *three Gods*; and with great justice, if words have any meaning. Dr. South came under the imputation of explaining away the Trinity, and falling into Sabellianism. The candid enquirer was unsettled and perplexed. He hesitated between the scheme of the former, which preserved a Trinity, but in which the unity was lost; and that of the latter, which under the terms "modes, subsistencies, and properties, &c." kept up the "divine Unity, but then lost a Trinity, such as the scriptures discover, at least with respect to the Father and

---

4   15 Lords' Journal, 332, 3d Jan. 1693. History of William III. vol. ii. p. 381. Proceedings of the House of Lords in the case of Benjamin Flower, p. 37, 38.

5   Burnet, vol. iv. p. 311.

the Son."[6] The Unitarians, availing themselves of Dr. South's explication, declared a readiness to assent to the liturgy and articles, if that was the kind of Trinity which the language of both was intended to circulate.[7]

Sentiments similar to those of Dr. Sherlock, so far at least as related to the distinction of persons, were advanced by an eminent divine among the dissenters, Mr. Howe; but he did not adopt Dr. Sherlock's idea of mutual consciousness as constituting the unity of the three divine persons; because that hypothesis left out, according to his expression, the *nexus*, or the connection by which they were united. His leading principles were, "that the persons in the Trinity are distinct numerical natures, beings, and substances; that there is a variety of individual natures in the Deity; that there are in the Godhead three distinct intelligent hypostases or persons, having each his own distinct, singular, intelligent nature; and these three divine persons, beings, essences, natures, substances, maintain a *delicious society*. No enjoyments being pleasant without *consociation* therein: and we must needs think this a most blessed state, or a more perfect idea of blessedness, than can be conceived in an eternal solitude." This, it has been observed, is Dr. Sherlock's doctrine; only with some more gross ideas and additions to it.[8] Mr. Howe's tract was entitled, "A calm and sober Inquiry concerning the

---

6   Emlyn's Works, vol. i. p. 15.

7   Lindsey's Apology, p. 73. 4th ed.

8   Unitarian Tracts, in 4to, 1695, p. 39, 40, vol. iii. This idea, gross as it may appear to some, was, in a short time after it was broached in a metaphysical disquisition, converted into a theme of devotional declamation by Mr. after Dr. Watts; and at the distance of twenty years, when he himself made an apology for having been carried away by the warm efforts of imagination further than riper years would probably indulge on so sublime and abstruse a subject, was delivered from the press in a sermon entitled, "The Scale of Blessedness; or blessed Saints, blessed Saviour, and blessed Trinity;" from Ps. lxv. 4. Having dwelt upon the thought, that knowledge and mutual love make up the heaven of the three divine persons, the pious author, borne away by a heated imagination, and lost in his subject, concludes it in this rapturous strain: "The nearness of the divine persons to each other, and the unspeakable relish of their unbounded pleasures, are too vast ideas for our bounded minds to entertain. 'Tis one infinite transport that runs through Father, Son, and Spirit, without beginning and without end, with boundless variety, yet ever perfect and ever present, without change and without degree; and all this, because they are so near with one another, and so much one with GOD." Sermons on various subjects, vol. i. No. xii. or p. 399, 12mo. ed. 1721.

possibility of a Trinity in the Godhead; in a letter to a person of worth." To which were added some letters formerly written to Dr. Wallis, on the same subject. 1694. Notwithstanding the prominent feature of agreement in the hypotheses of the two divines, Mr. Howe fell under the censure of Dr. Sherlock, as advancing such a notion of the unity of GOD as neither the scriptures nor the ancient church knew any thing of, and as scarcely needing a confutation. Yet he offered animadversions on it in his defence against Dr. South. It was also noticed in "Some Considerations on the explications of the Doctrine of the Trinity, in a letter to H.H." To both Mr. Howe replied; to the former in a "Letter to a Friend;" and to the latter, in "A View of those Considerations," in a letter to the friend whom he had before addressed. In this performance, with a fairness and liberality that did him much credit, he gave it "as his judgment, that much service might be done to the common interest of religion, by a free mutual communication of even more doubtful thoughts, if such disquisitions were pursued with more candour, and with less confidence and prepossession of mind, or addictedness to the interest of any party. If it were rather endeavoured to reason one another into or out of this or that opinion, than either by sophistical conclusions to cheat, or to hector by great words, one that is not of our mind. Or if the design were less to expose an adversary, than to clear the matter in controversy. Besides, that if such equanimity did more generally appear and govern in transactions of this nature, it would produce a greater liberty in communicating our thoughts about some of the more vogued and fashionable opinions, by exempting each other from the fear of ill treatment in the most sensible kind. It being too manifest that the same confident insulting genius which makes a man think himself to be competent to be a standard to mankind, would also make him impatient of dissent, and tempt him to do worse than reproach one that differs from him, if it were in his power. And the club or faggot arguments must be expected to take place, where what he thinks rational ones did not do the business." Mr. Howe by his publications in this controversy rose in esteem and respect with some; others, who highly valued his other publications, wished that he had left this argument untouched; a third set could scarcely refrain from charging him, as well as Dr. Sherlock, with heresy; a term, by which those who use it assume to themselves orthodoxy and infallibility, and fix a stigma on such as differ from them.[9] In the church, Dr. Sherlock's sentiments found advocates as well as opponents. On the feast of St. Simon and Jude in 1695, Mr. Bingham, rector of Headbourn-Worthy, near Winchester, and a fellow of University college in Oxford, afterwards eminent for his laborious investigations and learned publications on the antiquities of the Christian church, and for his meritorious services in behalf of the establishment to which he belonged, advanced, in a sermon before the university, the notions of Dr. Sherlock; and asserted that "there were three infinite distinct minds and substances in the Trinity; and also that the three persons in the Trinity were three distinct minds or spirits, and three individual substances." They who patronised and embraced the sentiments of Dr. South were offended with these assertions; and had sufficient influence to procure a solemn decree in convocation, judging, declaring, and determining "the aforesaid words to be false, impious, and heretical; disagreeing with and contrary to the doctrine of the Catholic church, and especially to the doctrine of the Church of England publicly received." The realists, instead of yielding to the decision and sentence of the convocation, entered a virtual protest against it; and answered, that "what the heads of Oxford had condemned as heretical and impious, was the very Catholic faith: that the decree was a censure of the Nicene faith, and of the faith of the church of England, as heresy; and exposed both to the scorn and triumph of the Socinians." Dr. Sherlock in particular said, "that he would undertake any day in the year, to procure a meeting of twice as many wise and learned men to censure their decree."[10]

Under these circumstances, neither the authority of the university, nor the solemnity with which the decree was issued, could secure the end proposed by it. It rather irritated the parties, than settled their differences. Dr. Tennison, who then filled the see of Canterbury, prevailed with the king to interpose by his authority, and to give the royal sanction to certain injunctions drawn up by himself, and addressed to the arch bishops and bishops, to be published in their dioceses, and enforced by their episcopal authority, to maintain the purity of

9 Calamy's Life of Howe, p. 198–209.

10 Ben Mordecai's Letters, vol. i. p. 70. 8vo. ed.

the Christian faith, and preserve the peace of the church. The proclamation directed,

That no preacher whatsoever in his sermon or lecture should presume to deliver any other doctrine concerning the blessed Trinity, than what was contained in the Holy Scriptures, and is agreeable to the three creeds and the thirty-nine articles of religion.

That in the explication of this doctrine they should carefully avoid all new terms, and confine themselves to such ways of explication as have been commonly used in the church.

The careful observance of the 53d canon, which prohibits public opposition between preachers, and especially bitter invectives and scurrilous language against all persons whatever, was particularly recommended. These rules were also enjoined on all who wrote on the disputed questions. These directions were not limited to the clergy alone to govern their conduct in the controversy, but were also levelled at those who were not of the clerical body, but who, it was understood, had presumed to talk and dispute against the Christian faith concerning the doctrine of the Trinity, or had written or published or dispersed books and pamphlets against it: And the clergy were strictly charged and commanded, together with all other means suitable to their holy profession, to use their authority according to law to repress and restrain such exorbitant practices.[11]

No decree of a council, no bull of a pope, could be more decidedly marked by claims to authority over conscience, and to infallibility of judgment in the enactors of either, than were these royal injunctions drawn up by an episcopal pen. The royal personage from whose court they were given, and the prelate whose spirit dictated them, though credit should be given to the purity of their motives, forgot that they were protestants. The only part of these injunctions that could possibly answer a valuable end, and that properly fell within the province of the civil magistrate, was the order to abstain from bitter invectives and scurrilous language. The other directions tended only to overbear the judgments of men, to suppress conviction, and to restrain inquiry.

The decree of the university and the injunctions of the king were not merely dead letters. The partizans of orthodoxy in

11   Tennison's Life, p. 49-53.

that day not only had recourse to censures, but adopted vigorous measures. In 1695 was published a tract, reprinted by the London Unitarian Society in 1793, entitled "The designed End to the Socinian Controversy; or a rational and plain Discourse to prove that no other person but the Father of Christ is GOD Most High:" by Mr. John Smith. "The author discovers, " says the editor of the modern edition, "a very considerable acquaintance with the Christian scriptures, and a mind influenced by the love of truth." These recommendations did not screen him or his work from resentment and the visitation of power. The work was seized, and the author was apprehended.[12] Dr. Trelawney, while bishop of Exeter, entered the lists with peculiar spirit against those who were deemed to be engaged in a conspiracy against the catholic faith, viz. Socinians, latitudinarians, and deniers of the mysteries; and he proceeded to the extreme measure of excommunicating Dr. Bury, who had been also solemnly condemned by the universities for notorious heresy.[13]

By these means the Trinitarian controversy had at last a temporary suspension; but not till the leading disputants in it, Dr. Sherlock and Dr. South, had been ridiculed in a popular ballad, called "The Battle Royal."[14] The various modes

12 Preface to the last edition.

13 A Letter to a Convocation Man, 1697; ascribed to Dr. Binckes. N. B. In a copy of this tract in Dr. Williams's Library, Red-Cross-street, London, the names of Trelawney and Bury are inserted in the margin; as one the actor, the other the sufferer.

14 This ballad was translated into several languages, particularly the Latin, by a curious hand, at the University of Cambridge; and presents were made to the author by the nobility and gentry. The ludicrous strain of it, which was very indecorous, considering the eminent and learned persons whom it reprimands, and the gravity of the questions debated by the disputants, is a proof that the dispute was regarded as the contention of theologues rather than as the sober investigation of sacred and important truth; and did not procure from all persons respect to the divines concerned in it. As it is a document that shews the spirit of the times, and the impression made by the controversy on the public mind, it may be acceptable to the reader.

"THE BATTLE ROYAL,"
To the tune of "*A Soldier and a Sailor.*"

A dean[16] and a prebendary[17]
Had once a vagary;
And were at doubtful strife, sir.
Who led the better life, sir,
And was the better man.

The dean, he said, that truly
Since BLUFF was so unruly,
He'd prove it to his face, sir,
That he had the most grace, sir,
And so the fight began, &c.

16 Dr. Sherlock.   17 Dr. South.

adopted for suppressing the works of the Unitarians occasioned one[15] who had written with acrimony against the friends of the Revolution, to remark "that certainly there must be something formidable in their books and some reasonings in them, which could not be well answered, that so much diligence was used to suppress them."[20]

THE CONTROVERSY ABOUT JUSTIFICATION

The dissenters had scarcely begun to enjoy peace, protection, and liberty, under the auspicious influence of the Revolution, than they disagreed among themselves. Division and dissention, always to be lamented, were in several views, at that time, particularly disgraceful and unseasonable. They furnished those who had predicted their disunion, if they were left to themselves, an opportunity of insulting and reproaching them. While the flames were breaking out in the Established Church, occasioned both by religious and practical animosities, if the dissenters had been wise and temperate enough to preserve harmony and union among themselves, they would have secured honour to their principles, preserved the consistency of their character as protestants, and acquired respectability and weight in the state. It had been presumed, that a foundation for

When PREB replied, like thunder,
And roar'd out, it was no wonder,
Since Gods the dean had THREE, sir,
And more by TWO than he, sir:
For he had got but one, &c.

Now, while these two were raging,
And in dispute engaging,
The Master of the CHARTER[18]
Said both had caught a tartar,
For gods, sir, there were none, &c.

That all the Books of Moses
Were nothing but supposes;
That he deserved rebuke, sir,
Who wrote the Pentateuch, sir;
'Twas nothing but a sham, &c.

That as for Father Adam,
With Mrs. Eve, his madam,
And what the serpent spake, sir,
'Twas nothing but a joke, sir,
And well-invented flam, &c.

That in the BATTLE ROYAL,
As none could take denial,
The dame for which they strove, sir,
Could neither of them love, sir,
Since all had given offence, &c.

She therefore, slyly waiting,
Left all THREE FOOLS a prating;
And being in a fright, sir,
RELIGION took her flight, sir,
And ne'er was heard of since.[19]

[18] Dr. Thomas Burnet, master of the Charter-House, who about this time published his Archæologia; in which he was charged by some with having impugned and weakened the divine truths of the Old Testament.
[19] South's Posthumous Works, Memoirs, p. 128–130.
[15] Dr. Hickes.
[20] Preface to the late edition of Smith's Divine End, &c. p. vi.

a permanent union had been laid, and that a cement of their mutual interests had been formed, by the heads of agreement, to which the body of the ministers, both presbyterian and congregational, in London and its vicinity, and in several parts of the country, had assented in 1691.[21] But strange as it may appear, the rise of their differences may be dated, it is said, from that agreement. Some few of the congregational denomination never either approved of those heads of agreement, or concurred in the union. They were not satisfied, moreover, with resuming their consent to the union, and preserving their own independency; but were assiduous in using their influence with their brethren, who entertained the same sentiments with themselves on certain doctrinal points, and had joined the union, to detach them from it; and they gave them no rest till this end was effected. The influence of the united ministers in London, on account of some differences and animosities to which the opinions broached by Mr. Davis, of Rothwell in Northamptonshire, had given rise, contributed on their side to heighten the dissatisfaction of the others, to widen the breach, and to precipitate a rupture. "They acted," says Dr. Calamy, "as if they had been under the secret influence of some who were fearful while the Established Church was divided, lest their own interest should gain a firm and permanent union." It had been observed in Germany, that "the book of concord," as a plan of union was called, was the occasion of great discord; so the attempted union among the dissenters was the occasion of new quarrels and divisions."[22]

Mr. Davis, of Rothwell, incurred the censure of his brethren in the neighbourhood for erroneous principles and irregular practices. The errors charged on him were these: "That the law of innocency was not able to save men at first: That justification upon believing is only a manifestation to the conscience of an antecedent justification; and so it is not the state of the soul, but its sense of its state, that is altered upon conversion: That justifying faith is a persuasion that our sins are pardoned; and when it is said we believe for pardon, it is meant for the knowledge of pardon: That this faith is not a consenting act of the will: That the law prepares not for conversion, and its convictions tend to drive men farther from

[21] See before, p. 99.

[22] Calamy, p. 512, 537. Howe's Life, p. 181, 182.

Christ: That the law of the gospel is the great law of electing grace, viz. I will have mercy on whom I will have mercy: That there be no preparatory humblings in order to faith: That we should begin our religion with high confidence of our interest in Christ, and must maintain it against all challenges or doubts from our sins or defects: That they are like Baal's priests, who put men on trying themselves by such marks, as sincerity, universal obedience, love to GOD and Christ and the brethren: That all believers at all times stand before GOD without sin; yea, when they are sinning against GOD, they are without spot before GOD; and when they have sinned and prayed for pardon, it is for the discovery thereof to their conscience, and not for what is properly forgiveness: That Christ fulfilled the covenant of grace for us, and he believed for us, as our representative."

On the subject of irregular practices, Mr. Davis was accused of sending forth preachers unfit for the ministry, and not approved by neighbouring ministers; of unchurching such churches as did not agree with his exorbitant methods and licentious principles; of wickedly railing at most of the orthodox laborious ministers, endeavouring to the utmost to prejudice the people against their persons and labours, as idolatrous, illegal, and antichristian; yea, of affirming that all the churches had gone a whoring from Christ, and that he was happy who was the instrument of breaking all the churches. He was particularly pressed, in one point, with a charge of holding an horrid opinion, and observing an unchristian practice: it was, that though he did not scruple to baptize the children of his own people, yet he rebaptized such adult members as were baptized in their infancy by any ministers of the Church of England. Against this charge he defended himself on these grounds; "that if any, the seed of strangers, and having no other baptism than that of the public, desired to submit to the ordinance, he dared not to refuse it: for he looked on that administered in public as null and void, on two accounts: first, that they and their unbelieving parents being in no sense or wise under the covenant, baptism could not be a seal; and, it not a seal, he apprehended it to be nothing, and therefore null and void. And secondly, that the administrators were none of Christ's sending, and that therefore what they did in matters of religion was nothing, as an idol is nothing." Mr. Davis argued, "by parity of reason, ordinances falsely administered are nothing; and, though baptism was performed by them in the name of the Father, Son, and Spirit; yet still they prophesied lies in the name of the LORD, for He never sent them." The strain and spirit of his assertion may be considered as a specimen and a proof of the charge alleged against Dr. Davis.

This statement of his principles and conduct formed part of a declaration published by the "United Brethren," at the instigation of the ministers in the country, to counteract the spread of his sentiments, and in testimony of their own fidelity and zeal for the truth of Christ. In this declaration they expressed their thoughts concerning his doctrines and practices, and entered their protest against them, as repugnant to the gospel, to the doctrine of the Church of England, and to other confessions, to which they had given their assent. They also stigmatized his principles as furnishing "strong temptations to carnal security and libertinism; as Satan's fiery darts, whereby he endeavoureth the ruin of those souls who are less subject to other snares; and as what would destroy the ministry which Christ hath appointed and prospered to the conversion of sinners." They disowned Mr. Davis himself, as neither then nor at any former time esteemed to be of the number of the united brethren.

The concluding paragraph of this declaration is strongly expressive of the views and spirit of those who published it, as to the subject before them. "It is our grief," they say, "that a man should with meer falsehood, clamour, and noise, prevail so far: It is no less our wonder, that he should generally set up for the only gospel preacher, reviling most others; and yet when charged with his assertions, he at times attempts, to unintelligent persons, to reduce those abominable assertions to what is the general opinion of such as he exposeth. But we shall earnestly pray for his repentance; and in the mean time, that that scripture may be verified in him, 2 Tim. iii. 9. 'He shall proceed no further, but his folly shall be manifest to all men:' which we are encouraged to hope the sudden accomplishment of, since he is given up to such trifling visions, enthusiastic pretences, self-contradictions, highest arrogancy and insolence, and many are awakened to see the wiles of the Devil by their visible effects; and most persons fit to judge thereof agree, it cannot be the interest of Christ that he serves, by the spirit he discovers, and the public scandal and mischiefs he so industriously promotes."[23]

The reader will judge how far the air of infallibility, and the tone of authority, which such a declaration carries in it, are calculated to convince or to conciliate. It is certain, that this paper had not the effect which it was meant to produce. Discontents existed among the united brethren themselves, and a difference of opinion about some doctrinal points soon discovered itself on an occasion which their sagacity could not anticipate, nor their influence prevent.

During the unhappy times of the civil wars, the subject of Justification had been warmly controverted by writers of the several religious parties: who disagreed in their ideas on the meaning, not of the word "*justification*" only, but of the terms "*faith* and good works," and in their construction of the language of the apostles Paul and James on this subject. Contests were started, that could have no object but to divide and alienate: various hypotheses were formed, which obscured the points that they were meant to elucidate: and the sense of the apostolical writers was perplexed by abundance of learned sophistry. Some who appeared in this controversy were censured as leaning to popery or judaism; others were regarded as advocates of antinomianism and libertinism; some again were charged with pelagianism and socinianism; and others, lastly, were considered as advancing the principles of manichæism and fatalism. The questions connected with this controversy had been agitated, with much contention, for about twenty years, when they attracted the attention of Mr. afterwards Bishop Bull; then 26 years of age, and engaged his close enquiries and assiduous study during eight or nine years. The result of his investigation was the publication of a work in Latin, entitled "Harmonia Apostolica," *Apostolical Harmony*; consisting of two dissertations, the first to explain and defend the doctrine of James on justification, the second to demonstrate the agreement and harmony of Paul with him on this point. The particular design of the first dissertation was to shew "that good works which proceed from faith, are a necessary condition required from us by GOD, to the end that by the new and evangelical covenant obtained by and sealed in

---

[23] Calamy, vol. i. p. 512-514.

the blood of Christ, the mediator of it, we may be justified according to his free and unmerited grace."

Though our young divine settled his own judgment, he was not equally successful in his endeavours to bring others to discern and acknowledge the truth of those conclusions on the point, to which he had himself been led by his review of the scriptures and of primitive antiquity: for notwithstanding all his caution in discussing a subject which the disputations of theologians had rendered abstruse, his performance created alarm both in the church and out of it. His interpretations of the sacred writers, and his method of reconciling the two apostles, were tried by the correspondence which they bore to the sentiments of Luther and Calvin, whose names, as the two apostles of the Reformation, carried with them an undue and overbearing influence. Though the evidence and strength of his arguments appeared to some in a clear and convincing light, hard censures were passed by others on the work and its author; and the doctrines maintained in it were condemned as pernicious and heretical, contrary to the decrees of the Church of England, and of all other reformed churches. Dr. Morley, bishop of Winchester, in a charge to his clergy, prohibited the reading of Mr. Bull's work; some heads of houses in the universities and some tutors warned the students against it. Dr. Barlow, Margaret professor at Oxford, and afterwards bishop of Lincoln, and Dr. Tully, principal of Edmund's Hall, an eloquent and learned writer, were the most zealous to oppose the pacific method which it offered in order to reconcile the different systems about attaining salvation. Among the dissenters, Mr. Joseph Truman, educated in the distinguishing doctrines that were ratified by the Westminster Assembly, and Mr. Tombes, a learned baptist minister, animadverted on the "Apostolical Harmony," as if a blow had been aimed by it at the ground-work of the Reformation. About a year after it was published, a copy of it was sent to the author with marginal annotations and animadversions from the hands of his diocesan Dr. Nicholson, bishop of Gloucester; written, it was afterwards discovered, by Dr. Charles Gataker, the son of the learned critic of that name, whose zeal for the principles which he had received, as authentic explications of the gospel, in the systems that he had studied, neither permitted him to think sedately, nor to write with temper. Dr. Lewis du Moulin, son of the famous Peter du Moulin, an independent, likewise attacked with great severity the principles and opinions advanced by Mr. Bull, in a pamphlet entitled, "A short and true Account of the several advances the Church of England hath made towards Rome; or a model of the grounds upon which the papists, for these hundred years, have built their hopes and expectations that England would ere long return to popery." London, 1680. This tract contained also virulent reflections on several eminent divines of the Church of England.[24] The ground of the strain in which this pamphlet and others in this controversy were written, was, that the solifidian doctrine was regarded by many as the main pillar of protestantism; which being once shaken, it was thought, there could be no possibility of its bearing up its head against popery, or of justifying the proceedings of Luther and the other first reformers. With this tract, the controversy, which had been continued for ten years, was terminated: as Mr. Bull did not judge it necessary to reply. He had particularly and fully answered the other writers, who had animadverted on his "Apostolical Harmony." His biographer says, "that with a very laudable diligence he spared no pains, that he might thoroughly and impartially examine all that his adversary could bring against him: nor could it be denied, that he made such just and reasonable concessions, as rendered his own cause the stronger, while they yielded to the opposite that which it might lawfully demand." In the discussions which originated with his work, the meaning of the terms, "justification, faith, and good works," was canvassed. The nature of the Mosaic law, and of its promises and threatenings, came under examination. These were proper subjects of enquiry; and the investigation of them tended to elucidate the scriptures, and to place the matter in debate on scriptural authority, its just and only obligatory ground. But with the discussions on these points were blended systematic principles and scholastic niceties. It must be added, to the disgrace of those who wrote in it, though too much in the spirit of all times and of all controversies, that their pens were often dipped in gall, and their arguments were accompanied with

---

[24]   It ought to be mentioned to the honour of Dr. Moulin, and as a pleasing instance of candour and ingenuousness, that on his death-bed, soon after the appearance of his pamphlet, he retracted all the personal reflections which he had cast in his book upon any divine of the Church of England; and directed his retraction to be made public after his death. This was accordingly done. Nelson's Life of Bishop Bull, p. 254.

heavy charges and invidious imputations. "The best cause in the world may be run down with clamour and confidence; but truth is never better supported, than by being modestly and simply proposed, with the arguments for and against it fairly represented, without reflection upon any for not thinking after the same manner with us."[25]

The controversy which was begun in the Established Church, and revived by the publication of Bull's "Harmonia Apostolica," was also taken up by the dissenters, and conducted with much warmth. So far back as the year 1649, Mr. Baxter had discussed the questions concerning the doctrine of justification, in a treatise, entitled, "Aphorisms of Justification and the Covenants." Exceptions were made to this work at its first appearance. It excited much attention; became a subject of obloquy with many; and several learned men, as Dr. John Wallis, Dr. Geo. Lawson, Mr. John Warren, and Mr. Christopher Cartwright, employed their pens in animadverting upon it. The "Aphorisms" were particularly answered by Mr. John Crandon, of Fawley in Hampshire, in a book, which he inscribed, "Mr. Baxter's Aphorisms exorcised;" and by Mr. Wm. Eyre, of Salisbury, in his "Vindiciæ Justificationis gratuitæ." Some of these writers delivered their sentiments at the desire of Mr. Baxter himself; upon which he published his suspension of these aphorisms; then his fuller explication and defence of them in his "Apology;" and afterwards an additional explication and defence of them, in his "Confession of Faith," and in his "Disputations of Justification." On his part the controversy was agitated, at different times, for forty years. In one of his publications, during this period, he entered the lists with Dr. Tully, one of Bishop Bull's opponents, in "A Treatise of Justifying Righteousness, in two books," in 1676. In this work, though he sometimes acknowledged the doctor to be a very worthy person, yet he hesitated not to charge his "Justificatio Paulina" as being "defective in point of truth, justice, charity, ingenuity, and pertinency to the matter." "It was the unhappiness both of Mr. Baxter and Dr. Tully," observes Mr. Nelson, "that they gave but too much reason for the imputation, under which they both equally lay, of being angry writers." Bull, Bellarmin, who also wrote on the same subject, and Baxter, were considered and represented by Dr.

---

25 For a full, candid, and succinct review of this controversy, see Nelson's Life of Bishop Bull, p. 89-257.

Tully as "the three great adversaries of the faith," engaged in "a triple league" to overthrow it.[26]

After the controversy, as it had been handled by some writers whom we have mentioned, had subsided, it revived again amongst the dissenters, and seems to have been confined within their pale. It was occasioned by the republication of the works of Dr. Crisp, by his son Mr. Samuel Crisp, sanctioned by the names of several presbyterian and independent ministers. When they were first published, the assembly of divines at Westminster desired them to be burnt. The author was a man of great piety, and exemplary purity of character; but the sentiments that he advanced and defended were, with reason, considered as very pernicious in their tendency, and as opening a door for great licentiousness of manners in those whom their passions might dispose to act upon the strict letter of them.

Dr. Crisp's scheme is stated to be this: "That by GOD's mere electing decree, all saving blessings are by divine obligation made ours, and nothing more is needful to our title to these blessings: That on the cross all the sins of the elect were transferred to Christ, and ceased ever to be their sins: That at the first moment of conception, a title to these decreed blessings is personally applied to the elect, and they invested actually therein. Hence the elect have nothing to do, in order to an interest in these blessings; nor ought they to intend the least good to themselves in what they do: sin can do them no harm, because it is none of theirs; nor can GOD afflict them for any sin."

On his scheme it was affirmed, "That sins are not to be feared as doing any hurt, even when the most flagitious are committed. Grace and holiness cannot do us the least good. GOD has no more to lay to the charge of the wickedest men, if they be elected, than he has to lay to the charge of a saint in glory. That the elect are not to be governed by fear or hope; for the laws have no promises or threats to rule them; nor are they under the impressions of rewards or punishments, as motives to duty, or preservatives against sin."[27]

These sentiments were stiled *Antinomian*, as impugning the excellence and subverting the obligations of the law. They exhibit an overstrained construction of Luther's doctrine,

---

[26]   Nelson's Life of Bull, p. 243–254.

[27]   Dr. Williams's Gospel Truth, p. 6, 7, 8.

which represents the merits of Christ as the source of man's salvation; and of Calvin's doctrine respecting divine decrees. Were there not reason to suppose that the advocate for them was sincere, though misled, one should be ready to impute to him an invidious design to caricature the opinions of those reformers, and to expose them to indignation or contempt. These opinions sprung up in Germany, and were broached by John Agricola, a native of Aisleben, and an eminent doctor of the Lutheran church. His followers were called *Antinomians*, i.e. "Enemies of the law." This sect was suppressed in its infancy by the fortitude, watchfulness, and influence of Luther: and Agricola acknowledged and renounced his pernicious system; though he is said to have returned to his errors, and to have preached them again with success after the death of Luther.[28]

These opinions had for many years lain dormant in England, when the republication of Dr. Crisp's works in or about 1690 revived them, and gave them a new and wide circulation, especially among the nonconformists, whose liberties were threatened on this account. Under the conduct of Mr. Davis the flame broke out with peculiar violence, and spread through eleven counties. Judicious and faithful ministers, who inculcated the necessity and obligations of righteousness, were deserted, and reproached as legalists; churches were divided, and town and country were filled with debates and noise. So high did the ferment rise, so widely did the infection spread in the city of London, that if a minister among the presbyterians preached a sermon in which hope was placed on conditional promises, or the fear of sin was pressed by the divine threatenings, he was immediately condemned and censured as an enemy to Christ and free grace. This censoriousness and violence of temper shewed itself particularly amongst the independents and baptists. One of the lecturers at Pinner's Hall preaching on repentance as necessary to the remission of sins, that pulpit was soon filled with the harshest censures against the presbyterians.[29]

Many of the ministers of that persuasion solicited Mr. afterwards Dr. Daniel Williams, to confute the principles of Dr. Crisp. This he undertook to do; and entered on his talk

---

28 Mosheim's Ecclesiastical History, vol. iv. p. 33.

29 Gospel Truth, preface, p. 27; and Bishop Bull's Life, p. 260.

first in a sermon at Pinner's Hall; and then in a treatise, entitled, "Gospel Truths stated and vindicated." The method in which this work was drawn up, was to state the *truth* and *error* under each head; to prove the latter to be the opinion of Dr. Crisp; then to shew wherein the difference did not lie, and this being done, to declare in what the real and proper difference did consist. Having thus explained and stated the case, the author confirmed the truth, which was opposed to a specific error, by the rule of faith received by both sides. To the direct proofs were added corroborating testimonies from the approved catechisms and confessions both of the presbyterian and independent body, viz. those of the assembly at Westminster, of the synod of New England, and of the congregational elders at the Savoy, besides those of such particular authors as were generally esteemed orthodox. And, lastly, he investigated the ground of Dr. Crisp's mistake. This plan of discussion was applied to about twenty-six points; it was executed with plainness and simplicity, and matters were stated with such fairness and impartiality, that his adversaries did not detect one instance in which the opinions of the doctor were misrepresented or mistaken.[30] The author himself declared, that he had carefully avoided any reflection on the late Rev. Dr. Crisp; "whom," he added, "I believe a holy man; and have abstained exposing many things according to the advantages offered, if by any means this book may become useful to such as most need it."

The points connected with the controversy, and discussed in this treatise, through as many chapters as the propositions amounted to, are "the state of the elect before effectual calling: GOD's laying sins on Christ: the discharge of the elect from sins, upon their being laid on Christ: the elect ceasing to be sinners from the time their sins were laid on Christ: the time when our sins were laid on Christ, and continued there: GOD's separation from and abhorrence of Christ, while our sins lay upon him: the change of person between Christ and the elect: the nature of saving faith, the free offer of Christ to sinners, and of preparatory qualifications: union with Christ by faith: justification by faith, with a digression about repentance: the necessity and benefit of holiness, obedience, and good works, with perseverance therein: intending our soul's good by the

---

[30]   Bishop Bull's Life, p. 261.

duties we perform: the way to attain assurance: GOD's seeing sins in believers, and their guilt by it: the hurt that sin may do the believers: GOD's displeasure for sin, in the afflictions of his people: the beauty of sincere holiness: Gospel preaching: legal preaching: exalting of Christ: the honour of the free grace of GOD."

Dr. Williams has been considered as Mr. Baxter's successor in the management of these disputes; and he incurred the same severe censures as had befallen that eminent writer, being accused of maintaining opinions inconsistent with the doctrine of Christ's satisfaction, and yielding up the cause to the socinians. Names that carried an odium with them were very freely bestowed on him; as if it were more the study of the partisans of Dr. Crisp's opinions to expose those with whom they had the dispute to reproach and obloquy, than to examine their arguments and discover truth.

Dr. Williams's work was first published in 1692, with testimonials of approbation by Dr. Bates, Mr. Howe, Mr. Alsop, Mr. Shower, and twelve other dissenting ministers. The names of double that number were added to the second edition. This was succeeded by a third edition, with other names; to which a large postscript was added, for elucidating sundry truths.[31]

Dr. Chauncy, and several who coincided with him in opinions, animadverted on Dr. Williams's performance: to whom Dr. Williams replied, in "A Defence of Gospel Truth," a performance which secured the approbation of able judges. But notwithstanding the conviction which it carried to some minds, it did not give the same satisfaction to all. Mr. Mather, an independent minister, published a sermon on justification, in which he asserted that believers were as righteous as Christ himself; that the covenant of grace was not conditional; with other opinions of the same tenor. Dr. Williams answered him in a tract, entitled, "Man made Righteous." To this work no one replied.[32]

On the publication of Dr. Williams's "Gospel Truth," instead of its serving to compose the differences which had

---

31 Mr. Orton recommended the treatise of Dr. Williams as the best that he knew, to enable a person to judge of those controversies. "He is," Mr. Orton added, "the clearest, fairest controversial writer I am acquainted with." Letters to a young Clergyman, letter xv.

32 Bishop Bull's Life, p. 262.

broken out among the lecturers at Pinner's Hall, a new and great clamour was raised; particularly on account of the interpretation given to Phil. iii. 9. At length a paper of objections to that work, signed by Mr. Griffith, Mr. Cole, Mr. Mather, Mr. Chauncy, Mr. Trail, and Mr. Richard Taylor, was delivered at a meeting of the united ministers. But no cognizance was taken of it. The reasons of passing it over without notice were, that three of the six objectors were not of the union; and that the material objections were not only considered to be ungrounded, but were expressed in words as recited from Dr. Williams's work, which were quite contrary to the letter of the expressions.[33] The doctor examined the paper in a post script to a third edition of his tract, and fully considered the objections it exhibited. But the silence with which the united ministers treated it, gave umbrage; and Dr. Chauncy, at a meeting about October 1692, using many warm words, assigned this neglect as a reason for leaving their meetings, and breaking off from their union. The more candid and pacific studied healing expedience; and after much consideration fixed on certain doctrinal articles, to which both sides agreed and subscribed, Dec. 16, 1692. These were published to the world under the title of "The Agreement in Doctrine among the Dissenting Ministers in London." This paper was far from answering the conciliatory end that was expected from it. The debates continued: one party was suspected of verging towards arminianism, and even socinianism. The charge of encouraging antinomianism was retorted on the other party. Separate weekly meetings were held. New creeds were framed; but they were objected to by some others "as too large or too strait, too full or too empty." Different papers were drawn up and subscribed, to effect an accommodation: but they created new altercations and fomented new differences. It seemed to be the aim and wish of some, that they might be thought to differ from their brethren, whether they really did so or not. The contending parties, in some instances at least, fancied their mutual differences to be greater than in fact they were. A letter was published in 4to. entitled, "A Vindication of the Protestant Doctrine concerning Justification, and of its preachers and professors, from the unjust charge of Antinomianism." But the hopes of free brotherly

33   Dr. Williams's Works, vol. iv. p. 322-324.

correspondence vanished away.[34] "Such were the effects of these wrangles at that time," observes Dr. Calamy, "upon the most common conversation, and so odd do the controversies that were then managed appear, if reviewed at a distance, as to convince considerate observers that there is no such enemy to peace as jealousy encouraged, and that indulged suspicion is an endless fund of contention."[35]

Though the controversy arose amongst, and was confined to, the dissenters; yet an appeal was made to the judgment of two celebrated divines in the established church, Dr. Stilling-fleet bishop of Winchester, and Dr. Jonathan Edwards, lately the principal of Jesus college, Oxford.

One point of debate which was started in the disputes of the day, related to a commutation of persons between Christ and believers. This, it was alleged, Dr. Stillingfleet had asserted and supported in his answer to Grotius on the doctrine of Christ's satisfaction; and this Dr. Williams was charged with denying, because he had denied what Dr. Crisp called a change of person, (not persons in the plural) *i.e.* a change of condition and state between Christ and a sinner; Christ thereby becoming as sinful as we, and we as righteous as he. Dr. Williams was induced, on this representation of his sentiments, to address a letter to the bishop, requesting his judgment on three questions: 1. What was his sense of commutation of persons? 2. Whether the author of "Gospel Truth" was chargeable with socinianism? and 3. Whether Dr. Crisp's sense concerning the change of person or persons were true or false? He supported his request by urging that his lordship's sentiments were pleaded against him. Mr. Lob, one of the independent party, though no direct antinomian, endeavoured also to secure the bishop as an umpire in their disputes; by a letter, informing him of the controversy then subsisting among the dissenters, in which a reference had been made to his lordship's sentiments; and soliciting him, that he would condescend to give them his impartial thoughts on the point, "as being likely on both hands to be so received as to compose the differences between them." Before this letter came to hand, the bishop had already answered Dr. Williams, and given his sentiments on the points

[34] Calamy, vol. i. p. 515, 516; Calamy's Life of Howe, p. 183; Nelson's Life of Bishop Bull, p. 260-263.

[35] Life of Howe, p. 184.

mentioned in both their letters with great freedom and impartiality, as well as with singular candour and judgment. This letter was, on the receipt of Mr. Lob's published in vindication of Dr. Williams against the heavy charges alleged against him. Mr. Lob on this addressed a second letter to the bishop, expressing much satisfaction with what he had written, and offering his thanks for it. He apprised his lordship, that to afford him a fuller state of the matters in controversy, and to furnish him with more ample means of composing their differences, he was preparing for the press an "Appeal" directed to his lordship; to whom he offered to send the sheets for his inspection in manuscript. This proposal the bishop waved. The Appeal, as soon as it was printed, was sent to his lordship; who, as a perfect master of the cause, considered it with great exactness, but did not live to finish his answer to it. What appeared gave the public a true state of the controversy, and fully vindicated both Mr. Baxter and Dr. Williams from the charge of going over to the camp of the socinians.[36] A paragraph on this point deserves to be quoted, as an evidence of the bishop's candour, and as an admonition to those who are ready in the present day to bring forward invidious charges.

"There is," said the bishop, "a remarkable story in the history of the Synod of Dort, which may not be improper in this place. There were in one of the universities of that country two professors, both very warm and extremely zealous for that which they accounted the most *orthodox* doctrine; but it happened that one of these accused the other before the synod for no fewer that *fifty* errors, tending to socinianism, pelagianism, &c. &c.; and wonderful heat there was on both sides. At last a committee was appointed to examine this dreadful charge; and upon examination they found no ground for the charge of socinianism, or any other heresy; but only that he had asserted too much the use of ambiguous and scholastic terms, and endeavoured to bring in the way of the schoolmen, in his writings; and therefore the synod dismissed him with that prudent advice, – Rather to keep to the language of the scriptures than of the schools."[37]

Dr. Edwards, to whom were sent the same questions, which had been laid before Bishop Stillingfleet, addressed in answer a

36   Bishop Bull's Life, p. 264-269.
37   Calamy's Life of Howe, p. 184, 5.

letter to Dr. Williams, in which he also fully acquitted him of giving any countenance to the opinions of Socinus; and justified him against his accusers, as having stated in a right and an orthodox manner the doctrine of Christ's satisfaction. But the progress of the controversy has been anticipated by introducing here the appeal made to those two eminent divines of the Established Church. For, previously to this stage of it, a design was formed to exclude Dr. Williams out of the lecture at Pinner's Hall, in 1694. A new lecture was set up at Salter's Hall: three of the old lecturers, Dr. Bates, Mr. Howe, and Mr. Alsop, accompanied him to the new lecture; and two others were added: and four were joined to the old lecturers, Mr. Mead and Mr. Cole, who remained at Pinner's Hall. The supporters of the new lectures consisted of the greatest part of the old subscribers, men of great piety and judgment, who perceiving the violence of the other party, when all pacific proposals and measures had proved abortive, removed to a more convenient place.[38] Thus the lecture was broken into two; Mr. Howe's friendly proposal, urged by him, both publickly and privately, to alternate the same lecture in both places, could not be carried; and the separation continued. A few years since the lecture at Salter's Hall, for want of support and attendance, was given up.

Besides Mr. Howe's conciliating proposal, another attempt for reunion was made, by an offer on one side to renounce Arminianism, and on the other Antinomianism; but this plan of harmony proved unsuccessful. Soon after, a few particular ministers of each party privately drew up a paper, with a hope that they should be able by their influence to prevail on both sides to sign it. But this measure, instead of extinguishing old differences, created new ones. Some were zealous for it, and complained much that it was not adopted. Others warmly opposed it, and, among various reasons, because they conceived of it as bearing hard upon Dr. Williams.[39]

It affords an unhappy instance of the asperity and malignity of party, that not only the sentiments of Dr. Williams were censured and stigmatized, but an attack was made on his reputation, an attack so peculiar as scarcely to admit of any precedent; which, observes Dr. Calamy, "was far from

38 Ibid. p. 194.
39 Calamy, p. 549.

recommending the dissenters, as to their candour or conduct, to standers by." But the ends of his adversaries were not answered. For after about eight weeks spent in an inquiry into his life by a committee of the united ministers, who received all manner of complaints against him, it was declared at a general meeting, as their *unanimous opinion*, and repeated and agreed to in three several successive meetings, that "he was entirely clear and innocent of all that was laid to his charge."[40]

It was subsequent to this, that a new clamour was raised against him: on which the appeal was made to Bishop Stillingfleet and Dr. Edwards, which has been already mentioned. Though that prelate vindicated the sentiments of Dr. Williams, he censured, in a charge to his clergy in 1696, the body of dissenters, as defective in their discipline, on account of their divisions: a censure, which seems to indicate that his lordship was inclined to apply coercive measures in such a case, instead of employing argument and persuasion to convince them of their errors, and leaving it to time and reflection to calm and compose their minds. In consequence of the appeal made to the learned members of the church, various publications on both sides issued from the press: but whether prejudices were softened, or passion had spent itself, or argument at length produced conviction, the dissenters became cool, and the controversy was terminated, at the instance of Mr. Lob, by Dr. Williams in 1698, who printed a few sheets entitled, "an End to Discord:" in which he stated the orthodox as also the socinian and antinomian notions as to Christ's satisfaction; and interpreted the confession of those more sober independents in as orthodox as a sense as their words with the most charitable construction could bear. It is almost incredible how much Dr. Williams was a sufferer in this controversy, from some who were too apt to act their principles against such as opposed them: for he had to contend with a strong party, who would leave nothing unattempted to crush him if possible. "But he had counted the cost;" as he wrote to a very respectable member of the Established Church, "even though his life had been 'sacrificed'." This integrity, zeal, and fortitude in opposing, under such circumstances, what appeared to him pernicious errors, displayed the energy of principle, and excellence of his own character. To his indefatigable and

40　Calamy, vol. i. p. 549. Bishop Bull's Life, p. 276.

zealous exertions it is in a great degree, ascribed, that within sixteen years after the close of this controversy, the number of antinomians among the dissenters was so reduced, that only three or four preachers of that denomination, and those men of no estimation, were left: the opposite principles could be advanced without exciting a clamour, and most of the independents and baptists in the metropolis preached against antinomianism.[41]

Another effect of this controversy was, that from the time of forming a new and separate lecture at Salter's Hall, the two denominations of presbyterians and independents became distinct communities, and acted separately with respect to their own denominations. And the ground of the separation being in doctrinal sentiments, the terms came afterwards to signify not a difference in Church Government, according to their original meaning, but in doctrinal opinions: the latter being applied to denote the reception of calvinistic, the former to signify the belief of arminian sentiments; or respectively of creeds similar to either system.

[41] Nelson's Life of Bishop Bull, p. 274-276.

AN END TO DISCORD
Daniel Williams

Epistle to the Reader.

If Arguments *might induce Christians to Peace, it were
enough to say, nothing is more expressly required than*
Christian Concord *by our Lord Jesus, or more commended
from its heavenly Original and happy Fruits; nor scarce any
thing more warned against, as obstructing the Kingdom of
Christ, advantageous to Satan's Interest, destructive to
Religion, yea to Civil Society, and repugnant to the very*
Design *and* Spirit *of the Gospel, as well as to the mutual
Usefulness of men, than uncharitable and dividing* Contentions *be. The only reason that can be suggested to acquit such*
Contenders *from notorious Guilt must be, that it is* for the
Faith of the Gospel *that they contend. But it's worth our
serious thoughts, that as even this cannot excuse a rigid,
censorious, envenomed Spirit, or unhallowed Methods in our
struggles for Truth; so no other than* a direct Opposition to
the Essentials of some fundamental Article *can warrant
Divisions, or refusals of Communion, on the account of mere
difference in the Faith, provided* no Assent to any real Error
is imposed on us as a Term of Union.

*It is too obvious to require Proof, that if a direct
Opposition to what is* not fundamental, *or to whatever*
remotely *belongs to that which is so; nay further, if opposing
by* denied Consequences *what is of the Essence of any
fundamental Article of Faith; be a warrant for* Separation *of
Ministers and Churches from each other, then the* instituted
Rules *of Christian Fellowship do not oblige us; the* approved
Instances *of Communion in the New-Testament-Churches
ought to be condemned; and all the Churches of Christ must
daily be more and more* rended *by Non-communion and
dividing Animosities, until the* Catholic Church *lose all shew
of* Unity, *or be reduced to a single Congregation, (and that
but for an uncertain moment,) even when vast numbers of*

Christian Societies *proclaim the advancement of our Saviour's conquest.*

Nor is their Folly less apparent, who (for excuse of this) surmise, that every Error *which they ought to rectify in themselves, and by just methods to reform in others, is a* Bar to Communion; *or yet, that* Separation *is one of those* just methods *in the case fore-mentioned, especially towards such over whom they pretend to no Authority. Oh when will men see, that* Christ's Royal Prerogative *is assumed, whenever* other Terms of, *or* Bars to Communion *are invented, than what He hath expressly made such, and that in a matter wherein his own Honour and his People's Interest are concerned, next to that of Union with himself!*

But alas! in contempt of Rules so necessary to the Churches Peace, many Ages are filled with Instances of assuming a right to account him for a Heathen, *who differs but in Trifles, and cannot pronounce their very* Phrases, *tho' scrupled because abused to support an Error, and the Truth designed by them is most expressly owned: A thing so thwarting a Christian Temper, that* Athanasius *and* Basil *profess they would break with none who refused the word* ομουσιος, *so they would by any words declare their soundness in the Doctrine of the* Trinity; *and yet that word had been adjusted, not by a few particular Authors, but by the great* Council of Nice, *in opposition to the Heresy of* Arius. *I scruple not to say, an* Antichristian *Spirit most effectually extinguisheth the like Moderation; and such Imposers, intrusted with the* Secular Sword, *would use it as they do their* Ecclesiastical, *however they condemn Severity while* themselves *are not the Persecutors.*

That there have been of late years great Divisions *among the* Dissenters, *is too publickly known: And I had rather share in the Imputation of an Accessary, than perpetuate them by the fullest Vindication; hoping that a calm Season will better fit all of us to reflect, and repent of our Faultiness, especially the* Unchristian *management of our Debates; for which, we have great reason to pray, God would not signally contend hereafter.*

But blessed be the Name of our God, that ere we be quite devoured by each other, *a fit Occasion is ministred for our healing; and tho' Self-preservation hath been my work ever since my temperate Confutation of Dr.* Crisp, *(and then too,) none will wonder I take hold of this Opportunity, to evidence that* further Contests *will be inexcusable. Nor is it a hard Province, when the* united Ministers, *and the* Congregational Brethren, *have so far acquitted themselves: The* first, *by sundry former Accounts (and now more enlarged, from any word in which I cannot suspect two will differ,) of their* Vindication *from* Errors *concerning the* Satisfaction *of* Christ, *and* Justification, *which are the only Points objected: The* last, *by their* Declaration against Antinomian Errors; *for which I am too thankful, to remark its Stings; and had it come out before my* Postscript, *I durst not have represented their Judgment by the Consequences of their Objections, (however natural,) as in some few things is done. That the* God of Peace *would give us Peace, is the unfeigned Prayer of*

Thy Servant in the Gospel, and Bro-
ther in the Kingdom and Pati-
ence of our Lord Jesus,
Daniel Williams.

Chap. I. The State of Truth and Error, (subscribed by near Fifty of us,) drawn up and published by Mr. Williams, *in a book called* Gospel-Truth stated and vindicated, *first printed in the Year* 1692.

Truth 1. It is *certain* from God's decree of election, that the Elect shall in time be justified, adopted, and saved *in the way* God hath appointed; and the whole meritorious cause and price of Justification, Adoption, and eternal Life, were perfect, when Christ *finished* the work of Satisfaction. Nevertheless, the Elect *remain* children of wrath, and subject to condemnation, *till* they are effectually called by the operation of the Spirit.

Error. The Elect are *at no time* of their lives under the wrath of God; nor are they subject to condemnation, if they should die *before* they believe; yea, when they are under the dominion of Sin, and in the practice of the grossest Villainies, they are *as much* the Sons of God, and justified, as the very Saints in Glory.

Truth 2. Tho' *our Sins* were imputed to Christ with respect to the *Guilt* thereof, so that he, by the Father's appointment, and. his own consent, became obliged, as Mediator, to bear the *Punishment* of our Iniquities; and he did bear those

Punishments to the *full Satisfaction of Justice*, and to our actual Remission when we believe; nevertheless, the *Filth* of our Sins was not laid upon Christ; nor can he be called the Transgressor, or was he in God's account the Blasphemer, Murtherer, &c.

Error. God did not only impute the Guilt, and lay the Punishment of the Sins of the Elect upon Christ; but he laid all the very Sins of the Elect upon Christ, and that, as to their *real Filthiness and Loathsomeness*; yea so, that Christ was *really* the Blasphemer, Murtherer, and Sinner, and so accounted by the Father.

Truth 3. The Atonement made by Christ, by the appointment of God, is that, *for which alone* the Elect are pardoned, when it is applied to them. But the Elect are not immediately pardoned upon Christ's being appointed to suffer for them, nor as soon as the Atonement was made; nor is that Act of laying Sins on Christ, God's forgiving Act, by which we are *personally discharged*.

Error. The very Act of God's laying Sins on Christ upon the Cross, is the very *actual discharge* of all the Elect from all their Sins.

Truth 4. An Elect person ceaseth not to be a Sinner, upon the laying of our Sins upon Christ; that is, he remains a Sinner, as to the *Guilt*, till he believes, if adult. He is a Sinner, as to the *Filth* of Sin, till he be sanctified. He is a Sinner, as to the charge of the sinful *Fact* he commits, and that even after Pardon and Sanctification. Nevertheless, he is free from the *Curse*, when he is pardoned; and shall be purged from all the Filth of Sin, when he is perfect in Holiness. And tho' Christ did bear the Punishment of our Iniquity, yet it never was Christ's Iniquity, but *ours*.

Error. The Elect upon the death of Christ ceased to be Sinners; and *ever since* their Sins are none of *their Sins*, but they are the Sins of *Christ*.

Truth 5. The *Obligation* of suffering for our Sins was upon Christ, from his undertaking the office of a Mediator, to the moment wherein he finished his satisfactory Atonement. The *Punishment* of our Sins lay upon Christ, from the first moment, to the last of his state of Humiliation.

Error. The time when our Sins were laid *actually* on Christ, was, when he was nailed to the Cross, and God actually forsook him; and they continued on him *till* his Resurrection.

Truth 6. Tho' God testified his threatened *Indignation* against Sin, in the awful Sufferings of Christ's Soul and Body in his Agony, and suspended those *delightful* Communications of the Divine Nature to the Human Nature of Christ, as to their wonted degrees; yet God was never *Separated* from Christ, much less during his Body's lying in the grave; neither was the Father ever displeased with Christ, and far less did he *abhor* him, because of the *Filthiness* of Sin upon him.

Error. Christ was on the account of the *Filthiness* of Sins, while they lay upon him, *separated* from God, *odious* to him, and even the Object of God's *Abhorrence*, and this to the time of his Resurrection.

Truth 7. The Mediatorial *Righteousness of Christ* is so imputed to true Believers, as that for the sake thereof they are pardoned and accepted unto Life eternal; it being reckoned to them, and *pleadable* by them for these uses, as if they had personally done and suffered what Christ did as Mediator *for them*; whereby they are delivered from the Curse, and no other Atonement nor meriting Price of saving Benefits can be demanded from them. Nevertheless, this Mediatorial Righteousness is not subjectively in them, nor is there a *Change of Person* betwixt them and Christ; neither are they *as righteous as he*, but there remain Spots and Blemishes in them, until Christ by his Spirit perfect that Holiness begun in all true Believers; which he will effect, before he brings them to Heaven. *See the 2d Truth; and note, it is only Dr. Crisp's Change of Person is denied, viz. a perfect Change which makes us as righteous as he, &c. but not Christ's dying in our stead, which in this Book is oft asserted.*

Error. Every Believer, or Elect person, is as righteous as Christ, and there is a *perfect Change* of Person and Condition betwixt Christ and the Elect; he was what we are, *viz.* as sinful as we; and we are what he was, *viz.* perfectly holy, and without spot or blemish.

Truth 8. I shall express it in the words of the *Assembly*: "The Grace of God is manifested in the *second Covenant*, in that he freely provideth, and offereth to Sinners a Mediator, and Life and Salvation by him; and requiring Faith as the *Condition* to interest them in him, promiseth and giveth his holy Spirit to all his Elect, to work in them that Faith, with all other saving Graces; and to enable them unto all Obedience, as the evidence of the truth of their Faith and Thankfulness to God, and as the way which he hath appointed them to Salvation." *Note, Reader, that these Divines do here join together the* Covenant of Redemption *with Christ, and the* Gospel-Covenant *whereby are dispensed to us the Benefits impetrated by Christ; which two distinguished would lead to clearer thoughts.*

Error. The *Covenant of Grace* hath *no Condition* to be performed on man's part, tho' in the strength of Christ: Neither is *Faith* itself the Condition of this Covenant; but all the saving benefits of this Covenant, are actually ours *before* we are born: Neither are we *required* so much as to believe, that we may come to have an Interest in the benefits of the Covenant.

Truth 9. I shall express this in the words of the *Assembly*, and *Congregational Elders* at the *Savoy*, of *saving Faith*: [Confess. & Decl. *chap.* xiv. a. 2.] "By this grace, a Christian *believeth* to be true whatever is revealed in the Word, for the authority of God speaking therein; and *acteth* differently upon that which *each* particular Passage thereof containeth; yielding Obedience to the Commands, trembling at the Threatnings, and embracing the Promises of God, for this life, and that which is to come. But the principal Acts of saving Faith, are *accepting, receiving,* and *resting* upon Christ alone for Justification, Sanctification, and eternal Life, by *virtue* of the Covenant of Grace."

Error. Saving *Faith* is nothing but our *Persuasion*, or absolute concluding within ourselves, that our Sins are pardoned, and that Christ is ours.

Truth 10. Christ is freely *offered* to be a Head and Saviour to the *vilest* Sinners, who will knowingly assent to the truth of the Gospel, and from a conviction of their Sin and Misery out of Christ are humbled, and *truly willing* to renounce all their Idols and Sins; and denying their own *carnal* Self and Merits, accept of Christ as offered in the Gospel; relying on him alone, for Justification, Sanctification, and eternal Life.

Error. Christ is offered to Blasphemers, Murtherers, and the worst of Sinners; that they, *remaining* ignorant, unconvinced, unhumbled, and resolved in their purpose to continue such, may be assured they have a full Interest in Christ; and this, by *only concluding* in their own minds upon this Offer, that Christ is theirs.

Truth 11. Every man is without Christ, or *not united* to Christ, until he be effectually called: But when by this Call the Spirit of God inclineth and enableth him willingly to accept of Christ as a Head and Saviour, a man becomes *united* to him, and a partaker of those Influences and Privileges which are peculiar to the members of the Lord Jesus.

Error. All the Elect are *actually united* to Christ, *before* they have the Spirit of Christ, or at all believe in him, even before they are born; yea, and against their Will.

Truth 12. Tho' *Faith* be no way a meritorious Cause of a Sinner's Justification, yet God hath promised to justify all such as truly believe; and requires Faith, as an indispensable qualification in all whom he will justify for Christ's merits; declaring, that Unbelief shall not only hinder men's *knowing* that they are justified, but that it is a bar to any person's *being* justified *while* he continues an Unbeliever.

Error. The *whole use* of Faith in Justification, is only to *manifest* that we were justified before; and *Faith* is no way necessary to bring a Sinner into a justified State, nor *at all useful* to that end.

In a Digression there about *Repentance*, is added,
Truth. Altho' neither Faith nor Repentance be any part of the meriting Righteousness *for which* we are justified; and the Habits of both are wrought at the same time, and included in the regenerating principle; and there must be an assenting act of Faith, before there be any exercise of true Repentance; and *Repentance*, as consisting in the fruits meet for it, *viz.* an external Reformation and a fruitful Life, must *follow Pardon*, as doth also an ingenuous Sorrow for Sin in the sense of Pardon: Nevertheless *Repentance*, as it consists in some degree of Humblings and Sorrow, from convictions of our lost State and the Evil of Sin, with a sincere purpose of Heart to turn from our Sin and Idols to God, is *absolutely necessary* in order to the forgiveness of Sin.

Error. Our Sins are forgiven *before* any Repentance; and Believers *ought not* to complain, or mourn, or sorrow for the Sins they have committed.

Truth 13. Tho' neither Holiness, sincere Obedience, or good Works, do make any *Atonement* for Sin; or are in the least the *meritorious Righteousness*, whereby Salvation is caused, or *for which* this, or any Blessing, becomes *due to us as of debt*: Yet as the Spirit of Christ freely worketh all Holiness in the Soul, and enableth us to sincere Obedience and good Works; so the Lord Jesus hath *of Grace*, and for his own Merits, promised to bring to Heaven such as are partakers of true Holiness, as perform this sincere Obedience, and do these good Works perseveringly; and appoints these as the way and means of a Believer's obtaining Salvation, and several other Blessings; *requiring* these as indispensable duties and qualifications of all such whom he will so save and bless, and *excluding* all that want or neglect them, or live under the power of what's contrary thereto, *viz.* Profaneness, Rebellion, and utter Unfruitfulness.

Error. Men have nothing to do *in order* to Salvation; nor is Sanctification a jot *the way* of any person to Heaven: Nor can the Graces or Duties of Believers, no, nor *Faith* itself, do them the *least Good*, or prevent the least Evil; nor are they of any use to their *Peace* or Comfort; yea, tho' Christ be explicitly owned, and they be done in the strength of the Spirit of God: And a Believer ought not to think, he is *more pleasing* to God by any Grace he acteth, or Good he doth; nor may men *expect any Good* to a Nation, by the Humiliation, earnest Prayer, or Reformation of a People.

Truth 14. Tho' we ought to intend *God's Glory* as our supream End in all our Duties, and to design therein the expressing our Love and *Gratitude* to God for his Benefits, with a great regard *to publick Good*: Yet we also lawfully may, and ought to strive after Grace, to grow in it, and to perform holy Duties and Services, with an *Eye to*, and *Concern for* our own spiritual and eternal Advantage.

Error. No man ought to propose to himself *any Advantage* by any religious Duty he performeth; nor ought he *in the least* to intend the Profit of his own Soul by any Christian Endeavours; it being vain and unlawful to do any thing with an Eye to *our spiritual* or *eternal Good*, tho' in *Subordination* to God's Glory in Christ.

Truth 15. The *ordinary way* whereby a man attaineth a well-grounded *Assurance*, is not by *immediate* objective Revelation, or an inward Voice saying, *Thy Sins are forgiven thee*: But when the Believer is *examining* his Heart and Life *by the Word*, the holy Spirit *enlightens* the mind there to discern Faith, and Love, and such other qualifications, which the Gospel declareth to be infallible *Signs* of Regeneration; and he adds such *power* to the Testimony of *Conscience*, for the truth and inbeing of these Graces, as begets in the Soul a joyful sense of its reconciled State, and some comfortable freedom from those Fears which accompany a doubting Christian: And according to the evidence of these Graces, *Assurance* is *ordinarily* strong or weak.

Error. Assurance is not attained by the *Evidence* of Scripture marks or *Signs* of Grace, or by the Spirit's *discovering* to us that he hath wrought in our Hearts any holy Qualifications: But *Assurance* comes *only* by an inward *Voice* of the Spirit, saying, *Thy Sins are forgiven thee*, and our believing *thereupon* that our Sins are forgiven.

Truth 16. The Sins of Believers have the *loathsomeness* of Sin adhering to them, which God *seeth*, and accounteth the *Committers* guilty thereby: And they ought to charge *themselves* therewith, so as to stir up themselves to Repentance, and renew their actings of Faith on Christ for Forgiveness. Nevertheless, they ought not thereby to fear their being *out of a justified State*, further than their Falls give them *just cause* of suspecting, that *Sin hath dominion* over them, and that their *first* believing on Christ was *not sincere*.

Error. God *seeth no Sin* in Believers, tho' he see the *Fact*; neither doth *he* charge them with any Sin; nor ought they to charge *themselves* with any Sin, nor be at all sad for them; nor confess, repent, or do any thing, as a *means* of their Pardon; no, nor in order to *assuring* themselves of Pardon, even when they commit Murther, Adultery, or the *grossest* Wickedness.

Truth 17. It is true of *Believers*, that if Sin should have *dominion over them*, they would thereby be subject to Condemnation: And tho' the Grace of God will *prevent* the dominion of Sin in every elect Believer, and so keep them from *eternal* Death: yet true Believers may by Sin bring *great hurt* upon themselves in Soul and Body, which they ought to *fear*; and they may expect a share in *national Judgments*, according as they have contributed to common Guilt.

Error. The *grossest* Sins that Believers can commit, cannot do them the *least harm*; neither ought they to *fear* the least hurt by their own Sins, nor by *national Sins*; yea, tho' themselves have had a hand therein.

Truth 18. Tho' God is not so *angry* with his people for their Sins, as to cast them out of his *Covenant-favour*; yet by their Sins he is so *displeased*, as for them to *correct* his Children, tho' he speaks *Instructions* by his Rebukes.

Error. None of the Afflictions of Believers have in them the least of God's *Displeasure* against their persons for their Sins.

Truth 19. Tho' the present sincere *Holiness* of Believers be not *perfect*, according to the *Precepts* of the Word; nor *valuable* by the *Sanction* of the Law of Innocency; nor any *Atonement* for our defects; and we *still need* forgiveness, and the Merits of Christ, for *Acceptance* thereof: Yet as far as it prevails, it's lovely in itself, and pleasing to God, and is not *Dung* or *Filth*.

Error. The *greatest Holiness* in Believers, tho' wrought in them by the *Holy Ghost*, is mere *Dung*, Rottenness, and Filthiness, as *in them*.

Truth 20. GOSPEL-PREACHING is, when the Messengers of Christ do publish to fallen Sinners the good news of Salvation by Christ, to be *obtained* in the way which he hath appointed in his Word; *freely* offering Salvation on his Terms; earnestly persuading and commanding men in the name of Christ, to comply with those Terms, as ever they would escape the Misery they are under, and possess the Benefits he hath purchased; directing all to look to him for *Strength*, and to acknowledge him as the only Mediator, and his Obedience and Sufferings as the *sole Atonement* for Sin, and *meriting Cause* of all Blessings; instructing them in all revealed Truth, and by Gospel-motives urging them to obey the whole Will of God, as a Rule of Duty, but especially to be sincere and upright, pressing after Perfection.

Error. GOSPEL-PREACHING is, to teach men, they were *as much* pardoned, and as acceptable to God always, as when they are regenerate; and while they were ungodly, they had *the same Interest* in God and Christ as when they believe; neither can Sin any way hinder their Salvation, or their Peace; nor have they any thing to do to further either of them, Christ having done all for them, and given himself to them, *before* any holy qualification or endeavour.

Truth 21. LEGAL-PREACHING is, to preach the Law as a Covenant of innocency, or *of works*; or to preach the *Mosaick* or *Jewish* Covenant of peculiarity: But it is not *Legal Preaching*, to require and persuade to faith, holiness, or duties, by Promises and Threatnings, according to the *Grace of the Gospel*, and to direct Men to *fear and hope* accordingly.

Error. LEGAL-PREACHING is, to call People to act any Grace, or do any Duty, as a required *means* of Salvation or inward Peace; or to *threaten* them with Death or any Affliction, to cause *Fear*, if they commit the grossest Sins, and backslide, and fall away; or to *promise* them any Blessing upon their Obedience to the Commandments of Christ; or to urge the *Threatnings*, to persuade Sinners to believe and repent.

THE ORACLES OF REASON
Charles Blount

To the most Ingenuous and Learned Dr. Sydnham *at his House near the* Pestle *and* Mortar *in the* Pall Mall

Sir,
The last time I had the happiness of your Company, it was your Request that I would help you to a sight of the Deists Arguments, which I told you, I had sometimes by me, but then had lent them out, they are now return'd me again, and according to my promise I have herewith sent them to you. Whereby, you'll only find, that human Reason like a Pitcher with two Ears, may be taken on either side. However, undoubtedly in our Travels to the other World the common Road is the safest; and tho' Deism is a good manuring of a Man's Conscience, yet certainly if sowed with Christianity, it will produce the most profitable Crop. Pardon the hast of
Sir,

Rolleston, May 14th   Your most Obliged Friend
1686.   and Faithful Servant,
C. BLOUNT.

A SUMMARY ACCOUNT OF THE DEISTS RELIGION

Chap. I. *The Deists Opinion of God.*
Whatsoever is Adorable, Amiable, and Imitable by Mankind, is in one Supream infinite and perfect Being: *Satis est nobis Deus unus.*

Chap. II. *Concerning the Manner of Worshipping God.*
First, Negatively, it is not to be by an Image; for the first Being is not sensible, but intelligible: *Pinge sonum*, puts us upon an impossibility; no more can an infinite mind be represented in matter.
    Secondly, Nor by Sacrifice; for *Sponsio non valet ut alter pro altero puniatur*: However, no such *Sponsio* can be made with a

bruit Creature; nor if God loves himself, as he is the highest Good, can any External Rite, or Worship re-instate the Creature, after sin, in his favour, but only Repentance, and Obedience for the future, ending in an Assimulation to himself, as he is the highest Good: And this is the first Error in all particular Religions, that external things or bare Opinions of the Mind, can after sin propitiate God. Hereby particular Legislators have endeared themselves and flattered their Proselytes into good Opinions of them, and Mankind willingly submitted to the Cheat; *Enim facilius est superstitiose, quam juste vivere.*

Thirdly. Not by a Mediator; for, 1*st*, It is unnecessary, *Misericordia Dei* being *sufficiens Justitiæ suæ.* 2*ly*, God must appoint this Mediator, and so was really reconciled to the World before. And 3*ly*, A Mediator derogates from the infinite mercy of God, equally as an Image doth from his *Spiritualitie* and *Infinitie.*

Secondly, Positively, by an inviolable adherence in our lives to all the things φυσ{ει} δικαία, by an imitation of God in all his imitable Perfections, especially his Goodness, and believing magnificently of it.

Chap. III. *Of Punishments after this Life.*
A Man that is endued with the same Vertues we have before mentioned, need not fear to trust his Soul with God after death: For first, no Creature could be made with a malevolent intent, the first Good who is also the first Principle of all Beings hath but one Affection or Property, and that is Love; which was long before there was any such thing as Sin. 2*dly*, At death he goes to God, one and the same being, who in his own nature for the Sins of the Penitent hath as well an inclination to Pity as Justice, and there is nothing dreadful in the whole Nature of God, but his Justice, no Attribute else being terrible. 3*dly*, Infinite Power is ever safe and need not revenge for self preservation. 4*thly*, However *Verisimile est, similem Deo a Deo non negligi.*

Chap. IV. *The Probability of such a Deist's Salvation before the credulous and ill-living Papists.*
I. To be sure he is no Idolator. The *Jew* and the *Mahometan* accuse the Christians of Idolatry, the Reform'd Churches, the *Roman*, the *Socinian* the other Reformed Churches, the *Deists* the *Socinian* for his *Deus satius*; but none can accuse the *Deist*

of Idolatry, for he only acknowledges one Supream Everlasting God, and thinks magnificently of him.

2dly, The Morality in Religion is above the Mystery in it; for,

I. The Universal sense of Mankind in the Friendships Men make, sheweth this; for who does not value good Nature, Sincerity and Fidelity in a Friend, before subtilty of Understanding; *& Religio & quædam, cum Deo amicitia*: An unity of nature and will with God, that is the Root of the Dearest Friendships. Then, *2dly*, it is an everlasting Rule that runs through all Beings, *Simile a simili amatur*, God cannot love what is unlike him. Now, *3dly*, here lies our trial, here is the scene of our obedience, and here are our conflicts with our Passions; if this be true, then the credulous Christian that believes Orthodoxly, but lives ill, is not safe.

3dly, If the *Deist* errs, he errs not like a fool, but *secundam Verbum*, after enquiry, and if he be sincere in his Principles, he can when dying appeal to God, *Te, bone Deus, quæsivi per omnia.*

Notæ Aliquot.

1. The Grand *Arcanum* of Religion among the *Pythagoreans* was, that the Object of Divine Worship is one, and invisible; *Plutarch* cites this in the Life of *Numa*, as the Dogma of *Pythagoras*, and accordingly his Followers used no Images in their Worships.

2. The Heathens, notwithstanding their particular and Topical Deities, acknowledged one supream God, not *Jupiter* of *Crete*, but the Father of Gods and Men: Only they said this Supream God being of so high a nature, and there being other intermediate Beings betwixt God and Mankind, they were to address themselves to them as Mediators to carry up their Prayers, and bring down his Blessings; so as the Opinion of the necessity of a Mediator was the foundation of the Heathen Idolatry, they could not go to the Fountain of Good it self. The Popish Religion stands on the same foundation; whereas the greatest Goodness is the most accessible; which shews that Popery was a Religion accommodated to the Sentiments of Mankind from precedent Religions, and not to infallible Reason drawn from the eternal respects of things. And Reason being the first relation of God, is first to be believed, not depending on doubtful fact without us, but full of its own light shining always in us.

3dly, It was the common sense of the wisest Philosophers, that things were good antecedent to all humane Compacts; and this Opinion, *Pyrrho* in *Sextus Empericus* argues against: Also Mr. *Hobbs* hath of late revived in the World *Pyrrho*'s Doctrin, tho' without reason; for as there are immediate Propositions, to which the understanding (*sine discursu*) assents, as soon as proposed, so are there things good and just which they will at first view, without deliberation, approve of and chose also, (*viz.*) the Veneration of an Almighty invisible Being, referring of our selves to him, with a (*fiat voluntas tua*) abhorrence of breach of contract with man, of a lye, as a violation of Truth; so as in my judgment, there is a sanction arising from the nature of things, before any Law declared amongst men: That there is a *generosum honestum* hid in all our Souls is plain from the *Epicurean* Deists themselves, for they labour to have their Vices imputed rather to a Superiority of their reason above that of others, than to a servitude of their reason to their own passions; which shews Vice is naturally esteemed a base and low thing. This appears from the Legislators of the World, as *Numa, Zamolxis, &c. A Jove Principium*; there they did begin, well knowing human Compacts were too weak to balance and restrain the passions of human nature; Offenders presuming to escape unpunished, and rightly enough were all Laws but human compacts. In two cases which ordinarily happen in human life, (*viz.*) when the fact is unevident, or when the Magistrate is too weak to punish. Hence is *Grotius* his description of the Law of Nature, *Lex est*, &c. The Law is a combination of the Vertuous to punish the Vicious. Here the Obligation must be lodged, and this appears in the Satyrs of the Poets, in the complaints of the Philosophers, and in the several ages of the World against the manners of Mankind; for without Vertue God is only a name amongst men, and no man without it can hope well of God.

4*ly*, I remember *Plutarch* speaking of *Aristides*'s Justice, complains thus, Men have commonly three Affections or Opinions of the Gods; the first that they think them blessed; the second, that they fear them; and the third, that they reverence them: They account them blessed, because they're Immortal; they fear them, because of their Power, and reverence them because of their Justice; yet of these three, men most desire Immortality, whereof our nature is uncapable: Also Power which dependeth upon fortune, the only Divinity man is capable of, they neglect, and undervalue, in that God is inimitable to us: And this is the difference betwixt Corporeal and intellectual Love. If the object of my Love be external beauty, a person or a face, that I cannot imitate; but if an Idea of Perfection, and Intellectual Beauty, that I may be assimilated to, and partake of. Besides the soul in Intellectual love suffers not with the object it loves, as in a Corporeal love it doth; because that its object the Soveraign God never suffers; and this is the chief true conversion which frees us from all evils, the *Mors Philosophorum*, which *Porphery* speaks of. Others are rolled as upon Cylinders from one appearance of Good to another, and live in a perpetual storm; for 'tis not the change but the choice of our Object that maks us happy.

5ly. Antoninus says, if the question be put to us, what is thy art or profession, our Answer should be, to be good; as God made the world; not for his own good (who was infinitely happy before) but for his Creatures good: So our Religion must necessarily be this, to do good to his Creatures; for therein we concur with the Will of God, and it is a grand truth, very proper for the Immortal Deist to consider, that all vice and wickedness is but a denial and disowning of God, to be the Supreme, Infinite Good; my Pride denies he has ever been good to me; my lust believes the low and base matter can with its pleasures make me happier than he can with all his goodness; my envy would not have him good to others, but would have him contract and shrink up himself from his Creatures; and lastly, my malice and revenge hates his Creatures, if they be but once imagined my Enemies, and would destroy those whom his goodness first and would have still to exist.

6ly and Lastly, *Campanella* in his Book *De Sensu Rerum*, observes *Aristotelem dicentem Deum non habere cum hominibus amicitiam (quoniam non est proportio finiti ad infinitum) Majestatem non bonitatem Dei considerasse.*

AN APOLOGY FOR WRITING AGAINST SOCINIANS, IN DEFENCE OF THE DOCTRINES OF THE HOLY TRINITY AND INCARNATION

William Sherlock

After a long silence, and patient expectation what *the Learned Writers of some Controversies at present* (as a late Author calls them) would bring forth, I intend by the *Assistance of the Holy Trinity, and the Incarnate Jesus*, whose Blessing I most earnestly Implore, to resume the *Defence of the Catholick Faith*; which I shall Publish in some few short Treatises, as I can find Leisure for it, that I may not discourage my Readers by too Voluminous a Work.

But before I venture to Dispute these matters any farther, it is necessary to make some Apology for Disputing; which is thought very Unchristian and Uncharitable, and of dangerous Consequence, especially when we undertake the Defence of the Fundamentals of our Faith, against the rude and insolent Assaults of Hereticks.

Sometime since, *A Melancholy Stander-by* would be a *Stander-by* no longer, but interposed *An Earnest and Compassionate Suit for Forbearance, to the Learned Writers of some Controversies at present*. These *Learned Writers of Controversy* are the *Socinians*, who ridiculed without any Learning or Common Sense, *the* Athanasian *Creed, and the Doctrines of the Trinity and Incarnation*: The *Forbearance* he desires, is, That no body should write against them; though Dr. *Wallis* and my self are more immediately concerned in this *Suit*.

Who this *Melancholy Stander-by* is, I shall not enquire, for my Controversy is not with Men, but with Doctrines; and I know by experience, that common fame is not always to be trusted, much less suspicions; but if he be a Divine of the Church of *England*, it seems very strange, that he should profess himself a *Stander-by*, when the Fundamentals of the Christian Faith are in question; and a *Melancholy* Stander-by to see some others undertake the Defence of it. I confess I am always very jealous of men, who are so very Tender on the wrong side; for observe it when you will, their Tenderness is always owing to their Inclination. But to defend our selves, let us briefly consider what he says.

[Earnest Suit, p. 1.] He thinks, *The open Dissentions of its Professors a great blemish to the Reformation:* That is, that it is a great blemish for any men openly to defend the true Faith, which others openly oppose, or secretly undermine; but certainly it would be a greater blemish to the *Reformation*, to have *Old Heresies* revived, and the true *Ancient Catholick Faith* scorned, and no body appear in the Defence of it. But we know his mind, That it is for the honour of the *Reformation* not to Dispute, though it be for the most Important Truths. Surely our *Reformers* were not so much against *Disputing*.

But if these Dissentions be so great a blemish to the *Reformation*, whose Fault is it? Theirs who dissent from the Truth, or theirs who defend it? This is a very plain case; for no body would oppose the Truth, if no body taught it: *The urging too strict an Union* in matters of Faith, *begets dissentions*: That is, to require an open and undisguised Profession of our Baptismal Faith in *Father, Son, and Holy Ghost*, as the Terms of Christian Communion, is the Criminal Cause of our Dissentions. Well: What shall we do then? Renounce the Faith of the Trinity, for the sake of Peace? This he dares not say, for that would pull off his disguise; but *Christianity must be left in that Latitude and Simplicity wherein it was delivered by our Lord and his Apostles* [P. 2.]. This had been a good Proposal, would he have told us what this *Latitude* and *Simplicity* is; for I am for no other Faith than what Christ and his Apostles taught: But I would gladly know what he means by the *Latitude* of Faith: For if the Christian Faith be such a broad Faith, must we not believe the whole breadth of it? Or has Christ and his Apostles left it at liberty to believe what we like, and to let the rest alone? To believe that *Father, Son, and Holy Ghost are One Supreme Eternal God*; or to believe that the *Father alone is the True God, the Son a mere Man, and the Holy Ghost nothing but a Divine Inspiration?* To believe that the *Eternal Word* was *made Flesh*; or that Christ was no more than a Man, who had no being before he was born of the Virgin *Mary*? He can mean nothing else by this *Latitude* of Faith, but that Christ and his Apostles have left these matters so ambiguous and undetermined, that we may believe what we please; and then indeed those do very ill, who dispute these matters: But this is such a breadth as had no depth; for such a Faith as this can have no foundation. Can we certainly learn from Scripture, Whether Christ be a *God Incarnate*, or a *mere Man*? If we cannot, Why should we believe either? If we can, then one is true, and the other false; and then there is no *Latitude* in Faith, unless Christ and his Apostles have left it indifferent, whether we believe what is true, or what is false; what they have taught us, or what we like better our selves.

In the same manner he leaves us to guess what he means by the *Simplicity* of the Faith. He is very angry with the *School-Doctors, as worse enemies to Christianity, than either Heathen Philosophers, or persecuting Emperors* [P. 2.]. Pray what hurt have they done? I suppose he means the Corruption of Christianity with those barbarous Terms of *Person, Nature, Essence, Subsistence, Consubstantiality,* &c. which will not suffer *Hereticks* to lye concealed under Scripture-Phrases: But why must the *Schoolmen* bear all the blame of this? Why does he not accuse the *Ancient Fathers and Councils*, from whom the *Schoolmen* learnt these Terms? Why does he let St. *Austin* escape, from whom the *Master of the Sentences* borrowed most of his Distinctions and Subtilties? But suppose these *Unlucky Wits* had used some new Terms, have they taught any new Faith about the *Trinity in Unity*, which the *Catholick Church* did not teach? And if they have only guarded the Christian Faith with a hedge of Thorns, which disguised Hereticks cannot break through, Is this *to wound Christianity in its very Vitals*? No, no: They will only prick the fingers of Hereticks, and secure Christianity from being wounded; and this is one great Cause why some men are so angry with the *School-Doctors*; tho the more general Cause is, because they have not Industry enough to read or understand them.

He says, *The first Reformers complained of this, and desired a purer and more spiritual sort of Divinity*. What? With respect to the Doctrine of the *Trinity and Incarnation*?

What *purer Reformers* were these? I'm sure not our *English* Reformers, whom he censures for *retaining Scholastick cramping Terms in their Publick Prayers*: He means the beginning of our Litany: *O God the Father of Heaven: O God the Son, Redeemer of the World: O God the Holy Ghost, proceeding from the Father and the Son: O Holy, Blessed, and Glorious Trinity, Three Persons and One God*: These are his *Scholastick, Cramping Terms*, which he would fling out of our Liturgy, when the reason of such blessed *Alterations* comes. I hope those Excellent Persons among us, who, I doubt not, for better Reasons did not long since think of some Alterations, will consider what a foul Imputation this is upon such a Design, when such a person shall publickly declare, That they ought to Alter and Reform the Doctrine of the Trinity out of our Prayers.

But the whole Mystery of this *Latitude and Simplicity* of Faith which he pleads for, is that plausible Project (which has been so much talked of of late) to confine our selves to *Scripture Terms and Phrases*; to use none but *Scripture Words* in our Creeds and Prayers, without any Explication in what sense those words are to be understood [P. 3.]: As he tells us *Certainly we may Worship God right well, yea, most acceptably, in words of his own Stamp and Coinage*. Now at the first Proposal few men would suspect, that there should be any hurt in this; though it would make one suspect some secret in it, to consider that Hereticks were the first Proposers in it, and that Orthodox Christians rejected it. The *Arians* objected this against the *Homoousion*, or *the Son's being of the same Substance with the Father*, that it was an Unscriptural Word; but the *Nicene Fathers* did not think this a good reason to lay it aside: For what reason can there be to reject any words, which we can prove to express the true sense of Scripture, though they are not found there? For must we believe the Words or the Sense of Scripture? And what reason then can any man have to reject the Words, though they be no Scripture-Words, if he believes the Sense contained in them to be the sense of Scripture? The *Homoiousion*, or *that the Son had a Nature like the Father's, tho not the same*, was no more a Scripture-Word, than the *Homoousion*; and yet the *Arians* did not dislike that, because it was no Scripture-Word; nor are the *Socinians* angry at any man who says, That Christ is but *a meer man, who had no Being before he was born of the Virgin* Mary; tho these words are no where in Scripture: And is it not strange, that a man who heartily believes, or at least pretends to believe, that *Father, Son, and Holy Ghost are One Eternal God,* should be angry with a *Trinity in Unity,* or *Three Persons and one God,* which do as aptly express the Faith which he professes, as any Words he can think of?

It is very odd to be zealous for Scripture Words without the Scripture Sense. If the Scripture have any determined Sense, then that which is the true Sense of Scripture, is the true Faith; and if we must *contend earnestly for the true Faith,* we must contend for the true Sense of Scripture, and not merely for its Words; and when Hereticks have used their utmost art to make the Words of Scripture signifie what they please, is it not necessary to fix their true Sense, and to express that Sense in such other Words as Hereticks cannot pervert?

There are but few words in common speech, but what are sometimes differently used, in a *Proper* or *Metaphorical,* a *Large* or a *Limited* Sense; and all wise and honest men easily understand from the circumstances of the place, in what sense they are used; but if men be perverse, they may expound words *properly* when they are used *metaphorically,* or *metaphorically* when they are used *properly;* and there is no confuting them from the bare signification of the word, because it may be, and oftentimes is used both ways; and therefore in such cases we must consider the Circumstances of the Text, and compare it with Parallel Texts, to find out in what sense the word is there used; and when we have found it, it is reasonable and necessary to express the true Christian Faith, not merely in Scripture words, which are abused and perverted by Hereticks, but in such other words, if we can find any such, as express the true sense in which the Scripture-words are used, and in which all Christians must understand them, who will retain the Purity of the Christian Faith. We do not hereby alter the Christian Faith, nor require them to believe any thing more than what the Scripture teaches, tho we require them to profess their Faith in other words, which are not indeed in Scripture, but express the true and determined sense of Scripture words. And this is all the *Latitude of Faith* which this *Stander-by* so tragically complains we have destroyed, *viz.* That we have brought the Scripture words to a fixt and determined sense, that

Hereticks can no longer conceal themselves in a *Latitude* of expression, nor spread their Heresies in Scripture words, with a Traditionary Sense and Comment of their own.

I would ask any man who talks at this rate about a *Latitude of Faith*, Whether there be any more than One True Christian Faith? And whether Christ and his Apostles intended to teach any more? Or whether they did not intend, That all Christians should be obliged to believe this One Faith? If this be granted, there can be no more Latitude in the Faith, than there is in a Unit; and if they taught but One Faith, they must intend that their words should signifie but that one Faith; and then there can be no *Intentional Latitude* in their words neither; and what Crime then is the Church guilty of, if she teach the true Christian Faith, that she teaches it in such words as have no Latitude, no Ambiguity of Sense, which Hereticks may deny if they please, but which they can't corrupt in favour of their Heresies, as they do Scripture words?

It is an amazing thing to me, that any man who has any Zeal, any Concernment for the true Christian Faith, who does not think it perfectly indifferent what we believe, or whether we believe any thing or not, should judge it for the advantage of Christianity, and a proper Expedient for the Peace of the Church, for all men to agree in the same Scripture words, and understand them in what sense they please; tho one believes Christ to be the Eternal Son of God, and another to be but a mere man; which it seems has no great hurt in it, if they do but agree in the same words: But if the Faith be so indifferent, I cannot imagine why we should quarrel about Words; the fairer and honester Proposal is, That every man should believe as he pleases, and no man concern himself to confute Heresies, or to divide the Church with Disputes; which is the true Latitude our Author seems to aim at; and then he may believe as he pleases too.

But pray, why should we not write against the *Socinians*? Especially when they are the Aggressors, and without any provocation publish and disperse the most impudent and scandalous Libels against the Christian Faith. He will give us some very wise Reasons for this by and by, when he comes to be *plain* and *succinct*; in the mean time we must take such as we can meet with.

He is afraid people should lose all Reverence for the *Litany*, should we go on to vindicate the Doctrine of the

Trinity in Unity [P. 3.]: I should not easily have apprehended this, and possibly some of the *common people* might have been as dull as my self, had he not taken care before he parted, for fear no body else should observe it, to teach people to ridicule the Trinity in their Prayers. Dr. *Wallis* would not undertake to say what a Divine *Person* signifies, as distinguished from *Nature and Essence*, only says, a *Person* is *somewhat*, but the *True Notion* of a *Person* he does not know: This Author commends this as *ever held to by all Learned Trinitarians*; for indeed all the Doctor meant by his *somewhat* is, That Three *Persons* signify Three *Real Subsistences*, and are *Real Things*, not a *Sabellian Trinity of mere Names*. And yet in the very next Page he teaches his Readers to ridicule the Litany with the Doctors *somewhats: O Holy, Blessed, and Glorious Trinity, Three Somewhats, and One God, have Mercy on us, &c.* [P. 16.]. Was there ever any thing more Senseless, or more Phophane! That because the Doctor would not undertake to define a *Person*, but only asserted in general, That a Divine Person was *somewhat*, or some Real Being, in opposition to a mere Nominal Difference and Distinction; therefore in our Prayers we may as well call the Three Divine Persons, Father, Son, and Holy Ghost, *Three somewhats. Nobis non licet esse tam disertis.* I am sure he has reason heartily to pray, That these *Three somewhats*, as he prophanely calls them, *would have Mercy on him.*

In the next place he says [P. 3.], *He is well assured, that the late* (Socinian) *Pamphlets would have died away, or have been now in a few mens hands, had not divers persons taken on them the labour to confute them.* But did his *Socinian* Friends, who were such busie Factors for the Cause, tell him so? Did they print them, that no body might read them? Were they not dispersed in every Corner, and boasted of in every Coffee-house, before any Answer appeared? However, were it so, is there no regard to be had to Hereticks themselves? And is it not better that such Pamphlets should be in an hundred hands with an Answer, than in five hands without one? I should think it at any time a good reward for all the labour of confuting, to rescue or preserve a very few from such fatal Errors; which I doubt not but is a very acceptable service to that *Merciful Shepherd*, who was so careful to seek one lost and straggling Sheep. Heresies and Vices dye by being neglected, just as Weeds do; for we know the Parable, That *the Devil sows his tares, while men sleep.* But this is no new Charge; the good Bishop of *Alexandria* met with the same Censures for his Zeal against *Arius*; for it seems that Heresie would have died too, if it had not been opposed. I doubt this Author judges of other mens Zeal for Heresy, by his own Zeal for the Truth, which wants a little rubbing and chafing to bring it to life; but Heresy is all flame and spirit, will blow and kindle it self, if it be not quenched.

But yet if what he says be true, That by our unskilful way of confuting Heresie, we *run into those very Absurdities which our Adversaries would reduce us to*; This I confess is a very great fault, and when he shews me any of those Absurdities, I will thankfully correct them; for all the Obloquies in the world will never make me blush to recant an Error: But before he pretends to that, I must desire him, that he would first read my Book, which I know some men censure without reading it. Such general Accusations are very spiteful, and commonly have a mixture of spite both against the Cause, and against the Person.

His next Argument is very observable: We must not dispute now against *Socinians*, because *these Controversies* about the Trinity *have been above Thirteen hundred years ago determined by two general Councils* (*the* Nicene, *and first* Constantinopolitan), which are owned by our Church, and their Creeds received into our Liturgy. *Ergo*, we must not defend this Faith against Hereticks, because it is the Faith of two General Councils which are owned by our Church. Did *Athanasius* think this a good Argument against Writing and Disputing against the *Arians*, after the *Council of Nice* had condemned *Arius* and his Doctrines? Did St. *Basil, Gregory Nazianzen, Nyssen*, St. *Chrysostom*, St. *Jerom*, St. *Austin*, think this a good Argument, who wrote so largely against these Heresies, which former Councils had condemned? But this Author thinks the best way is to *let the Matter stand upon this bottom of Authority*; that is, let Hereticks ridicule our Faith as much as they please, we must make them no other answer, but that this is the Faith of the *Nicene* and *Constantinopolitan* Councils, and the Faith of the *Church of England*. And can he intend this for any more than a Jest, when he knows how *Socinians* despise the determinations of Councils, and particularly with what scorn they treat the *Nicene Fathers*? Is this an Age to resolve our Faith into *Church Authority*? Or would he himself believe such absurd Doctrines as they represent the *Trinity in Unity* to be, merely upon *Church Authority*? For my part I declare I would not. I greatly value the Authority of those Ancient Councils, as credible Witnesses of the *Traditionary* Sense of the Church before those Controversies were started; but were not these Doctrines taught in Scripture, were they manifestly repugnant to the plain and evident Principles of Reason, all the Councils in the World should never reconcile me to them, no more than they should to the Doctrine of *Transubstantiation*. And therefore methinks he might have at least allowed us to have challenged the Scriptures as well as General Councils on our side; and to have vindicated our Faith from all pretended absurdities and contradictions to Reason. But would any man of common sense, who had not intended to expose the Faith of the Holy Trinity, have told the world at this time of day, That we have no other safe and sure bottom for our Faith, but only the Authority of General Councils? Nay, That the Council of *Nice* it self, on whose Authority it must rest, had little else themselves for their Determinations but only Authority, That *it was Authority chiefly carried the Point*. And thus for fear we should have believed too much upon the Authority of Councils, which is the only bottom he will allow our Faith, he gives them a secret stab himself, and makes their Authority ridiculous. That the several Bishops declared, what Faith had been taught and received in their Churches is true; That this Authority *chiefly* carried the Point, is false: *Athanasius* grew famous in the Council for his learned and subtile Disputations, which confounded the *Arians*; and what Arguments he chiefly relied on, we may see in his Works: And whoever does but look into the *Fathers*, who wrote against the *Arians* in those days, will find that their Faith was resolved into Scripture and Reason, and not meerly or *chiefly* into Authority.

And thus he comes to be *Plain* and *Succinct*, and tells us [P. 5.], that *of all Controversies we can touch upon at present, this of the Trinity is the most unreasonable, the most dangerous, and so the most unseasonable.*

It is the most *Unreasonable: I. Because it is on all hands confess'd, the Deity is Infinite, Unsearchable, Incomprehensible; and yet every one who pretends to Write plainer than another on this controversy, professes to make all Comprehensible and easy.*

I perceive he is well versed in Mr. *Hobbs*'s Divinity; though I can discover no marks of his skill in Fathers and Councils. For this was Mr. *Hobbs*'s reason, why we should not pretend to know any thing of God, nor inquire after his Attributes, because he has but one Attribute, which is, that he is *Incomprehensible*; and as this Author argues, *It is a small favour to request of Persons of Learning, that they should be consistent with, and not contradict themselves*: that is, That they would not pretend to know any thing of God, whom they acknowledge to be *Incomprehensible*, which is to pretend to know, what they confess cannot be known. Now I desire to know, Whether we may Dispute about the Being and Nature of God, and his essential Attributes and Perfections: and vindicate the Notion of a Deity from those *Impossibilities*, *Inconsistencies*, *Absurdities*, which some *Atheistical Philosophers* charge on it, notwithstanding that we confess God to be *Incomprehensible*? And if the Incomprehensibility of the Divine Nature does not signifie, that we can know nothing of God, and must inquire nothing about him; the Trinity of Divine Persons is as proper an object of our Faith, and modest Inquiries, as the Unity of the Divine Essence, for they are both Incomprehensible. And to say, That *every one who pretends to write plainer than another on this Controversy, professes to make all comprehensible and easy*, may with equal Truth and Authority be charg'd on all those who undertake to vindicate the Notion and Idea of a God, or to explain any of the Divine Attributes and Perfections. A finite mind cannot comprehend what is infinite; but yet one man may have a truer and more perfect Notion of the Nature and Attributes of God than another: God is Incomprehensible in Heaven as well as on Earth, and yet Angels and Glorified Spirits know God after another manner than we do. There must be infinite degrees of knowledge, when the object is infinite; and every new degree is more perfect than that below it; and yet no Creature can attain the highest degree of all, which is a perfect comprehension: So that the knowledge of God may increase every day, and men may Write plainer about these matters every day, without pretending to make all that is in God, even a Trinity in Unity, *comprehensible and easy*.

This is a spiteful and scandalous imputation, and is intended to represent all those who undertake to write about the Trinity, and to vindicate the Primitive Faith of the Church from the scorn and contempt of Hereticks, as a company of vain-conceited, presuming, but ignorant Scriblers; who pretend to make the *Incomprehensible* Nature of God, *comprehensible and easy*. But the comfort is, we have so good Company, that we are able to bear this Charge without blushing; even General Councils, and those great Lights of the Church, *Athanasius*, St. *Hillary*, St. *Basil*, the *Gregories*, St. *Chrysostom*, St. *Austin*, and many others, besides all those who in all succeeding Ages to this day, have with equal Zeal and Learning defended the same Cause; and yet never profess'd to make *all comprehensible and easy*. All that any man pretends to in vindicating the Doctrine of the Trinity, is to prove that this Faith is taught in Scripture, and that it contains no such Absurdities and Contradictions, as should force a Wise man to reject it, and either to reject the Scriptures for its sake, or to put some strained and unnatural senses on Scripture to reconcile it to the Principles of Reason; and this, I hope, may be done by those, who yet acknowledge the Divine Nature, and the Trinity in Unity to be Incomprehensible.

But here he had a very fair opportunity, had he thought fit to take it, to correct the Insolence and Presumption of his *Learned Writers of Controversy*; who will not allow the Divine Nature to be *Incomprehensible*, and will not believe God himself concerning his own Nature, beyond what their Reason can conceive and comprehend: Who deny *Prescience* for the same Reason, that they deny the *Trinity*, because they can't conceive it, nor reconcile it with the liberty of Human Actions; and for the same reason may deny all the Attributes of God, which have something in them beyond what we can conceive: especially an Eternity without beginning, and without Succession, which is chargeable with more Absurdities and Contradictions, than the Trinity it self: For a duration, which can't be measured; and an eternal duration, which can be measured; and a Succession without a Beginning, a Second or Third without a First, are unconceivable to us, and look like very plain and irreconcilable Contradictions. This is the very use of the *Incomprehensibility* of the Divine Nature; not to stop all Enquiries after God, nor to discourage our Studies of the Divine Nature and Perfections: for we may know a great deal, and may every day increase our knowledge of what is Incomprehensible, tho we cannot know it all; but to check the presumption of some vain Pretenders to Reason, who will not own a God, nor believe any thing of God, which their Reason cannot comprehend; which must not only make them Hereticks, but, if pursued to its just Consequences, must make them Atheists, or make such a God, as no body will own, or worship, but themselves, a God *adequate and commensurate to their Understandings*, which must be *a little, finite, comprehensible God*.

In the next place, to prove how unreasonable it is to Dispute in Vindication of the Trinity, he observes again, That *this Matter has been sufficiently determined by due Authority*: but having answered this once, I see no need to answer it again.

To back this he adds, That *the present issue shews, that in this World it never will be better understood*: for it seems, as he says, *The Master of the Sentences*, and some Modern Writers, have made very sad work of it. And yet he does not seem to be very intimately acquainted with *the Master of the Sentences*, nor some of these Modern Writers. But all that he means is, that no body can say any thing to the purpose of so absurd a Doctrine, as *a Trinity in Unity*; and therefore he plainly adds, *The more Men draw the disputacious Saw, the more perplexed and intricate the Question is*; and therefore the only secure way is, to leave off disputing for the Trinity, and let *Socinians* Dispute against it by themselves. But such Stuff as this, deserves another sort of Answer than I can give it.

But he concludes this Argument of *Unreasonableness* very remarkably [P. 7.]. *And Lastly, Hereby our Church at present, and the Common Christianity (it may be feared) will be more and more daily exposed to Atheistical Men; for this being but the result of the former particulars, and such kind of Men daily growing upon us, it cannot be believed, they can over-look the advantages which is so often given them.* The sum of which is, That to Vindicate the Doctrine of the Trinity against *Socinians*, will make Men Atheists. This is a very bold stroke for a Christian, and a Divine, and I shall beg leave to expostulate this matter a little freely with him.

1st, I desire to know, whether he thinks the Doctrine of the Trinity to be defensible or not? If it be not defensible, why does he believe it? Why should we not rather openly and plainly reject the Doctrine of the Trinity, which would be a more effectual way to put a stop to Atheism, than to profess to believe it, but not to defend it? If it be defensible, and there be no fault in the Doctrine, but that some Men have defended it ill, would it not much more have become him to have defended it better, than only to quarrel with those who have defended it, as well as they could?

2dly, Why does he not tell the *Socinians*, what injury they do to common Christianity, by ridiculing the Faith of the Holy Trinity, and exposing it to the scorn of *Atheists*? Does he think that they are no Christians, and ought not to be concerned for common Christianity? Or does he think, that Atheists will like the Doctrine of the Trinity ever the better, for its being despised by *Socinians* as an absurd contradictory Faith, without having any Defence made by *Trinitarians*? Or does he think, that the Defences made by *Trinitarians* expose the Faith more than the Objections of *Socinians*? I wish I knew his mind, and then I could tell what to say to him.

3dly, How are *Atheists* concerned in the Disputes of the Trinity? Or how are we concerned to avoid scandalizing Atheists, who believe that there is no God at all? Must we be afraid of defending the Faith of the Trinity, lest Atheists should mock at it, who already mock at the Being of a God? What shall we have left of Christianity, if we must either cast away, or not defend every thing, which Atheists will mock at? Surely he has a very contemptible Opinion of the Doctrine of the Trinity, that he thinks all the Defences that are, or can be made for it, so ridiculous, that they are enough to make Men Atheists.

But I can tell him a Secret, which possibly he may be privy to, though in great modesty he conceals his knowledge, *viz.* That *Atheists* and *Deists*, Men who are for no Religion, or at least not for the Christian Religion, are of late very zealous *Socinians*; and they are certainly in the right of it: for run down the Doctrine of *the Trinity* and *Incarnation*, and there is an end of the Christian Religion, and with that an end of all Revealed Religion; and as for Natural Religion, they can make and believe as much, or as little of it as they please. And this is one Reason, and I am sure a better than any he has given against it, why we are, and ought to be so zealous at this time in opposing *Socinianism*, because it is the common Banner under which all the Enemies of Religion and Christianity unite. This makes that little contemptible Party think themselves considerable, that all the Atheists and Infidels, and licentious Wits of the Town, are their Converts; who promise themselves a glorious Triumph over Christianity, and particularly over the Church of *England*, by decrying and scorning the Catholick Faith of the Trinity and Incarnation.

II. Thus much for the *Unreasonableness* of this Controversie about the Holy Trinity; in the next place he tells us the *Danger* of it [P. 7.]: and he has thought of such an Argument to evince the danger of Disputing for the Holy Trinity, as I believe, was never dreamt of before; and that is, That it is *One of the Fundamentals of Christian Religion; now to litigate touching a Fundamental, is to turn it into a Controversie; that is, to unsettle, at least endanger the unsettling the whole Superstructure.* Now I am perfectly of his mind, that it is a dangerous thing to unsettle Foundations; But is it a dangerous thing too, to endeavour to preserve and defend Foundations, when Hereticks unsettle them, and turn them into Dispute and Controversie? Let us put the *Being of God* instead of *the Holy Trinity*, and see how he will like his Argument himself. The *Being of a God* is the Foundation of all Religion, and therefore it is dangerous to dispute with Atheists about the Being of God, because this is *to turn a Fundamental into a Controversie, that is, to unsettle, or to endanger the unsetling the whole Superstructure*: And thus we must not dispute against Atheists, no more than against Socinians: And what is it then we must dispute for? What else is worth disputing? What else can we dispute for, when Foundations are overturned? What is the meaning of that Apostolical Precept, *To contend earnestly for the Faith*? *Jud.* 3. What Faith must we contend for, if not for Fundamentals? What Faith is that which can subsist without a Foundation?

But I would desire this Author to tell me, whether we must believe Fundamentals with, or without Reason? Whether we must take Fundamentals for granted, and receive them with an implicite Faith, or know for what Reason we believe them? If our Religion must not be built without a Foundation, like a Castle in the Air, it is certain, that the Fundamentals of our Faith ought to have a very sure Foundation, and therefore we are more concerned to understand and vindicate the Reasons of our Faith, with respect to Fundamentals, than to dispute any less Matters in Religion, for the Roof must tumble, if the Foundation fail.

What shall Christians do then, when *Atheists*, *Infidels* and *Hereticks*, strike at the very Foundations of their Faith? Ought not they to satisfie themselves, that there is no force in the Objections, which are made against the Faith? Or must they confirm themselves with an obstinate Resolution, to believe on without troubling themselves about Objections, in defiance of all the power and evidence of Reason? This is not to believe like Men; Christianity had never prevailed against Paganism and Judaism upon these Terms; for they had Possession, Authority, and Prescription on their side, which is the only Reason and Security he gives us for the Faith of the Trinity, That *the Established Church is in possession of it* [P. 8.].

If private Christians then must endeavour to satisfie themselves in the Reasons of their Faith, when Fundamentals are called in question, is it not the Duty of Christian Bishops and Pastors to defend the Faith, and to defend the Flock of Christ from those *grievous Wolves* St. *Paul* prophesied of? Is not this their proper Work and Business? And when the Faith is publickly opposed and scorned in Printed Libels, ought it not to be as publickly defended? When Hereticks dispute against the Faith, must we be afraid of disputing for it, for fear of making *a Controversie of Fundamentals*? Thanks be to God, our excellent *Primate* is above this fear, and has now in the Press a Defence of that Faith, which this Writer would perswade all Men to betray by silence; and I hope so great an Example may at least prevail with him to let us dispute on without any more *earnest and compassionate Suits*.

III. His last Argument is, The *Unseasonableness* of this Controversie [P. 8.]. He says, all Controversies are now *unseasonable*; and I say a little more, that they are always so; for there is no Juncture *seasonable* to broach Heresies, and to oppose the Truth: but if Hereticks will dispute against the Truth *unseasonably*; there is no time *unseasonable* to defend Fundamental Truths. But why is it so *unseasonable* in this

Juncture? Because *under God, nothing but an union of Councils, and joyning Hands and Hearts, can preserve* the*Reformation, and scarce any thing more credit and justifie it, than an Union in Doctrinals.* To begin with the last first: Is *the Union in Doctrinals* ever the greater, that *Socinians* boldly and publickly affront the Faith of the Church, and no body appears to defend it? Will the World think that we are all of a mind, because there is disputing only on one side? Then they will think us all *Socinians*, as some *Forreigners* begin already to suspect, which will be a very scandalous Union, and divide us from all other *Reformed Churches.* Let *Union* be never so desirable, we cannot, we must not unite in Heresie; those break the Union, who depart from the Faith, not those who defend it. When Heresies are broached, the best way to preserve the Unity of the Church, is to oppose and confute, and shake Heresie and Hereticks, which will preserve the Body of Christians from being infected by Heresie, and the few there are, who forsake the Faith, the greater Unity there is in the Church.

But *nothing but Union of Counsels, and joyning Hands and Hearts, can preserve the Reformation.* Must we then turn all *Socinians*, to preserve the *Reformation?* Must we renounce Christianity, to keep out Popery? This Stander-by is misinformed, for *Socianism* is no part of the *Reformation*; and so inconsiderable and abhorred *a Party*, when they stand by themselves, that all Parties who own any Religion, will joyn *Counsels, and Hands and Hearts* to renounce them.

But what he would insinuate is, that we shall never joyn against a common Enemy, whose Successes would endanger the *Reformation*, while there are any Religious Disputes among us. I hope he is mistaken, or else we shall certainly be conquered by *France*, for twenty such *compassionate Suits* as this, will never make us all of a mind; and whether we dispute or not, if we differ as much as if we did dispute, and are as zealous for the Interest of a Party, the case is the same. But he has unwarily confess'd a great Truth, which all Governments ought to consider, That every Schism in the Church, is a new Party and Faction in the State, which are always troublesome to Government when it wants their help.

But *these Disputes about the Trinity make sport for Papists.* It must be disputing against the Trinity then, not disputing for it; for they are very Orthodox in this point; and never admitted any Man to their Communion who disowned this Faith, or declared, that he thought it at any time *unreasonable, dangerous*, or *unseasonable* to dispute for it, when for it was violently opposed.

A SHORT DISCOURSE OF THE TRUE KNOWLEDGE OF CHRIST JESUS
Samuel Bold

Philip. III. 8. Yea doubtless, and I count all things but loss for the excellency of the knowledge of Christ Jesus my Lord.

The Apostle doth not here speak of any thing that was *proper* to himself either as an *Apostle* or a *Christian* of an *extraordinary growth*, but what was *common* to *him*, with every *True Believer*, or sincere *Christian*. For these words are but part of the *Illustration* he annexes of that *Property* of true Believers or *Christians* he had laid down in the last Cause of the third Verse of this Chapter, who *have no confidence in the Flesh*.

In the seventh Verse he relates the different *Opinion* and *Judgment* he had of Matters with relation to *Justification* and *Salvation* before he was *Converted*, from what he had of them after his *Conversion*. Those things which before his *Conversion* he reckon'd *Gain*, *i.e.* which he thought were the *matter* of a Persons *Righteousness*, the things which being enjoy'd would *Justifie*, and render a Person *acceptable* to God, and *warrant* his being *confident* of *Salvation*, he accounted *Loss*, after he was effectually *Regenerated*: Because he then knew that *Christ* alone is our *Righteousness*, and that he only can *save* us.

In these words he declares again, with great *Earnestness*, that he looks upon the possession and enjoyment of all those things he formerly thought would *constitute* Persons *Righteous* and Happy, and every thing else *distinct* from *Christ*, that any can place their confidence in, to be of no more *moment* and consideration to these *Purposes* than heaps of *Dung*, and *Dross* can be to the *nourishing* of a Man's *natural Life*, and to the making of him *Wealthy*. And as *Christ* alone is our Righteousness, and he only can *justifie* and *save* us, so it is by the *knowledge of Christ*, that we come to be *interested* in *Him*, and to receive from him *those*, and all those singular and inestimable *Benefits* and *Blessings* He is *intrusted* to *dispense*. This knowledge of Christ Jesus is so *adapted* to this *end*, hath such a *Connexion* with us, by Divine *Ordination* and *Appointment*, hath such an *Excellency* in it, such a *Power, Efficacy*, and *Virtue* for the deriving of these Mercies and Blessings to us from *Christ*, that all other things are perfectly *insignificant* to this purpose, but when *depended* on for *Justification* and *Salvation*, are a very great *Detriment* and *Damage*.

In order to a more distinct understanding of these words, I will briefly consider four things in them, and then conclude with shewing some *Uses* we should make of what shall be discoursed.

The Four things I shall briefly consider are, First, *The matter of this Knowledge the Apostle speaks of:*

Secondly, *What kind of Knowledge it is of this point, which the Apostle doth thus* magnifie *and* extol, *and give such a preference to?*

Thirdly, *Wherein the* excellency *of this Knowledge doth consist?* And,

Fourthly, *The account the Person who knows Christ Jesus aright, doth make of all other things.*

First, I shall consider what is the *matter* of this Knowledge the Apostle here speaks of, or what is the *object* to be known. This he expresseth in these words, *Christ Jesus*, that is, that the *Person* God had promised to send into the World to be the *Saviour of Sinners*, was *Him* who is *generally known*, and was *signally distinguished* from other People by this Name *Jesus*; or that He who is commonly known, and peculiarly spoken of by this name *Jesus*, is the Person God did design, and promise to send into the World to be the Saviour of Sinners. That this *Jesus* is the *Christ*, the Person God hath *anointed* and *commissioned* to this *Office*; and that He isthe *only* and the *all-sufficient*, and most *gracious Saviour* of *Sinners*. That *Jesus is the Christ* (the Person God hath commissioned to be the Saviour of Sinners) is the *Proposition* I conceive the Apostle here speaks of, the object of that Knowledge here commended. And this is the *Gospel* strictly and most properly considered, *Luk. 2. 10, 11.*

Act. 4. 12. The fulfilling of the *Prophecies* which went before concerning the *Messiah*, or the Person God had promised to *send*, in this *Jesus*; and his declaring that he was that *Person*, and doing *such things* to confirm the truth of what he *Taught*, as could not be *wrought* and effected but by the *extraordinary* and *immediate Power* of *God*, afford sufficient *Evidence* to perswade Men of the truth of this *Proposition*, that *Jesus is the Christ.* This I take to be the matter or object of that Knowledge the Apostle here speaks of. Not that I think a bare *speculative Knowledge* of this *Article* or *Proposition* is the *Knowledge* the Apostle doth thus *magnifie* and set such a *value on.* Therefore I shall consider,

Secondly, What *kind of Knowledge of this Proposition it is, the Apostle doth here speak of.* And it is such a Knowledge as doth effectually determine the Person; and cause him to *resign* up himself *entirely* to *Christ Jesus* to be saved by him in his *own way.* Such a knowledge of him, as makes the Person to *take* him for *his Lord*; so that he will use his *serious, honest,* and *best endeavours* to understand what he hath taught and revealed, and will *assent* to, *believe* and *observe* whatever he shall attain to know He hath taught or revealed, and will *depend* wholly on *Him* to receive from *Him* in his *own way,* the *benefits* He is *intrusted* to *dispense.* The notional and speculative knowledge of Christ Jesus, hath its *usefulness,* being the Foundation on which the other is builded, but it may be without the latter, and therefore is not *saving,* but the *latter* cannot be without the *former,* no more than a *Superstructure* can be without a *Foundation.*

3rdly. *In the singular and inestimable Benefits which do accrue unto us upon our thus knowing of Christ Jesus.* Of which Benefits I will now name but these two.

1. *God's justifying of us, and owning us to be in the Covenant of Grace.* By Justification, I do mean something more than his Pardoning all our past Sins, even a *change* of our *State,* his acquitting and discharging us from the *Laws of Works,* as a *Covenant of Life.* Were all my Sins freely pardoned, and I left under the Law of Works, this *Pardon* would not *avail* me anything, if my *Life* were at all *continued,* for my very next *performances* would fall so *short* of what that *Law requires,* I should immediately be in the *same state* I was in before my *Pardon.* We are all under the

Law of Works till we do so know Christ Jesus, as to yield up our selves unreservedly unto his Conduct. Indeed, we are not now so under the Law of Works, as our first Parents were immediately on their *Transgression*, and before that *gracious Promise* that *the Seed of the Woman should break the Serpent's head*, was given them, for till then they were purely under the Law of Works, and had no *remedying Law* to make use of for their *Relief*. We are naturally still under that Law of Works, only we have this *advantage*, that now there is a Law of Pardon, or a *remedying Law concurrent* with it, if we will make use of it. But till we comply with, and accept of that Law, *i.e.* do yield up our selves absolutely to *Christ Jesus*, the other Law stands in full force against us.

Our so knowing of *Christ Jesus* as hath been mentioned, is our *actual consenting* to the *gracious tender* and *offer* God hath made to all Sinners, without excepting any, whereby we come to be really in the *Covenant of Grace*. What is ordinarily called the *Covenant of Grace*, is only the *Declaration* and *Testament* which Christ hath made of the *Grace of God*, or the *Blessings* he will bestow on all those who do or shall *unfeignedly consent* to yield up themselves *absolutely to Him*. It is a *Covenant* only with those who do thus *consent* unto *it*. And upon our *giving* up our selves thus to *Christ*, God owns us to be in Covenant with Him. Of this *Covenant Christ Jesus* is the *Mediator*, to whom it pertains to see, that *both parts* of the *Covenant* thus consented to be *performed*. We are to do what is assigned to us, *i.e.* we must *follow Christ's Conduct* in every thing we shall *know* he hath *ordained* for *us*, and therefore must use our *honest endeavours* to understand what he hath *taught*; and upon our doing *so*, we come to be *entitled* to the *Benefits God* hath *promised*, which *Christ* is also to see *accomplished*, and made *good* unto *us*. When we know *Christ Jesus* aright, we are *delivered from the power of darkness, and translated into the Kingdom of his dear Son*, Col. 1. 13.

2. *Power to perform such Obedience as God will graciously accept.* This *knowledge* of *Christ Jesus*, which is a special effect of the Holy Spirit, is not a *dead notion*, but the *Light of Life*, a divine *vital principle*, which hath an *influence* on all the *Powers* of the *Soul*, and *Faculties* of the *whole Man*, spiriting and directing them all in a *good measure*, in ways suitable to its own *Nature*, and the *end* for

which it is *given*. It possesseth the Soul with a predominant *Love* to *Christ*, and influences the Person to *labour* after a *Conformity* to Him. It puts the Person upon considering and enquiring what things *He*, whom he hath taken for his *Lord* hath *revealed*, what he doth Command, and in what manner it *behoves* him, now he hath thus *resigned* himself to Him, to *behave* himself; and it furnishes him with *ability* to execute the same, by *deriving* fresh supplies of *strength* from that *Holy Spirit* who is the *Author* of this divine *vital Principle*. It disposeth and enclineth him to do those *good Works* Christ hath *commanded* him, and to use those *means* Christ hath enjoyned in order to his receiving greater measures of the influences of the Holy Spirit, *Eph.* 2. 10. Such a Person's Good Works and Obedience are *accepted* with God, not because of their *intrinsick worth*, but only for the *merit* of *Christ*, who hath *procured the Law of Grace*, and is the *mediator* of the *new Covenant*. Our best Works cannot merit Salvation, that is the *purchase* of *Christ's Blood*. We are justified and saved by *Faith*, and that is the *Gift* of *God*; so that we have nothing to *boast of*, tho very much for which we are to be *thankful*. Our *good Works* are an *evidence* of the *truth* of our *Faith*, and that our *knowledge* of Christ is of the *right kind*: And such is the *Grace* of *God* through *Christ*, that the *more* we *abound* in them, the *greater* shall our *Reward* be; not because of their *Merit*, but because of his *gracious Promise*, assigning *degrees of Glory*, in proportion to our *abounding* in *new Obedience*. We do not derive *Power* from Christ to *merit* any thing for our selves, but we receive from Him *Power* to perform such *Obedience* as shall for *his sake* be *accepted* and *rewarded*. Upon our performing such *Obedience*, we shall receive *freely* the *Blessings He* hath *merited*, and which for his sake are made over to us in the *Covenant of Grace*. Our *Works* of *Righteousness* and *Goodness* do not *make* us *Righteous* and *Good*, but they prove and discover us to be *so*, *i.e.* that we are endu'd with a *divine Principle*, have our *Natures changed*, and do *know Christ Jesus* aright, as *vital acts* do not *make* a *living Creature*, but they prove that the *Creature* which performs them hath a *principle of Life* from which those *acts* do *flow*.

4*thly*. Another excellency of this knowledge is, that *it puts a check to vain Curiosity, to a search after empty and less* *necessary Speculations, and delivers us from all carnal and groundless Confidence, and engages us to a commendable Diligence, by determining our enquiries after such things as are most certain and true in themselves, and will be most useful and profitable unto us, by advancing us both in intellectual and moral Accomplishments and Perfections.* For it obliges us to employ our honest and best endeavours to *understand*, and make a *right use* of what *Jesus Christ* hath *taught* and *revealed*; which are matters of such *excellency*, that all *other things* are of *little account* with those who understand the *use* and *importance* of *these*, as the Apostle plainly testified, when he said, he accounted all things *but loss*, &c. Which brings me to consider,

Fourthly, What account he who knows *Christ Jesus* aright doth make of all other things. The *Sence* a sincere Christian hath of the *excellency* of this *knowledge*, discovers it self in a great *alteration* it makes in his *Opinion* and *Judgment* of all other things from what they were before. He doth set now a *just estimate* upon all *worldly Enjoyments*, and *outward Privileges* relating to *Religion*, and *external performances* in *Religion*, according to their several Natures, Places, and Ranks, to their use and ends. He does not absolutely condemn them, as evil in themselves, or as altogether useless to any good purposes, for should he *do so*, he would be *faulty*. He owns them to be the *good Gifts* of *God*, that a very *good use* may be made of them, is *thankful* to God for them, if he enjoys them, and *praiseth God* for bestowing them on others. He acknowledges they have a *beauty* and *excellency* considered in their *proper place* and *season*. But then he esteems them as the Apostle did, as *altogether useless* to the *business* here spoken of, *viz.* to be the matter of our Confidence, yea, extremely *hurtful* when depended on for Justification. To be but *loss*, yea *dung* when compar'd with, and set in opposition to this *knowledge* of *Christ Jesus*, which hath an *excellency* in it, unspeakably greater than all other things have, and which alone can avail and profit us to *Justification* and *Salvation*. That *divine Light* which discovers *Christ Jesus* to a Person, as the Person commissioned by God to be the Saviour of Sinners, and effectually causeth him, from a sense of his own Sin and Guilt, to yield up himself entirely to Him, to he saved by Him in his own way, doth discover all other things to him in such a *true* and *disparaging manner*, that he plainly perceives they cannot bear any *proportion* with *Christ*, and therefore he accounts them to be *loss*, as to the business of *Justification*. If I do not esteem Christ Jesus worthy enough to be the *sole object* of my *dependence*, I do *not know him aright*. And if I set up any thing in the World, as that I will trust to and depend on for Justification more than Christ, or equally with Him, or I acknowledge a greater or an equal virtue and efficacy in that with what I pretend to believe is in Christ for this purpose. Or if I depend on anything together with Christ, tho' in an *inferiour degree*, I do not take him to be the *only and sole sufficient Saviour of Sinners*, and so have not that knowledge of Christ Jesus here spoken of. Indeed, there are *other things* we may *depend on*, and make the *ground* of our *Perswasion* and *Confidence*, that we are *Justified* and shall be *Saved*, as those which are *sure, certain*, and *never-failing Evidences* of our *Interest* in *Christ*, as our *Saviour*, and that we do know Him aright. But there is not any thing but *Christ* and *his Righteousness*, we may trust to, and depend on for *Justification* and *Salvation, i.e.* as *that*, for the *sake of which* we shall be Justified and Saved.

From what hath been discoursed we may take notice,

First, *That Persons may have great Measures of speculative Knowledge concerning Christ Jesus, and what he hath taught, and not be True Christians*. The Apostle indeed doth tell us, that *whosoever believeth that Jesus is the Christ, is born of God*, which is the same with his being a *True Christian*, 1 *John* 5. 1. but it is evident, beyond all doubt, by his following discourse, that he doth not speak of a bare *speculative Knowledge*, but of such a Knowledge and Faith as I have been giving an account of. Such a Knowledge or Belief that Jesus is the Christ, that is, the *Person God hath commissioned to be the Saviour of Sinners*, as doth effectually cause a Person to resign up himself entirely to Him, doth *constitute* him a *True Christian*. Whatever Knowledge or Faith People may have, which falls short of this, will not profit them to *Justification*, nor have a due effect and influence on their Lives. The most *pompous Presences* will not prevail for our *acceptance* with *Christ*, where this is wanting, *Mat.* 7. 22, 23. Therefore,

Secondly, *We ought to make a thorough and impartial search concerning our selves, whether we be true Christians.*

Whether we are so fully perswaded that *Jesus is the Christ*, that we do *sincerely* yield up our selves, without any *reservation* to follow his *Conduct*. It is not enough that we call our selves *Christians*, and *pretend* to own him for our *Lord*, as *Mat*. 7. 22, 23. discovers. But we must justifie the *Truth* of our owning him to be *our Lord*, by employing our selves heartily to *understand* what He hath taught, and to *believe*, and make *such use* of what we attain to *know* He hath *taught*, as we shall perceive he intends and appoints. For,

Thirdly, *Tho' a right knowledge of this one point, that Jesus is the Christ, doth constitute and make a Person a Christian; yet there are many points Jesus Christ hath taught and revealed, which every sincere Christian is indispensibly obliged to endeavour to understand, and make a due use of.* When a Person becomes a True Christian, he doth resign himself (as you have been told) entirely unto *Christ Jesus* as his *Lord*, and obligeth himself, without any reservation, to use his *serious, honest*, and *sincere endeavours* to know what he hath revealed, and to *assent* unto, and make *such use* of what he shall attain to *know* he hath *revealed*,.as the *nature*, or *particular intendment* thereof (so far as he shall know the same) doth *direct*. He doth not *capitulate* and *compound* with *Christ*, that he will assent unto, and make such use as he orders, of *just* such a *number* of *Articles*, but will be excus'd from concerning himself to *extend* his *knowledge*, or *practice* any *further*. It is out of my *Reach* (and I am perswaded it is out of the reach of any Man, or Body of Men) to assign a *precise number* of *Articles* which are necessary to be *explicitly known* and believed by all *sincere Christians*, and *beyond* which no Christian is obliged to endeavour to *proceed* in his *Faith* and *Obedience*. Peoples *Capacities, Opportunities*, and *Advantages* are very *various* and *different*. Many things may be *necessary* for some Christians to *believe*, which are not *necessary* to be believed by *others*, because some do attain to the knowledge of them, and a great many more may never attain to the knowledge of them, and this not because of any *faulty omission* or *neglect* to use their *honest endeavours* to understand what *Christ* hath made known to the World, but from *something else* which will not be *reckoned* to them for a *fault*. I think a certain number of Articles cannot be fixed on (besides this, that Jesus is the

Christ) which we may *peremptorily* determine must of necessity be explicitly known and believed, or *no Person can be saved*. For the *belief* of the other *Doctrines* Christ hath *taught*, doth not *constitute* or *make* a Person a *True Christian*.

SOME THOUGHTS CONCERNING THE SEVERAL CAUSES AND OCCASIONS OF ATHEISM

John Edwards

I might in the last place take notice of a Plausible Conceit which hath been growing up to a considerable time, and now hath the fortune to come to some maturity. Not to speak of its reception, (if not its birth) among some *Foreign* Authors, chiefly *Socinians*, it seemed among our selves to be favour'd by that Learned, but Wavering, Prelate who writ the *Liberty of Prophesying*, and afterwards by another of his Order who compos'd[1] *The Naked Truth*. Lately it hath been revived by the Author of *the Naked Gospel*: and since more particularly fully and distinctly it hath been maintain'd by the late Publisher of *the Reasonableness of Christianity, as deliver'd in the Scriptures*. He gives it us over and over again in these formal words, *viz.* that *nothing is required to be believed by any Christian man but this, that Jesus is the Messiah*. He contends that there is no other Article of Faith necessary to Salvation; this is a Full and Perfect Creed, and no person need concern himself in any other. This takes up about three quarters of his book, for he goes through the History of the *Evangelists* and the *Acts of the Apostles*, according to the order of Time (as he thinks) to give an account of this Proposition. But yet this Gentleman forgot, or rather wilfully omitted a plain and obvious passage in one of the Evangelists, *Go teach all nations, baptizing them in the name of the Father, and of the Son, and of the Holy Ghost, Mat. 28. 19.* From which it is plain, that all Proselites to Christianity, all that are adult Members of the Christian Church, must be *taught* as well as baptized, into the Faith of the *Holy Trinity*, Father, Son, and Holy Ghost. And if they must be *taught*, this Doctrine (which is the peremptory Charge and

[1]   Chap. 1. Concerning the Articles of Faith.

Commission here given to the Apostles, *Go teach*, &c.) then it is certain that they must *believe* it, for this Teaching is in order to Belief. This will be denied by none, I suppose, and consequently more is required to be believed by Christian men, and Members of Christ's Church, than that *Jesus is the Messiah*. You see it is part of the *Evangelical Faith*, and such as is necessary, absolutely necessary, to make one a Member of the Christian Church, to believe a Trinity in Unity in the Godhead; or, in plainer terms, that though God is One as to his Essence and Nature, yet there are Three Persons in that Divine Essence, and that these Three Persons are really the One God: for we can't imagine that Men and Women should be required to be baptized into the Faith and Worship of any but the Only True God. This Epitomizer of the Evangelical Writings left out also that famous Testimony in *John* 1. 1. *In the beginning was the Word* (Christ Jesus) *and the Word was with God, and the Word was God*. Whence we are obliged to yield assent to this Article, that *Christ is the word of God*. And there is added in Verse 14. another indispensable Point of Faith, *viz.* that the *word was made Flesh*, i.e. that God was Incarnate, the same with 1 *Tim.* 3. 16. *God manifest in the Flesh*. And it follows in the same Verse of this first Chapter of St. *John*, that this *Word* is *the only begotten of the Father*: whence we are bound to believe the *Eternal*, though ineffable, *Generation of the Son of God*. Our Author likewise takes no notice that we are commanded *to believe the Father and the Son*, Joh 14. 10, 11. and that *the Son is in the Father, and the Father in the Son*, which expreses their *Unity*. This is made an Article of Faith by our Saviour's particular and express Command. And other eminent parts of Christian Belief this Writer passes by, without having any regard to them, and yet pretends to present the World with a Compleat and Entire Account of all that, is the matter of our Faith under the Gospel. This cannot but seem very strange and unaccountable to any man of deliberate Thoughts, and who expects Sincerity from a Writer who makes some shew of it?

But this is not all: this Learned Gentleman, who with so much industry amasses together Quotations out of the *Gospels* and the *Acts of the Apostles*, yet is not pleas'd to proceed to the *Epistles*, and to give an Account of them as he did of the others; though the *Epistles* are as considerable a part of the *New Testament* as the *Gospels*, and the *Acts*, and the Pen-men of them were equally inspired by the Holy Ghost. Can there be any Reason given of this partial dealing? Yes, it is most evident to any thinking and considerate person that he purposely omits the *Epistolary Writings* of the Apostles because they are fraught with *Other Fundamental Doctrines* besides that One which he mentions. There we are instructed concerning these Grand Heads of Christian Divinity, *viz.* the Corruption and Degeneracy of Humane Nature, with the True Original of it (the Defection of our First Parents) the Propagation of Sin and Mortality, our Restoration and Reconciliation by Christ's Blood, the Eminency and Excellency of his Priesthood, the Efficacy of his Death, the full Satisfaction thereby made to the Divine Justice, and his being made an All-sufficient Sacrifice for Sin. Here are peculiar Discoveries concerning Christ's Righteousness, and our Justification by it, concerning Election, Adoption, Sanctification, or the New Birth, and particularly Saving Faith, which is so signal a part of it. Here the Nature of the Gospel, and the New Covenant, the Riches of God's Mercy in the way of Salvation by Jesus Christ, the Certainty of the Resurrection of Humane Bodies, and of the Future Glory, are fully displayed. These are the Matters of *Faith* contain'd in the *Epistles*, and they are essential and integral parts of the Gospel it self: and therefore it is no wonder that our Author, being sensible of this, would not vouchsafe to give us an Abstract of these Inspired Writings, but passes them by with some Contempt. And more especially (if I may conjecture) he doth this because he knew that there are so many and Frequent, and those so illustrious and eminent Attestations to the Doctrine of the ever to be Adored *Trinity* in these Epistles.

Nor is this any uncharitable conjecture, as the Reader may easily satisfie himself if he takes notice that this Writer interprets *the Son of God* to be no more than the *Messiah*; he expounds *John* 14. 9. &c. after the Antitrinitarian mode, whereas generally Divines understand some part of those words concerning the Divinity of our Saviour. He makes *Christ* and *Adam* to be *the Sons of God* in the same senses, *viz.* by their Birth, as the *Racovians* generally do, and so he interprets *Luke* 1. 35. *John* 5. 26. according to their Standard. When he proceeds to mention the *Advantages* and

Benefits of Christ's Coming into the world, and appearing in the flesh, he hath not one syllable of his Satisfying for us, or by his Death purchasing Life and Salvation, or any thing that sounds like it. This and several other things which might be offered to the Reader, shew that he is all over Socinianized; and moreover that his design was to exclude the belief of the Blessed *Trinity* in this Understanding of his, *viz.* to prove that the believing of Christ to be the Messiah is the only Point of Faith that is necessary and saving. All the other Articles and Doctrines must fall a sacrifice to the Darling Notion of the Antitrinitarians, namely that Christ is not the True God, and coessential with his Father. For the sake of this one Point they are all dispatch'd out of the world, and are made by him Martyrs to this Cause. One could scarcely imagine that a person of Ingenuity and Good Sense should go this way to work. Which enclines me to think that the Ingenious Gentleman who is suppos'd by some to be the Author of this Treatise is not really so. I am apt to believe that the world is impos'd upon in this matter, for in this present Attempt there are none of those Noble Strokes which are visible in that Person's Writings, and which have justly fain'd him a fair repute. That Vivacity of thought, that Elevation of mind, that Vein of Sense and Reason, yea and of Elocution too which runs through his Works are all extinct here: only he begins as 'twere to recover himself about the Close when he comes to speak of the Laws of Christian Morality. Some may attribute this Flatness to the Ill Cause he manages; but for my part, I question whether we have the right Author, I can't perswade my self but that there is an *Error of the Person*: at least I will charitably presume so, because I have so good an opinion of the Gentleman who writ of *Humane Understanding* and *Education*.

But what is the ground of the foresaid Assertion? What makes him contend for One Single Article, with the Exclusion of all the rest? He pretends it is this, that all men ought to understand their Religion. And I agree with him in this; but I ask him, may not a man understand those Articles of Faith which I mention'd out of the *Gospel* and *Epistles*, if they be explain'd to him, as well as that One which he speaks of? Why then must there be but One Article, and no more? But he, notwithstanding this, goes on, and urges that there must be nothing in Christianity that is not plain, and exactly level to all mens Mother-wit and common apprehension. For [2] *God considered the poor of the world, and the bulk of mankind: the Christian Religion is suited to vulgar capacities*, and hath only [3] *such Articles as the labouring and illiterate man may comprehend. The Writers and Wranglers in Religion fill it with Niceties, and dress it up with Notions,* (viz. the Trinity, Christ's Satisfaction, &c.) *which they make necessary and fundamental parts of it.* But the bulk of mankind have not leisure for Learning and Logick: and therefore there must be no such doctrine as that concerning the *Trinity, the Incarnation of the Son of God*, and the like, which are above the capacity and comprehension of the Vulgar. And in the Entrance of his book he hath the same notion, for he tells us that the Scriptures are *a collection of writings designed by God for the instruction of the illiterate bulk of mankind*, (for he is much taken with this phrase, you see, *the bulk of mankind*) whereby he understands the Ignorant and Unlearned Multitude, the *Mob*, as he calls it in another place. Surely this Gentleman is afraid of *Captain Tom*, and is going to make a Religion for his Myrmidons: and to please them he gives them as little of this kind as he possibly can, he contracts all into One Article, and will trouble them with no more. Now then the sum of all that he aims at is this, that we must not have any Point of Doctrine whatsoever in our Religion that the *Mob* doth not at the very first naming of it perfectly understand and agree to. We are come to a fine pass indeed: the Venerable *Mob* must be ask'd what we must *believe*: and nothing must be receiv'd as an Article of Faith but what those Illiterate Clubmen vote to be such. The *Rabble* are no *System-makers*, no *Creed-makers*; and therefore away with *Systems* and *Creeds*, and let us have but One Article, though it be with the defiance of all the rest, which are of equal necessity with that One.

Towards the close of his Enterprise he hath a fling (and that a Shrewd one) at the *Dissenters*, telling them that [4] *their Congregations and their Teachers understand not the Controversies at this time so warmly manag'd among them.* Nay the Teachers themselves have been pleas'd to make him their

[2]   P. 157.

[3]   P. 157.

[4]   P. 157-8.

Confessor, and to acknowledge to him that *they understand not the difference in debate between them*. Why? because they (as well as the Conformists) have Obscure Notions and Speculations, such as *Justification*, the *Trinity, Satisfaction*, &c. terms that all the *bulk of mankind* are unacquainted with: whereas Religion should have no Difficulties and Mysteries in it. The very Manner of every thing in Christianity must be clear and intelligible, everything must be presently comprehended by the Weakest noddle, or else it is no part of *Religion*, especially of *Christianity*, which yet is call'd the ⁵ *Mystery of Godliness*: but this being in the *Epistles*, it is no great matter; we are not to mind what they say.

Thus we see what is the Reason why he reduces all Belief to that one Article before rehearsed: as if the other Main Points which I produced were not as *easily learnt* and *understood* as This; as if there were any thing more difficult in this Proposition [The Father, Son and Holy Ghost are One God, or Divine Nature] than in that other [Jesus is the Messiah]. Truly if there by any Difficulty, it is in this latter, for here is an *Hebrew* word first to be explain'd before the *Mob* (as he stiles it) can understand the Proposition. Why therefore doth this Author, who thinks it absurd ⁶ *to talk Arabick* to the Vulgar, talk *Hebrew* to them, unless he be of opinion (which no body else is of) that they understand this Language better than that? Or, suppose he tells the Rabble that *Messiah* signifies *Anointed*, what then? Unless he explains that word to them, it is still unintelligible. So that it appears hence that this Article which he hath spent so much time about, is no more level to the understanding of the Vulgar than that of the *Holy Trinity*, yea it is not so much.

To conclude, this Gentleman and his fellows are resolved to be *Unitarians*; they are for *One* Article of Faith, as well as *One* Person in the Godhead; and there is as much reason for one as the other, that is, none at all. But it doth not become me perhaps to pronounce this so peremptorily, and therefore I appeal to the Judicious and Impartial Reader; desiring him to judge of what I have suggested. But this I will say, if these Learned men were not highly prejudiced and prepossessed,

⁵ 1 Tim. 3. 16.

⁶ P. 157.

they would discern the Evil and Mischief of their Assertion: they would perceive that when the Catholick Faith is thus brought down to One Single Article, it will soon be reduced to none: the Unit will dwindle into a Cypher.

EXCEPTIONS OF MR. EDWARDS, IN HIS CAUSES OF ATHEISM, AGAINST THE REASONABLENESS OF CHRISTIANITY

Anonymous

To the Author of the Reasonableness of Christianity, as deliver'd in the Scriptures.

Sir,
In reading your Book of that Title, I readily perceived your Design, intimated in your Preface, to be therein most industriously and piously pursued: So that you have, with full Evidence of Scripture and Reason, shewed, against the manifold obscure and tedious Systems, that the Fundamentals of Christian Faith, necessary to constitute a Man a true Member of Christ's Church, are all comprehended or implied in this plain Proposition, That Jesus is the Messiah: *Whereby you have happily provided for the Quiet and Satisfaction of the Minds of the honest Multitude or* Bulk *of Mankind, floating in Doubts and Fears, because either they cannot understand, or can find no clear Evidence in Holy Scripture, of those intricate Points requir'd to be explicitly believ'd upon pain of eternal Damnation. You have also argued clearly the Reasonableness and Usefulness of the Christian Revelation against Atheists and Deists. These things consider'd, 'twas no marvel, that the Systematical Men, who gain both their Honour and Profit by the Obscurity and Multitude of their Fundamental Articles, should raise an Outcry against you, like that of the* Ephesians *magnifying their* DIANA. *They have more cause for it than* Demetrius *had. But that they should traduce your Work as tending to Atheism or Deism, is as strange from Reason, as many of their Articles are from Scripture. And that Mr.* Edwards *has done it, and forc'd it in among his Tendencies to Atheism, is, I think, to be imputed to the Co-incidence of*

your Book's being publish'd, and striking strongly upon his inventive Faculty, just when it was in hot pursuit of the Causes of Atheism, rather than to any the least Colour or Inclination that way, which Mr. Edwards *can spy in it in his cool Thoughts: For I am much perswaded on the contrary, that there is no Atheist or Deist in* England, *but, if he were ask'd the Question, would tell Mr.* Edwards, *that their obscure and contradictious Fundamentals were one Cause or Inducement to his casting off and disbelief of Christianity.*

In this Mind I have undertaken to vindicate your Doctrine from the Exceptions of Mr. Edwards *against it. But whether I have done it as it ought to have been done, I cannot be a competent Judg. If I have mistaken your Sense, or us'd weak Reasonings in your Defence, I crave your Pardon: But my Design in this Writing was not to please you, (whom I know not) nor any Man whatsoever, but only to honour the One God, and vindicate his most useful Truths. I am,*

SIR,

Your very humble Servant.

Mr. Edwards's *Exceptions against the Reasonableness of Christianity, examined, &c.*

It seems to me, that Mr. *Edwards*, printing his *Causes of Atheism*, whilst the *Reasonableness of Christianity* was newly publish'd, was put upon it by his Bookseller, to add some Exceptions against that Treatise so much noted for its Heterodoxy; that so the Sale of his own Tract might be the more promoted: whence it comes to pass, that his Notes being writ in haste, are not so well digested as might be expected from a Person of his Learning and Ingenuity. In *pag.* 180 he takes notice of A PLAUSIBLE CONCEIT, *which hath been growing up a considerable Time*, &c. but tells not his Reader what that Conceit was, till he hath charged it upon a very *Learned* and famous Author, whom he is pleased to call *a wavering Prelate*, and *another of the same Order*, and a Third of a lower Degree; but more *particularly, fully and distinctly*, upon the late Publisher of *The Reasonableness of Christianity*, &c. Here at length in his next Page, he tells us, That *this Author gives IT us over and over again, in these formal words*, viz. *That nothing is required to be believed by any Christian Man but this*, THAT JESUS IS THE

MESSIAH. I think if he had not been in haste, he would have cited at least two or three of those Pages, wherein we might find those formal Words, but he has not one, and I do not remember where they are to be found; for I am almost in as much haste as Mr. *Edwards*, and will not seek for them. It's true, he says, *That all that was to be believed for Justification*, or to make a Man a Christian, by him that did already believe in, and worship one true God, maker of Heaven and Earth, *was no more than this single Proposition, That Jesus of Nazareth was the Christ or the Messiah.* But then he takes to be included in this *Proposition*, 1. All synonimous Expressions, such as, the Son of God; The King of *Israel*; The sent of God; He that should come; He of whom *Moses* and the Prophets did write; The Teacher come from God, *&c.* 2. All such Expressions as shew the manner of his being the Christ, Messiah, or Son of God, such as his being conceived by the Holy Ghost and Power of the most High; his being anointed with the Holy Ghost and Power; his being sanctified and sent into the World; his being raised from the Dead, and exalted to be a Prince and Saviour after the time he was so, &c. 3. Such Expressions as import the great Benefits of his being the Messiah; as having the Words of Eternal Life; his having Power from the Father to remit Sins, to raise the Dead, to judg the World; to give eternal Life; to send the H. Spirit upon the Apostles whereby they might work Miracles, and preach the Light of Life to *Jews* and *Gentiles*, and the like. For all those Quotations of Scripture which the Author (as Mr. *Edwards* observes) *has amassed together out of the Gospels, and the Acts of the Apostles, which take up about three quarters of his Book*, for the proof of his Proposition, are indeed expository of the meaning of that Proposition, and are included in it. Not that it was necessary that every one, who believed the Proposition, should understand and have an *explicite* Faith of all those particulars: for neither the Believers during the Life of Christ, nor the Apostles themselves understood many of them, no nor presently after his Death and Resurrection; for they had still divers erroneous Opinions concerning the Nature of his Kingdom, and the preaching to the *Gentiles*, and other things. And in the beginning of Christ's preaching, though *Philip* believ'd that *Jesus was the Messiah*, the Son of God, the King of *Israel*; yet he seems to be ignorant of his being born of a

Virgin, for he calls him the Son of *Joseph, John* 1. 45. But as
he that believes that *William* the 3*d* is the true King of
England, &c. believes enough to make him a good Subject,
though he understands not all the grounds of his Title, much
less all his Power and Prerogatives that belong to him as
King: So he that believes upon good Grounds that *Jesus is the
Messiah*, and understands so much of this Proposition as
makes him, or may make him a good Subject of Christ's
Kingdom, though he be ignorant of many things included in
that Proposition, he has all the Faith necessary to Salvation,
as our Author has abundantly proved.

But Mr. *Edwards* says, *This Gentleman forgot, or rather
wilfully omitted a plain and obvious Passage, in one of the
Evangelists,* GO TEACH ALL NATIONS, *&c.* Mat. 28. 19.
From which it is plain (says he) *that all that are adult
Members of the Christian Church, must be Taught as well as
Baptiz'd into the Faith of the Holy Trinity, Father, Son and
Holy Ghost, and then they must believe it: and consequently
more is required to be believed by Christian Men, than that
Jesus is the Messiah.* He infers from this, *You see it is part of
the Evangelical Faith, and such as is necessary, absolutely
necessary to make one a Member of the Christian Church, to
believe a* TRINITY *in Unity in the God-head; or, in plainer
Terms, that though God is one as to his Essence and Nature,
yet there are three Persons in that Divine Essence, and that
these three are really the one God.* I must confess, that if Mr
Edwards's *reasoning* be good, the Author is totally confuted,
three quarters of his Book at least are writ in vain, and the
old Systems must stand good; and the *Bulk of Mankind* will
certainly be damned, or it will be a wonder if any of them be
saved. But give me leave to tell him I do *not see*, what he says
we do see: that Text will well enough consist with our
Author's Proposition. For I would ask him, whether the
Apostles follow'd this Commission or not: If they obey'd it,
then in Baptizing in the Name of *Jesus the Messiah*, and
exhorting those to whom they preached, to be baptiz'd in the
Name of the *Messiah*, after their preaching the *Messiah* to
them, they did in effect baptize in the Name of the Father,
Son and Holy Ghost, otherwise they did not pursue their
Commission; for we never find them baptizing in those
express Terms, but always in the Name of *Jesus the Messiah*,
or the Lord Jesus, or the Lord, and the like. So that

Mr. *Edwards* must either charge the Holy Apostles with Ignorance *of*, or Disobedience *to* their Lord's Command, or acknowledg that they did really baptize in the Name of the Father, and of the Son, and of the Holy Ghost, when they did but expressly baptize in the Name of the Son or *Messiah*; forasmuch as all that were so baptiz'd, did believe in the Father of that Son of God, as implied in the Son, and in the Holy Ghost, as the Anointing of the Son, and which also was given to those that were so baptiz'd. But as for his Inference, *viz.* That *it's absolutely necessary to believe a Trinity in Unity in the Godhead*; or *that God is one as to his Essence and Nature, yet there are three Persons in that Divine Essence, and that these three Persons are really the one God*: This will condemn not only the Unitarians, and *the Bulk of Mankind*, but the greater part of Trinitarians, the Learned as well as the Vulgar. For all the real Trinitarians do not believe *one Essence*, but three Numerical Essences. Here Dr. *Sherlock*, Dr. *Cudworth*, the Bishop of *Gl.*, the late Archbishop, Mr. *H–w*, and all that hold as the Council of *Nice* did, with that Council it self, and the whole Church (except some Hereticks) for many Centuries, are by Mr. *Edwards* expung'd out of the Catalogue of Christian Believers, and consequently condemn'd to the horrible Portion of Infidels or Hereticks. The Mystery-men, or *Ignoramus Trinitarians*, they are condemn'd too; for they admit not any Explication, and therefore not Mr. *Edwards*'s. There remains only Dr. *South*, and Dr. *Wallis*, and the Philosopher *Hobbs*, who (Mr. *Edwards* says) *is the great Master and Lawgiver of the profess'd Atheists*, pag. 129. and that Party which have the absolutely necessary Faith of three Persons in one Essence. But if you ask these Men what they mean by three Persons: Do they mean according to the common sense of Mankind, and especially of the English Nation, three singular intellectual Beings? No, by no means, that is Tritheism, they mean three *Modes* in the one God, which may be resembled to three *Postures* in one Man; or three external Relations, as Creator, Redeemer, Sanctifier; as one Man may be three Persons, a *Husband*, a *Father* and *a Master*. This is that Opinion of Faith, which the Antients made Heresy, and *Sabellius* the Head of it. Thus it is absolutely necessary to make a Man a Christian, that he be a *Sabellian* Heretick. But perhaps Mr. *Edwards* may be of Mr. *H–w*'s Mind, for he says, *These three Persons are really the one God*; but then, no one of them singly is so, but every one *a Third of God*: If so, Mr. *Edwards* is indeed a Unitarian, for he gives us one God only; but then he is no Trinitarian, for he has put down the Father himself from being God singly, and so the Son and Holy Ghost.

As to what he says of being Baptized into the *Faith and Worship* of none *but the only true God*, that has been answer'd a hundred times. He cannot look into any of the Unitarian Books, but he will find a sufficient Answer to that Inference. Were the *Israelites* baptiz'd into the Worship of *Moses*? but they were *baptized into* Moses, 1 *Cor.* 10. 2. Or when the Apostle *Paul* supposes he might have *baptized in his own Name*; Did he mean that he should have baptized into the Worship of himself as the most high God?

Then Mr. *Edwards* minds his Reader, that the Author had left out also that famous Testimony in John 1. 1. *In the beginning was the Word* [Jesus Christ] *and the Word was with God, and the Word was God.* Whence (saith he) we are obliged to yield assent to this Article, *That Christ the Word is God.* Here Mr. *Edwards* must mean that this is a Fundamental Article, and necessary to Salvation; otherwise he says nothing against his Author, who has prevented his urging any other Text, not containing a Fundamental, in his Answer to the Objection from the Epistles and other Scriptures. For (saith he) *pag.* 156. *They are Objects of Faith – They are Truths, whereof none that is once known to be such may be disbelieved. But yet a great many of them, every one does, and must confess a Man may be ignorant of; nay disbelieve, without Danger to his Salvation: As is evident in those who allowing the Authority, differ in the Interpretation and Meaning of several Texts. – Unless Divine Revelation can mean contrary to it self.* The whole Paragraph ought to be read, which I have abridged. And if this Text of *John* 1. 1. be not one of those, that by reason of its difficulty and variety of Senses, may not be disbeliev'd in Mr. *Edwards*'s Sense, then I will be bold to say, There's no such Text in the whole Bible. To it I say, 1. He dares not trust his Reader with the clear Text, but thrusts in his own Sense, *In the beginning was the Word* (Jesus Christ:) and then 2. Makes his Fundamental Article not from the Text, but from what he has inserted into the Text thus, *Christ the Word is God.* But will Mr. *Edw.*

stick to that? Is he of *Socinus*'s Mind, that by the Word is meant the Man Jesus Christ, born of the Blessed Virgin, and anointed with the Holy Ghost? I think he is not. Or does he mean that Christ was *the First-born of every Creature*, as he is called, *Col.* 1. 14. *The beginning of the Creation of God*, *Rev.* 3. 14. *By* whom God made the Worlds, and is therefore *a God*? I think Mr. *Edw.* might be call'd an *Arian*, if that were his Sense. What then does he mean? He does not mean that either the Body or Soul, or both united to constitute a Man, or the Anointing of the Holy Ghost added to that Man, was the *Word*; though by reason of those he had the Name of *Jesus*, and by reason of this he had the Name of *Christ*. He means by the Word, *a second Person or Mode of God.* Now how fairly he calls this second Person a Mode of God, *Jesus Christ*, when it was neither Jesus nor Christ, nor any part of him, let his Reader judg. *In the beginning was the Word* [that is, (according to him) before the Beginning, and therefore from Eternity, God in a second Mode or Person did exist: *and the Word was with God*] *i.e.* God in the second Mode was present with God, even himself in the first Mode or Person: *and the Word was God*] i.e. God in his second Mode was *himself*; or otherwise, was the Father himself and the Holy Ghost; for he tells us before, that the three Persons [or Modes] *are really the one God*: but if the *Word* is really the one God, as Mr. *Edw.* understands the Term *God* in this Text, then the *Word* is the three Persons, or else he is not really the one God, which the three Persons only are. Now if this be a clear Text to build an Article necessary to Salvation, and the Worship of another Almighty and only wise Person upon, besides the God and Father of our Lord Jesus Christ; let all that have any reverence for God or his Gospel judg! Besides, can he alledg one Text out of all the Old Testament, or out of the three former Gospels, where ever by the WORD or *Logos* (as they love to speak) is meant any such preexistent eternal Person? If there be none such, it seems to be no little Defect in the Holy Scriptures, that the World should be 4000 Years old, before any part of it heard any thing of a second personal God, equal to the First, and who had therefore as much Right to be known and worshipped as the First: Nay, and that that Person, *the Word*, should have no mention made of him in the Gospels or Sermons of Christ or the Apostles till above threescore Years after the Ascension; for it was so long (as Ecclesiastical Historians tell us) before the Gospel of the Apostle *John* was written, all the Churches and Believers we read of in Scripture, having been gather'd and converted before.

Next Mr. *Edw.* tells us (*p.* 107. [181]) *there is added* in verse 14. *another indispensable point of Faith*, viz. *That the Word was made Flesh*, i.e. *That God was incarnate, the same with* 1 Tim. 3. 16. *God manifest in the Flesh.*

One would have expected that Mr. *Edw.* undertaking in short to confute a Proposition, that the Author had spent *three quarters of his Book* (which consists of 300 Pages) in proving; and for which he had alledg'd perhaps an hundred clear Texts of Holy Scripture, should have produc'd some clear Texts against him, and not such as need Explanations; and when he has explain'd them, leaves them far more difficult than before. We have spoken already of the *Word* that was said to be God in the first verse of that Chapter; and now in the 14th the *Word* must signify God: but, 1. Are not the same Words and Terms taken in different senses in the same Context, and that too, when they come nearer together than at thirteen verses distance? Thus the word *Light* in *ver.* 5. signifies an impersonal Thing; but in the 7, 8, and 9*th* verses, it denotes a Person, which *John* was not, but Jesus was, to wit, the Revealer of the Word or Gospel. 2. The Father was God too, and if God was *Incarnate*, how will it be avoided that the Father was *Incarnate?* And if it cannot, then Mr. *Edw.* will be a *Patripassian* Heretick. 3. It must be acknowledged, that Mr. *Edw.* has given a wonderful learned explanation of the Phrase – *was made Flesh*; far more Learned than that of the old Justice – *Invasion is Invasion.* The Vulgar and Unlearned may understand something, when it is said that one Thing is made another Thing, as when *Water was made Wine*; but I doubt they will stare and know nothing, when one tells 'em that *a Person was Incarnate*; much more when they read Mr. *Edw.* saying, That *God was Incarnate*, will they not gladly return from the Explanation to the Text? and then it will run thus, *God was made Flesh.* But was God indeed turn'd into Flesh, and *ceased to be God*, as the Water turn'd into Wine ceased to be Water? I'm sure Mr. *Edw.* never intends to make that an *indispensable Point of Faith*, as he calls this, *That God was Incarnate.* But this is a very hard case, that the generality of the World (which *God* *so loved, that he gave his only begotten Son, that whosoever believeth in him should not perish, but have everlasting Life*) their Salvation or Damnation should still depend on the belief of, not only *obscure* Texts, but of *much more obscure* Interpretations of those Texts. Whither shall we go for the Sense of *God was Incarnate?* He sends us to 1 Tim. 3. 16. *God manifest in the Flesh.* But he might know that that reading of the Word *GOD* in that Text is a Corruption, and that instead of *God* was read *which* in the Council of *Nice*, as the accurate Examination against Mr. *Milbourn* has fully prov'd; however allowing that reading, has given a rational Sense of it. Thus we are sent for the Sense of an obscurer Interpretation of an obscure Text, to a corrupt One. Whither shall we go next? It's very like that Mr. *Edw.* may next time send us to the *Athanasian Creed*, when the Scriptures fail him; That *Creed* saith, *It is necessary to everlasting Salvation, that one believe rightly the INCARNATION of our Lord Jesus Christ, -* That he *is God and Man - perfect God and perfect Man - One Christ, not by Conversion of the Godhead into Flesh, but by taking of the Manhood into God:* So then the sense of *the Word was made Flesh*, will be this, *God was Incarnate*, that is, not by being made Flesh or Man, but by taking Man into God; that is, God is now perfect God and Man. Well, but since God is a Person, and Man another Person; perfect God and perfect Man must unavoidably be two Persons: but this is the Heresy of *Nestorius* Arch-Bishop of *Constantinople, An. Dom.* 428. but how shall we help it? For to believe God and Man not to be two Persons, we directly contradict our Belief of God's being *perfect God* and *perfect Man.* If we say with *Apollinarius, An. Dom.* 370. That God and Man are not two Persons but one, because the Man had no Human Soul or Understanding, then we contradict God's being a perfect Man, and are condemn'd to eternal Damnation, as *Apollinarian* Hereticks. And if for solving these Difficulties, we should think good to hold, that indeed there were two natures in Christ when God was made Flesh, but upon the Union the Human was swallowed up of the Divine, and so there was one Nature made of two; then we incur the *Anathema* of the *Eutichian* Hereticks.

"And it follows (saith Mr. *Edw.*) in the same verse of this first Chapter of St. *John*, that *this Word is the only begotten of the Father*; whence we are bound to believe the Eternal, tho ineffable, *Generation of the Son of God.*"

Answ. Could Mr. *Edw.* be so weak as to think any Body but one deeply prejudiced, would approve of either of his Inferences from that Clause? either the Eternal Generation, or that we are bound to believe it as an Article necessary to Salvation? Does he not know that Jesus is the *only Son* of God, by reason of that Generation which befel him in Time? Does he read of any other Son that God generated of a Virgin but Jesus? See *Luke* 1. 35. Did God ever *sanctify and send into the World* in such *a Measure and Manner*, any that were called Gods or Sons of God, as he did Jesus our Lord? See *John* 10. 35, 36, 37, 38. and *Chap.* 3. 34. Did he ever give such Testimony to any other? Did God ever beget any other Son by raising him from the Dead to an immortal Life (*Acts* 13. 33.) *by anointing him with the Oil of Gladness above his Fellows*, Heb. 1. 9. By *setting him on his Right-hand*, making him *to inherit a more excellent Name than Angels*, even that of *SON* in a more excellent Sense, *Heb.* 1. 3, 4, 5. By *glorifying* Christ, making him *an High-Priest*, saying unto him, *Thou are my Son, this Day have I begotten thee?* Is not *Isaac* call'd the only begotten Son of *Abraham*, though *Abraham* had other Sons? But for Mr. *Edw's* Eternal Generation, there is not one Tittle either in this Text, or in all the Bible; and yet he has the Confidence to bind the Belief of it upon Mankind, upon pain of Damnation: I wish he would not be so rash, but more reverent in so tremendous a Point.

Next, he finds our Author faulty in not *taking notice, that we are commanded to believe the Father and the Son*, John 14. 10, 11. *and that the Son is in the Father, and the Father in the Son, which expresses their Unity.* Wonderful! Did our Author indeed take no notice that we are commanded to believe the Father and the Son? when he all along in his Treatise makes the *Messiah, Christ, Son of God*, terms synonimous, and that signify the same thing; and cites abundance of Texts to that purpose; so that the belief of the Father & the Son, is required by him in the whole three quarters of his Book, which Mr. *Edw.* takes notice he spent in proving his Proposition. Did Mr. *Edw.* write these Remarks? Or did some body else add them to his Book *of the Causes of Atheism?* As for the *Unity of the Father and Son, exprest* he says by these words, *The Son is in the Father, and the Father in the Son;* Does he think his Reader never read that Text in John 17. 21. *That they* [Believers] *all may be one, as thou Father art in me, and I in thee, that they also may be one in us*, with *ver.* 23. Or that other Text, 1 *John* 4. 16. *He that dwelleth in Love, dwelleth in God, and God in him?* But for the word *Unity*, which he uses, if he means by it any more than a close Union, it implies a contradiction, that two should be one; that a Duality should be an Unity. *This* (saith he) *is made an Article of Faith by our Saviour's particular and express Command.* He must mean, that Mr. *Edwards's* own sense of that Text is commanded as necessary to Salvation, else he says no more of that than the Author allows concerning both that and other Scriptures. If he means his own sense, then I think he's an inconsiderate and rash Man; for I have shew'd that his sense is contradictious.

Here Mr. *Edw.* calls in question the sincerity of our author, and, *pag.* 109 [182]. says, "It is most evident to any thinking and considerate Person, that he purposely omits the *Epistolary Writings* of the Apostles, because they are fraught with *other Fundamental Doctrines*, besides that one which he mentions."

I will not question Mr. *Edwards's* sincerity in what he writes, but I question much his due considering what he writes against. Does not our Author make in effect the same Objection against himself, *pag.* 151. and answer it in fourteen pages, even to the end of his Book? but Mr. *Edw.* takes notice of very little of it. And the most of that he does take notice of, he answers with a little Raillery upon the *Bulk of Mankind*, the *unlearned Multitude*, the *Mob*, and *our Author*. His note upon these Phrases, is, *Surely this Gentleman is afraid of Captain* Tom, *and is going to make a Religion for his Myrmidons. – We are come to a fine pass indeed; the venerable* Mob *must be ask'd what we must believe.* Thus he ridicules the Doctrine of Faith, on which the Salvation or Damnation of the Multitude depends, and the Grounds of our Author's Design; who finding in Holy Scripture, *that God would have all Men to be saved, and come to the KNOWLEDG of the Truth; the Gospel was preach'd to the Poor, and the common People heard Christ gladly; that God hath chosen the Poor in this World, rich in Faith*; he concluded (when he had overcome the prejudices of Education, and the contempt of the Learned, and those that think themselves so) that the Gospel must be a very intelligible and plain Doctrine, *suted to Vulgar Capacities, and the State of Mankind in this World destin'd to Labour and Travel; not such as the Writers and Wranglers in Religion have made it.*

Another Evidence of Our Author's being *Socinian*, is (according to Mr. *Edw.*) that *he expounds* Joh. 14. 9, &c. *after the Antitrinitarian Mode, whereas generally Divines understand some part of those words concerning the Divinity of our Saviour.* He says, – *generally Divines*, &c. By this mark those Divines that do not so interpret, must be *Socinians*: the *Socinians* owe Mr. *Edw.* their thanks, for adding to their Number many Learned and able Divines; but I doubt those Divines will not thank him for it. But Mr. *Edw.* has Courage enough to call a most Learned and right Reverend Father, *Wavering Prelate*, and to bring in his Doctrine about Fundamentals, as favouring the Causes of Atheism, if he and those other Divines agree not with him in their Sentiments.

Another mark of Socinianism is, that our Author *makes Christ and* Adam, *to be the Sons of God – by their BIRTH, as the Racovians generally do.* That they both make Christ to be the Son of God by his Birth, and that truly according to that Text of *Luke.* 1. 35. cannot I think be denied by any that duly considers the Place; but that either the one or the other make *Adam*, who was never born to be *so*, in like manner by his *Birth*, is Mr. *Edwards's* Blunder, and not their Assertion.

I have not taken notice of the other Fundamentals which Mr. *Edw.* reckons in his System, (divers of which are not found in Holy Scripture, either Name or Thing, expressly, or by consequence) because he insists chiefly on the Doctrine of the Trinity; which however it is believed by Learned Men, to be in some sense or other (they cannot agree in what sense) a Truth; yet some of the most Learned of them do not believe it a Fundamental and necessary Truth, particularly Mr. *Limborch* (than whom this present Learned Age does not afford a more Learned and able Divine) could not defend Christian Religion, in his most famous and weighty Disputations against the Jews, without waving that Point; one of which we have in his *Amica Collatio cum erudito Judæo*, &c. the ablest Jew (I presume) that ever wrote in Defence of *Judaism* against Christianity. Another Conference I am informed we may hope shortly to see, in his Reduction of an eminent Person, who was upon the Point of forsaking the Christian Religion, and embracing for it that of the Jews at *Amsterdam*, when first the ablest Systemers had tried their utmost skill and could not effect it. Perhaps Mr. *Edw.* means him for one, when he says, our Author's *Plausible Conceit* found *reception (if it had not its birth) among some*

Foreign Authors besides *Socinians*, pag. 104 [180]. Indeed he had cause enough, for Mr. *Limborch* tells the Jew expressly (in the Book I named, *Chap. 9. Pag.* 218). *Quando exigitur fides in Jesum Christum, nusquam in toto novo Testamento exigi ut credamus Jesum esse ipsum Deum, sed Jesum esse Christum, seu Messiam olim promissum, vel quod idem est, esse Filium Dei; quoniam appellationes Christi & filii Dei inter se permutantur.* "When we are requir'd to believe in Jesus Christ, we are no where in all the New Testament requir'd to believe that Jesus is the very God, but that Jesus is the Christ or the *Messiah*, that was of old promised, or which is the same, that he is *the Son of God*; because those Appellations of *Christ* and of *Son of God* are put one for another." So that in Company of Mr. *Limborch* and other eminent Divines, as well as our English Bishops and Doctors, our Author may still believe the Doctrine of the Trinity to be a Truth, though not *necessary, absolutely necessary to make one a Christian*, as Mr. *Edwards* contends.

But why does he make mention of only the Right Reverend Fathers, one Reverend Doctor, and the foreign Divines and *Socinians*, as Favourers of this *Plausible Conceit, of making nothing necessary and Fundamental*, but what is *EVIDENTLY contain'd in Holy Scripture as such*; and so is accommodated to the apprehension of the Poor, that hear and read the Scriptures, making them also capable of being saved, though they are either ignorant of, or do not believe aright those Truths, which, though deliver'd in Scripture, are yet either hard to be understood, or difficultly infer'd, or have no mark of Fundamental, either in themselves, or in Divine Revelation; and for those Reasons cannot be made evident to the *despised* common People, which the Lord Jesus came to save as well as the Learned? He might also have charg'd the sixth Article of the Church of *England* with this *Plausible Conceit*, which has so much *Evil and Mischief in it, tending to reduce the Catholick Faith to nothing*, pag. 122 [186]. For that Article saith thus; "Holy Scripture containeth all things necessary to Salvation, so that whatsoever is not *read* therein, nor may be *proved thereby*, is not to be required of any Man, that it should be believed as an *Article* of Faith." Observe here, that every necessary Article must be *read* expressly, or at least *proved thereby*, and to whom is this Proof to be made? even to the WEAKEST NODDLES of those that are requir'd to believe it.

Absolutely there is not one Man or Woman of the *venerable Mob*, that (according to Mr. *Edw*.) can be saved, because they cannot possibly have the Article of *the three Persons that are one* prov'd to them from Scripture; for it's evident the Learned, even of the Clergy, cannot prove it to one another, much less to vulgar Understandings. And Mr. *Chillingworth* (the ablest Defender of *the Religion of Protestants*, that the Church ever had) says (and ingeminates it) – *The BIBLE, the BIBLE, I say the BIBLE only is the Religion of Protestants; whatsoever else they believe besides it, and the plain IRREFRAGABLE and INDUBITABLE Consequences of it, well may they hold it as a Matter of Opinion, but not as a Matter of Faith or Religion; neither can they with consistence to their own Grounds believe it themselves, nor require the Belief of it from others, without most High and most Schismatical Presumption,* Ch. 6. N. 56. Will Mr. *Edwards* say, His Fundamentals are such irrefragable and indubitable Truths, about which there are among Protestants such hot and irreconcileable Contentions? Again, that most judicious Author lays this as the unmoveable Foundation of his whole Discourse against the Papists, viz. *That all things necessary to Salvation are* evidently *contain'd in Scripture*; as the Church of *England* does, (see *Pref. N.* 30.) And he shows in the following Paragraphs, to *N.* 38. That all the Jesuits Arguments against Protestants are confuted by it. But that's not all, the same Author after Dr. *Potter* affirms, *That the Apostles Creed contains all those points of Belief, which were by God's Command of Necessity to be preached to all, and believed by all*: And yet he says in the same Paragraph, *That all Points in the Creed are not thus necessary*; See Chap. 4. N. 23. Now what more or less hath our Author asserted in his whole Book? For I have shewed out of him, and it's evident to the Impartial; that his Proposition, that *Jesus is the Messiah or Christ*, does comprehend or clearly imply all the Articles of necessary Christian Faith in the Creed. For, though it was sufficient to constitute a Believer during the Life of Christ, to believe him to be the Christ, although they had no explicit Belief of his Death and Resurrection to come; yet afterwards those Articles *were necessary, being undoubted Evidences of his being the Messiah*, as our Author *pag.* 20. And therefore Mr. *Edw.* is very injurious to him, in representing his Proposition, as if it were only the believing the Man called *Jesus* to be *the Messiah*, an *Hebrew word*, that signifies in English *Anointed*, without understanding what is meant by that Term, see *pag.* 121 [185]. But why should I expect that Mr. *Edw.* should have any regard to Mr. *Chillingworth's* Judgment, and all those, the Vice Chancellour, the Divinity professors, and others that licensed and approved his Book, when he has none for the Pious and Learned Bishop *Jer. Taylor*, and those others? Nay, when those numerous plain Testimonies, which our Author has quoted out of the Holy Scriptures themselves, do but provoke his Opposition and Contempt; though the Divine Writers add these Sanctions to the Belief of our Author's Proposition, or of those Words and Sentences that are of the same Import, and comprehended in it, viz. *He that believeth shall be saved*, or *shall never thirst*, or *shall have eternal Life*, and the like: On the contrary, *He that believeth not shall be condemned*, or *shall die in his Sin*, or *perish*, and the like. However I doubt not but my impartial Reader will consider both what my Author, and what my self have said in this Point.

Having thus made it appear, that the reducing of the Fundamentals of Christian Faith to a few, or even to one plain Article deliver'd in Scripture expressly, and often repeated there, and in divers equipollent Phrases, easy to be understood by the POOR, and strongly enforcing the Obedience of the *Messiah*, (as is our Author's Proposition) is far from having any tendency to Atheism or Deism; I shall now retort this charge upon Mr. *Edw.* and show that on the contrary, the multiplying of speculative and mysterious Articles as necessary, which are neither contain'd in Scripture expressly, nor drawn thence by any clear and evident Consequence, but are hard to be understood, especially by the *common People*, having no rational Tendency to promote a good Life, but directly to the high Dishonour of the one God, the God and Father of our Lord Jesus Christ, and the subversion of the Hope and Peace of Christians, as I have manifested in one and the chief of Mr. *Edw*'s Fundamentals, and of other Systemers: This I say has been, and is one great Cause, or chief occasion of that Atheism and Deism that is in the World.

1. Mr. *Edw.* himself tells us, That "Undue Apprehensions of a Deity join'd with superstition, are the high road to Atheism, *pag.* 34 – Therefore imposing of false Doctrines, concerning the Attributes of God, is very pernicious, for they are destructive of his very Being and Nature." But I have shew'd

that the imposing of the Doctrine of *three Almighty Persons*, or personal Gods, is a false Doctrine, and destroys one of the chief Attributes of God, therefore is (according to Mr. *Edw.*) *destructive of his very Being and Nature*, pag. 35. Again, another of Mr. *Edw*'s Fundamentals is, *That full Satisfaction is made by the Death of Christ to the Divine Justice*; which Doctrine does clearly destroy the Attribute of the *Divine Mercy*: for every one may readily perceive, that full satisfaction to Justice by Punishment, cannot consist with Pardoning Mercy; when a Judg punishes according to full Justice, he does not at all forgive or shew Mercy. But that they may not be seen to destroy altogether the Mercy of God, they make him to inflict that Punishment upon himself in a Human Body and Soul. Will not these *false conceptions of the Deity expunge at last the Belief of the true one*? Mr. *Edw.* says false ones will.

2ly. Another occasion, Mr. *Edw.* says, *Atheists take from our Divisions, Broils and Animosities, from the many Parties and Squadrons of Sects that are in the World, to bid defiance to all Religion.* And is it not manifest that those Divisions, &c. arise chiefly from those Doctrines that are Mr. *Edw*'s Fundamentals? I have intimated already, there are many Divisions of Trinitarians, and how hotly they contend with one another, and upon Unitarian Principles. And whoever shall but peep into Ecclesiastical History, may soon see that their *Trinity* has been such a bone of Contention as has exercis'd the Wits and Pens of Churchmen these 1400 Years; for so long it is, and longer since Christians departed from the simplicity of the Faith, as it was preached by our Lord Christ and his Apostles. And now when the Unitarians and our Author would bring Christians back to that simplicity, in which the *Gospel was preached to the Poor*, and they understood it and receiv'd it; this pious Design is ridicul'd, and the Salvation of the Bulk of Mankind is set at nought; Mr. *Edw.* may well conclude that this conduct gives occasion to Atheistical Persons.

3ly. He says, *pag.* 63. *When Persons observe that the very Divinity of our Blessed Lord and Saviour is toss'd and torn by rude Pens – what can they think of the other great Verities of Christianity?* But Mr. *Edw.* mistakes, it's not the opposition that is made to the supreme Divinity of the Son of God, but the asserting it, that inclines Men to disbelieve Christianity. Had many that are now Deists, been sooner acquainted with the Doctrine of one God even the Father, and of one Man the

Mediator between God and Men, it's very probable they would have continued Christians; for there are some that of Deists have been reconcil'd to the Christian Faith by the Unitarian Books, and have profess'd much Satisfaction therein. But I must confess it's a very handsome rebuke Mr. *Edw.* gives to his own Party, when he blames the *Antitrinitarians, That they have provok'd some of them to an undecent sort of Language concerning these Holy Mysteries: so that some of these latter have hurt the Cause, it may be almost as much by their Defending it, as the others have by their Opposing it.* I must lay up this for a curious Figure in Rhetorick: He cuts some dignified Persons through the Unitarians sides; and so whoever is in Fault, they must bear the Blame. But if the Unitarians have *Truth,* and *necessary Truth* on their side, then they are not faulty, even as Christ and the Apostles were not faulty, though they preach'd the Gospel which set *the Son against the Father,* &c. and produc'd not *Peace but a Sword*: And the Reformers were not faulty in vigorously opposing the Popish Faith, even unto Blood. But whoever will attentively consider it, may see it's the Nature of the Trinitarian Doctrine, that it cannot be defended without being exposed, so that when the most Learned of the Party labour to defend it, they necessarily run into one Absurdity or another; which being perceived by the next Learned Man, he exposes him: and a Third sees the weakness of each of them: and a Fourth Man spies Flaws in every of them. This produces various Hypotheses, and makes them a Scorn to Atheists, and enclines others to Deism. For the obscuring of a Contradiction will not take it away. Contradictions are stubborn things, and will never yield to any Reconciliation whatsoever. God will never be more than One real Person, and One Person will never be Three real Persons. And if Trinitarians will (as they do) make that a Fundamental of Religion, which contradicts the best Reasonings of Mankind, whereby they prove the Existence of God and his Unity, *viz. That he is that Being which IS necessarily and by himself, and so consider'd not in Kind, but in Act; wherefore if you suppose more Gods, then you will necessarily find nothing in each of them why any of them should be.* Grotius de verit. Chr. Relig. in initio. And if the Trinitarians cannot explain their Doctrine to one another, so as to clear it from introducing more Gods than one, no marvel then that loose Men (who yet reason as the incomparable *Grotius,* and other Learned Men do) do thence deny there is *any God at all.* The Learned allow there is not necessarily any God, if you suppose more than one: The Trinitarians say he is more than *one*; Men who think it their Interest there should be no God, conclude thence, it's equal in reason to believe there is no God as three. And Mr. *Norris* joins them with his Suffrage in the Point; *I think it* (saith he) *a greater Absurdity, that there should be more Gods than one, than that there should be none at all. Reason and Relig.* p. 59.

And if some Men take occasion from such reasonings as these to turn Atheists it may easily be conceiv'd, that Men that are more Sober, and find strong and irresistible Reasons for the Existence and Unity of God, but see clearly that Christians worship Three, and besides that, hold divers other absurd Doctrines for Fundamentals; such Men (I say) must of necessity forsake Christianity, and turn Deists. Thus it's most manifest, that the Unitarians take the direct Course to prevent Atheism and Deism, by letting the World see, that those Fundamentals are no Doctrines of Christ; but that the necessary Faith of Christ is a plain and short Doctrine, easy to be understood by the Poor, and clearly exprest in Scripture, most reasonable in it self, and most agreeable to the Unity and Goodness of God, and other the Divine Attributes.

I shall now in the 4*th* Place shew how the Obscurity, Numerousness, and Difficulty of understanding Systematical Fundamentals promotes Deism, and subverts the Christian Faith, and that in a notorious Instance. It's matter of Fact, and evident to the whole World, that the *Quakers* are a very numerous People, and form'd into a compact Body, in which they exercise strict Discipline, as to what concerns their Party. They will not own any other Denomination of Christians or others for *the People of God,* but themselves *only*; all others are of the World. They utterly disown the Scriptures as the Rule of Faith; they decry it as *Letter, Carnal, Dust,* &c. Their Principle is, that their Religion is taught them by Inspiration or Revelation of a Light within, whereof every Man has a Measure, but *they* only hearken to it, and obey it; They give the Scripture the place of bearing witness to their inward Light, as the Woman of *Samaria* to Christ. They turn the Gospel into an Allegory, and consequently make use of the Words and Phrases of the Scripture, as that *Christ is the Word, the light, the Teacher, the Word in the Mouth and Heart; that Christ* *died, and rose, and ascended, and is in Heaven*; and the like; but all in a mystical or spiritual Sense, as they call it. By all which things, and indeed by the whole Tenour of their Books, Preachings and Professions, they appear to be *Deists* and not Christians. *George Fox*'s Book, titled, *The great Mystery*, will give full satisfaction in this Point. And they have all along been charg'd by other Denominations to be *no Christians*, and that *Quakerism is no Christianity*. However retaining still the Words wherein the Christian Faith is exprest, though in an *equivocal* Sense; and having some among them (as *George Keith* and others) who still believ'd the Gospel in the proper Sense, they made a shift to be reputed *generally* Christians. And indeed this Conduct of theirs deceived even many of their own Party, which is manifest in *William Rogers* of *Bristol*, *Francis Bugg*, *Thomas Crispe*, *John Pennyman*, and especially in *George Keith*; who having been a Quaker about 30 Years, yet did not till within these three or four Years discover the Infidelity of the Primitive and true Quakers, who are deservedly call'd *Foxonians*, because holding the Principles of *George Fox* their Author. But *G. Keith* living in *Pensylvania*, (where the Quakers were *Governours*, and might be free to open their Minds plainly) did then perceive they did not believe the Doctrine of *the Apostles Creed*, the summary of Christian Faith, which made him preach it and contend for it more earnestly. This provok'd the *Foxonians* so far, that it came to a Breach and Separation, and at length to Impeachment, Fines and Imprisonment. Then *G. Keith* returns to *London*, where the matters in Contest between him and the *Foxonians* of *Pensylvania*, was taken into Consideration, and had divers Hearings by the General Annual Meeting of Quakers, 1694, who gave a kind of a Judgment in the Case, but no clearer Determination of the principal Matter concerning *Christ within*, and *Christ without*, and the other Articles of Christian Faith, than their former *equivocal* Expressions. The next Year 1695, at the like General Meeting, they absolutely excommunicate *G. Keith*, and make this the Ground of it, *viz.* that he had not given due observance to their former Order, and was troublesome to them in his Declarations, &c. For he had still continued to preach frequently *Christianity* as before. See a late Book, titled, *Gross Error and Hypocrisy detected*, &c. The Reader I hope will excuse it, that I have detain'd him in this long Story, because it was necessary for me first, to prove the Quakers are *Deists*, and then to proceed and shew,

Secondly, That the Obscurity, Ambiguity, and Numerousness of *Systematical* Fundamentals, is that which is the chief Cause of their being *so*: For not being able to satisfy themselves in understanding and determining the Truth and Certainty of those Fundamentals, for the proof of which Scriptures were alledg'd; but *those* of so doubtful a sense, and variously interpreted by opposite Parties, that they readily embrac'd *George Fox's* only Fundamental of *the Light in every Man*; that is in reality the *natural Light*, whereby we distinguish between Good and Evil in ordinary; whence it is that (as saith the Apostle *Paul*) *We* (as *the Gentiles*) *are a Law to our selves, and our Thoughts accuse or excuse*, Rom. 2. 14, 15. Which is in Truth an excellent Doctrine, and has great certainty and clearness in it. But *G. Fox* preaches this, not as a natural Principle, but 1. As a supernatural Revelation: And 2. Christ being call'd in Scripture, *the Light that lighteth every Man*, and the *Light of the World*, because he brought the Light of the Gospel into the World; *George Fox* applies these Terms and Phrases, and almost every thing that is spoken of Christ, to *the Light in every Man*, and so turns the plain sense of the gospel into a Parabolical or Mystical Sense, and makes the Christian Scripture to speak nothing but Deism. 3. *G. Fox* adds certain Observances of giving no respect in Word or Gesture, or Title, nor speaking as others speak, nor saluting as others salute, nor paying Tithes, nor using the Sword, nor swearing in common Form, &c. and all as inspired Dictates, that so the *only People of God* might be separated from all the World, and they serve admirably for that purpose. Now if you consider the experimented *certainty* of their Principle, *the Light within*, that accuses and excuses, and their Perswasion that it was *a Divine Inspiration*, which also was confirm'd to them by their giving *obedience* to those Ceremonies which were so contrary and offensive to the World, and expos'd them to much Suffering; [All suffering for Religion, and especially for a clear Revelation from God, confirming the Sufferers in their Perswasion:] You may clearly perceive it was the Uncertainty, Obscurity, and Intricacy of their former Principles, which induced them to embrace *G. Fox's* Religion, which is all dictated by the Spirit of God in every Man. Whence it is, they upbraid other Professors with *Doubtfulness* and *Fallibility*; and every one of them counts himself *as infallible* as the Papists do the *Pope*. *How can ye but delude People* (says *G. Fox*) that *are not infallible?* Myst. p. 33.

Lastly, The Obscurity, Uncertainty, and Multiplicity of Fundamentals, is that which has given an Argument to Popish Priests and Jesuits, wherewith to seduce Protestants to Popery. For evidence of *this*, I shall mind you of a Paper written by a Jesuit, in the late King *James*'s time, titled, *An Address presented to the Reverend and Learned Ministers of the Church of England*, &c. The purport of which is, *That all things necessary to Salvation are not clearly contained in Scripture*, as Protestants hold; because the *Belief of a Trinity, one God and three Persons, is necessary to Salvation, but not clearly contain'd in Scripture*. Then he goes about to shew, that the Scriptures commonly alledged for the Trinity, admit of another sense. He goes the same way in the Article of the *Incarnation*. Thus supposing these Articles to be necessary to Salvation (as Protestants hold) and not clearly contain'd in Scripture; it follows that the undoubted Certainty of them must be found in the Determinations of the Church; and then that Church which professes *Infallibility* is the only Refuge; and *I believe as the Church believes*, supplies all other Articles. No Certainty any where else; but Certainty must be had in these Points. Here the making of those Articles Fundamental, which cannot be clearly prov'd from Scripture, subverts the Sufficiency and Clearness of Scripture, and sends poor Protestants to *Rome*, for the Certainty and Infallibility of the Christian Faith.

They did so glory in the strength of this Argument, that the Jesuit-Preacher in *Limestreet*, read their Paper, and made the same Challenge in his Pulpit, where he had a great number of Protestants that went out of Curiosity to hear him

Having thus (as I presume) vindicated our Author, and shewn the Mischiefs of Mr. *Edw*'s Fundamentals, I may now take my leave of my Reader. Only I am first willing to let Mr. *Edw.* know, that I have not undertaken this Defence out of any ambitious Humour of contending with so Learned a Man as he is; nor would I have made opposition to him in any other Point of Learning or Divinity: but Fundamentals every Man is concern'd in, and ought to know, and to be assured that he holds them all. *Eternal Salvation* is a greater thing by far than any Empire, and will therefore justify and exact our utmost Care and Endeavour for the obtaining it. So that in these

Considerations of Mr. *Edw*'s Exceptions – I have done my Duty to my self; and that I have publish'd them, I am perswaded I have therein done a great Charity to my Neighbours, *the Poor and Bulk of Mankind*, for whose Salvation (I hope) I should not think it too much to lay down my Life, however Mr. *Edw.* speaks so scoffingly of them, even where there eternal Happiness or Misery is deeply concern'd.

THE END.

SOCINIANISM UNMASK'D
John Edwards

The Introduction.

The following Discourse (which was finish'd above two months ago, but by reason of some Intervening Occurrences found not its way to the Press) is design'd against the undertaking of a late Author in his book which bears the Title of *the Reasonableness of Christianity*, &c. But the Writer himself is wonderfully pleased with his Lying hid, and being No Body. I grant there may be Reasons why a man may sometimes conceal his Name, and not prefix it to the Book he is Author of. But there are some Reasons that are proper and peculiar to this Writer's circumstances, for this is perfectly after the Mode of our late *English Racovian* Writers, who constantly appear *Nameless*, and accordingly herein he shews himself to be of the right *Racovian* breed. And another good reason is this (which indeed argues something of Modesty) he would not set a *Christian Name* before that book wherein he so grossly abuses *Christianity*, and renounces the greatest part of it.

I will not waste time, and trouble the Reader and my self about guessing who this Writer is. Out of Christian good will and charity I am backward to believe that he who is vogued to be the Father of these Extravagant Conceits, is really so. I will still perswade my self that there is *an Error of the Person*; upon which account I shall be more free than otherwise I should have been.

[*A Late Writer's Unreasonable Opinions confuted.*]

Chap. I

I Will now betake my self to the Task which is before me, after I have told the Reader, that I intend not to imitate our Nameless Author in his Childish Flourishes, in his Spruce and Starched Sentences, and in his Impotent Jestings, which are sprinkled up and down his *Vindication*. Nor will I follow him in his Impertinencies and Incoherencies, in his trifling Excursions to eke out his two sheets and a half. I will not resemble him in his Little Artifices of evading, in his weak and feeble Struglings with a Strong Truth. I will not personate him in the Confusion and Disorder of his Reply, for it seems he had forgot, that it is one sign of a *Well-bred, a Well taught Man,*[1] *to answer to the first in the first place*, and so in order. I will not imitate him in his Dry Common Places, in his Set of Words and Phrases, of Sayings and Apothegms, which would have serv'd on any other occasion, as the Intelligent Reader cannot but take notice. Much less will I comply with him in his Angry fits and Passionate Ferments, which, tho he strives to palliate, are easily discernible, for he feels himself Wounded, and is not able to disguise it. I will betake my self, I say, to the present Concern with great application and mindfulness, fully making good my *Former Charges* against his Book, and clearing my own from those sorry Objections and Cavils which he hath since rais'd against it. In the whole management I will sincerely acquaint the Reader first with *his own words*, and then offer my Refutation of them: and all along I will be careful to banish all Indecent Reflections; unless those shall be counted such which are purely grounded on his own expressions, and which his Freedom of Language necessarily and unavoidably administers to me.

The Main *Charges* are these. 1. That he unwarrantably crowded all the Necessary Articles of Faith into *One*, with a design of favouring *Socinianism*. 2. That he shew'd his good will to this Cause by interpreting those Texts which respect the *Holy Trinity*, after the Antitrinitarian mode. 3. That he gave proof of his being *Socinianiz'd* by his utter silence about *Christ's satisfying for us*, and purchasing Salvation by vertue of his Death, when he designedly undertook to enumerate the *Advantages* and *Benefits* which accrue to mankind by Christ's coming into the World. And in the making good of these Particular Charges, I shall (as I did before) evidence to the World that this Writer hath not only a design to cherish *Socinianism*, but at the same time to make way for *Atheism*.

[1]　*Mishn. Tract. Avoch.* c. 5.

I begin with the First, on which I will enlarge more than on any of the rest; because it comprehends in it several other Particulars, and because in discussing of this, I shall have opportunity to lay open the Sophistry and Dissimulation of this *Vindicator*, and likewise to discover to the Reader how Mischievous and Pernicious his Design is. First, it is observable that this Guilty Man would be shifting off the Enditement by excepting against the *formality of the Words*, as if such were not to be found in his Book. But when doth he do this? In the close of it, when his matter was exhausted, and he had nothing else to say, *Vindic.* p. 178. Then he bethinks himself of this Salvo, whereas he had generally before pleaded to the formal Enditement, and had thereby owned it to be True. And indeed he can do no other, for it was the main work he set himself about to find but *One Article* of Faith in all the Chapters of the four *Gospels* and the *Acts of the Apostles*: and accordingly he over and over again declares, that there is but that One Truth (viz. *Jesus is the Messiah) necessarily to be assented to by Christians*, or (as he sometimes words it) *absolutely required to make a man a Christian, or a member of Christ. This is the SOLE Doctrin press'd and requir'd to be believ'd in the whole tenour of our Saviour's and his Apostles preaching.* p. 102. of his *Reasonableness of Christianity.* And again in the same place. *This was the ONLY Gospel Article of Faith which was Preached to them.* This he often inculcates, having left out several considerable passages in the very *Gospels*, and having thrown aside the *Epistles*, as if they were no part of the New Testament, hoping that some of his Readers would be bubbled by this means.

And when I told him of his *One Article*, he knew well enough that I did not exclude the Article of the *Deity*, for that is a Principle of *Natural Religion*; whereas, I only took notice of his passing by and wholly omitting those points which are *Evangelical*. Yet he willfully mistakes me in this, p. 174. of his *Vindication*, and saith he doth not deny the necessary belief of a *Deity*, or *One only True God*; and so the belief of the *Messias* with that makes Two Articles. Thus he would perswade the Reader, that I misunderstood him, and that I tax'd him with setting up One Article, when he acknowledges two. But the Reader sees his Shuffling; for my Discourse did not treat (neither doth his Book run that way) of Principles of

Natural Religion, but of the *Revealed one*, and Particularly the *Christian*. Accordingly this was it which I taxed him with, that of all the Principles and Articles of Christianity he chose out but *One* as necessarily to be believed to make a Man a Christian.

And though since he hath tried to split this One into two, p. 175. yet he labours in vain, for *to believe Jesus to be the Messias* amounts to the same, with *believing him to be a King or ruler*, his being *Anointed* (*i. e.* being the *Messias*) including that in it. Yet he hath the Vanity to add in great Characters, THESE ARE ARTICLES, as if the putting them into these *Great Letters* would make one Article two. Such is the fond fancy and conceitedness of the Gentleman, whereas in other places he hath formally declared, that there is but *One Article* that is the necessary Matter of Faith. This I had just reason to except against; and now I will give a farther account of my doing so, by shewing that, besides that One Fundamental Principle or Article which he so often mentions, there are *Others* that are as necessarily to be believed to make a Man a *Christian*, yea to give him the denomination of a *Believer*, in the sense of the Gospel. Several of these I particularly, but barely enumerated in my former *Discourse*, and now I will distinctly insist on the most of them, and let the Reader see, that it is as necessary for a Convert to Christianity to give assent to *them*, as to that other he so frequently specifies.

This Proposition, that *by one man sin entred into the World, and death by sin*: and this which follows, *Death passed upon all men, for as much as all men have sinned*, Rom. 5. 12. and that other, that even *the Regenerate* (for the Apostle speaks of himself and the Converted Ephesians) *are by nature the Children of wrath, as well as others*, Eph. 2. 3. these, I say, are as absolutely necessary to be known, assented to, and believed, in order to our being *Christians* as this Proposition, *Jesus is the Messias, or Sent of God*. For I ask, what was the end of his being sent? Was it not to Help Mankind, to rescue and deliver them from some Evil? And where can we be inform'd concerning the Rise and Nature of this Evil, but in the Sacred and Inspired Writings? And do not these foresaid Texts, which we find in St. *Paul's Epistles*, which acquaint us with the true Source and Quality of our condition by nature? Do they not discover the Root of Mans

Misery, *viz.* the Apostacy of *Adam* (for he is that *one Man*)
and the dreadful Consequences of it, expressed by *Death* and
Wrath? And is this set down to no purpose in these Inspired
Epistles? Is it not requisite that we should know it and believe
it? Yea, is not this absolutely requisite? For it is impossible
any one should firmly imbrace or so much as seriously attend
to the Doctrin of the *Messias*, unless he be persuaded that *He
stands in need of him.* And can he be persuaded of this unless
he be acquainted with his Degenerate and Miserable State,
his universal Depravity and innate Proness to what is
Vitious, and with the true Original of it? *viz.* The voluntary
Defection and Fall of our First Parents, and with that the loss
of our Happiness. The word *Messias* is an insignificant term
till we have a belief of this: Why then is there a Treatise
published to tell the World, that the bare belief of a *Messias*
is all that is required of a Christian?

Again, it is not only necessary to know that *Jesus is the
Messias*, but also to know and believe *who* this *Jesus*, this
Messias is, *viz.* whether he be *God* or *Man*, or both. For
every one will grant that there is a Vast Difference between
the one and the other, as much as there is betwixt Infinite and
Finite; and therefore that we may have a due apprehension
concerning the *Messias*, it is absolutely necessary, that we
should believe him to be what he is declared to be in the
Infallible Writings, *viz.* God as well as Man. *The Word was
God*, John 1. 1. *The Word was made Flesh*, v. 14. And this
Word is *the Only begotten of the Father*, in the same Verse.
God was manifest in the Flesh, 1 Tim. 3. 16. He is called not
only *God* in these places, and in several others, but he is stil'd
the True God, 1 John 5. 20. and *the Great God*, Tit. 2. 13.
The Lord of all, Acts 10. 36. *God blessed for ever*, Rom. 9.
5. Hence we must conclude, that there is a necessity of
believing the *Messias* to be *the very God*, of the same Essence
with the Father and the Holy Ghost, for these are the two
other *Persons* included in the Deity. So that hence it will
follow, that it is requisite to believe the Holy *Trinity*, i.e. that
there are in the Godhead Three Persons, Father, Son and
Holy Ghost; which is the Doctrin that our Saviour himself
taught (and he taught it, that it might be *believed*) *Mat.* 28.
19. where the Celebration of *Baptism*, which is a solemn part
of Divine Worship, is commanded to be *in the name of the
Father, and of the Son, and of the Holy Ghost*, who are

One God, 1. John 5. 7. *These Three are One*, one Essence or
Being, as the word Ev imports. Those words of the Apostle
are observable, 1 *Cor* 1. 13. *Were ye baptised in the name of
Paul?* As much as to say, *Baptism* is in the name of *God*, and
not of a Man: Therefore when it is said, *Go and Baptize in
the name of the Father, Son, and Holy Ghost*, it is included,
that these Three are *God, i.e.* Three Persons in one and the
same Deity. Thus it is manifest, that the believing of *Jesus*'s
being the *Messias*, or *Anointed* is not sufficient to make a
Man a Christian Believer, but he must further believe these
Propositions or Articles, *viz.* that the Son of God was made
flesh, *i.e.* assumed our Human Nature; that Christ is True
God; and He with the Father and the Spirit are One God; for
these are not only expressed in the *Gospels* and *Epistles* (out
of both which we are to gather the Fundamental Articles of
Faith) and consequently are to be assented to by all
Christians, but the very Nature of the thing it self dictates
that we ought to have a firm belief of these Truths; for
otherwise when a Man professes his belief in the *Messias*, he
is yet ignorant of the *Person* he pretends to believe in. He
doth not know whether he believes in a *God* or in a *Man*, or
to which of these he is beholding, for the Good he looks for
by the Messias's coming. Now, Sir, you with your *Reasonableness of Christianity*, what do you think of this? Is it not
reasonable that a Christian should (as the Apostle speaks of
himself) *know whom he hath believed?* 2 Tim. 1. 12. Nay, is
it not indispensably necessary, that he should know whether
it be a *Divine*, or *Human*, or *Angelical* Power that he is
obliged to, that so he may accordingly proportion his
Affections and Service? for (what ever the late Set of
Socinians hold) there must be a *difference* made between the
Homage which is paid to a Creature (such as they declare
Christ to be) and that which is due only to the Creator. I will
refer the Reader to the Incomparable Bishop *Pearson* on the
Second Article of the *Creed*, where he shews, the "*Necessity
of our believing Christ to be the Eternal Son of God, and God
himself*, 1. For the directing and confirming of our Faith
concerning the *Redemption of Mankind*. 2. For the right
informing of us about that *Worship* and *Honour* which are
due to him. 3. For giving us a right apprehension, and
consequently a due value of the *Infinite Love* of God the
Father in sending his Only-begotten Son into the World to die

for us." Thus this Judicious Writer. But our Nameless Author would persuade us, that there is no necessity of believing any such thing.

Then in the next place, we are to have a right conception concerning our *Recovery* and *Restauration* by this *Messias*, who is God-Man. And here those several Scriptures will furnish us with Articles, *As by the offence of one, judgment came upon all men to condemnation, even so by the righteousness of one the free gift came upon all men unto justification of life. For as by one mans disobedience many were made sinners, so by the obedience of one shall many be made righteous*, Rom. 5. 18, 19. *He appeared to put away sin by the sacrifice of himself*, Heb. 9. 26. *Christ was once offered to bear the sins of many*, Heb. 9. 28. *Christ hath once suffered for sins, the just for the unjust*, 1 Pet. 3. 18. *He gave himself a Ransom for all men*, 1 Tim. 2. 6. *Ye are redeemed with the precious blood of Christ*, 1 Pet. 1. 18, 19. And to it is prefix'd *ye know*, to let us understand that this Article is to be known and assented to. *We are bought with a price*, 1 Cor. 6. 20. and 7. 23. *We are reconciled unto God by the Death of his Son*, Rom. 5. 10. *By him now we have received the Atonement*, v. 11. *By one offering he hath perfected for ever them that are sanctified*, Heb. 10. 14. *It behoved Christ to suffer, and to rise from the dead the third day*, Luk. 24. 46. *Christ must needs have suffered, and risen again from the dead*, Acts 17. 3. *He was taken up into heaven, and sat on the right hand of God*, Mark 16. 19. These and the like places afford us such Fundamental and Necessary Doctrins as these are, that by and for the Meritorious Righteousness and Obedience of Christ (the Second *Adam*) we are accounted Righteous and Obedient in the sight of God: That Christ was a Sacrifice for us, and suffered in our stead: That he satisfied Divine Justice by paying an Infinite Price for us; That by vertue of that Payment all the Debts, *i.e.* all the Sins of Believers are perfectly absolved: That hereby the anger of the Incensed Deity is pacified, and that we are entirely Reconciled to him: That we have an assurance of all this by Christ's rising from the dead, and ascending triumphantly into Heaven. These are *Principles of the Oracles of God*, Heb. 5. 12. These are part of the *Form of sound words*, 2 Tim. 1. 13. which are indispensable Ingredients in the *Christian Faith*, which you may know by this, that if a man be obliged to the belief of the Messias's Coming, it is undeniably requisite that he should know *what* the Messias came to do for him, and that he should firmly yield assent to it. This I think no Man of Reason will deny: and then it will follow that these Articles which I have last mentioned are the Necessary and Unexceptionable object or matter of the Faith of a Christian Man. And here likewise it were easie to shew, that *Adoption, Justification, Pardon of Sins*, &c. which are Privileges and Benefits bestowed upon us by the *Messias*, are necessary matters of our Belief, for we can't duly acknowledge him for our Benefactor and Saviour, unless we believe, that these Great Prerogatives are confer'd upon us.

Moreover, it is of undoubted necessity in order to our being *Christians*, that we know and believe what the *Messias requires of us*; which is contained in such general Texts as these, *That ye being delivered out of the hands of your enemies may serve him* (Christ our Deliverer) *without fear, in holiness and righteousness before him all the days of our life*, Luke 1. 75. *The grace of God which bringeth salvation, teacheth us, to deny ungodliness and worldly lusts*, &c. Tit. 2. 11, 12. *He gave himself for us, that he might re-redeem us from all iniquity*, &c. Tit. 2. 14. *This is the will of God, even your sanctification*, 1 Thess. 4. 3. *Without Faith it is impossible to please God*, Heb. 11. 6. *Without holiness no man shall see the Lord*, Heb. 12. 14. Which places yield us such Propositions as these, that the *Messias* who vouchsafed to come into the World to redeem lost Man, requires of him universal Holiness and Righteousness, and the abandoning of all sin and ungodliness: That it was one grand end and design of Christ's visiting the World to redeem men from their iniquities, to sanctifie their Natures, and to make them entirely godly, sober and righteous in their Lives: That without these there is no Salvation, no Seeing of God in the regions of Glory, no hopes of Everlasting Happiness. The disbelieving of these *Articles* hath made so many Sorry *Christians* as we see every where, such as lay claim to that Honourable *Title*, but are regardless of that Holiness which should accompany it. We must not only believe that *Jesus is the Messias*, but we must believe this also that we can have no Benefit by this Messias unless we by Faith and Obedience adhere to him.

Chap. II.

Thus I have briefly set before the Reader those *Evangelical Truths*, those *Christian Principles* which belong to the very Essence of Christianity. I have proved them to be such, and I have reduced most of them to certain *Propositions*, which is a thing the *Vindicator* call'd for, *p.* 169. If what I have said will not content him, I am sure I can do nothing that will. And therefore, if he should capriciously require any thing more, it would be as great Folly in me to comply with it as it is in him to move it. From what I have said it is evident that he is grossly mistaken when he saith, *Whatever doctrines the Apostles required to be believed to make a man a Christian, are to be found in those places of Scripture which he hath quoted in his book*, *p.* 166. The places which he quotes are made use of by him to shew that there is but *One Article* of Belief, *viz.* that *Jesus is the Messiah*: but I think I have sufficiently proved that there are Other Doctrines besides That which are requir'd to be believed to make a man a Christian. Why did the Apostles *write* these Doctrines? Was it not that those they writ to might give their *Assent* to them? Nay, did they not require Assent to them? Yes verily, for this is to be proved from the Nature of the things contained in those Doctrines, which were such as had *immediate* respect to the Occasion, Author, Way, Means, and Issue of their Redemption and Salvation, as any impartial judg by examining the several Particular Articles and Propositions will readily grant. So that the sum of all amounts to this, The belief of those things without the knowledg of which a man cannot be saved is absolutely Necessary: but the belief of the foregoing Particulars is the belief of such things without the knowledg of which a man cannot be saved; Therefore the belief of these Particulars is absolutely necessary. None will be so refractory, I suppose, as to deny the first Proposition in this Syllogism; therefore I am to prove the Second, which is easily effected thus. The belief of those things which have *Immediate* respect to the Occasion, Author, Way, Means, and Issue of our Salvation, and which are necessary for knowing the True Nature and Design of it, is the belief of such things without the knowledg of which a man cannot be saved: but such is the belief of the preceding Articles, *Ergo*.

Chap. IV.

It is likely I shall further exasperate this Author when I desire
the Reader to observe that this *Lank Faith* of his is in a manner
no other than the *Faith of a Turk.* For the [2] *Alcoran*
acknowledges that the *Spirit of God bore witness to Christ the
son of Mary: a Divine Soul was put into him. He was the
Messenger of the Spirit, and the Word of God.* And in another
place *God* is brought in declaring that *he had sent Christ the
Son of* Mary, &c. And in other places he is mention'd as a
Prophet, as a *Great Man*, one Commission'd by God, and *sent
by him* into the world. This is of the like import with what our
good *Ottoman* Writer the *Vindicator* saith of our Saviour, and
this he holds is the sum of all that is Necessary to be believ'd
concerning him. The *Mahometans* call themselves *Musselmen*,
or rather (according to the true account of the *Arabick* word)[3]
Moslemim, i.e. *Believers*; and what difference is there between
one of them and our Author's *Believer?* The former believes
that Christ is a Good Man, and not above the nature of a Man,
and sent of God to give Instructions to the world: and the Faith
of the latter is of the very same scantling. Thus he confounds
Turky with *Christendom*; and those that have been reckon'd as
Infidels are with him *Christians.* He seems to have consulted
the *Mahometan Bible*, which saith,[4] *Christ did not suffer on
the cross, did not die*; for he and his Allies speak as meanly of
these Articles as if there were no such thing. The Alcoran often
talks (particularly see the *Last Chapter* of it) against Christ's
being *the Son of God by Generation.* It is one of the First
Principles of *Mahometism* that there is but *One God neither
begetting nor begot.* See *Sylburgius's Saracenica.* This is it
which our Author drives at when he labours to prove the
Messias and *the Son of God* are terms synonymous, as you
shall hear by and by. This reminds me of that Affinity and
Correspondence which hath been between the *Turks* and this
Gentleman's Party.[5] *Servetus* conferr'd notes with the *Alcoran*,
when he undertook to fetch an Argument out of it to disprove

[2]   Azoar 1. Azoar 67.

[3]   From the Arabick verb *islam, credidit*, whence the Mahometan Religion is
call'd *Islamisimus.*

[4]   Alcor. Azoar. 11.

[5]   De Trin. I. 1.

the *Deity* of our Saviour. It is observable that those Countreys of *Europe* which border on the *Sultan's* dominions, as *Hungary, Transilvania,* &c. abound with *Socinians* and *Antitrinitarians.* The inhabitants of these places accommodate themselves to their Potent Neighbours, they make some approach to the *Conqueror's Creed.* Some of these men have lately got footing in *England,* and because they and the *Great Turk* disbelieve the *Trinity,* therefore we must all be Proselytes to their opinion. They are making way for this by taking away all the Articles of the Christian Faith but One. And our late Writer is the Instrument they make use of for this purpose. This Great Mufti hath given us a Hopeful Draught of *Christianity*; and it was fit the English Reader should know that a *Turk* according to him is a *Christian,* for he makes the same Faith serve them both.

Nay, in the last place, let us take notice that this Gentleman presents the world with a very Ill notion of *Faith,* for the very *Devils* are capable of all that *Faith* which he saith makes a *Christian man,* yea of more, for we read that they *believed Jesus to be the Son of God,* Mat. 8. 29. They cried out to him, *Thou art Christ the Son of God,* Luke 4. 41. which latter words in both places denote his *Divinity,* as I shall shew afterwards. But besides this *Historical Faith* (as it is generally call'd by Divines) which is giving credit to Evangelical Truths as barely reveal'd, there must be something else added to make up the True Substantial Faith of a *Christian.* With the Assent of the Understanding must be joyn'd the Consent or Approbation of the Will. All those Divine Truths which the Intellect assents to must be allow'd of by this Elective power of the Soul. True Evangelical Faith is a hearty Accepting of the Messias as he is offer'd in the Gospel. It is a sincere and impartial submission to all things requir'd by the *Evangelical Law,* which is contain'd in the *Epistles* as well as the *other Writings.* And to this Practical Assent and Choice there must be added likewise a firm Trust and Reliance in the Blessed Author of our Salvation. But this late Undertaker, who attempted to give us a more perfect account than ever was before of *Christianity as it is deliver'd in the Scriptures,* brings us no tidings of any such *Faith* belonging to *Christianity,* or discover'd to us in the *Scriptures.* Which gives us to understand that he verily believes there is no such *Christian Faith,* for in some of his Numerous Pages (especially 101, 102, &c.) where he speaks so much of *Belief* and *Faith,* he might have taken occasion to insert *one word* about this Compleat Faith of the Gospel.

Having thus represented how Defective, how *Narrow*, how *Erroneous*, how *Mistaken* this Unknown Writer's *Christianity*, and especially his *Faith* is; I will now proceed to shew how *Dangerous* and *Pernicious* this sort of Doctrine is. Here is a Contrivance set up for the bringing in of *Darkness* and *Barbarism* into the Christian world. The only Necessary Point of Belief that the *Old Testament* delivers, is, according to these Gentlemen that *there is One God*: and all the *New Testament* affords us as matter of Necessary Faith is this, that *Jesus is the Messias*. Carry but these Two Articles along with you, and you are a True Christian. There is no *Necessity* at all of being acquainted with the Reveal'd Doctrine concerning the Cause of Mankinds Degeneracy and Corruption, which gave occasion to the *Messias*'s Coming into the world. There is no Necessity of knowing whether this *Messias* be God or Man, or both: there is no Necessity of understanding whether he came to suffer and dye in our stead, and to satisfie the Divine Justice, and to purchase Salvation for us by his Blood: There is no Necessity of believing that without Faith and Evangelical Obedience we cannot have any Benefit by the Messias: There is no Necessity of being perswaded that our Salvation springs from the mere Grace and Bounty of Heaven: There is no Necessity of believing the Privileges and Rewards (both here and hereafter) which are entail'd on Christianity. There is but a *Single Article of Belief*, and this a very Short one too, *viz.* that *Jesus is the Messias*; and if you assent to This you are as *Sound a Christian* and as *Good a Believer* as this Gentleman can make you. One would think that seeing there are so many Branches of the Evangelical Faith commended to us and urged upon us by the Apostles in their Epistles (some of which our Saviour himself in the Gospel, had made mention of) one would think, I say, that a man that hath a True Sense of Christianity, and is a Lover of Souls should endeavour to display before the world these Several Parts of the *Christian Belief*, and should be earnest with men to embrace them All, and not to omit or neglect any of them, seeing they all so nearly concern their Everlasting Wellfare. But here comes One that makes it his great business to beat men off from taking notice of these Divine Truths, he represents them as wholly Unnecessary to be believed, he cries down all Articles of Christian Faith but One. He at this time of day, when *Christianity* is so bright, strives to darken and eclipse it; he hides it from the faces of mankind, draws a thick Veil over it, will not suffer them to look into it, takes the Holy and Inspired *Epistles* (which are as much the Word of God as the *Gospels*) out of their way, and tells them again and again that a *Christian man* or *Member of Christ* need not know or believe any more than that One Individual Point which he mentions.

Hear O ye Heavens, and give ear O Earth, judg whether this be not the way to introduce *Darkness* and *Ignorance* into Christendom, whether this be not blinding of mens eyes, and depriving them of that Blessed Light which the Writings of the Evangelists and Apostles should illuminate mens minds with. Which makes me think sometimes (and perhaps the Reader doth so too) that this Writer and the other Confederates are Under-hand-Factors for that Communion (though they would seem to be much against it) which cries up *Ignorance* as the mother of Devotion and Religion. If they had not some such design, why do they labour so industriously to keep the people in Ignorance, to tell them that One Article is enough for them, and that there is no *Necessity* of knowing any other doctrines of the Bible? Thus by following their *Italian* Master *Socinus*, they trade for that *Countrey*. And this *Vindicator* among the rest trafficks very visibly for it whilest he blasteth so substantial a part of the New Testament as the *Epistolary* Writings are. Would not one be apt to suspect that (as their *Roman* Masters have done) they would afterwards not only keep a part, but the Whole Scripture from the people? And so we shall travel to *Rome* by the way of *Racovia*.

But what may be the Reason why both the *Exotick* and *English Unitarians* agree to maim the Head of Christianity, to contract its Articles, and to reduce it into so small a compass? Seeing there are *Several* Fundamental Truths appertaining to the Christian Religion, why are they not all pronounced Necessary to be believed and assented to? They have several reasons for this; first, they are compell'd to do it because otherwise they can't maintain that which so many of them profess to believe, *viz.* the Salvation of all men, of whatsoever Perswasion they are. This is an extravagant Principle which they have taken up, and it is the Modish Opinion at this day, but if they should hold that there is a

Necessity of believing a considerable number of Articles in Christianity, they could not possibly entertain this Fashionable Notion. Secondly, they cunningly keep up this Conceit of the necessity of but One Article, because it makes for their own Preservation and Safety, that neither the Magistrate nor Ecclesiastical Power in any Country may take occasion to animadvert upon them: for why should they trouble and molest them for holding such doctrines as are not of the Foundation of Religion, as are of no Necessity to be believed? This makes them forward to propagate their Notion. And hence also we see what is the reason of their talking so warmly for *Liberty*: This is done to Secure themselves that though they broach never so Pernicious Opinions they may not fall under the lash of the Magistrate. In brief, they would not be Punish'd here, and they think they have made sure of hereafter by another Tenent of theirs. Thirdly, by vertue of this Expedient they can throw off any Doctrine when they please, especially those Main Articles of the *Holy Trinity*, of *Christ's Satisfaction*, &c. for it is but saying that they are not necessary to be believed, (there being a Necessity of believing but One) and the business is done. Thus you see how it is their Concern to hold up their One Article.

But who sees not that hereby they depress Christianity, and unspeakably injure the Faith of the Gospel? What is the meaning of *Catechizing*, which hath been so universally commended and practised by the Ancients? There were in the Primitive Church particular persons that made it their business to instruct and inform the ignorant in a *Catechetical* Way: yea, it was a Distinct Office among the Christians of old. Saint *Mark* in the Church of *Alexandria* was a *Catechist*, *Pantænus* succeeded him, then *Origen* had the same Employment there, and *Heraclius* after him. What! was this only to teach *One Article* of Faith? Who but a *Socinian* can believe this? Is it not enough to rob us of our *God*, by denying *Christ* to be so, but must they spoil us of all the Other Articles of Christian Faith but One? Who would think that the Popular Man, who pretends to take such care of the *Multitude*, should do them the greatest Mischief imaginable, whilest he makes a shew of being extraordinarily kind to them? for a greater Mischief there cannot be than to put them off with One Article of Christian Belief, when there are Many others of absolute necessity.

Chap. VIII.

Having now dispatch'd my Main Business, and found the Bill against the Criminal, not by *Innuendo's*, but by Plain Express Proof, I am at leisure to account with him for some Other Passages in his *Vindication*. He insinuates that I would represent every one as an *Atheist*, or a *Promoter of Atheism* that doth not think as I do, *doth not just say after me, p.* 161, 162. Which is a groundless Calumny, and might be confuted from that *Freedom* which I professed, *p.* 77. even in that *Discourse* which he excepts against. I have always been averse to *Bigotism*, I never shew'd my self a Dogmatizer, but always declar'd for an Ingenuous Liberty, such as doth not audaciously encroach upon the Necessary and Fundamental Points of our Religion. Therefore this *Vindicator*'s wilful mistaking of what I said, thereby to represent me as extremely Censorious and Uncharitable, looks like Spleen. But I need say no more than this, that the Reader is convinc'd (I question not) from what hath been premised that this Writer will say any thing that comes into his head. This seems to be natural to him every where: and he can be no more without it than a Spaniard without his Guittar.

To be *Orthodox* is a great Scandal, it seems, and he often objects it to me: which, as the Learned know, was the very language and idiom of the *Arrians* of old, and of that sort of men who are since known by the name of *Socinians*. He speaks in the very Stile of the *Old Antitrinitarians*; though it may be he will say he doth not know it. He publickly prides himself in his *Heterodoxy*, and hates even with a deadly hatred all *Catechisms* and *Confessions*, all *Systems* and *Models, p.* 165. He laughs at *Orthodoxy, p.* 169, 172. and derides *Mysteries*, which are infallible marks of a *Racovian* Brother. And O how he grins at the *Spirit of Creed-making? p.* 170 *Vindic.* the very thoughts of which do so haunt him, so plague and torment him that he cannot rest till it be conjured down. And here, by the way, seeing I have mention'd his rancour against *Systematick books and writings*, I might represent the *Misery* that is coming upon all *Booksellers* if this Gentleman and his Correspondents go on successfully. Here is an effectual Plot to undermine *Stationers Hall*; for all *Systems* and *Bodies* of Divinity, Philosophy, &c. must be cashier'd: whatever looks like *System* must not be bought or sold. This will fall heavy on the Gentlemen of St. *Paul's Church-yard*, and other places.

This Author often finds fault with me for my *Zeal*, p. 163, 170, 178. It is likely he hath heard that when the Gospel was heretofore read in the Churches in *Poland* (before it was *Socinianized*,) it was usual to draw their Swords, to shew that they would defend it against all that opposed it. I do but draw my Pen in defence of the *Gospel*, yea and the *Epistles*, and I am censur'd as a *Zealot* by him. And it is not strange, for he must needs declare against *Zeal* that is *Indifferent*. Besides, according to this Judicious Casuist there is but *One* Point of Christianity that a man can be zealous for, if he would. Queen *Mary's* Martyrs foolishly threw away their lives, for neither *Bonner* nor any of their Persecutors did so much as desire them to renounce this Article *Jesus is the Messias*: and as for all the rest, this Gentleman tells us that they are *not necessarily to be believ'd*, and consequently not to be acknowledg'd and profess'd; and then who will shew any *Zeal* for them, especially such as will carry a man into the Flames?

He often talks of *my being in his bosom, and knowing his heart and thoughts*, p. 167, 168, 172. (which by the by is more than his Brethren will allow *God himself* to know, for *Free Acts being uncertain they can't be certainly understood by God* (as the Gentleman whom I shall speak a word with anon tells us.) This sort of Talk argues that he is much troubled that I have penetrated into his *Thoughts*, and have discovered to the world what his Intention and Design is. And yet he intimates also by this way of speaking that it is an Impossible thing to do this. How impossible then is it for himself *to know his heart*? for this is a certain Maxim, It is the Punishment of a Dissembler to deceive himself, for his endeavouring to do so to others. I wish this Writer would consider of it, and learn for the future to be free, open and fair, and then others (as well as himself) would have a window into his breast, and see that which they are sorry they find no appearance of now.

And I wish this were not too common a fault of the Party, at least of many of them. They inure themselves to Sophistry, Cunning, and Artifice, when they either interpret Texts, or Argue in favour of their Darling Opinions. They then too palpably impose upon other mens minds, as well as upon their own. And yet at the same time they pretend to great Simplicity and honest dealing. Thus you find them applauding themselves in their late Prints: ⁶ *the Unitarians* (say they of themselves) *are plain fellows, and have Countrey Consciences, and do not like juggling.* You Gentlemen of the *City*, look to it: these *Unitarians*, these *Socinians* have a very bad opinion of you, for here they would have it believ'd that *City-Consciences* are false and perfidious, deceitful and juggling. It is a course Complement, and Rustick enough which these *Plain Fellows* put upon you. It is not the first time they have struck at you: *London* must be disciplin'd by *Racovia*. And the *Vindicator* is one of these *Plain Fellows*, for as he hath shew'd himself an *Unitarian*, so he makes it appear that he hath a *Country-Conscience* in the sense that these men ultimately mean it in, *viz.* a knack of Cheating in a Rustical plain way, as when he pretends to make a Religion for the *Rabble*, an *Easie Plain Religion*, a *Creed with One Article*, and no more; pretending thereby to gratifie *them*, but under hand subverting *Christianity*.

Nor have I yet done with him. I find him to be a Man of a very Uneven Temper: sometimes he is very Low and Whining, and will be *asking pardon*, and *desiring me*, &c. at other times he is Imperious and Magisterial, and *requires me*, &c. Sometimes he talks very demurely, as about being *in earnest, p.* 165. *being serious and grave, p.* 173, 174. and in a Pedantick Humour he undertakes to censure and correct my *Stile, p.* 173. But this fit of Gravity doth not last long; he every where shews himself Light and Freakish, Ironical and Abusive as far as he is able, and nibbles at Wit according to his mean Talent. He inveighs forsooth against *Declamatory Rhetorick, Wit and Jest*, &c. *p.* 173. *Vindic.* and yet at the same time is Wanton and Frolick, Starting any thing to sport himself with. In that very place before mention'd where he seems to put on his Gravity, he hath not forgot *the Merry time of Rope-dancing and Puppet-Plays*, at which he was good in the days of yore. It is likely he had been a little before conducting some of his Young Brood to *Bartholomew Fair*, and thence this precious idea came into his head.

Without doubt he thought he was not a little Ingenious in that waggish expression, *p.* 164. *a Known Writer of the brotherhood*: which is meant of the Brethren of the Clergy who have writ against the *Socinian* Cause, the same with the *Popular Authorities and Frightful Names* which he speaks of,

⁶ The Trinitarian Scheme of Religion, *page* 21.

p. 172. The professed Divines of *England* you must know are but a pitiful sort of folks with this great *Racovian Rabbi*. He tells us plainly that he is not mindful of what *the Generality of Divines declare for, p.* 172. He labours so concernedly to engratiate himself with the *Mob*, the *Multitude* (which he so often talks of) that he hath no regard to these. *The generality of the Rabble* are more considerable with him than *the generality of Divines, the Writers of the brotherhood.* Though truly a Wise Man that hears any one judg thus, will think he deserves as well to be rewarded with a pair of Ears of the largest size as *he* did who judg'd on *Pan*'s side against *Apollo.* But there is more yet in this term of *brotherhood* than this, for here it is implied (and his thoughts may be suppos'd to be upon it when he wrote) that he himself is a Writer of an *Other Fraternity*; and truly this Stile is very proper, for the men of that Party (as 'tis well known) have labour'd to signalize themselves (in the Writings that they have publish'd) by the Title of *Brethren*. It is agreed then; we will for the future take him for a *Polonian Brother.* And I ask the Reader whether this *Brother* be not of kin to the Order of *Friers* in *Italy* who were call'd *Fratres Ignorantiæ, viz.* because, they professed to teach the people as little as possibly they could, as suppose *One Article of Religion*, and no more.

I might proceed further, and shew that this Author, as Demure and Grave as he would sometimes seem to be, can scoff at the Matters of Faith contain'd in the Apostles *Epistles, p.* 169. *l.* 4. &c. To coakse the *Mob* he prophanely brings in that place of Scripture, *Have any of the Rulers believ'd in him? p.* 177. Ridiculously and Irreligiously he pretends that *I prefer what he saith to me to what is offer'd to me from the Word of God, p.* 173. What is there that this Gentleman will not turn into Ridicule or Falsity? What is there that he will not take hold of to be Sportive and Gamesome? We may further see how Counterfeit his *Gravity* is whilst he condemns *frothy and light discourses, p.* 173. *Vindic.* and yet in many pages together most irreverently treats a great part of the *Apostolical Writings*, and throws aside the Main Articles of Religion as unnecessary. From all which it is clear that he contradicts and opposes himself. Whence by the by we may gather that when he saith he is *no Socinian*, we must take his meaning to be that *he is one*, for he is made up of Contradictions. I observed before that the *Dissenting Ministers confess'd to him* (if you will believe[7] him) *that they understood not the difference in debate among them*: but this Gentleman can't be brought to *confess* any thing, he will not own that he is *a Writer of the brotherhood*. No: there is some great Reason (if it may be call'd so) for this, that he would not be thought to be of *Sozzo*'s side: though the Marks and Tokens are so plain that he may be apprehended without a Hue and Crie.

Come, Good Sir, do not act a part any longer: They have been desirous to put you upon service, and you were as willing to be employ'd in it: but now at last Confess it. Appear no more in Masquerade: away with this Mummery, and shew your self what you are. You have let the world see (and so far we are beholding to you) that *Socinian* is a Reproachful Title; that any one may gather from your being so backward to own it. You would never have taken so much pains to shift off this Character if it were not a very Scandalous One. Throw off your Vizour then, and speak out like a Man. Be free and ingenuous, and dissemble not with Heaven as well as Men. I have, Sir, been very free with you, which you may impute to your not being so with your self. You know the Rule among the Men of Art, The Heart is known by the Pulse. I have made bold to usurp upon the Faculty, I have been feeling your Pulse, and I have found that it strongly beats after the *Racovian* tone. This I have told you with some plainess, and you are obliged to me for representing you to your self. I know you did not expect an Assault, for it was your self (however you apply it to me) that was thought to be one of [8] *the most Priviledged sort of men*. But, Sir, in the Reign of Truth *Protections* are not of any use. It is a laudable way sometimes to fight the Enemy in his Trenches. There are some Criminals that must be snatch'd from the horns of the Altar, especially when they injure the Altar it self, when they abuse that which is Holy, and trample upon our Sacred Faith and Religion.

To conclude, I have said nothing out of prejudice or disgust, much less out of bitterness and ill will, for I am in Entire Charity with you, and the more so because I have spoken so freely. If you complain now (as you did before) that you are

---

[7] Reasonableness of Christianity, *p.* 158.

[8] Vindic. *p.* 170.

hardly dealt with, I have only this to say, A Plain Down-right Adversary might perhaps have met with another usage, but such a Stubborn Dissembler could not expect *fairer quarter*.

A Brief Reply to Another Socinian Writer, Whose Cavils bear this Title, [The Exceptions of Mr. Edwards in his Causes of Atheism against the Reasonableness of Christianity, &c. Examin'd.]

There came lately to my hand this Writer's Sheets in the true *Racovian Print*: but I having been so large upon the *Vindicator*, this *Double-Column'd* Gentleman, who pretends to be an *Examinator*, cannot expect I should spend much time about him. In the first place we are to observe that he most humbly and reverentially *dedicates* his Papers to the New Patron of the Cause, and takes upon him the Defence of what he hath said in his *Reasonableness of Christianity*. He highly applauds him for his being so serviceable to the *Socinian* and *Antitrinitarian* Interest. And it is part of his Panegyrick that *he hath happily provided for the quiet and satisfaction of the minds of the honest multitude, p. 3* [187]. That is, he hath not troubled and molested them (as some have done) with propounding Several Articles of Christian Belief but hath told them that *One* is enough for them, and bids them rest contended with that, like good honest Ignorant Souls. Thus *he hath provided* (but how *happily* let the Reader judg) *for their quiet and satisfaction*. But though the *Examinator* heaps great Commendations on the *Vindicator*, yet he professes if (you'll believe him, you may) that *he knows him not, p. 4* [188]. Only at a venture he takes his part, he now being become one of the *Brotherhood*, and may prove a very Substantial Tool and Engine in the great Work they are now about, *viz.* the subverting of our Saviour's *Divinity*, the laying aside the *Apostolical Epistles*, the shutting out the *Necessary Matters of Faith* contain'd in them, and the setting up and idolizing of *One Article*, with defiance of all the rest as any ways Necessary to be believ'd. This is the New *DIANA* that is set up by our *Ephesians*, especially by their late *Demetrius*.

Now next let us see how the *Examinator* licks over the *Vindicator*'s Article, and tells us that the belief of *Jesus*'s being the *Messias comprehends* and *implies several other things, p. 3* [187]. Here he sweats to bring off his Brother handsomly and with credit by letting us know that his Bold Assertion which runs through his whole book is to be *qualified* after this manner, 1. *All synonymous expressions*, &c. and so he sets them down one, two and three. But I ask him this Question (and let the Reader be pleas'd to observe the issue of it) Why did not the Gentleman himself make use of these *Qualifications* when he vented the Proposition, and insisted upon it in the bulk of his book, yea why did he not mention these *Qualifications* in his *Answer* to any Exceptions against his book? He knew what he had asserted, and he defends (as well he can) his doing so, but you will find in no part of his *Vindication* that he betakes himself to these *Evasions*, though he hath enough of Others of a different sort. How then come you, Mr. *Examinator*, to invent these things for him? Do you not hereby proclaim to the world that you will put off the Reader with any idle and groundless Conceit of your own?

When he repeats my words, *p*. 6, 7 [190, 191]. wherein I took notice of the Gentleman's *willful omitting of plain and obvious passages in the Evangelists* (out of whose Writings he had drawn a Whole Article) *which contain the belief of the Holy Trinity*, he saith not a word to excuse his *Omission*, but by his silence (for he would have spoken without any doubt if he had had any thing to say in his Friends defence) he owns it to be wilful and blameable. Only he comes with the Trite and Common Answer of the Party to those Texts; but before he enters upon the Second of them, *viz. John* 1. 1. he declares *there is no such Text in the whole Bible, p*. 9 [192]. He said rightly that *he was bold to say it*, for a man shall scarcely hear a more Audacious word, though 'tis true he endeavours to mollifie it with an *if*.

In the next place he will turn *Critick*, and see whether he can thrive in this employment, seeing he hath so ill success in his former attempts. His nice palate disgusts the word *birth*, as applyed to *Adam, p*. 38 [198]. but thereby he only shews his want of skill in the Denotation of words. He is so poor a Dabbler in *Grammer* and *Criticism* that he knows not that by the Hebrew *jalad*, and the *Greek* γίνεδης and γεννᾶδης, and the Latin *nasci*, and accordingly our English [*to be born*] are signified in a *general* way the *Origin, Rise*, or *Beginning* of things or persons, and consequently *Birth* or *Nativity* is not to be taken always in the Vulgar Sense. He might have read in *Genethliack* Writers that the word is applied even to *Cities* and *Houses*. But

I need not go so far to defend the Expression. The use of it, and that in the very way that I have applied it, is to be found in Scripture: *art thou the first man that was born? Job* 15. 7. Or we may read it, if we please, more exactly according to the Original, *Art thou born as the first man, or Adam,* i.e. (as the Context will shew it) art thou as understanding as the man that was *first born, viz.* as our First Parent *Adam?* By reason of this *birth Adam* is call'd *the son of God, Luk.* 3. 38. Whence the *Socinians* would gather that *Christ* hath that name upon the like account, because of his Extraordinary *Original,* because of his Miraculous *Birth.* Thus we have found that this Gentleman is ignorant of the true meaning of words in *Common Authors,* that he doth not know the acception of them in *Holy Scripture,* nay that he doth not know what his *own Authors* say, which evinces him to be triply a *Blunderer,* and that he deserves no more to be call'd an *Examinator.*

Then he thinks he doth mighty things, *p.* 39 [199]. by quoting *Limborch* a very Learned Foreigner (a *System-maker* for he hath compiled a Large *System* of Divinity, though he gives it another Name; and why then doth this Gentleman talk so reproachfully of *Systems? p.* 44 [206]. &c.) but this his Author is a *Second Episcopius*; and therefore it was wisely done to bring him in to tell us what are the *Fundamentals* of Religion.[9]

But it was more cunningly done in the next Paragraph to fetch in the *Sixth Article* of the *Church of England* in favour of the *Vindicator's* Conceit. Surely this his Patron, at whose feet he lays his Papers, will give him little thanks for this, for he jeers him rather than defends his Cause. Thus though they are agreed, and understand one another so far as to Impose upon the world, yet they cannot (and never will) agree to speak Truth. And indeed this Worthy Writer foresignified something of this nature. He is a *boding* sort of man, you may perceive, for thus he speaks in his Humble Dedicatory to the Vindicator, *If I have mistaken your sense, or used weak reasonings in your defence* (and behold! here he doth both) *I crave your pardon.* And so you may, and I will tell you for your comfort, he will soon forgive you, for he knows that your heart is right, *i.e.* for the Good Cause, and therefore a little Mistaking of him out of weakness is pardonable.

---

[9] who is so near a-kin to one that is voted a Socinian in the Brief History of the Unitarians.

Then he hales in *Mr. Chillingworth* by head and shoulders, *p.* 200. pronouncing him very definitively *the ablest defender of the Religion of Protestants that the Church ever had*; which is too high a Character for him, though he was a person of Great Parts and Learning. Why must he be said to be *the Ablest Defender* when we can name so many Eminent Writers in other Countreys that have perform'd this task? Or, if he means the *Church of England*, why must he have the absolute Preference to Others that we can name here, especially that Great Ornament and Glory of our Church, whom I had occasion to mention before, who hath so Learnedly defended the *Religion of Protestants?* I, but he writ against *Crellius*, and therefore he must not be the *Ablest Defender*. Again, there is a reason well known to the world why Mr. *Chillingworth* hath the *Preheminence* in the opinion of this Writer and his Confederates, but of that at some other time perhaps. Let us now go on, and see what this Gentleman gets by his producing of Mr. *Chillingworth*; and it is no other than this, a plain confutation of the *Vindicator's* Project concerning the reducing of Religion to a Point, and no more. For these are that Worthy Man's words, *The Bible, the Bible, I say the Bible only is the Religion of Protestants.* And I say so too, but this Gentleman and the Author of *the Reasonableness of Christianity* are of another opinion, for according to them it is not the *Bible*, but a very *Small Portion* of it that is the *Religion of Protestants.* They acknowledg that Some few Verses in several Chapters of the *Four Evangelists* and the *Acts* are matter of Faith or Religion, but they do not cry *the Bible, the Bible, the Bible*, they do not think that All and Every one of the Fundamental Truths in the Whole Scripture are the necessary matter of our Belief. Thus I think this Reverend Scribe might have spared the quoting of Mr. *Chillingworth*, unless he delights in confuting himself and his New Convert.

Afterwards he nibbles at some other passages in my Discourse, but flies off into Impertinencies. Only one thing I meet with that is very Remarkable, and I request the Reader to attend to it. *There are* (saith he) *some that of Deists have been reconciled to the Christian faith by the Unitarian books, and have profess'd much satisfaction therein, p.* 42 [203]. You may perceive that they are making of *Proselytes* as fast as they can, and among the rest some *Deists* come in to them, and so (as the Apostle speaks of Seducers and those that are

Seduced, 2 *Pet*. 2. 20) *the latter end is worse with them than the beginning*: for whereas before they owned a *Natural Religion*, now they become guilty of perverting and prophaning a *Revealed* one. They are so far from being *reconciled to the Christian Faith*, that they oppose and contradict it, and even defie the *Main Articles* of this Religion which is owing to Divine Revelation. Such Converts as these have no reason to *profess much satisfaction in the Unitarian books*, unless Corrupting the Christian faith be to be chosen before plain *Theism*. To speak the plain truth (and it is the design of these Papers to do so) and that which every Thinking and Considering Man cannot but discern, the *Socinians* are but the Journeymen of the *Deists*, and they are set on work by them, for these latter hope to compass their Design, which is to impair the Credit of the *Christian Religion* and those *Inspired Writings* which give us an account of it, they hope (I say) effectually to compass this design by the help of such Good Instruments as they find the *Socinianiz'd* Men to be. You see then what ground this Gentleman hath to think that the *Deists* are Proselytes to the *Unitarians*.

Then he proceeds to make a long harangue about the *Obscurity of Systematical Fundamentals*, p. 44 [206]. &c. but never was poor Creature so bewildred as he is. Only he happily lights upon the *Quakers*, p. 44, 45 [206, 207]. where it is worth observing that the man doth not know his Friends from his Foes, nor these from them. He rails against this sort of men (who he saith would be counted *the only People of God*) and yet it is certain that they are his brethren-*Socinians*. *They utterly disown the Scripture as the Rule of Faith*, he saith: and doth not our late *Socinian* Writer symbolize with them when he declares that the Divine Truths contained in the *Epistles* of the Holy Apostles (which are a considerable part of *Scripture*) are not the Necessary matter of Faith? He complains that *the Quakers turn the Gospel into an Allegory*; but the foremention'd Author doth much worse, for he represents the greatest Part of the Gospel-discoveries as Superfluous and Needless. In giving us the farther Character of the *Quakers*, he in lively colours represents the *Socinians*, for these are his words concerning them, *Retaining still the words wherein the Christian Faith is expressed, though in an Equivocal Sense, they have made a shift to be reputed generally Christians.* Certainly there could not be a better Pourtraiture of the

Racovian Writers, for it is known that they are crafty and sophistical, and quote Scripture only to pervert it. They acknowedg *Christ* to be *God*, and an *Expiatory Sacrifice*, but they mean it *Equivocally*; they quit the true *sense* of Scripture though they retain the *words*, and by reason of this latter *have made a shift* (as this Author speaks) *to pass for Christians.* These men (whatever some few *English* Writers of the *Racovian* way hold of late) exactly side with the *Quakers* in crying down of *Water-Baptism* (for so they both call it in derision.) In the Grand Point of the *Trinity* they both concur, *i.e.* to reject it, witness *W. Pen's Sandy Foundation*, by which he means the doctrine of the *Blessed Trinity*. In a quibbling manner, wherein he shews both his Ignorance and Blasphemy, he thus speaks,[10] *If God, as the Scriptures testifie, hath never been declared or believed but as the* HOLY ONE, *then it will follow that God is not an* HOLY THREE. *Neither can this receive the least prejudice from that frequent, but impertinent distinction, that he is One in Substance, but Three in Persons or Subsistencies.* To which all *Socinus*'s followers say *Amen*. The same Gentleman derides the doctrine of *Satisfaction*, and scoffingly calls the Asserters of it [11]*Satisfactionists*: and who knows not that *Transylvania* agrees here with *Pensylvania*? *The Man that suffer'd at Jerusalem* is the *Socinian* as well as the *Quakers Stile*: And generally as to the main things that relate to our *Saviour*, they perfectly accord, *viz.* in making nothing of them. If *Quakerism* then *be no Christianity*, as this our Writer reports it in the same place, then we may with much more reason conclude that *Socinianism is none*. By this it appears that *Socinus* and *Fox* are well met, and that they are very Loving Friends. But they must seem to disagree, as here in this Gentleman's Papers.

Lastly, let us see the wonderful hand of God in suffering this Unthoughtful Writer to produce *a Paper written by a Jesuite in the late Reign, entituled an Address*, &c. And in this Address, he saith, *he goes about to shew that the Scriptures commonly alledg'd for the Trinity, admit of another sense. He goes the same way in the Article of the Incarnation.* What! had he not enough of the *Quaker* but he must bring in the *Jesuite*? And must he tell the world that the *Jesuitical* Writers take the part of

10   W. Pen's Sandy Foundations, *p.* 12.
11   Sandy Foundat. ibid.

the *Socinians?* must he publickly give notice that they both carry on the same work, and joyntly conspire to pervert the *Scriptures* in order to it? For the credit of the Cause, it had been better to have placed this under a former head, and to have told the Reader that some *Jesuites* (as well as some *Deists*) are *Converts* to *Socinianism.* But he hath blurted it out that *Ignatius Loyola* and *Faustus Socinus* were of kin. Surely this Author must not be employ'd any more to write in defence of the Cause. He must be no longer a *Double-Column'd* Writer: they must look out for a man that is not so Open-hearted, one that can handle his Weapon with more Cunning, for this man hath stabb'd his own Cause.

But because this Writer in the beginning and towards the end of his Papers is pleas'd to use some words of Deference and Respect, I will not be backward to return his Civility in the same kind by letting him know that I suppose him to be a *Person of Ingenuity and Learning* (only I wish he had *shew'd* it in his late Undertaking) and that *I would not have made opposition to him in any other Points* but These which are the Foundation, Basis and Ground-work of *Christianity*, and the very Life and Soul of our *Religion*, and therefore none is to be permitted to treat them *irreverently* and *scoffingly*, as he and his Associates have lately done. But I entertain some hope that this Unsavoury *Tang* will wear off in time.

And this I have finished both my *Replies* to the Gentlemen's Writings against me: and I have wholly confined my self to these, and not ventured to guess at their Persons, or make any Reflections of that kind, for that is a thing which I abhor. Nay, though the *Vindicator* by his reflecting upon my *Degree*, p. 24. and 36. and *Calling*, p. 36, and before, p. 26, and before that, p. 9. had given me occasion to enquire into his Quality and Character, yet I purposely forbore to meddle with any such Considerations. And so as to the *Examinator*, I could easily have traced his Person and Station, and offer'd some Remarks upon either, but I made it not my business to observe Who they were that wrote, but what they had written. And it was necessary to do this latter with some Salt and Keenness, that the levity of their Arguments might be the better exposed, and that I might in a lawful innocent way retaliate that Liberty which they had taken. And indeed the *Socinian* Gentlemen must shew themselves very Disingenuous (which I will not presume of them) if they be dissatisfied with me for my

Freedom of discourse, when in all their Writings they profess to use it. And it is plain that they make use of it: for who sees not that [12] they have been very sharp upon some of the most Eminent and Venerable Persons of our Church? They have handled the late Archbishop and some of his Reverend Brethren (who in their Writings shewed their dislike of the *Socinian* doctrines) with no excess of Respect: And they represent them and the whole Clergy as Mercenary, Timerous, and False hearted: They would perswade the world that the doctrine of the *Trinity* is defended by them merely because they are bribed or forced to it. And others of their Writers have been very severe upon the *Trinitarians* in their late Prints. And therefore with good reason some of These have been free with them again, especially that Worthy Person who undertook the Defence of the *Archbishop* and the *Bishop of Worcester*, and hath with great Vivacity and Sharpness reflected on the *Socinian* Errors, and with as great Solidity and Composedness establish'd the contrary Truths, and hath not spared that Socinian Author whom he grapples with, no not in the least. I suppose none will grudg *me* that Freedom which this Gentleman and others have taken in their *Replies* to the *Racovian* Writers, especially seeing I have not (as I conceive) made ill use of it. But of that let the Reader judg.

FINIS.

---

[12] Considerations on the Explications of the doctrine of the Trinity.

SOME PASSAGES IN THE REASONABLENESS OF CHRISTIANITY, &C. AND ITS VINDICATION

Samuel Bold

To the Reader.

After I had Preached the foregoing Sermon, Mr. Edwards's Book *against the* Reasonableness of Christianity *falling into my Hands, occasioned my perusing of that Treatise again a second time with more attention; Whereby I came to be furnished with a Truer, and more just* Notion *of the main design of that* Treatise, *than I had, upon my looking over it* Cursory *presently after it was published.*

If the following Papers shall help any to understand the true State *of the* Controversie *betwixt those two* Celebrated Writers, *and induce People to consider more sedately the* Just grounds *of our believing* Jesus *to be the* Messias, *and the indispensable Obligation those who do believe in him are under to search after the Knowledge of what he hath Taught and Commanded, and to believe and obey the same, by Virtue of the aforesaid* Belief; *I shall not be sorry that I have spent a few days in reading deliberately the* Books *to which they* Relate. *I am a perfect Stranger to both Authors. I am not certain that I ever heard the* Name *of the Author of the* Reasonableness, *&c. mentioned. I am persuaded I never saw* Mr. Edwards. *But he is a Person for whom I have a* Particular *and* Great Respect, *because of several* Treaties *he hath published, which do not abound with* Magisterial Rant, *but discover him to be an* Excellent Critick, *a Person of great* Reading, *and of good Judgment. I hope he will oblige the* Publick *with more* Treatises, *Enrich'd with such* Solid Learning, *as his former* Books *are replenished with, and beautified with that* Calmness *of Temper, which did peculiarly adorn his first Productions.*

That there are more Truths *taught in the* New Testament *than this,* That Jesus is the Messiah, *and which are therefore to be Learned and Believed, is most certain; and to make this Demonstrably Manifest (which I fancy was Mr.* Edwards's *great design) when it is denied, or called in question, is a very* Laudable Undertaking, *but it doth not at all* affect *the* Reasonableness of Christianity, &c. *which excellently discovers what is to be* believed, to make Men Christians, *that hereby they may be engaged to acquaint themselves well with the* True Reasons and Grounds *of our believing that* Point, *and may not any longer* wear *the* Profession of Christianity, *as they do their* Cloaths, *but become* Understanding *and* Judicious Christians, *upon* sound Conviction; *and so perceive the Obligation they are under to* Study *diligently the* Holy Scriptures, *that they may advance in the Knowledge, Belief and Practice of what,* that Jesus *hath revealed,* whom they believe to be the Messias. *And could People be brought to* this, *the* Adversaries, *to some of the* Great Doctrines *taught in our* Bibles, *would have little ground to hope they should do any great* Exploits, *by their insisting on* small Critical Niceties, *or making a* Clamour, *because no more can be known at present, concerning some* Doctrines, *they have* no liking to, *than what is* Revealed. *For it is enough for a* good Christian, *to believe what is* Revealed. *To know Christ Jesus aright, and follow his Conduct sincerely, are so necessary, and of such Efficacy to our Safety, Establishment and Comfort at present, and to our future Blessedness, that you cannot be prompted to attend to any thing of equal moment, by*

Your Faithful
Servant, *&c.*

S. B.

SOME PASSAGES IN THE REASONABLENESS OF CHRISTIANITY, AS DELIVERED IN THE SCRIPTURES.

In this Treatise we have as clear, distinct, and full Proof (I think) as can with Reason be desired, That Jesus, and his Apostles did not teach any thing as necessary to be believed, *to make a Man a Christian,* but only this one Proposition, *That Jesus of* Nazareth *was the Christ, or the Messiah.* That the proof of this Point, was the principal thing aimed at, and intended in that Treatise, seems so clear to me, I cannot imagine how any Man can doubt of it, who attentively peruses these Words, in Page 102. "I challenge them, to shew that there was any other Doctrine (*viz.* than this, That *Jesus* of *Nazareth* was the *Messiah*) upon their assent to which, or disbelief of it, Men were pronounced Believers, or Unbelievers, and accordingly received into the Church of Christ, as Members of his Body, as far as meer believing could make them so, or else cast out of it." That it is not a bare notional Knowledge of the before-mentioned Proposition, that is discoursed of in this Treatise, is very evident, by the Author's frequent declaring, that by believing this Proposition, he means such a Faith as makes the Person believing it, *to receive Jesus for his King and Ruler*: As in Pages 51, 111, &c. The Author doth no where teach (that I do observe) that Jesus Christ, and his Apostles did not deliver any Doctrines to be believed besides this *one*, or that Christians are not obliged to believe any more Doctrines but this one. He saith expressly, "The other Parts of Divine Revelation are Objects of Faith, and are so to be received. They are Truths whereof none that is once known to be such, may, or ought to be disbelieved", Page 156.

SOME ANIMADVERSIONS ON MR. EDWARDS'S
REFLECTIONS ON THE REASONABLENESS OF
CHRISTIANITY, AS DELIVER'D IN THE SCRIPTURES.

Mr. *Edwards* begins his *Reflections* on the *Reasonableness of Christianity*, &c. Page 105 [180]. of *some Thoughts concerning the Causes of Atheism*; where he affirms, that "the late Publisher of the Reasonableness of Christianity, &c. gives it (*viz.* The plausible Conceit he took no notice of, Page 104 [181].) us over and over again in these formal Words; *viz.* That nothing is required to be believed by any Christian Man, but this, That Jesus is the Messiah." Then Mr. *Edwards* bestows some Pages in reporting several Propositions taught by our Saviour in the Gospel, which the Author of the Reasonableness of Christianity, &c. hath omitted. "These (he tells us) are Matters of our Faith, under the Gospel." And he adds an account of what he takes to be the sense of these Articles. Tho' I have read over the Reasonableness of Christianity, &c. with some Attention, I have not observed those *formal Words* in any part of that *Book*, nor any *Words* which are *capable* of that *Construction*; provided they be considered with the Relation they have to, and the manifest dependance they have on what goes before, or follows after them. I acknowledge the Scriptures Mr. *Edwards* doth mention, do contain *Matters of Faith* to be believed by those who *are Christians*, and attain to know that Jesus Christ did teach them. But that Mr. *Edwards* should have proved, to make his Discourse reach the Reasonableness of Christianity, &c. was This, That the *explicite Knowledge*, or belief of those *particular Scriptures*, or his *Interpretation* of them, *is necessary* by *Christ's Appointment*, to *constitute*, or *make a Person a Christian*. These Scriptures do effectually overthrow, or confute that Proposition Mr. *Edwards* hath started, and then charged on the Author of the Reasonableness of Christianity, &c. but they do not affect any Proposition that Author hath advanced, that I know of.

In the next place Mr. *Edwards* finds fault with the Author of the Reasonableness, &c. "because he did not proceed to the Epistles, and give an account of them, as he did of the Gospels, and the Acts of the Apostles:" And saith, "It is most evident to any thinking and considerate Person that he purposely omits the Epistolary Writings of the Apostles, because they are fraught with other Fundamental Doctrines, besides that one, which he mentions, P. 109, 110 [182]."

Now what Mr. *Edwards* doth mean by Fundamental Doctrines, is not very clear to me. If he means all the Doctrines taught in the Epistles, or all the Propositions delivered in the Epistles concerning just those particular Heads, he immediately mentions, it lies upon him to prove, that Jesus Christ hath made it necessary, that every Person must have an explicite Knowledge and Belief of all these, before he can be a Christian; which I do not see he hath attempted. If by Fundamental Doctrines, Mr. *Edwards* doth mean some Doctrines which are of special Importance, and which for that Reason, sincere Christians should principally endeavour to get the knowledge of, it cannot with any Justice be laid to this Author's charge, that he did not proceed to the Epistles, and give us an account of those Doctrines from them: Because that did not pertain to his Undertaking; who was not enquiring what Doctrines are of greatest moment to be understood, and believed by them who are Christians, but what was necessary to be known and believed to a Person's being a Christian. If what Mr. *Edwards* doth alledge, can be assigned for the Reason why this Author did purposely omit the Epistolary Writings, methinks it is most evident to any thinking and considerate Person, that it would

have kept him from giving the World that account he hath
given, of what the Gospels and the Acts of the Apostles deliver
concerning the Subject of his Enquiry and Discourse: For there
are many important Doctrines taught both in the Gospels and
the Acts, as well as in the Epistles, besides this, That Jesus is
the Messiah. But how many soever the Doctrines be which are
taught in the Epistles, if there be no Doctrine, besides this,
That Jesus is the Messiah, taught there, as necessary to be
believed, to make a Man a Christian, all the Doctrines taught
there, will not make any thing at all against what this Author
hath asserted, nor against the Method he hath observed:
Especially considering we have an Account in the Acts of the
Apostles of *what* those Persons, by whom the Epistles were
writ, did teach as necessary to be believed to People's being
Christians. And whereas Mr. *Edwards* speaks, p. 111 [182]. of
this Author's "not vouchsafing an Abstract of these Inspired
Writings; *viz.* The Epistles:" This Author doth not appear to
have had a Design of giving an Abstract of any of the Inspired
Books, if by Abstract be meant a summary Account of all the
Doctrines contained in them. As to the Gospels, and the Acts of
the Apostles, he gives an Account of what they inform us, was
taught by Christ and his Apostles as necessary to be believed to
the making of a Man a Christian. And if he had proceeded to
give the like account of the Epistles, that would have been as
little satisfactory, as what he hath done already, to those who
are resolved not to distinguish betwixt what is necessary to be
believed to make a Man a Christian, and those Articles which
are to be believed by those who are Christians, as they can
attain to know that Christ hath taught them. We believe Jesus
to be the Christ, or Messiah, not barely because he said he was
the Messiah, but because of other Evidences, manifesting and
confirming that Truth. But he that is a Christian, believes other
Doctrines, because he knows that Jesus, whom he believes to
be the Messiah, hath taught them. Now had this Author
quoted all those Passages in the Epistles that are for this
purpose, as 1 *Cor.* 3. 11 and 1 *Joh.* 5. 1. he would still have left
out all those Doctrines Mr. *Edwards* doth reckon up: And no
just occasion could any Man have had from thence, to charge
him with disowning those Doctrines, or passing those parts of
the Epistles where they are delivered, by, with contempt.

   If there by any true Reasoning in what Mr. *Edwards* doth
further write in this Discourse against the *Reasonableness of*

Christianity, &c. it is to me so clouded, by his way of expressing himself, I am too dull to perceive what his Reasons are, and wherein the strength of them doth lie. And therefore shall say little to his other Pages, till you come to Page 120 [185]. where Mr. *Edwards* doth hint, that there is *not any thing more difficult in this proposition [The Father, Son, and Holy Ghost are one God, or Divine Nature] than in that other [Jesus is the Messiah.*] Now let that be as Mr. *Edwards* saith, yet I see no proof, that the belief of the former Proposition is, that which doth constitute and make a Man a Christian. No nor that the belief of that, and all the other Propositions he hath mentioned in his Discourse, either exclusive of, or in conjunction with the latter, doth make a Man a Christian. That which is to be proved in opposition to the *Reasonableness of Christianity*, &c. is this, That Jesus Christ and his Apostles have taught that the belief of some one Article, or certain number of Articles, distinct from this, that *Jesus* is the *Messiah*, either as exclusive of the belief of this, that *Jesus* is the *Messiah*, or in conjunction with the belief of this Article, doth constitute and make a Person a Christian. But that the belief of this, that *Jesus* is the *Messiah*, alone doth not make a Man a Christian.

Whereas Mr. *Edwards* saith, *p.* 115 [183]. The Author of the *Reasonableness of Christianity*, &c. "pretends to contend for one single Article, with the exclusion of all the rest, for this reason, because all Men ought to understand their Religion." I cannot perceive any ground for such an assertion. The Author of the *Reasonableness*, &c. assigns why he asserts and contends that it is the believing that *Jesus* is the *Messiah*, which makes a Person a Christian, is this (if I understand him aright) because God doth not require the belief of any thing but this, to make a Man a Christian, or that Jesus Christ and his Apostles did not propose or teach any thing but this, as what was to be believed to make a Man a Christian. The Authors words are these, "*God* out of the Infiniteness of his Mercy has dealt with Man as a compassionate and tender Father. He gave his Reason, and with it a Law. – But considering the frailty of Man, apt to run into Corruption and Misery, He promised a Deliverer, whom in his good time He sent, and then declared to all Mankind, that whoever would believe Him to be the Saviour promised, and take him rais'd from the Dead, and constituted the Lord and Judge of all Men, to be their King and Ruler, should be saved." *Reasonableness of Christianity*, &c.

p. 157. So that the Reason why he contends that nothing
more is absolutely necessary to be believed to Salvation, or to
make a Person a Christian is, because God hath declared, this
is all that He absolutely requires to be believed to this
purpose. Which I think is as good a Reason as can possibly be
given. Then the Author of the *Reasonableness*, &c.
observed, that "The All-merciful God seems herein to have
consulted the Poor of this World, and the Bulk of Mankind."
Which words are not propos'd as a. Reason why nothing
more is necessary to be believed to make a Person a
Christian, but as a Pious Reflection, or Inference how
evidently the Goodness of Mankind appears, in that He
requires no more to a Persons being a Christian, than *the
belief of that plain intelligible Proposition* before mentioned.
So far is this Ingenious Author from aiming at what Mr.
Edwards affirms, *p.* 117 [184]. *viz.* "That we must not have
any point of Doctrine whatsoever in our Religion, that the
Mob doth not at the very first naming of it perfectly
understand, and agree to"; That he declares himself in these
very words: *The other parts of Divine Revelation, are
Objects of Faith, and are so to be received*, Reasonableness,
&c. *p.* 156. which is so far from *excluding* all *other Articles
of Faith*, or from setting up one Article with the *defiance of
all the rest*, that it attributes the just Honour to every thing
that can be the Object of a Christian Belief. The Question is
not, how many Articles may be necessary to be believed by one
who is a Christian? But whether any thing more than this, *that
Jesus is the Christ or Messiah*, is of necessity to be believed, to
make a Man a Christian? And I do not perceive, that Mr.
Edwards hath offered any thing that is at all cogent for the
Affirmative.

SOME ANIMADVERSIONS ON MR. EDWARDS'S BOOK ENTITULED, SOCINIANISM UNMASK'D.

The Introduction doth not prompt me to expect any great
strength of Argumentation in the following Discourse, if the
Author keep on in the strain in which he hath writ these pages,
and make his whole Book of a piece with his Beginning.

Chap 1. were a Man obliged to judge of the Vindication of
the Reasonableness of Christianity, &c. and of this Book Stiled
Socinianism Unmask'd, by the account given of them in the
second and third pages, and part of the fourth of this Chapter,

he would be apt to determine the former, one of the illest Books, and worst writ, that was ever published: And the latter, the most Accomplished Treatise amongst Humane Writings. Mr. *Edw.* p. 5 [211]. persists in his representing this Proposition, *There is but this one Truth* (viz. *That Jesus is the Messiah*) *necessarily to be assented to by Christians* (which is his own Proposition) and this Proposition, *There is but this one Truth* (viz. *that Jesus is the Messiah*) *absolutely required to be believed, to make a Man a Christian*; (which is the Authors Proposition he sets himself to oppose) to be the very same. Yet if he prove in the following part of his Book, that no person can be a Christian, or Member of Christ, till he explicitly understands, and actually assents to every thing that any Christian may be obliged to assent unto, or indeed to any one Article distinct from this, *That Jesus is the Messiah*; I shall acknowledge he hath effectually confuted the main point insisted on, in the *Reasonableness of Christianity*, &c. and its *Vindication*: But whereas Mr. *Edw.* produces some lines out of p. 101. of the *Reasonableness of Christianity*, &c. to justifie his charging that Author with the *formal words* (spoken of before) I shall refer any intelligent and fair Reader, to peruse that page, and try whether he can discern any ground (considering what goes before and after) to put such a construction on that Authors words, as Mr. *Edw.* doth; for I confess I am not sagacious enough to perceive it. Yet if Mr. *Edw.* had set down the Authors Challenge (which I have already transcribed) which is placed just between those words he doth quote; I think he would have done the Author a great deal of right, and have assisted his Reader, in conceiving duly, what it is the Author of the *Reasonableness*, &c. doth insist on; and what the point is his Adversary is to speak to, in order to his confuting that Book, and invalidating the large Evidence there produced, from Christ, and his Apostles for the confirming of what that Author asserts.

Mr. *Edw.* undertakes, p. 7 [212]. to shew that besides that one Fundamental "Principle or Article which the Author of the *Reasonableness*, &c. so often mentions, there are *others* that are as necessarily to be believed, to make a Man a Christian;" yea, to give him the denomination of a believer in the Sense of the Gospel. Now, this is the point Mr. *Edw.* is to keep to; and if he prove this, which he professeth he hath undertaken to prove, he doth effectually confute the *Reasonableness of*

Christianity, &c. if I am capable of making a Judgment in the case. Yet within a few lines, Mr. *Edw*. saith, "He will let the Reader see, that it is as necessary for a Convert to Christianity to assent to them (*viz*. most of those other Articles he had barely enumerated in his former Discourse) as to that other he (*viz*. the Author of the *Reasonableness*, &c.) so frequently specifies." But this is quite another point. For the Question is not, what Articles a Convert to Christianity may be obliged necessarily to believe, for he must necessarily believe as many Articles, as he shall attain to know that Christ Jesus hath taught. The Question is, what is necessary to be believed to make a Man *a Convert to Christianity?* For a *Convert to Christianity*, is, I conceive, the same with a *Christian*.

Mr. *Edw*. then lays down several Propositions, which are indeed Divine Truths, and of great use and moment to be known and believed, by those who are Christian; even such Propositions, that the Knowledge of them may conduce much to dispose People to be Christians. But I do not see any Proof he produceth, that the believing of all or any of those Propositions doth *make a Man a Christian*, or that the believing of these, together with this, *That Jesus is the Christ*, is necessary to *make a Man a Christian*: So that the due believing that Jesus is the Christ, or Messiah, doth not of it self constitute a Man a Christian, which was the thing he undertook to Prove. Yet.

Chap. 2. Mr. *Edw*. saith, p. 22. "He thinks he hath sufficiently proved that there are other Doctrines besides that; That Jesus is the *Messiah*, which are required to be believed to make a Man a Christian." But I think the utmost he hath proved, is only this, that there are other Doctrines which those who are Converts to Christianity, are obliged to believe, which is far enough from being the matter in Debate. And then Mr. *Edw*. asks, "Why did the Apostles write these Doctrines? Was it not that those they writ to, might give their assent to them?" To which it may be answered in his own words, *Yes verily*. But then it may be asked again, were not these Persons Christians, to whom the Apostles writ *these Doctrines*, and whom they required to assent unto them? *Yes verily*. And if so, what was it that made them Christians, before their *assent* to *these Doctrines* was *required?* If it was any thing besides their believing *Jesus to be the Messiah*, that ought to be instanced in, and made out. And not those Doctrines they were *afterwards* required to assent to, upon Jesus his Authority, and by *virtue* of their *believing Him* to be the *Messiah*. In p. 23 [217]. Mr. *Edw.* sums up all he had said (in the former Chapter) of his necessary Propositions into a *Syllogism*, and saith, "The proof of the second Proposition in that *Syllogism*, is easily effected thus. The belief of those things which have immediate respect to the Occasion, Author, Way, Means, and Issue of our Salvation; and which are necessary for knowing the true Nature and Design of it, is the belief of such things, without the knowing of which, a Man cannot be Saved. But such is the belief of the preceding Articles, *Ergo*." Here Mr. *Edw.* stops, whereas he should have proceeded to prove that Jesus Christ, or his Apostles have taught, that no Man can be a Christian, or shall be Saved, unless he had an explicit Knowledge of all those things which have immediate respect to the Occasion, Author, Way, Means, and Issue of our Salvation, and which are necessary for our knowing the true Nature and Design of it. But this he hath not done. It is a very good Argument, to another purpose: But without another *Medium* it will do no *Feats* in the present Case. Mr. *Edw.* p. 24. takes notice, "That in Vindication of the *Reasonableness*, &c. p. 171. the Author asks this Question, Whether these which you have set down under the Title of Fundamental Doctrines, are such (when reduced to Propositions) that every one of them is required to be believed, to make a Man a Christian; and such as without the actual belief thereof he cannot be Saved?" And the Substance and Strength of Mr. *Edw.* Answer (if I apprehend him aright) is this, "That no Man besides himself ever started such a thing;" representing the Question, as if the Author had asked, Whether those Propositions must be *always actually believed*; whereas the Question is only, Whether a Person cannot be Saved, without the actual belief of those Propositions? Now, that a Man can believe particular Propositions, and not actually believe them, is much above my capacity to understand. It is acknowledged those *Propositions* are in our *Bibles*; and they are there for this *purpose*, that they may be *believed*, as Mr. *Edw.* saith, and so is every other Proposition, which is taught in our Bibles. But how will it thence follow, that no Man can be a Christian, till he particularly know, and actually assent to every Proposition in our Bibles?

Chap. 4. What Mr. *Edw.* here saith of *Turks* and *Devils*, &c. is writ after such a rate, I think it needless for me to say any thing to it. If you read p. 102, 103. and 156, 157. of the

Reasonableness, &c. I think you will easily perceive the *Reasonableness of Christianity* administred no just ground for such Discourse. Yet the most considerable and best Expressions (excepting strict Scripture-Quotations) I have yet met with in this whole Discourse, happen to be dropt amongst the *Stuff* with which this Chapter is crowded, *viz.* Those which declare Mr. *Edwards*'s Notion of Evangelical Faith. As, "That a true Evangelical Faith is a hearty accepting of the *Messiah* as he is offered in the Gospel", p. 56 [219]. But whereas Mr. *Edw.* saith "this Author brings us no tidings of any such Faith belonging to Christianity, or discovered to us in the Scriptures, which gives us to understand that he verily believes there is no such Christian Faith, p. 56, 57 [219]." I think Mr. *Edw.* is much mistaken both in his Assertion, and his Inference, for such I conceive is the Sense of his latter words. If the Author of the *Reasonableness*, &c. had not brought any tidings of such a Faith, I think, it could not be thence justly and regularly inferr'd, that he verily believes there is no such Christian Faith. Because his enquiry and search was not concerning *Christian Faith*, considered *Subjectively*, but *Objectively*, what the Articles be which must be believed to make a Man a Christian? And not with what sort of Faith, these Articles are to be believed? So that if he had not said one word concerning Faith Subjectively considered; he might have as true and just a conception, and belief concerning this matter, as any Man living. And tho' Mr. *Edw.* could not find *one word about this compleat Faith of the Gospel in those pages*, (viz. 101, 102. &c.) where he expected it; yet there are several words about it in that Book. As in all those pages where he speaks of *taking and accepting Jesus to be our King and Ruler*. Where can you find a truer or more exact account of Christian Faith, than what this Author hath given us in these words, *But considering the frailty of Man, apt to run into corruption and misery, he* (i.e. God) *promised a Deliverer, whom in his good time he sent, and then declared to all Mankind, that whoever would believe him to be the Saviour promised, and take him now raised from the dead, and constituted the Lord and Judge of all Men, to be their King and Ruler, should be Saved*, p. 157.

Chap. 5. Mr. *Edw.* continues in this Chapter to give vent to something, to which I will not adventure to assign a *Proper Name*, and pretends it is all against what the Author of the *Reasonableness of Christianity* hath writ; when it is all against a conceit of his own framing, and there is not any thing that I can find in the *Reasonableness*, &c. that hath any likeness to it, *viz.* what he affirms (in the former Chapter) "The Author of the *Reasonableness*, &c. tells Mankind again and again, that a Christian Man, or Member of Christ, need not know, or believe any more than that one individual point which he mentions, p. 59 [221]." If any Man will shew me those words, in any part of the *Reasonableness*, &c. I shall suspect I was not awake all the time I was reading that Book. And I am as certain as one awake can well be, that there are several passages in that Book, directly contrary to those words. And there are some expressions in the Vindication of the *Reasonableness*, &c. one would think, if Mr. *Edw.* had observed them, they would have prevented his mistake.

Mr. *Edw.* p. 73. certifies, "He design'd his Papers for the satisfying of the Reader's doubts about any thing occurring concerning the matter before us, and for the establishing his wavering Mind; and for that reason will answer a Quæry or Objection, which some, and not without some shew of ground may be apt to start; *viz.* how comes it to pass, that this Article, of Faith, *viz.* That Jesus is the *Messias*, or Christ, is so often repeated in the *New Testament*? Why is this sometimes urged without the mentioning of any other Article of Belief?" I think the Quæry should be put thus, Why did Jesus Christ and his Apostles require assent to, and belief of this one Article alone, *viz.* That Jesus is the *Messias*, to constitute and make a Man a Christian, or true Member of Christ (as it is abundantly evident they did, from the *Reasonableness of Christianity*) if the belief of more Articles is absolutely necessary to make and constitute a Man a Christian?

Mr. *Edw.* to clear this Objection (as he hath framed it) and to give a full and satisfactory answer to all doubts in this affair, offers these ensuing particular.

1. "It must be considered, that the believing of Jesus to be the promised *Messias*, was the first step to Christianity, and therefore this, rather than any other Article, was propounded to be believed by all those, whom either our Saviour or the Apostles invited to embrace Christianity, p. 74". But here it may be Queried, by whose Authority are we obliged to consider, *That the believing of Jesus to be the promised Messias, is but a step* or *the first step to Christianity*? And not Christianity it self! If Mr. *Edw.* had proved that Jesus Christ or

his Apostles had taught so, the Controversie had been at an end: But he offers nothing of this nature, only gives us his own word for it. As p. 50. he had said, that "the belief of Jesus's being the *Messias*, was one of the first and leading Acts of Christian Faith." Now Christian Faith here, must be the belief of something or other; and if it be the belief of any thing besides this, that Jesus is the Christ, or *Messias*, that other thing should be specified, and it should be made appear, that the belief that Jesus is the *Messias* or *Christ*, without the belief of that other Proposition, is not Christian Faith. Now I apprehend that Christian Faith, and Christianity, considered subjectively (and an act of Christian Faith, I think, cannot be understood in any other sense) are the very same. And how an act of Christian Faith can be but a step to Christianity, is above my Capacity to conceive. For Christian Faith, or Christianity (if I be not mistaken) is that which constitutes a Man a Christian. But Mr. *Edw.* perhaps by Christianity and Christian Faith, doth not mean that Faith which constitutes a Man a Christian, but the belief of all, or a considerable number of Propositions, which are of great importance to be known and believed by those who are Christians. Now that Faith which constitutes a Man a Christian, differs very much in the *ground* of it, from that Faith, whereby one that is a Christian, believes the particular Doctrines which Christ and his Apostles have taught. A Christian believes what Propositions he attains to know that Jesus hath taught, for this reason, because he knows they were taught by that Jesus, whom he believes to be the *Messias*. But a Man believes Jesus to be the *Messias*, because of the evidence and Proof that is given, that this Jesus was the *Messias*. And the believing Jesus to be the *Messias*, is so far from being but a *step to Christianity*, or a *leading act of Christian Faith*, it is Christianity it self, or Christian Faith it self. That which constitutes and makes a Man a Christian, a Believer, a Disciple, or Subject of Christ, is his believing Jesus to be the Christ, so as to yield himself unreservedly to believe and practise whatsoever he shall attain to know he hath taught and commanded him. This is all that is necessary to make a Man a Disciple, or Subject, &c. to one who appears to be Commissioned to admit Persons into such Capacity and Relation on those terms: If by *Christianity* we understand the particular Doctrines or Articles Jesus Christ hath proposed to be believed by those who are Christians: The belief of any or all of these

Doctrines, is not *strictly Christian Faith*, but *the Faith of Persons who are Christians*. And to determine which is the first act of this sort of Faith, we must have recourse to particular Persons, unless it can be proved that every Christian, doth undoubtedly obtain the knowledge of one certain Proposition Christ hath taught, before any of them doth know any other. For if one Christian attains in the first place, to know that Jesus hath taught, that by dying on the Cross, he offered up himself a Sacrifice to satisfie Divine Justice for the Sins of the World; his believing this point, because he knows Jesus hath taught it, is the first act of Christian Faith in him, taking Christian Faith in this larger sense. But if another Christian doth not attain to know in the first place, that Christ hath taught this Doctrine; nor till after he knows several other Truths which Christ hath taught: His belief of this, when he comes to know Christ hath taught it, will be so far from being the first act of Faith in him, that all the Doctrines he knew Christ had taught, before he knew that he hath taught this, must take place, and be reckon'd in the order of his believing before this. That Faith which is strictly Christian Faith, and makes a Man a Christian, *viz.* believing Jesus to be the Christ, doth not barely *make way for the embracing of all other Articles, or become a passage to all the rest*, as Mr. *Edw.* expresseth himself, p. 75. but it lays an indispensible obligation upon the Person, to embrace and believe whatever Articles he shall attain to know Jesus Christ hath taught, and to use his best endeavours to acquire such knowledge. This is Christianity, properly so call'd. And the several Truths which Christ, and his Apostles have revealed, are the Doctrines, which those who are Christians, must endeavour to understand and believe, because Jesus, whom they believe to be the Christ, or *Messias*, hath taught and delivered them to the World, and for the special use of his Disciples and Followers. A Man may believe several of the Doctrines taught by Christ and his Apostles, who does not believe that Jesus is the *Messias*; but then he does not believe them with the Faith of a Christian; that is, for that reason why a Christian must and doth believe them, *viz.* his knowing that they were taught by that Jesus whom he believes to be the Christ, or *Messiah*.

2. Mr. *Edw.* saith, "It is to be remembred, that though this one Proposition or Article be mentioned alone in some places, yet there is reason to think and be persuaded, that at the same

time, other matters of Faith were proposed, p. 76." Supposing
is no Proof in this case. You may suppose as many matters of
Faith discoursed of at one and the same time as you please; but
the point to be proved is this, That some other Point or Article
of Faith besides this, that Jesus is the Christ, was proposed to
be believed, to make them Christians. It is all along
acknowledged, there are many Articles proposed for Christians
to believe, but the Proof is wanting, that more than this one
Article was proposed to be believed, to make Men Christians.
If there be reason to think and be persuaded, that other matters
of Faith were discoursed of at the same time, it seems very plain
and evident to me, that there was not any Article but this one,
that Jesus is the *Messiah*, the belief whereof was necessarily
required to make them Christians, because there is nothing but
this Recorded, which was insisted on for that purpose.

3. Mr. *Edw*. saith, "This also must be thought of, That
though there are several Parts and Members of the Christian
Faith, yet they do not all occur in any one place of Scripture,
p. 76. – *And consequently*, if we would give an impartial
account of our Belief, we must consult those places of Scripture
where the Articles of the Christian Faith are; and they are not
all together, but disperst here and there: Wherefore we must
look them out, and acquaint our selves with the several
particulars which make up our Belief, and render it entire and
consummate, p. 77." That there are several Propositions and
Articles delivered by Christ and his Apostles; which Christians
must endeavour to know and believe, is very true; as also that
these do not all occur in any one place of Scripture, and
therefore Christians must look them out, &c. But this is no
Proof that all that is absolutely necessary to be believed to
make a Man a Christian, is not to be found in any one place of
Scripture; much less that no Man can be a Christian, till he
hath an explicite knowledge of every Proposition Christ and his
Apostles have taught. The place of Scripture Mr. *Edw.* here
quotes, *viz. Rom.* 10. 9. I take to be a full confirmation of
what the Author of the *Reasonableness of Christianity*, &c.
asserts. The words are these, *If thou shalt confess with thy
Mouth the Lord Jesus, and shalt believe in thy Heart, that God
hath raised him from the dead, thou shalt be saved.* The plain
meaning and sense of which words, I think is this, If thou shalt
confess, or make profession with thy Mouth, that thou dost
take Jesus for thy Lord, and this verbal Confession, proceeds

from, and is the genuine Fruit of an unfeigned hearty belief, grounded upon solid, substantial Evidence, such as God's raising him from the dead is, that he is the *Messias*, thou shalt be saved. But how this Scripture should have such a construction fastened to it as this, if thou believe Christ's Resurrection, and all other Truths he and his Apostles have taught, thou shalt be saved, so as to exclude every Man from Salvation, that believes Jesus to be the *Messias*, and yet attains not to an explicite knowledge and belief of every thing Christ and his Apostles have taught, is not obvious to me.

4. Mr. *Edw.* saith, "This (which is the main answer to the objection) must be born in our minds, that Christianity was erected by degrees, according to that Prediction and Promise of our Saviour, *That the Spirit should teach them all things*, Joh. 14. 26. *And that he should guide them into all truth*, Joh. 16. 13. We are not to think that all the necessary Doctrines of the Christian Religion were clearly published to the World in our Saviour's time, p. 78." It is true, all the Doctrines which Christ and his Apostles taught, were not delivered at once, but gradually, and at several times. But what is this to the proving, that all that was necessary to be believed to make a Man a Christian, was not clearly published in our Saviour's time? Will not that make a Man a Christian now, which made the Apostles themselves Christians? Christians in different times may be furnished with a less or greater number of Truths and Doctrines, which they must endeavour to understand and believe. But the Belief of *that*, which makes one Man a Christian, or ever did make any Man a Christian, will at any time to the end of the World, makes another Man a Christian. The Faith of Christians may encrease and extend to a greater number of Objects, or Articles, as they are discovered and made known, but there can be no difference as to *that*, the belief *whereof*, doth make a Man a Christian. What is absolutely necessary to be believed to make one Man a Christian, at any time, is absolutely necessary to be believed to make others Christians, at any time, and in every part of the World. And nothing else is or can be absolutely necessary to be believed; to make any Man a Christian. If Mr. *Edw.* instead of *distinguishing of times*, had distinguished between what is necessarily to be believed, to make a Man a Christian, and what Doctrines have been taught and delivered by Christ and his Apostles, which those who are Christians must labour to

understand and believe, I fancy he would not have been of the Opinion, that the enlarging of the *Revelation*, did make more necessary to be believed, to make a Man a Christian at one time, than was necessary for that purpose at another.

Chap. 6. Here Mr. *Edw.* falls foul with the Author of the *Reasonableness*, because he did not treat of matters, which pertained not to his Subject. Because he did not discourse of the *Trinity*, and the *Deity of our Saviour*, which are particular Doctrines proposed to be believed by them who are Christians. Whereas that Author's business was to enquire, not what points are proposed to be believed by Christians, but what is necessarily to be believed, to make a Man a Christian. Mr. *Edw.* appears mightily out of humour also, because the Author of the *Reasonableness*, &c. did not mention some passages in the Gospels which did not belong to his Enquiry, and because he did not explain some Scriptures, as he would have them explained. Now I think it appears evidently enough, by some of the former Papers, that there is no just ground to accuse any Man to be an *Anti-Trinitarian*, or a *Socinian*, because he asserts that believing Jesus to be the *Messias*, is all that is necessarily required to make a Man a Christian. I farther add, that the belief of the *Trinity*, and that Jesus *the Son of God, is God*, doth not constitute a Man a Christian. Nor can any Man believe these Doctrines, or any other Doctrines taught in the Gospel, with the Faith of a Christian, till he is a Christian, and believe them, because he knows they were taught by Jesus Christ, whom upon just grounds he believes to be the *Messias*. It is not fair and just to charge a Man with rejecting these Doctrines meerly because he does not interpret some particular Texts to the same purpose others do. For he may believe these Doctrines, though he does not think all those Scriptures cogent proofs of them, which some may alledge for the proof of them. The Author of the *Reasonableness*, &c. had observed that *the Messias, and the Son of God, were synonymous Terms amongst the* Jews *in our Saviour's time*, p. 23, 29, 30. Hence Mr. *Edw.* takes occasion to write many pages about these *terms*. But I do not perceive that he pretends to offer the least proof that these terms, were not synonymous terms amongst the *Jews* at that time, which is the point he should have proved, if he designed to invalidate what this Author saith about that matter.

Chap. 7. In this Chapter Mr. *Edw.* seems much disturbed, because the Author of the *Reasonableness*, &c. "Makes nothing of the force of that Demonstration (as he calls it) of his being a Disciple of *Socinus*, viz. That when he mentions the advantages and benefits of Christ's coming into the World, he hath not one syllable of his satisfying for us, or by his Death purchasing Life and Salvation, or any thing that sounds like it, p. 94." The Scripture Doctrine of Christ's Satisfaction, is of mighty importance, for a true Christian to be well acquainted with. But that a Person must be a *Socinian* because he omitted that *particular*, when discoursing of the advantages and benefits of Christ's coming into the World, unless he had expressly promised to name every one of them, does not appear *Demonstratively* unto me, supposing Christ's Satisfaction were in *Strictness* to be reckoned amongst the *Benefits and Advantages* which accrue and redound, either to Sinners or Believers, from Christ's coming into the World. For the mentioning of *some*, is no denial of *other* Advantages. But I conceive, *Satisfaction* is not so *strictly* to be termed an *Advantage*, as the *Effects* and *Fruits* of it are, and the ends themselves, for which this Satisfaction was made. Some of the *main ends* for which Christ came into the World, were these. To procure us the *Pardon of Sin*. The *Holy Spirit* to enable us to walk in all pleasing before God, and to secure to us *Everlasting Glory and Blessedness*. These are the great Benefits and Advantages (speaking strictly) of Christ's coming into the World. Of the two last the *Author of the Reasonableness*, &c. hath discoursed amongst the Benefits, &c. of Christ's coming into the World; and the other he hath spoken of in the former part of his Book. The Doctrine of Satisfaction, instructs us in the *way*, how Christ did by Divine Appointment, obtain these Advantages for us.

Chap. 8. This is the last Chapter Mr. *Edw.* writes directly against the *Reasonableness of Christianity*, and its *Vindication*, or rather against the *unknown Author*. But this Chapter is so entirely of the same *strain* with those foregoing pages I have past over in silence, I shall say no more of it; but that my dulness is such, I cannot discern the least appearance of reasoning in it.

If you believe Mr. *Edwards's* account of the *Reasonableness*, &c. you will conclude it likely to do abundance of *hurt*, especially to St. *Paul's Churchyard*. And indeed, I am persuaded it will as certainly be the *Cause* of very much *mischief* as *Tenterton-Steeple* was the *Cause* of the *Goodwin Sands*.

Were the *Reasonableness of Christianity*, &c. generally read with *deliberation*, and rightly understood, and (what I apprehend to be) its *main design* well followed, it would be of eminent use, amongst other *good purposes*, to these two.

First, *To effect an happy alteration in particular Persons*. For if more time and pains were employ'd, in bringing *People* to a *sound Conviction*, and *full persuasion*, that *Jesus is the Christ*, and only Saviour of Sinners, and of their *own personal need of Him*, and less of each in *Squabling* about *Terms*, Men have *devised* to express their own *Conceits* relating *Points* which *Christ* and his *Apostles* have delivered in *easie* and *unaffected words*, there would not be such great numbers every where, who *pretend* to be *Christians* meerly because it is the *Fashion* and *Mode* of the Country to make that *Profession*; but we might upon good grounds *expect* that multitudes would be *Christians* upon a *Rational* and *Wise Choice*: From whence it would follow, that as they would be *able* to *justifie* their *Faith*, and give a *good Reason of their Hope* to any who should discourse with them concerning the *same*; so they would be more *inquisitive* after, and *observant* of the *Laws* of *Christ*, and would be *disposed* to yield a *becoming Assent* and *Submission* to the several *Truths* and *Doctrines* they shall attain to know were taught by *Him*.

Secondly, *To overthrow and ruine Faction in Religion, and promote that Concord, and good Affection amongst Christians, which would render them mightily serviceable to one another, put them into a condition, to reap singular advantage from all Publick ministrations, which would make the whole number of Christians appear to the World as one entire and well compacted Body, and effectually remove those pernicious Prejudices against our most Sacred Profession, which too many take occasion to entertain, from the humoursome Separations, and groundless Devisions which do most unmercifully prevail amongst Christians. The Men of Art* in all the *Parties*, appear agreed (how distant soever they be one from another in other matters) not to speak in *favour* of the *Reasonableness of Christianity*, &c. But if this *Agreement* of theirs doth arise from the *obvious tendency* that Book hath to promote the *Happy Concord* beforementioned, what can be thought better of it, than that it is an *Evil Conspiracy* to continue and maintain *Unchristian Discords*, for private *Selfish Ends*, to the exceeding great *Detriment* of *Religion*, and the *Publick Good*? In short, if the *Reasonableness of Christianity, as deliver'd in the Scripture*, doth merit no worse a *Character*, on any other account, than it doth justly deserve, because it advanceth and so fully proveth this Point, *That Christ and his Apostles did not propound any Articles as necessarily to be believed to make a Man a Christian, but this, That Jesus is the Christ, or Messias*, I think it may with great Justice be reputed, one of the *best Books* that hath been published for at least *these Sixteen Hundred Years*.

THE END

A DISCOURSE OF FUNDAMENTALS, BEING THE SUBSTANCE OF TWO CHARGES DELIVERED TO THE MIDDLESEX CLERGY, AT THE EASTER VISITATIONS OF 1734 AND 1735

Daniel Waterland

Reverend Brethren,

Upon a serious and attentive review of the general state of religion amongst us, and of the particular controversies now depending, I could not think of any subject more useful, or at this time more seasonable, than the subject of *fundamentals*. The name is a noted name, frequently occurring in religious debates: but the notion is often left obscure, and the application is so various among contending parties, that it may be difficult to fix any certain rule for it, though it is allowed, on all hands, that much depends upon it.

Lord Verulam, at the beginning of the last century, expressed his judgment of the great *importance* of distinguishing rightly between points *fundamental* and points of *further perfection*; so he worded the distinction, though, I think, not accurately. At the same time he complimented the Divines of that age, as having done their parts to entire satisfaction upon that article[1]. But upon the more mature consideration, twenty years after, or nearly, he apprehended that some further improvement was still wanting, and so he recommended it, among the *desiderata* in theology, to the care and diligence of succeeding Divines[2].

The subject has since passed through many learned and judicious hands[3], most of them complaining of the perplexities

---

[1] See Advancement of Learning, p. 320, 321. first ed. A.D. 1605.

[2] Augmentum Scientiarum, lib. ix. p. 532, 533. ed. Paris. A.D. 1624.

[3] 1635. Mede's Letters, Opp. vol. ii. p. 1064–1074.
     1638. Chillingworth, part i. chap. 3rd, p. 115.

appearing in it, but all bearing testimony to the great weight and importance of it.

The very name of *fundamental* carries in it some confuse general idea of *weight* and *significancy*; which again rises in proportion to the dignity of the subject whereunto it belongs. Every *art* or *science*, every *society, system*, or *constitution*, has its *fundamental* rules, laws, principles, or constituents, which it rests upon, and whereby it subsists. The word *fundamental*, in such cases, seems to mean the same thing with *essential*, and to denote that wherein the very *essence* or *subsistence* of the subject spoken of is contained. And as there is a just distinction to be made between *essentials* and *circumstantials*, so is there the like just distinction to be made between *fundamentals* and *extra-fundamentals*, or *non-fundamentals*. When we apply the epithet *fundamental* either to religion in general or to Christianity in particular, we are supposed to mean something *essential* to religion or Christianity; so necessary to its being, or at least to its well-being, that it could not subsist, or not maintain itself tolerably without it.

There is in Scripture itself, as well as in the reason of the thing, ground sufficient for distinguishing between points fundamental to Christianity and points of small moment. There are the *weightier* matters, and the matters *less weighty*; some things deserving our most *earnest heed*, others requiring no more than ordinary or common care. I shall not take up your time in commenting upon the several *texts* which appear to have intimated the distinction, or to have expressed it in terms. The whole tenor of the New Testament abundantly authorizes the distinction, while it lays a very particular stress upon some doctrines more than upon others, and while it condemns the contrary tenets as *subversive* of the Gospel, or as *frustrating* the *grace* of God, or as rendering the false teachers

1650. Johann. Hoornbeeck, Socin. Confut. tom. i. lib. 1. cap. 9. p. 181. Exercitat. Theolog. p. 712, &c.
1654. Dr. Hammond, Opp. vol. i. p. 275.
1665. Bp. Stillingfleet, Rat. Account, part i. chap. 2, 3, 4.
1680. Lambert. Velthuysius, Opp. vol. i. p. 693.
1682. Dean Sherlock, Vindic. of Stillingfleet, chap. 5.
1693. Dr. Clagett, vol. ii. Serm. second and third.
1694. Frid. Spanheim. Fil. Opp. tom. iii. p. 1289, &c.
1696. Puffendorf. Jus feciale Divinum: sive de Consensu et Dissensu Protestantium.
1697. Witsius. In Symbolum Apostol. p. 9, &c.
1719. Alphons. Turretin de Articulis Fundamentalibus.

altogether unworthy of Christian communion. The whole conduct of our Lord's Apostles sufficiently declares the same thing: but I shall instance only in St. Paul, that I may not be tedious in a plain case. There were in the days of the Apostles, Judaizers of two several kinds; some thinking themselves obliged, as Jews, to retain their Judaism along with Christianity, others conceiving that the Mosaical law was so necessary, that it ought to be received, under pain of damnation, by all, whether Jews or Gentiles. Both the opinions were wrong; but the one was *tolerable*, and the other was *intolerable*. Wherefore St. Paul complied in some measure with the Judaizers of the first sort, being willing, in such cases, "to become all things to all men[4]:" and he exhorted his new converts of the Gentiles to bear with them, and to receive them as brethren[5]. But as to the Judaizers of the second sort, he would not "give place to them by subjection, no not for an hour, lest the truth of the Gospel" should fatally suffer by it[6]. He anathematized them as subverters of the faith of Christ, and as a reproach to the Christian name[7]. This single instance may suffice to point out the distinction between *fundamentals* and *non-fundamentals*: and to illustrate the use of it in practice.

The primitive churches afterwards had the same distinction all along in their eye, as might be made appear from numerous and plain testimonies. But their ordinary conduct in admitting persons to communion, or rejecting them from it, according to that rule, is a plain and sensible argument drawn from certain fact, which supersedes all further inquiries. Unity in the *fundamental* articles of faith was always strictly insisted upon as one necessary condition of church membership: and if any man openly and resolutely opposed those articles, or any of them, he was rejected as a deserter of the *common faith*, and treated as an *alien*.

From hence then it may appear, that the *distinction* which we are now upon is *ancient* and *well grounded*: and of what *moment* it is may be collected from hence, that the previous question, in almost every dispute concerning *church communion*, depends upon it. Nor need we wonder if much pains have

---

4   See 1 Cor. ix. 19–23. Acts xvi. 3. xxi. 21–26.

5   See Rom. xiv. xv. Coloss. ii. 16, 17.

6   Gal. ii. 5, 21.

7   Gal. i. 7, 8, 9. v. 12.

been taken by many to perplex and entangle it: for they who are most afraid of being condemned by the rule will declare against it, or will warp and pervert it, to make it serve their own purposes. Hence it is that we have almost as many different rules for determining *fundamentals*, as there are different sects or parties; and that which might otherwise serve (if all men were reasonable) to end all differences, has itself been too often made one principal bone of contention.

But though perverse disputers may at any time raise clouds and darkness, and there is no rule so clear, but a wrangler may contrive a thousand ways to perplex and entangle it: yet if the point can but be once settled upon a *rational* foot, the clearing it so far will suffice among the *honest* and *reasonable* part of mankind; and it is an end worthy of our thoughts and care. It is morally certain that all schemes or projects for any *perfect union* of Christians, however well intended or wisely laid, will at length fail in the issue, (through the almost infinite variety of capacities, tempers, interests, passions, prejudices,) just as all schemes for an *universal peace* throughout the world (or only over all Europe) will of course fail of effect: nevertheless, we ought evermore seriously to seek after *peace*, whether religious or secular, and to promote the same by instruction, counsel, and endeavour, as far as *possible*, or *reasonable*, leaving the event to God. And therefore there is no reason for throwing aside any *useful* means of making peace, though some persons will not admit of them, and others may turn them into a matter of more strife.

As the distinction between doctrines *fundamental* and *non-fundamental* is undoubtedly just in the general, and is confessed, in a manner, by all parties to be a good *precious* rule for settling the terms of *Christian communion*, there is certainly a way of clearing it from all *reasonable* exceptions, however difficult it may be to come at that way. *Error* may run men into inextricable mazes, and commonly does so: but *true* and *right* principles, regularly and aptly pursued, will always find a clear exit. I proceed then to the business in hand.

It will be needless here to distinguish between the fundamentals of *natural* and *revealed* religion, because revealed takes in both, and both, so considered, fall into one. It will be equally needless to distinguish nicely between the several fundamentals of *faith, worship*, and *morality*, because all of them indifferently are *essential* to Christianity, and ought equally to be insisted upon, as terms of *Christian communion*. But it may be highly needful to distinguish fundamentals considered in an *abstract* view, as essentials of the Christian *fabric* or *system*, (in which view it is, that they are most properly called *essentials* and *fundamentals*,) and fundamentals considered in a *relative* view to particular persons, in which respect they are frequently called *necessaries*, as being ordinarily necessary to salvation. For though the *fundamentals* and the *necessaries* do really coincide, and are indeed the same thing, (*equal* capacities and opportunities *supposed*,) yet so great is the variety of capacities and opportunities in different persons, that one rule and measure of *necessaries* will not equally serve for all. The want of observing this very useful distinction between *fundamentals* as such in an *abstract* view, and *necessaries* as such in a *relative* view, has unhappily occasioned much confusion in our present subject: and therefore the surest and readiest way to clear it up to satisfaction will be to attend carefully to the distinction now mentioned[8]. Fundamentals in their *abstract* view are of a fixed determined nature as much as Christianity itself is, and may be ascertained by plain and unalterable rules; but fundamentals in their *relative* view to persons will always vary with the *capacities* and *opportunities* of the persons. There is no certain judgment to be made as to particular men, either with respect to their *heads* or their *hearts*: neither can we presume to determine in special how far the Divine mercies may extend towards *idiots*, or men next to *idiots*; towards *enthusiasts*, or others not far from *enthusiasts*; towards even sensible and learned men erring *fundamentally*, but under some *unconquerable* prejudice or disorder of mind[9]. In this view, there is no

8   Bp. Stillingfleet means the same thing in the main, though he words it differently, where he distinguishes between what things are *necessary* to the salvation of men *as such*, or considered in their *single* or *private* capacities; and what things are *necessary* to be owned in order to salvation by *Christian societies*, or as the *bonds* and *conditions* of *ecclesiastical communion*. Whereupon he further adds: "The want of understanding this *distinction* of the necessity of things has caused most of the perplexities and confusion in this controversy of fundamentals." *Stillingfleet, Rat. Account*, part i. chap 2. p. 49.

9   It may be noted, that though the Scripture says absolutely, "He that believeth not shall be damned," and the Athanasian and other creeds have followed the like absolute form of expression, yet from other places of Scripture, and from the nature of the thing, it is plain that such forms of expression are always to be understood with grains of allowance for

fixed measure of *fundamentals*: or to speak more properly, though *fundamentals* as such are fixed and established in the very nature or reason of things, yet *necessaries* as such are not so; neither need they be. The way then is, to abstract from *persons*, and to consider *fundamentals* under a distinct view, as referring to the *fabric* of Christianity. All parties almost one way or other, one time or another, do admit of the like distinction, making the *terms* of *communion* somewhat stricter than the necessary *terms* of *salvation*: that is to say, they exclude many from communion as erring *fundamentally*, whom notwithstanding they do not, they dare not condemn absolutely to everlasting perdition.

The reason is, because they can make no certain estimate of the *infirmities* or *incapacities* which the men may unhappily lie under, nor of the *allowances* which an all-seeing God may please to make to them upon that score. The Romanists, who are commonly the most severe in their censures of any men whatever, yet sometimes do make a distinction between excluding men absolutely from *Christian communion*, and peremptorily sentencing the same men to *eternal damnation*. The Remonstrants, who in debate, and to serve a cause, love to confound *fundamentals* with *necessaries*, or *fundamentals* of *communion* with *fundamentals* of *salvation*, are yet observed to distinguish them in practice; for they receive not Jews, Turks, Pagans, or wild sectaries professing Christianity, as friends or brethren, and yet they presume not to exclude them absolutely from all possibility of being saved. All which shews, that a distinction ought to be made between *fundamentals* considered in their *abstract* nature, as *essential* parts of the Christian system, and *fundamentals* considered in a *relative* view to the salvation of particular persons.

Having thus far cleared the way, by separating from the subject what belongs not to it, (but has been unwarily or insidiously brought in, to perplex and confound it,) I may now proceed to the explaining the *ratio* of a *fundamental* truth or error, and to the fixing some certain *rule* whereby to discover

invincible ignorance or *unavoidable infirmity*, as all the Divine *laws* concerning either matters of *faith* or matters of *practice* are to be understood: they bind according to what a man *hath*, or *might have* if he would: and not according to what he *hath not* and *could not* have. This exception is so just and evident, that it was sufficient for *Scripture* or *creeds* to *suppose* it generally, rather than to *mention it*: for every one's common sense will readily supply it.

or determine what kind of doctrines or positions properly fall under such denomination.

"A *fundamental doctrine* is such a doctrine as is in strict sense of the *essence* of Christianity, without which the whole building and superstructure must fall; the belief of which is necessary to the very being of Christianity, like the *first principles* of any *art* or *science*[10]." So says a learned and judicious writer: and this may serve for a good general description of what *fundamental* means, as likewise for a first principle or *postulatum*, to proceed upon in our further inquiries.

The next step we advance to, and which bears an immediate connection with the former, is, that such doctrines as are found to be *intrinsical* or *essential* to the *Christian covenant* are *fundamental truths*, and such as are plainly and directly *subversive* of it are *fundamental errors*.

To be more particular, the *Christian covenant* may be considered as containing or including the several articles here following. 1. A Founder and principal Covenanter. 2. A subject capable of being covenanted with. 3. A charter of foundation. 4. A Mediator. 5. Conditions to be performed. 6. Aids or means to enable to performance. 7. Sanctions also, to bind the covenant, and to secure obedience.

I. The first article to be considered is, the *Founder* and principal Covenanter: for without this, there could be no such *covenant* as is here supposed; a covenant of grace and salvation made with mankind by God the Father, in and by Christ Jesus[11]. Hence it is evident, that the *existence* of a *Deity* is a *fundamental* article of doctrine; and to deny or to disbelieve it is to err *fundamentally*. In the belief of a Deity is included the belief of all such *perfections* or *attributes* as without which God cannot be understood to be *God*: and therefore to disown such perfections as are necessarily and plainly contained in the idea of a *Divine* Being, is the same in effect with disowning the *existence*, and so is erring fundamentally. To this head belongs the belief of God's being our *Creator, Preserver,* and likewise

---

10 Sherlock, Vindicat. of the Def. of Stillingfleet, p. 256.

11 How the Christian religion carries in it a *covenant* of this kind, see explained at large by Baron Puffendorf, Jus feciale Divinum, sect. xx. p. 92, &c. sect. xxxvii, p. 134, &c. English translation, entitled, An Essay towards the Uniting of Protestants, p. 87, &c. 129, &c.

Inspector over our thoughts, words, and actions: and consequently the denial of any one or more of these articles must be numbered among the errors *fundamental*.

But besides the *existence* and *providence* of some Divine Being thus considered in the general, (which even the soberer kind of Pagans made part of their creed,) it is further *fundamental* in the *Christian system* to acknowledge a Deity in *special*; namely, *Jehovah*, God both of the Old and New Testament, and *Father of Christ*, in opposition to the false Gods, either of *heathens* or *heretics*. For it is not sufficient for a *Christian* barely to know or believe that there is a God, but to understand also *who* is God. Faith in *Jehovah* as being both *God of Israel* and *Father of Christ Jesus*, is an *essential* in Christian theology, and *fundamental* to the Christian covenant: from whence also it is evident, that the Simonians, Cerinthians, Marcionites, Manichees, and as many others as presumed to contest this article, erred *fundamentally*.

II. A covenant between God and man supposes and implies that man is a party *capable of being covenanted with*, has *freedom* of *will* sufficient to denominate him a *moral* agent, apt to discern between *good* and *evil*, and *choosing* which he pleases. Therefore the doctrines of *free-will* (thus understood) and of the *essential* differences between *moral good* and *evil* are *fundamental* verities; and to disown them, or either of them, is to err *fundamentally*[12].

III. The *charter* of *foundation* is undoubtedly an *essential* of the covenant: and therefore, of course, the admittance of the *sacred oracles*, which are the *charter* itself, (or at least the only *authentic* instrument of conveyance,) is essential to the covenant: consequently, to reject, or disbelieve the *Divine authority* of sacred Writ, is to err fundamentally.

IV. The belief of a *Mediator* of the Christian covenant is manifestly an *essential*, and needs no proof. The acknowledging of the blessed *Jesus* as *Messiah* and *Mediator* is plainly *fundamental*, according to the old tenor both of the Old and New Testament; and to deny it is to throw up Christianity at once.

But further, the acknowledging such a Mediator as the Scripture very clearly describes, a *Divine* Mediator, a Mediator who is *very God* and *very man*, while one Christ, is

[12] See Clagett, vol. ii. Serm. 2. p. 56, 57, 58. Velthuysius, p. 75.

fundamental also in the Christian system. "We must know and believe of this Mediator, that he is *true God* and the second Person in the sacred Trinity, and that he is also a true man, and that the same, who is both God and man, is yet but one Person. The places of Scripture are numberless which prove that the Mediator of the new covenant is *God*, which give to him that name in the *proper sense* of it, and ascribe to him such *works* as can be ascribed to none but God. And this indeed is what the very nature of the *covenant* required, for as much as no *creature* whatever could be of so great dignity as to be worthy and fit to bear the person of all mankind with an effect so great as even to equal the creation of them[13]."

To deny the real and proper *Divinity* is of consequence to err *fundamentally*. It is in effect "rejecting the chief Person of the covenant upon whom our salvation depends, and does therein overthrow the whole covenant[14]."

To this head belongs the doctrine of *expiation, atonement,* or *satisfaction,* made by Christ in his blood: a *fundamental* article of Christianity, fully expressed, frequently and earnestly inculcated quite through the New Testament. To advance one's *own* righteousness in *opposition* to justification by the *meritorious* sacrifice of Christ, or as *sufficient* without it, is plainly altering the *terms* of *acceptance*, and *frustrating* the covenant in Christ's blood, as it is making him to have "died in vain[15];" which is subverting the whole Gospel.

"A religion *with a sacrifice*, and a religion *without a sacrifice*, differ in the whole kind. The first respects the *atonement* of our past sins and our daily infirmities; it respects God as the *judge* and *avenger* of wickedness, as well as the rewarder of those who diligently seek him: the other is a kind of *philosophical* institution, to train men up in the practice of piety and virtue. A religion *without a sacrifice* is at most but half as much as a religion *with a sacrifice*: and that *half* wherein they agree are of quite different nature from each other. – The *practical* part of religion is vastly altered by the *belief* or *denial* of the sacrifice and expiation of Christ's death[16]." In a word, to

---

13   Puffendorf. sect. xli. p. 145. Lat. edit. 138. Engl. edit. Compare Sherlock, Vindicat. &c. p. 261–270.

14   Puffendorf. ibid. p. 143. Lat. p. 135. Engl.

15   Gal. ii. 21. Compare Gal. i. 6, 7, 8, 9.

16   Sherlock, Vindicat. p. 282, 283.

deny the *expiation*, or *satisfaction*, is to renounce the Christian covenant, and is refusing to be saved upon the Gospel terms; which undoubtedly must be erring *fundamentally*.

V. The conditions of the covenant on our part are very plainly *essential* to the covenant itself. Consequently, the doctrines of *repentance* and a *holy life* are fundamental doctrines. Whatever tenets or principles do directly and evidently overthrow the necessity of *holiness*, or of *evangelical obedience*, do at the same time subvert the Gospel covenant, and are therefore grievous and fatal errors, errors in the *foundation*.

VI. The *aids*, or enabling *means*, without which the covenanter cannot perform the conditions, must of course be looked upon as *essential* to the covenant. The *two Sacraments* in this view, considered as enabling *means* of *grace*, are essential to the covenant: therefore the discarding of *two Sacraments*, or either of them, and the denying their *use* or *necessity*, is erring fundamentally[17]. I might perhaps come at the same conclusion more directly, by considering the *Sacraments* as *seals of the covenant*, and so bearing in that view an immediate relation to it and connection with it. But I know not whether the premises might not admit of some dispute; besides that a metaphorical expression is not so clear a ground to build an argument upon: though at the same time I make no question but that the *two Sacraments* are very justly styled, and really are, *seals of the covenant*.

Among the necessary *aids* must be reckoned the assistance or guidance of God's *Holy Spirit*, as the chief of all aids, and what contains all other: this therefore is a *fundamental* principle. And because this cannot be rightly understood without admitting that the Holy Spirit is *omnipresent, all-sufficient*, and, in a word, strictly *Divine*, therefore the *Divinity* of the Holy Ghost is a *fundamental* article of the Christian covenant, and to disown it is to err *fundamentally*[18].

And since it is manifest from the whole tenor of Scripture, that there is but *one God*, one Lord *Jehovah*, it is evident that the doctrine of *three* real Persons in *one* eternal Godhead is a *fundamental* doctrine of Christianity. Of this I have largely

---

[17] Of Baptism in particular, see Puffendorf. Jus. fecial. sect. lii. liii. and Clarke's Sermons, vol. ix. p. 86. Of the Eucharist as essential, see Puffendorf. ibid. sect. lvii. and Velthuysen, p. 800.

[18] See Sherlock, Vindicat. p. 271, 294. Velthuysius, p. 783, 789, 794.

treated elsewhere[19]; but I may here take leave to add the excellent words of Baron Puffendorf, a person of exquisite judgment, and very far from being a bigot to any churchmen: "In this article of *three Persons* in *one Divine essence* lies the *foundation* of genuine Christian religion; which being taken away this falls to the goround, and nothing will remain but somewhat of an exact *moral philosophy*. For if there are not more Persons than one in the Divine essence, there is *no Saviour, no redemption, no faith, no justification*." Good reason there is why the Christian churches would never communicate either with the Samosatenians and Arians of old time, or with the Socinians of later date: a noble writer of our own has very justly observed, "That by this very thing, that they disbelieve the article of the *Holy Trinity*, they make themselves uncapable of the *communion* of other Christian people of the Nicene faith: and we cannot so much as join with them in good prayers, because we are not agreed concerning the Persons to whom our devotions must be addressed. And Christendom never did so lightly esteem the article of the *Holy Trinity*, as not to glory in it, and confess it publicly, and express it in all our Offices. The *Holy Ghost*, together with the *Father* and the *Son*, must be worshipped and glorified." But I proceed.

VII. In the seventh and last place, I am to observe, that the *sanctions* proper to bind the covenant, and to give it its due force and efficacy, must needs be looked upon as *essential* to the covenant. Accordingly, the doctrine of a *future state* must be a fundamental doctrine, as it is the principle of all religion: for without it there can be no sufficient inducement to the *constant* and *conscientious* practice of virtue and piety. The doctrines also of a *resurrection*, and final *judgment* by Christ our Lord, together with the doctrines of a *heaven* for the righteous, and a *hell* for the ungodly, are *fundamental* points of Christian theology. To deny or disbelieve these doctrines is to overturn the *covenant*, because it directly tends to defeat and frustrate the *end* and *use* of it, undermining its binding force, and sapping its influences, depriving it of its life, strength, and energy.

Thus far I have proceeded in pointing out some of the *fundamental verities*, together with the *fundamental errors*

---

[19]   Importance of the Doctrine of the Trinity, vol. iii. p. 389.

opposite thereto, and known by their contraries. By the same rule, and upon the same general principles, it may be easy to draw out more, as often as occasion shall require. It is not necessary to exhibit any complete *catalogue*[20] either of fundamental truths or errors: it is sufficient that we have a *certain* rule to conduct by, whenever any question arises about church communion, heresy, schism, or the like. The ablest physicians would not perhaps undertake to give us an exact catalogue or determinate number of all the *essentials* of human life, or of all the *fatal* distempers or *mortal* wounds incident to the animal frame: but they could easily give in a competent list of either kind; and when any particular case comes before them, they can for the most part judge, by the rules of their art, what means may be necessary to preserve life, and what will as naturally tend to destroy it. In like manner, though Divines take not upon them to number up with exactness all the verities *essential* to the life of Christianity, or all the errors *subversive* and *destructive* of it, yet they can specify several in each kind with unerring certainty, and have certain rules whereby to judge, as occasion offers, of any other; and this suffices in the essentials of *faith*, as well as in the essentials of *practice*.

There may be some difficulty in marking out the exact partitions which divide *fundamentals* from *non-fundamentals*, as they differ only in the degree of *more* and *less* weighty: but then there is also the like difficulty in settling the precise boundaries between *lawful* and *unlawful, right* and *wrong, virtue* and *vice*, in many particular instances; which yet is no just objection to the undertaking, nor accompanied with such difficulties as need make any considerate casuist despair.

Besides, whatever perplexities may sometimes arise in *theory*, there will be few or none in *practice*, since in case of just and reasonable *doubt*, whether such or such an article be *fundamental* or otherwise, the known rule is, to choose the *safer* side. If it be further asked, which is the *safer* side, that of *truth* or of *peace*; I scruple not to give it on the side of *peace*, which ordinarily is of greater value (as more depends upon it) than the supporting or securing the outward profession of a *non-fundamental* truth, or which does not certainly *appear* to be fundamental. When I speak of *doubtful* cases, I would not be understood of *doubtful doctrines*, (for such are not

[20]   See Chillingworth, part i, cap. 3. sect. 13, 53.

fundamental,) but of such cases where the *truth* of the doctrine is at least *morally certain*, and the *importance* of it only *doubtful*. In such cases and instances, reasons of *peace* and *charity* (as I humbly conceive) ought to prevail, rather than break communion for the sake of such truth as cannot be clearly proved a *fundamental* one. Till good proof can be made of its being *fundamental*, it may reasonably pass for a *non-fundamental*: and they who reject it, or refuse to accept it, may notwithstanding be received as *Christian brethren*, yea and ought to be received as such, if there be no other greater reason for excluding them. For I may note by the way, that though a disagreement in *fundamentals* is one bar to communion, and a very just one, yet it is not the only one which may be supposed. If any *non-fundamental* error should be rigorously insisted upon, so far as to *require* us to deny any certain truth, or if any *sinful* terms whatever be imposed: a breach of communion must follow of course, (since it is necessary to avoid a *lie*, and to obey *God* rather than *man*,) and the *imposers* in such cases are the *dividers*. So likewise in case of *impure* worship or flagrant *immoralities*, (though all the *essentials of faith* might remain secure,) it may be necessary to refuse communion with such and such men, or bodies of men. But I have no occasion to consider those or the like cases, which lie out of the compass of our present inquiry. The subject of *fundamentals* was all that I undertook to state and clear as briefly as might be, and to observe how far *Church communion* hangs upon that single article, waving the consideration of other articles, as foreign to the point in hand. I am willing to hope that what has been said may be found sufficient with persons of discernment, for determining the *formal reason* of a fundamental truth or error; and for the settling a safe and easy rule to distinguish the same from what is not fundamental. I have not room to consider particular cases and instances, wherein some difficulties may occur: but if the *general* rule laid down be right and clear, that suffices; neither is the rule to be rejected on account of *accidental* difficulties which may sometimes happen to arise about the application of it.

But for the further illustrating or confirming the rule laid down, it may be now proper to compare it with *other rules*, some differing in *words* only, (being the same in *substance* with it,) others differing in the main thing, and some of them very widely. As to those other rules which appear to coincide with what I have offered, or scarcely to differ from it, it will be sufficient barely to mention them in passing.

Some learned and judicious writers resolve the *ratio* of a fundamental article into its essential connection with the general and comprehensive article of *salvation by Christ*[21]: which in reality amounts to the same with resolving it, as I have done, into the nature of the *Christian covenant*. Others characterize fundamental doctrines as being "necessary to the love of God towards us, or to that love of ours towards him, which consists in keeping his commandments." Which again comes to the same with resolving the *ratio* of a fundamental into the *covenant* of grace: for maintaining that *covenant* in all its *essential* parts or branches, is most effectually maintaining the principles of consummate *amity* between *God* and *man*. Our very judicious Mr. Mede resolves the *formal reason* of a fundamental into the necessary connection which it has with the acts and functions of *Christian life*: but he owns at the same time that if it be resolved into the necessary connection it has with the *Christian covenant*, it is all one with the other, differing only in the manner of expression. Baron Puffendorf, in his excellent treatise upon the subject of Union among Protestants, every where resolves the *ratio* of a fundamental, just as I have, into the doctrine of the *Christian covenant*. But I proceed to consider several other *rules* or *ratios* which have been offered by learned men, and which are more or less widely differing from what I have laid down. It will be proper not only to mention them, but to confute them likewise, by pointing out their faults or defects.

I. Some, to make short work, and to cut off all disputes at once, have been pleased to refer us to the *definition of the Church*, as the surest or the only rule for determining what is *fundamental*, and what not. But it is certain that the *definition* even of the *primitive churches*, after the Apostles, is merely *declarative*, not *effective*; makes no fundamental article, but declares only what was supposed to be so previously to that declaration: and therefore we must look higher for the *formal reason* of a fundamental. The judgment of the *primitive churches* is, no doubt, of great use and weight, as they drew from the fountain head, and well understood the true and genuine principles of the Christian system: and it is of great

---

[21]   Dean Sherlock, Vindicat. p. 259, 302.

moment to observe what doctrines they *received* as fundamental truths, and what they *rejected* as fundamental errors; because there is good reason to believe, all circumstances considered, that they judged very rightly in both cases. But still since their judgment must finally be submitted to the test of *Scripture* and *right reason*, and cannot be admitted but as consonant thereto, it is very plain that the *ratio* of a fundamental rests not ultimately in their *judgment* or *definition*, but in the nature of the doctrine itself, and the credentials which it brings with it, by which all the rest must be tried. The *definition* therefore even of the *primitive churches* can never be justly looked upon as the proper or adequate rule.

As to the *definition* of any modern church, (the Roman for instance,) the pretences urged in favour of it are altogether frivolous and vain. To boast of *infallibility* against a thousand demonstrations that such church *may err*, and in fact *has erred*, and yet *does err*, is a ridiculous *vanity* at the best, not call it by a worse name. And it is very odd to imagine that their *definitions* are an unerring rule, when they cannot be more certain, on one hand, that any such definitions were ever made, or are now extant, than we are, on the other hand, that they are *false* and wrong, and some of them even palpably *absurd*[22].

II. There are those who take *Scripture truths* and *fundamental truths* to be tantamount and reciprocal, conceiving that every thing asserted in *sacred Writ* is *fundamental*, because the whole Scripture *was written for our learning*[23], and cannot be *contradicted* in any part, without giving the lie to the *Holy Spirit* of God. But this opinion, however pious in appearance, is none of the most solid or judicious. It confounds the *truth* or *usefulness* of what is said with the *importance* or *necessity* of it; as if there were no difference between the *weightier* matters and the matters *less weighty*. Scripture contains points of an *inferior* moment, as well as those of an *high nature*: and all the truths contained in it are neither equally *clear* nor equally *important*. There are many incidental verities, *historical, geographical, genealogical, chronological,* &c. which common Christians are obliged rather implicitly to admit, or not to deny, than explicitly to know, or treasure up

[22]   If the reader would see more in answer to this first pretence, he may please to consult Bishop Stillingfleet, Rat. Ac. part i. c. 2. p. 47.

[23]   Rom. xv. 4.

in their minds. There may be thousands or millions of these *inferior* truths[24] in sacred Writ, which it may suffice to believe in the gross, under this one general proposition. *Whatsoever Scripture declares, or teaches, is infallibly true and right.* If any person, without any ill meaning, should dispute or deny many of those occasional *inferior* points, (misinterpreting the texts, and retaining all the while a just veneration for the *authority* of holy Scripture,) he might be thought a bad critic or commentator, rather than a bad Christian: but were the same person to dispute or deny the *necessity of holiness*, or the doctrine of a *resurrection*, or of a *future judgment*, (misinterpreting the texts whereon those doctrines are built,) he might be, and would be justly suspected as guilty of *profane levity* and *heretical pravity*, notwithstanding any pretended veneration for Scripture he might presume to boast of. And what is the reason of the difference in the two cases now mentioned? plainly this: that in one case, the *main substance* of the Christian faith, worship, morality would suffer little or no detriment, but in the other case would suffer very much. Some truths are valuable for the sake only of *greater*, which they may accidentally be joined with, or resolve into; while those *greater* are valuable for their own intrinsic weight and worth. Hence it is, that *creeds, catechisms, confessions*, and other *summaries* of true religion, take in only the principal *agenda* and *credenda*, leaving out the truths of an inferior class; though *scriptural*, and *infallibly* certain, and of the same *Divine authority* with the other. Those inferior points may by *accident* become fundamental[25], if the denying them, in some certain

---

[24] "Accidental, circumstantial, occasional objects of faith, millions whereof there are in holy Scripture: such as are to be believed not *for themselves*, but because they are *joined with others* that are necessary to be believed, and are delivered by the *same authority* which delivered these." *Chillingworth*, chap. iv. sect. 3. p. 172.

"Such as pastors are not bound to teach their flocks, nor their flocks bound to know and remember; no nor the pastors themselves to know them or believe them, or not to disbelieve them, *absolutely* and *always*, but *then only* when they do see and know them to be delivered in Scripture as Divine revelations." *Chillingworth*, ibid. p. 173.

[25] "To acknowledge any proposition to be of *Divine* revelation and authority, and yet to *deny* or *disbelieve* it, is to offend against this *fundamental* article and ground of faith, that *God is true*. But yet a great many of the *truths* revealed in the Gospel – a man may be *ignorant* of, nay *disbelieve*, without danger to his salvation; as is evident in those who, allowing the *authority*, differ in the *interpretation* and meaning of several

circumstances, should inevitably carry with it a denial of the *Divine authority* of sacred Writ: but that, and the like *accidental* circumstances excepted, they are of slight moment in comparison, neither would it be justifiable to break communion with any man for differing from us in things only of that kind.

I may further add, that the rule which I have been here considering appears to be faulty in *defect*, as well as in *excess*: for as every Scripture tenet is not fundamental, so neither does Scripture, strictly speaking, contain *all* fundamental truths. The *certainty* of the *canon* in general, and the *authenticity* of the sacred code, are *fundamental* articles, and are *previous* to those which Scripture itself contains: and our obligation to receive them resolves into this *fundamental* principle of *natural* religion, that we are bound to receive with reverence whatever God shall *sufficiently* make known to us as his law, word, and will. But I proceed.

III. A third pretended rule for determining *fundamentals* is to admit every thing *expressly* taught in Scripture, and nothing but what is so: which differs from the former, as there is a difference between saying *every thing* taught, and every thing *expressly* taught. However this rule also is faulty, and that both in *excess* and *defect*. It is faulty in *excess*, as making many more fundamentals than there really are: for there may be thousands of very *express* verities in holy Scripture which in themselves are not fundamental, having no *immediate* connection with the Christian *covenant*, no direct concern with or influence upon faith, worship, or morality. It is faulty likewise in the other extreme, of *defect*, as not taking in *all* that is really fundamental. The *sense* of Scripture is *Scripture*; and such sense may be *certain* and *indubitable*, when it is not *express*: and if the point of doctrine contained in it be of the *important* kind, nearly affecting the *vitals* of Christianity, it is a *fundamental* article. Some *consequences* are so direct, plain, and immediate, that they even force their way into every attentive and well disposed mind. It has been frequently manifested, and ought now to be acknowledged as a *ruled* case, that clear *consequential* proof is very little short of *express* text, (if it be at all so,) either as to value or certainty: not to mention that *express* text, (or what some may call so,) may often

texts of Scripture not thought fundamental." *Locke, Reas. of Christianity*, p. 156.

mislead us, if we make not use of *reason* and *argument*, that is to say, of *consequences*, to draw out and ascertain the true and just meaning. It may indeed be allowed, that *fundamental* doctrines ought not to be rested upon consequences really *obscure*, or very *remote*: neither ought persons to be charged with *capital* errors for holding some tenets, which *obscurely*, or at a *distance* only, appear to strike at the foundation. Therefore Divines have distinguished fundamental errors into two sorts, as being either *in the foundation*, or *near the foundation*; while those which are more remote, being *besides* the *foundation*, or *distant* from it, are reckoned among the *non-fundamental* errors, as not affecting the *vitals*, or *essentials* of Christianity, except it be in *so distant* or *obscure* a manner, that a person may reasonably be supposed *not to see* such consequence, or seriously to *abhor* it. But if any person holds a tenet which plainly, directly, and at *first consequence*, destroys a *fundamental* article, he is altogether as blamable as if he erred against the *express* text, in a point of like *importance*. But I pass on.

IV. Another pretended rule is, that whatever Scripture has expressly declared *necessary*, or commanded us to believe under pain of *damnation*, or of *exclusion* from Christian communion, that is *fundamental*, and nothing else is. Now as to the first part, it is certain, that whatever Scripture has thus strongly bound upon us is *fundamental*: but it is not true, on the other hand, that whatever Scripture has not so bound upon us is *not fundamental*. So then this rule is faulty in *defect*, as narrowing the foundation more than is just or proper. God's plainly revealing any doctrine carries in it the force of a strict *command* to assent to it as true, whenever we think of it as revealed: and if such a doctrine be found to bear an *intrinsical* or *essential* connection with the doctrine of the *Christian covenant*, that single consideration, added to the former, is sufficient to make out its *importance*, and to signify to every man of common discernment the *fundamental* nature of such article, without any additional declaration from sacred Writ. However it may perhaps be justly said, that, in a general way, all the *essentials* of the Gospel are declared to be *necessary to salvation* in one single text, which declares the belief of the Gospel necessary: "He that believeth *it* not, shall be damned." Mark xvi. 16. What are the essential articles must be learned from other places, or from the nature of the thing itself; but whatever they are, they are here declared to be *necessary*. But of this matter I have professedly treated elsewhere[26], and need not repeat; except you will give me leave, thus far, to say, what I there prove, that "the *importance* of any doctrine is not to be judged of merely from the *declarations* of Scripture concerning its *necessity*, but from the *nature* and *quality* of the doctrine itself, and the *relation* it bears to the *other parts* of revealed religion, and from the mischiefs likely to ensue upon the opposing of it."

V. Some very considerable Protestant writers[27], in their disputes with the Romanists, have often referred to the Creed called the Apostles', both for the *rule* and the *sample* of fundamentals. But then it ought to be observed, in the first place, that the most which those excellent persons intended by it is, that the Creed contains all *necessary* matters of *simple belief*: which if admitted, does not sufficiently answer our present purpose with respect to the question of *Church communion*: for fundamentals of *worship* and of *Christian morality* must be considered in this case, as well as fundamentals of *mere faith*. Add to this, that the Apostles' Creed rather *supposes* than *contains* the article of the *Divine* authority and inspiration of Scripture, and therefore is no complete catalogue or summary of fundamentals. Besides, it may be justly questioned whether it really contains or includes all the fundamentals of *simple belief* which are to be found in holy Scripture: or if it does now, it did not always; for it was once much *shorter*. And creeds never were intended as perfect *catalogues* of *fundamentals*, but were compiled with other views and for other purposes[28]. I may add further, that were the Roman Creed ever so complete a catalogue of fundamentals, when *rightly* understood, yet since that creed is *verbally* admitted by all parties and denominations of Christians, and by some that err *fundamentally* even in point of *simple belief*, (as by Arians, Socinians, Sabellians, &c. who warp the general expressions of the Creed, as they do Scripture texts also, to their respective persuasions,) the Creed so

---

26   Importance of the Doctrine of the Trinity, vol. iii. c. 3. p. 446–450.

27   Such as Petit, Usher, Davenant, Calixtus, Chillingworth, Stillingfleet, Tillotson, Whitby, &c.

28   See my Sermons, vol. ii. p. 188. Crit. Hist. of the Athanas. Creed, vol. iii. p. 252. Remarks on Clarke's Catechism, vol. iv. p. 39. Importance, vol. iii. p. 536.

misinterpreted and misapplied will be of very little service to us, for the distinguishing *fundamental* articles from *non-fundamental*. Those learned Divines, who have spoken the most highly of its perfection and use, have always supposed that it ought however to be rightly understood, according to the true meaning and intent of the compilers that drew it up, and of the churches which made use of it: otherwise the design of it is in great measure lost or frustrated.

From what hath been observed, we may certainly conclude that the *rule* which refers us to the Apostles' Creed is a wrong rule, as it is faulty in *defect*, shortening the number of *fundamentals* more than is meet: at the same time it appears also, in some other respects, to be peccant in *excess*, taking in some articles which seem not to merit a place among *fundamentals*. Such for instance are the articles of Christ's suffering under Pontius Pilate, and of his *descent into hell*, whatever it means: for though they are *Scriptural truths, theological verities*, or *articles of religion*, yet that they are properly *articles of faith*, of the essential and fundamental kind, (more than several other *Scripture truths* left out of the creeds,) does not appear; neither does their *perspicuity*, or intrinsic *dignity*, or *use*, give them a clear preference above many less noted articles of religion which might be named.

VI. Some have been of opinion, that the sixth chapter of the Epistle to the Hebrews, in the two first verses, gives us a complete list of fundamentals, under four or five articles, viz. *repentance, faith in God, baptism* with *confirmation, resurrection*, and *judgment*[29]. But this opinion appears to be founded

[29] "The doctrine of *fundamentals* (about which learned and contentious men have raised great disputes) is really from this passage of the Apostle exceedingly clear and manifest. For the *only* fundamental doctrines of Christianity (viz. those covenanted about at Baptism) are plainly these: that *we have faith towards God*, that we *repent from dead works*; that we have the acceptableness of this repentance assured to us through Christ in the ministration of the *Word* and *Sacraments*, styled here by the Apostle the doctrine of *Baptisms* and of *laying on of hands*; and, lastly, that we live as becomes such persons as are in continual expectation of a *resurrection from the dead*, and of *eternal judgment*: these, I say, are plainly the *only* fundamentals of Christianity: about these there can be no controversy; in these there can be no ignorance, no not among persons of the *meanest* capacity. And besides these, whatever other doctrines are *occasionally* taught, or eagerly *disputed* about, they cannot be of the *foundation* of religion, but men may *differ* concerning them with *peace* and *charity*, and yet every one hold fast the *root* of their *confidence*, the *assurance* of their

only in the *equivocal* sense of the name *fundamental*, and the want of distinguishing between the *elementaries* and the *essentials* of Christianity. The Apostle is there speaking of *milk* as opposed to *strong meat*, of doctrines proper to *babes* in Christ, as opposed to doctrines fit for *grown men*: he is not speaking of points *essential* to the Christian system, as opposed to points *not essential*. The first *elements* of Christianity are not the same with *fundamentals*, in the sense we here take the word, as signifying *essentials*: therefore that passage out of the Hebrews is wide of our present purpose, and mostly foreign to the business in hand. It may indeed be allowed, that the *elementary* doctrines there specified are so many *essentials* likewise: but there are other *essentials* besides those; neither was it the Apostle's design to number them up in that place. In that short summary of *elementary* principles, no express mention is made of the doctrine of Christ *crucified*, which the Apostle elsewhere lays a very particular stress upon[30]; no mention of *justification* by the merits and death of Christ, in opposition to justification by mere works, though an *essential* of the Gospel in St. Paul's account[31]; no express mention of any thing more than what some *heretics* condemned by St. Paul as such[32], and others in like manner condemned by St. John[33], might have owned, or probably did own. Therefore the Apostle's list of *elementaries* in that place is no list of *fundamentals* properly so called, no catalogue of *essentials*. And whereas it is suggested, that those were the *only* fundamental doctrines stipulated in *Baptism*, that cannot be true, since it is acknowledged that what concerns the *dignity of the person of Christ* is omitted in that catalogue[34]: for who can imagine that *Baptism* in the name of the Father, Son, and Holy Ghost, does not carry in it a plain intimation of the *dignity of the person of Christ*, and a stipulation to pay him the like honour, worship, and service, as we pay to the *Father*; or that such doctrine and such worship are not *essentials* in the

salvation in these undisputed doctrines of faith and obedience." *Clarke's Posthumous Sermons*, vol. ix. serm. iv. p. 90.

[30]   1 Cor. ii. 2.

[31]   Gal. i. 7, 8, 9. Gal. v. 4. Phil. iii. 8, 9.

[32]   Gal. i. 7, 8, 9.

[33]   2 John 10.

[34]   Clarke's Sermons, vol. ix. p. 71, 94.

Christian system? And whereas it is further suggested, that those four or five articles there mentioned by the Apostle are such as admit of *no controversy*, and that in these there *can be no ignorance*, no not among persons of the *meanest capacity*; it may pertinently be replied, that there was great *controversy*, even in the Apostles' days, about one of them, namely, about the doctrine of the *resurrection*, which some *heretics* of that time interpreted to a *metaphorical* sense, and in effect vacated and frustrated it: and it is notorious at this day, that some *Christians*, so called, do very *ignorantly* (for it were hard to say that they do it *maliciously*) reject *water-baptism*, and throw off the *use* or *necessity* of both *Sacraments*. So that it is in vain to offer any catalogue of *fundamentals* which may not or has not been *controverted*, in whole or in part, by some that call themselves *Christians*; or to think of settling the rule of fundamentals by considering what may be called the *undisputed* doctrines of faith and obedience. But this by the way only; we shall have more of that matter presently, in its proper place. All I shall observe further here is, that if the articles in Hebr. sixth are to be understood in the *inclusive* way, and with all that they may be supposed to comprehend, or contain, then indeed they may be said to include all the fundamentals, and more; for even the single article of *faith towards God*, in the reductive way, contains every thing: but if they are to be taken in the *exclusive* way, (as is plainly intended by those who refer to them as a rule for fixing *fundamentals*,) then it is certain, that they come vastly short of a complete catalogue. But I proceed.

VII. Some persons observing, that converts in the apostolical times were admitted to Baptism upon the confession of a single article, namely, that *Jesus is the Messiah*, with two or three concomitant articles, have concluded from thence, that such a *general* belief is sufficient to *make* a man a *Christian*, and therefore also to *keep* him so: from whence also it is further insinuated, that such a confession gives a man a claim to *Christian communion*, and that nothing beyond that ought to be absolutely insisted on as *fundamental*, or made a *term* of communion[35].

---

[35] "The belief of *Jesus of Nazareth to be the Messiah*, together with these concomitant articles of his *resurrection*, *rule*, and coming again to *judge the world*, are all the faith required as *necessary* to justification." *Locke*, p. 151.

But this reasoning is faulty in many respects. 1. It proves too much to prove any thing: for, by the same argument, there would be no absolute need of any belief or confession at all; *Baptism* alone (as in *infants*) is sufficient to *make* one a Christian, yea, and to *keep* him such, even to his life's end, since it imprints an *indelible* character in such a sense as never to need repeating. 2. Admitting that a very short creed might suffice for *Baptism*, it does not follow that the same may suffice all along to give a man a right to *Christian fellowship*; especially when he is found to hold such principles as tend to *overthrow* that very confession. The whole of Christianity may be virtually implied or included in that single article, of admitting *Jesus* to be *the true Messiah*; and therefore the denying any *important* point of the Christian faith is in effect revoking or recanting that very article. 3. The *forms* of admission into any society, (though they commonly draw after them an obligation to submit to all the *fundamental* laws, rules, or maxims of such society,) are not properly the *fundamentals* themselves: and though a man may have a right to be *received* as a member upon his passing through such forms, it does not follow that he has a right to *continue* a member, and to participate of the privileges thereto belonging, while he refuses to submit to the *essential* rules or maxims of that society, or makes it his endeavour to subvert or destroy them. It is one thing to say what may be barely necessary at *admission*, and another to say what may be necessary *afterwards*. General professions may suffice at first, as a pledge and earnest of more *particular* acknowledgements to come after: and if those do not follow, it amounts to a kind of retracting even that *general* security. 4. It may be further observed, that neither Simon Magus, nor the ancient Judaizers whom St. Paul anathematized[36]; neither Alexander, nor Hymenæus, nor Philetus, (who denied the general *resurrection* and were delivered over to Satan for it[37],) neither the Docetæ of the apostolical age, who denied Christ's *humanity* and were rejected by St. John[38]; nor even the impious Nicolaitans whom our Lord himself proscribed as unfit for Christian communion: none of those (so far as appears) ever directly threw up their

---

[36]   See Importance &c. vol. iii. p. 401.

[37]   Ibid. p. 402, 459.

[38]   Ibid. p. 402, 547.

baptismal profession, or denied, in such a sense, that *Jesus* was the *Messiah*, or ceased to be *Christians* in the large import of the name, so as to want to be *rebaptized*: and yet certainly they had forfeited all right to *Christian communion*, and were justly rejected as deserters and aliens, for teaching doctrines *subversive* of the Christian religion. Therefore again, that short creed, or single article, however sufficient it might be to *make* a nominal Christian, or to *keep* him so, was yet never allowed sufficient to entitle a subverter of the faith to the right hand of fellowship, or to supersede an explicit acknowledgment of other Gospel doctrines, as *fundamental* verities. 5. Lastly, I observe, that to deny *Jesus to be the Messiah*, is in effect to renounce Christianity, and to revert to *Judaism*, or *Paganism*, or worse: and therefore the insisting upon that confession only without any thing more, as a *term* of *communion*, is as much as to say, that all but downright *apostates* are to be received as *Christian brethren*, so far as *faith* is concerned: a consequence too absurd for any sober and considering man to admit; and so I need not say more of it, but may pass on to a new article.

VIII. Another pretended rule or criterion for determining fundamentals, is *universality of agreement* among *Christians* so called: to throw out what is *disputed*, and to retain only what *all agree in*. A rule as *uncertain* in its application and use, as it is *false* in its main ground: for how shall any one know what all sects and denominations of Christians agree in, or how long they shall do so? Or if that could be known, are we to be guided by the floating humours, fancies, follies of *men*, or by the unerring wisdom of *God*? What article of faith is there which has not heretofore, or may not again be disputed? Or what *creed* can there be pitched upon, be it ever so short, that can please all, or that some perverse sect or other may not controvert? The Romanists allow the *Church governors* to augment the number of *fundamentals* at discretion by their *definitions*: on the other hand, these Universalists, still worse, seem to allow any the wildest sectaries to *abridge* the number as they please, (by disputations,) and not for themselves only, but for all Christendom: for whatever is *disputed* by any of them, is by the supposition to be thrown out as *unnecessary* or *non-fundamental*. A strange expedient for healing differences: a remedy much worse than the disease. It must be owned that a *comprehension* or *coalition* of religious parties is a thing very desirable in itself; and so far as it can be effected by throwing out *circumstantials* and retaining only *essentials*, it is well worthy of every good man's thoughts and care: but to attempt the doing it by relaxing the *rule* for *essentials*, or leaving us no rule at all, or what is next to none, is a wild undertaking. If it may be called *uniting*, it is uniting in nothing but a *cold indifference* towards the *weighty* concerns of God and a world to come, which of course will be accompanied with so much the *warmer* pursuit of *secular* emoluments; for, in the same proportion as *religious* fervours abate, *secular* will succeed in their room. I forbear to be more particular in answer to this so popular pretence, because the learned Spanheim is beforehand with me, and has in a manner exhausted the argument under nine several articles. To recite what he says, at length, would be trespassing too far upon your patience, and to abridge what is so close and so well written would be doing it an injury, and much impairing its force. So I pass on to another head.

IX. There is another pretence, which proceeds upon a like bottom with what I last mentioned, but is looser still, and much more extravagant. For as that pitched upon the *universal agreement* of *Christians* so called, for its mark or rule to steer by, so this still fetching a wider compass, pitches upon the *universal agreement* of the whole race of *mankind* (or of the soberer part at least) in all ages, for its measure of *fundamentals*. Throw out all that has been *disputed*, not only between Christian and Christian, but between *Christians* and *Pagans*, or between *Christians* and *Jews*, or *Mahometans*, and make a short creed of the remainder, and there is your list of *fundamentals*, your *terms* of *communion*, reducible to *five* articles of *natural* religion, as is pretended. 1. The *existence* of a *Deity*. 2. Some kind of *worship* to be paid him. 3. The practice of *moral virtue*. 4. *Repentance* for sins past. 5. Belief of a *future* state of rewards and punishments.

I shall not here waste your time in confuting a notion which confutes itself, and which ought rather to be *exploded* at once with abhorrence, than seriously answered. If *infidelity* in the worst sense, carried up to *apostasy*, is not a *fatal* delusion, or if *Christianity* itself is not a *necessary* term of communion, it is in vain to attempt to prove any thing, or to say any thing upon the subject of *fundamentals*. But from hence we may observe what mazes of error the minds of men (and sometimes men of excellent sense otherwise) are exposed to, when once they recede from true and sound principles, and are set afloat to follow their own wanderings. The effect is natural, as error is infinite, and knows no bounds: and when vain presumption once gets the ascendant, and makes men full of themselves, God leaves them to themselves, and to their own inventions.

X. There is one pretence more which I have reserved for the last place, being as loose as any, and yet carrying so fair a face with it, that it may be most apt to deceive. It is to throw off all concern for a *right faith*, as insignificant, and to comprise all *fundamentals* in a single article of a *good life*, as they call it; to which some are pleased to add *faith* in the *Divine promises*. Well: but can we say any thing too much, or too high, in commendation of a *good life*, the flower and perfection of all religion, and the brightest ornament of every rational mind? I do not say that we can ever think or speak too highly of it, provided only that it be *rightly understood*: but the more valuable a thing it is, the greater care should be taken to *understand* what it means, and not to repose ourselves on an *empty name*, instead of a *real* thing. There is not a more equivocal or ambiguous phrase than this of a *good life*: every different sect almost has its own peculiar *idea* of it: and though they may perhaps agree in some *few generals*, yet none of them agree in all the *particulars* that should go in to make up the one collective notion or definition of it. *Jews, Turks, Pagans*, and *Infidels*, as well as *Christians*, all talk of a *good life*, and each in their *own* sense: and the several denominations of Christians, as *Papists* and *Protestants, believers* and *half believers*, the soberest *churchmen* and the wildest *sectaries*, all equally claim a title to what they call a *good life*. But do they all mean the same thing by it? No certainly: and there lies the fallacy. To be a little more particular, it is observable, that the infamous Apelles, of the Marcionite tribe, in the second century, (a man that discarded the *prophecies* of the Old Testament, and who denied the *real* humanity, or incarnation, of our blessed Lord, yet) pleaded this for a *salvo*, or cover for all his execrable doctrines, that a *good life*, together with a reliance upon *Christ crucified*, was *sufficient* for every thing. It is certain that he left out of his idea of a *good life* one essential ingredient of it, viz. a *sincere* love of *truth*, accompanied with an *humble submission* of his own conceits to the plain and salutary doctrine of the Gospel. So again, professed Deists have put in their claims, along with others, to the title of a *good life*, and have valued themselves upon it, under a total contempt of all *revealed* religion. It is manifest, they must have left out of their idea of a *good life*, the best ingredient of it; namely, the *obedience of faith*. No doubt but *moral probity* is in itself an excellent quality, and I should be apt to value even a *Turk*, a *Jew*, or a *Pagan*, who enjoys it in any competent degree, more than the most orthodox *Christian* who is a stranger to it: but still it is but a *part* (though an essential part) of a *good life*, in the proper *Christian* sense; for nothing comes up to the true and full notion of a *good life*, but *universal righteousness* both in faith and manners[39]. A *right belief* (in *fundamentals* at least) is implied and included in *true obedience*, as *believing* is submitting to Divine authority, and is *obeying* the commands of God[40]. It is a vain thing therefore to speak of a *good life*, as separate from *saving* belief or knowledge, where such knowledge may be had[41]. The pretence to it carries this twofold *absurdity* along with it: it supposes the *end* already attained without the previous *necessary* means, and makes the *whole* to subsist without the *essential* parts. In short, there is no judging of a *good life*, but by considering first what it contains, and whether it answers its *true idea* or *definition*, or means only a *partial obedience*. A belief of *fundamentals* ought to make *part* of the *idea*, ordinarily at least: which therefore must be determined before we can form a just estimate of a *good life*. To deny or disbelieve the *fundamental* articles of Christianity, is a contradiction to the very nature and notion of true *Christian obedience*, and will always be a stronger argument against the supposition of a *good life*, than any other circumstances can be for it. Or if we may sometimes charitably hope or believe that such and such persons, erring fundamentally, and propagating their errors, are yet strictly *honest* men, and accepted by the great Searcher of hearts, as holding what is *sufficient* for *them*, and as doing the best *they can*; yet

39   See Importance &c. vol. iii. p. 478, &c. 566.

40   Ibid. p. 433, &c.

41   A late ingenious writer well expresses this matter as follows: "It is in vain to pretend to real *purity* of *heart* or *life*, without a *belief* of the *truth*. – How is it possible that the man can be really *good*, who is constantly offering the *highest affronts* to his *Maker*, and by a disbelief of the *plain* and *important* articles of faith, is loudly proclaiming him a liar? *He that believeth not God, hath made him a liar, because he believeth not the record that God gave of his Son.* 1 John v. 10." *Dunlop's Preface to Westminster Confession*, p. 168.

this can be no rule for the Church to proceed by, which must judge by the nature and tendency of the doctrines, what is *fundamental* in an *abstract* view to the Christian *fabric*, as before intimated. As to what is so in a *relative* view to particular persons, God only is judge, and not we; and therefore to him we should leave it.

Having thus, my Reverend Brethren, recited, and competently examined the several *improper* or *erroneous* rules suggested by some learned writers for determining *fundamentals*, and having pointed out (in as clear a manner, and in as short a compass as I well could) their principal *defects*; I may now return with the greater advantage to the rule before laid down, and there abide. Whatever verities are found to be plainly and directly *essential* to the doctrine of the *Gospel covenant*, they are *fundamental verities*: and whatever errors are plainly and directly *subversive* of it, they are *fundamental errors*. By this rule, as I humbly conceive, we may with sufficient *certainty* fix the *terms of communion* with the several denominations of Christians. As to the precise *terms of salvation*, they may admit greater variety and latitude, on account of particular circumstances of diverse kinds: and there is no necessity of absolutely excluding all from *uncovenanted* or even *covenanted* mercies[42], whom we may be obliged to exclude from *brotherly communion*. God will have regard in judgment to *invincible* ignorance, incapacity, infirmity: but *men* ought to have no regard to them, in settling the *terms* of *communion*; because they ought never to look upon any ignorance &c. *as invincible*, while it is in their power to apply any *probable* or *possible* remedies; and among the possible or probable remedies, *Church censures* may be justly reckoned, as carrying both *instructions* and *admonition* along with them. Whether the errors be *vincible* or *invincible*, whether the parties erring be *curable* or *incurable*, in many cases, God

---

[42] Persons *unbaptized* and without the pale of the Church, doing all that humanly speaking could be expected in their circumstances, we exclude not from *uncovenanted* mercies.

Persons admitted into *covenant* by *Baptism*, and erring *fundamentally*, but with an *honest* mind, and under some *unavoidable* infirmity or incapacity, we exclude not even from *covenanted* mercies: for they that are unavoidably, unaffectedly *blind*, are not chargeable with *sin* so far; and a man shall be accepted (as I observed above, p. 261.) according to what he *hath* or *might have*, not according to what he *hath not* and could not have. This rule is a *Gospel rule*, and so makes a part of the *Christian covenant*.

alone can know; Church governors do not, and cannot; and therefore they are to proceed in the same way, and to make use of the same expedients, (under direction of Scripture,) as if they were *certain* that the error is *conquerable*, and the party *capable* of *cure*.

But besides the consideration of the *offending* party, there are several more things of moment to be looked to in this business, viz. the preserving *others* from going astray, and the keeping ourselves *pure* and *undefiled*, and the maintaining *truth* and *godliness* in the face of the world, every man according to his abilities, and according to the station wherein God has placed him: for "since the conservation of such things as are *united* is the end of *union*, it is evident that we are not to entertain any *union* but only with them who may help it forward. If therefore there be any, who, under colour of the blessed name of Christ, *subvert* his *doctrine*, *annihilate* his *authority* and our *salvation*; it is so far from being our duty to *unite* ourselves to them, that, on the contrary, we are obliged to *part* with them: because, to *unite* with them, were in effect to *disunite* from *Christ*, and from his *body*; and instead of coming to *salvation*, to fall into *eternal ruin*. – Both the *discipline* of *Jesus Christ*, and the laws of *civil societies*, and even those of *nature* itself, permit us to *avoid* the *communion* of such as, under any pretence, name, or colour whatever, go about to *destroy* and *ruin* Christianity[43]."

---

[43]   Daillé, Apology for the Reformed Churches, p. 4, 5.

LIBERTY
Contemporary Responses to John Stuart Mill
Edited and Introduced by **Andrew Pyle**

ISBN 1 85506 245 3 : Pb : 466pp : **£14.95/$24.95**
Key Issues No. 1

POPULATION
Contemporary Responses to Thomas Malthus
Edited and Introduced by **Andrew Pyle**

ISBN 1 85506 344 1 : Hb : 320pp : **£45.00/$72.00**
ISBN 1 85506 345 X : Pb : 320pp : **£14.95/$24.95**
Key Issues No. 2

GROUP RIGHTS
Perspectives since 1900
Edited and Introduced by **Julia Stapleton**

ISBN 1 85506 403 0 : Hb : 320pp : **£45.00/$72.00**
ISBN 1 85506 402 2 : Pb : 320pp : **£14.95/$24.95**
Key Issues No. 3

AGNOSTICISM
Contemporary Responses to Spencer and Huxley
Edited and Introduced by **Andrew Pyle**

ISBN 1 85506 405 7 : Hb : 310pp : **£45.00/$72.00**
ISBN 1 85506 404 9 : Pb : 310pp : **£14.95/$24.95**
Key Issues No. 4

LEVIATHAN
Contemporary Responses to the Political Theory of Thomas Hobbes
Edited and Introduced by **G. A. J. Rogers**

ISBN 1 85506 406 5 : Pb : 318pp : **£14.95/$24.95**
Key Issues No. 5

THE SUBJECTION OF WOMEN
Contemporary Responses to John Stuart Mill
Edited and Introduced by **Andrew Pyle**

ISBN 1 85506 409 X : Hb : 338p : **£45.00/$72.00**
ISBN 1 85506 408 1 : Pb : 338pp : **£14.95/$24.95**
Key Issues No. 6

THE ORIGIN OF LANGUAGE
Edited and Introduced by **Roy Harris**

ISBN 1 85506 438 3 : Hb : 344pp : **£45.00/$72.00**
ISBN 1 85506 437 5 : Pb : 344pp : **£14.95/$24.95**
Key Issues No. 7

PURE EXPERIENCE
The Response to William James
Edited and Introduced by **Eugene Taylor**
and **Robert H. Wozniak**

ISBN 1 85506 413 8 : Hb : 294pp : **£45.00/$72.00**
ISBN 1 85506 412 X : Pb : 294pp : **£14.95/$24.95**
Key Issues No. 8

GENDER AND SCIENCE
Late Nineteenth-Century Debates on the Female Mind and Body
Edited and Introduced by **Katharina Rowold**

ISBN 1 85506 411 1 : Hb : 344pp : **£45.00/$72.00**
ISBN 1 85506 410 3 : Pb : 344pp : **£14.95/$24.95**
Key Issues No. 9

FREE TRADE
The Repeal of the Corn Laws
Edited and Introduced by
Cheryl Schonhardt-Bailey

ISBN 1 85506 446 4 : Hb : 372p : **£45.00/$72.00**
ISBN 1 85506 445 6 : Pb : 372pp : **£14.95/$24.95**
Key Issues No. 10

HUME ON MIRACLES
Edited and Introduced by **Stanley Tweyman**

ISBN 1 85506 444 8 : Hb : 180pp : **£45.00/$72.00**
ISBN 1 85506 443 X : Pb : 180pp : **£14.95/$24.95**
Key Issues No. 11

HUME ON NATURAL RELIGION
Edited and Introduced by **Stanley Tweyman**

ISBN 1 85506 451 0 : Hb : 350pp : **£45.00/$72.00**
ISBN 1 85506 450 2 : Pb : 350pp : **£14.95/$24.95**
Key Issues No. 12

Key Issues

ALSO IN THE SERIES

HERBERT SPENCER AND THE LIMITS OF THE STATE

The Late Nineteenth-Century Debate between Individualism and Collectivism
Edited and Introduced by **Michael Taylor**

ISBN 1 85506 453 7 : Hb : 280pp : **£45.00/$72.00**
ISBN 1 85506 452 9 : Pb : 280pp : **£14.95/$24.95**
Key Issues No. 13

RACE

The Origins of an Idea, 1760–1850
Edited and Introduced by **Hannah Augstein**

ISBN 1 85506 455 3 : Hb : 298pp : **£45.00/$72.00**
ISBN 1 85506 454 5 : Pb : 298pp : **£14.95/$24.95**
Key Issues No. 14

RELIGIOUS SCEPTICISM

Contemporary Responses to Gibbon
Edited and Introduced by **David Womersley**

ISBN 1 85506 509 6 : Hb : 282pp : **£45.00/$72.00**
ISBN 1 85506 510 X : Pb : 282pp : **£14.95/$24.95**
Key Issues No. 15

JOHN LOCKE AND CHRISTIANITY

Contemporary Responses to The Reasonableness of Christianity
Edited and Introduced by **Victor Nuovo**

ISBN 1 85506 539 8 : Hb : 282pp : **£45.00/$72.00**
ISBN 1 85506 540 1 : Pb : 282pp : **£14.95/$24.95**
Key Issues No. 16

Key Issues

JOHN LOCKE AND CHRISTIANITY

Contemporary Responses to
The Reasonableness of Christianity